SNACKY TUNES

MUSIC IS THE
MAIN INGREDIENT

By

Darin   Greg
Bresnitz   &   Bresnitz

with
Khuong Phan

Forewords by
Jeff Gordinier
&
Jaime "El-P" Meline
of Run The Jewels

Phaidon Press Limited
2 Cooperage Yard
London E15 2QR

Phaidon Press Inc.
65 Bleecker Street
New York, NY 10012

phaidon.com

First published 2020
© 2020 Phaidon Press Limited

ISBN 978 1 83866 136 6

A CIP catalogue record for this book
is available from the British Library
and the Library of Congress.

Commissioning Editor: Emily Takoudes
Project Editor: Anne Goldberg
Production Controller: Sarah Kramer
Design: Omnivore

Printed in Italy

Phaidon would like to thank Carrie
Bradley Neves, Linda Bouchard,
Ken Della Penta, and Caitlin Arnell
Argles for their contributions to
this book.

JEFF GORDINIER

The music mattered. The food mattered. ● We cared about what we were going to eat and we cared about which bands we were going to hear. The Clash, the Rain Parade, Fishbone, X, Uncle Tupelo, R.E.M. Fish tacos from a truck in Highland Park, borscht downtown from Gorky's Russian Cafe, Thai boat noodle soup from Sapp Coffee Shop, hickoryburgers from the Apple Pan. It all mattered. My friends and I were Pasadena kids, Reagan Era preppies from the same Southern California town where Julia Child had grown up, but the choices we made— back then during that brief Ringwaldian utopia known as the Eighties—repre- sented our small way of letting people know (or at least letting ourselves know) who we really were (or at least who we really wanted to be). ● The music and the food were all mixed up. ● It's still that way. What you eat and what you listen to— I mean can you think of any more reli- able indicators of identity and aspiration, of intellectual curiosity and emotional openness? Therein lies the insight of these *Snacky Tunes* dudes, the brothers behind this book, Darin and Greg Bresnitz. They get it. They understand that food and music dovetail like chocolate and pea- nut butter in that old TV candy commer- cial. They're two things so intimately in harmony that they might as well be *fused*.

They saw it. The Bresnitz brothers sensed, back when they hatched *Snacky Tunes* on Heritage Radio in Brooklyn in 2009, that the subatomic alignment of food and music had coalesced into a sort of move- ment, or at least a ripe opportunity to catch lightning in a bottle. The bands wanted to talk about what they ate. (James Murphy of LCD Soundsystem would go on to open a wine bar in Brooklyn.) The chefs wanted to talk about what they listened to. (David Chang paid maniacal attention to the playlists in his Momofuku restau- rants.) It wasn't so much that "chefs were the new rock stars"—that bromide was always too easy. It was that the creative comradeship of cool music and cool food, whose seed had been planted by Gen Xers back in the '80s, truly started to bear fruit in the early decades of the 21st century. ● And so the idea behind *Snacky Tunes*, really, is that a playlist and a menu *are the same thing*: avenues of personal expression, delivery systems that deliver pleasure. ● The food matters. The music matters. ● We know you agree, because you're here.

JAIME "EL-P" MELINE

OF RUN THE JEWELS

In the mid '90s, during the period of time that I was writing what would ultimately become my first full-length album, me and my best friend/roommate John were so broke that we made the unspoken decision to sleep until 5 p.m. every day. It was, I felt, an elegant solution to a clear problem. The longer we were awake, the more expensive it was, and between the two of us we had a post-rent per diem of just about ten bucks. Every day around 5:30 p.m. we would shuffle out of the building and over to a deli in our neighborhood to spend the first five bucks of our budget on our food for the day. The other half was allotted to the neighborhood weed dealer. He had pretty decent stuff, and his nickel bags were plump and always in stock. ● When you're operating on a five-dollar food budget for two you really only have one shot to get it right. This was going to be our only meal of the "day" (early evening), and it needed to hold us down all night. There was music to make, and ideas to write in the studio (a.k.a. my bedroom), and we literally couldn't afford being bothered by hunger pangs. We had to carefully vet our choices and balance them perfectly between "under five bucks for two people," "filling enough to not eat again until tomorrow," and lastly: good. Sure, we were broke as hell, but that didn't mean we were savages. Besides, if there is one thing New Yorkers know, it's that eating well absolutely does not have to cost much. After a little experimentation, we ultimately settled on the only food that fit all our criteria, and at the local deli we would each order one toasted bagel with cream cheese, and a small cup of coffee. I took two sugars and cream, John drank it black, and as we sat on the neighboring stoop to silently devour our catch, the sun would set over Brooklyn, signaling that our day had begun. Perfect. The first traces of sound would start to dart around my consciousness... tonight I work.

Time passed and I finished an album, and my career took off, and the world opened up to me. Years down the line while I was promoting my fourth studio album, *I'll Sleep When You're Dead*, I was asked to perform on a cable TV show called *Dinner With The Band*. The concept was pretty cool, I thought. I was not only going to be the musical guest on the show, but I was also going to cook something of my choosing with the host. The way it was put to me was that they wanted to know what I most missed when I was on the road... the food that meant more about home to me than anything else. The thing I couldn't really get anywhere else. ● Late nights wired and young and ready to say something... having nothing and needing nothing but a shot at a future and something decent to keep us going until it came... ready for something... to gather up whatever was around us and assemble it in to some sort of moment... some sort of life... the calm of the Brooklyn sky when the sun slides below the building tops... ● Let's make bagels, I told them. That feels right.

One of the most important ways people define themselves is by how they connect, both to themselves and to the world at large. For us, and many of the chefs who have appeared on our podcast *Snacky Tunes*, those connections have been expressed by their life-long, intertwined relationships with food and music. ● Food and music have been central to everything we have cared about in life, and we have our parents, Gloria and Eddy, to thank for that. Their love for these disciplines really opened our eyes to the larger world beyond our Philadelphia suburb. Our mom is an incredible cook who put up three-course, European-inspired dinners every night. Our dad provided the soundtrack with his thoughtfully curated record collection. It was apricot chicken and Talking Heads. Rabbit stew and Santana. Mushroom salad and Al Jarreau. Outside of our house, it was Peking duck at Sang Kee in Chinatown followed by The Pretenders at the Tower Theater. Whatever we did, wherever we went, food and music were always involved. ● In high school in the '90s, we were pulled into the orbit of the DIY/punk scene, which was fueled by shows in basements or at the First Unitarian Church, and cheap bites. No night was really complete until we sang along to our favorite lyrics, picked up a 7-inch at the merch table, and dug into a hoagie from WaWa, or a plate of 2 eggs, hash browns, toast, and bottomless coffee at our local Llanerch Diner. The scene also showed us we could create something on our own. We realized you didn't need someone's permission to make music, or design a T-shirt, or put on a show; you could have an idea, build something out of nothing, and be a part of that creation. ● In the early 2000s, we saw that same creative shift in the food industry and culinary media. We were in college, passing around a dog-eared copy of *Please Kill Me: The Uncensored Oral History of Punk* by Legs McNeil and Gillian McCain, when *The Naked Chef* and the original *Iron Chef* debuted on TV. These programs proved to us there could be a different type of cooking show: one with a DIY approach or an absurd sensibility that still respected and aptly told the story of the food it presented. This, mixed with the create-whatever-you-want-attitude we were soaking up from the stories of the original punk scene, gave us our first inclination we could make something original combining our passions for food and music. ● In 2009, Darin created *Dinner with the Band*, the world's first food-and-music cooking show, which we sold to IFC. In true DIY fashion, we put together a small team—Elena, Sam, Eric, Luke, Matty, Emily, Erik, Jeanne, Beck, and Pablo—and went to work creating something from nothing. We built the set, helped craft the recipes, and booked all of the bands, many of whom we had met DJing around New York City. In each episode our legendary host, Chef Sam Mason, would invite musicians like Sharon Jones & the Dap-Kings, the Murder City Devils, and Rufus Wainwright over to his loft for a meal and a musical performance. Sam would cook them a dish inspired by their life on the road, and, in kind, they would perform some of our favorite songs. Instead of renting a studio, we found one of Williamsburg's last dilapidated warehouses and built a culinary loft which we affectionately dubbed The Rising Tide. We used it for our show, rented it out to other productions, and eventually opened it to the community for dinner parties, salons, and the occasional all-night fête. Both the show and the loft were a culmination of our lifelong obsessions with food, music, and the punk spirit. ● In many ways, our radio show *Snacky Tunes* was a continuation of what we sought to do with *Dinner with the Band*. Greg had been hosting radio shows since he was 18 (starting out at the University of Oregon's KWVA), so we knew the format was perfect for the type of program we wanted to create: a show where we could talk about food and music, and create a space for chefs, restaurateurs, bands, and other like-minded artists to share their stories. A nascent Heritage Radio Network, now a well-known producer of culinary radio shows, had just started broadcasting. With the trust and support of Patrick Martins and Jack Inslee (with an infamous layup from Brandon Hoy, the co-founder and co-owner of Roberta's, the beloved Brooklyn pizza restaurant where Heritage has their recording studio), we aired our first episode on July 13, 2009. Since then, we've had the honor of interviewing over a thousand guests, recording hundreds of live music performances and sharing their stories about how they grew up, why they fell in love with food, and how music has inspired them creatively. ● This book is an homage to those inspirations, and conversations. It's a tribute and a recording of the intersections where food and music come together. In brand-new interviews, each chef and restaurateur in these pages has shared never-before heard stories about the music that has motivated them, and recipes for the food they have been inspired to create. Sharing food and music connects people not just to a larger community, but also to their truest selves. We hope that you'll find a piece of yourself somewhere in these stories, and be moved to create something of your own to share with the world.

BY

DARIN BRESNITZ

AND

GREG BRESNITZ

MATT ABERGEL

At the beginning of his career, Matt worked in Japanese kitchens throughout Canada before moving to New York City to work under Masayoshi Takayama at Masa. When Matt moved to Hong Kong in 2009, the food culture of the city inspired him to open his own restaurant and in 2011, he opened Yardbird Hong Kong with his business partner Lindsay Jang. Matt and Lindsay opened their second restaurant, RŌNIN, in 2013.

Good Old Daze Playlist ▶
Enough said.

1.	Nautilus	Bob James
2.	Watermelon Man	Herbie Hancock
3.	Wind Parade	Donald Byrd
4.	Mister Magic	Grover Washington Jr.
5.	Chase the Devil	Max Romeo & the Upsetters
6.	You Don't Love Me (No No No)	Dawn Penn
7.	Darkest Light	Lafayette Afro Rock Band
8.	I Got a Thing, You Got a Thing, Everybody's Got a Thing	Funkadelic
9.	Holy Ghost	The Bar-Kays
10.	Brothers on the Slide	Cymande
11.	Everybody Loves the Sunshine	Roy Ayers
12.	Wildflower	Hank Crawford
13.	Rock Creek Park	The Blackbyrds

Quail Karaage with *Sansho Peppercorns and Orange*

▼ Matt Abergel

This dish is one of only two non-fish offerings on the menu at RŌNIN. We definitely didn't want to put any chicken on the menu, but we were getting really amazing fatty quail from France, so we were inspired to develop this recipe. You can substitute pigeons, guinea hens, or even spring chickens, too, if you can't get nice big quails. *Karaage* is a Japanese style of deep-frying that typically involves a light marinade and a flour and/or starch breading. We cook the breasts to medium-rare or medium, but you can adjust the frying time if you prefer them well done.

Serves 2 to 3

2 fresh whole quail, about 250 g each

200 ml sake

200 ml fresh orange juice

10 g dried sansho peppercorns

3 litres vegetable oil, for frying

■ For the flour blend:

300 g karaage ko flour mix (available in most Japanese groceries and online)

75 g potato starch

70 g tempura flour

7 g finely ground sansho pepper

Sea salt, for serving

Ground sansho pepper, for serving

Zest of 1 orange, for serving

To cut each quail into serving pieces, using a sharp boning knife, run the flat side of the blade along the outer part of a wing and cut down the ribs, gently taking off the breast. Fillet the breast, keeping the wing attached to the outer piece. Set aside and repeat to remove and fillet the other breast half and wing. Remove the legs, trying your best to keep as much of the meat as possible.

In a large bowl, whisk together the sake, orange juice, and sansho peppercorns. Reserve 100 ml of the mixture in a medium bowl and set aside. Add the quail pieces to the marinade in the large bowl, turn to coat, and marinate in the refrigerator for at least 2 hours.

When you're ready to fry, in a deep-fryer or other heavy-bottomed saucepan over medium-high heat, heat the oil to 175°C (350°F).

Meanwhile, to make the flour blend, in another large bowl, combine the karaage ko, potato starch, tempura flour, and ground sansho pepper and whisk to mix well.

Remove the quail from the marinade and discard the marinade. Pat all of the pieces dry. Separate the legs, breasts, and fillets into separate piles, as they have different frying times.

When the oil is hot, first, dip the legs into the reserved sake mixture and then dredge in the flour blend to coat on all sides. Drop carefully into the fryer and set a timer for 1½ minutes. When the timer goes off, coat the breast pieces in the sake and flour mixtures the same way, add to the hot oil with the legs, and fry for another 1 minute. Dip and dredge the fillets, drop them into the oil, and cook for 30 seconds longer. Using tongs or a slotted spoon, take out the legs first, then the breasts, then the fillets, transferring all to paper towels to drain. Arrange on plates and season with salt, sansho pepper, and orange zest. Serve immediately.

I spent a lot of time growing up in bars and clubs where our friends were DJs, so I got to see firsthand the hard work that went into being really good at it. Another influence that shaped my identity was this massive, extensive, world-famous record shop in Calgary called Recordland. It's owned by this Moroccan Jewish family and I'm also Moroccan Jewish. They were the most eccentric, hilarious people. The store is still there. Back in the day, I would go with a good friend of mine, Dean Clark. He's still a musician and DJ in Calgary. I was maybe fifteen at the time and he was a good fifteen years older than I. Dean showed me what music IS. The music I discovered through Dean and Recordland became the lifetime foundation of the music I love. ● Dean and I spent hours and hours looking at albums at Recordland, going back over and over, researching and listening and listening some more. When we noticed that the same people played on twenty different albums we loved, we began to connect to the idea that music is something bigger and deeper than just individual records. Seeing how musicians used the same producer or the same drummer helped us understand that good things are created through collaboration. We could feel the passion of these players—perhaps especially in jazz and reggae, where the musicians were not afraid of sampling or indirectly copying other people's work. They were just being inspired by the music that was going on at that time. In those contexts, we found different versions of the same song over and over again, on maybe fifty different albums. But it never felt like an ego thing… it was just people trying to do their own version of a song and show respect to it. ● My point is, I think that's a lot like cooking. While we chefs always hope to avoid copying anyone else, at the same time, there's no such thing as an original dish—unless you're making a floating balloon filled with pineapple smell, or if you're creating something with food just to be original. It is important for me to remember to stay focused on craft. To be good at one thing while taking a lot of influence from a lot of different places. Being really true to your craft, practicing, respecting the path, knowing what it takes and knowing the history of what you're doing is all that matters. ● Another big musical inspiration for me was seeing Toots and the Maytals. Toots was pretty old at that point, and seeing someone so energetic, so passionate, playing in a small room, showed me how I could do what I loved forever, without compromising my ideals. This guy had a fifty-year career and was playing at this tiny club in Calgary, Alberta. I don't think that he ever focused on money or fame or any of those things, which is probably why he was playing a club in Calgary when he was sixty-five years old. But he also seemed to really be enjoying it. I remember him dancing, singing, and beaming. I really understood then that if you're talented and you follow your passion and you have a good attitude, all the other stuff will fall into place and you will be rewarded for holding on. ● Like being a musician, being a chef means being both selfless and super selfish. There may be years and years in a musician's life where they don't have to care about anybody else. Same with chefs—things we love, like our relationships, might go to shit. We often abuse drugs, alcohol, things of that nature. If you hold on long enough, maybe there's a turning point where people start to appreciate what you're doing; they get you. Then you can turn around and have some success. But by then, you're also supporting a lot of people. ● For musicians, there's the band touring with you, or even for solo artists, there's your team. For chefs, it's the staff, and the customers. I think there's a real similarity between what musicians and chefs go through—a lot of hardship, and often a lot of shitty treatment. A lot of people saying that it's not going to work. Creative people often get pretty self-destructive, a push to fall in and feel. You work super hard, maybe falling into a certain kind of vice-led trap. In the end, you come out on top or you don't. And at that point, you realize what's important. Once you know, once you get out of your own head, a lot of good things can happen, if you can make it through, if you find clarity. But a lot of the time it's just you finding precious clear moments within those struggles, combined with the fact that you know what you love. Even though you might not act like you know what you love, you do know. ● When we first opened RONIN, the idea was that all of our food would just be "versions," the basis, or basics, of a dish defined through various rhythms. Like a rendition of a song, you're putting a spin on a dish. When you think about it, how much time did these guys have in a studio in Jamaica? How many songs were they trying to get out? It was more about showcasing the fact that they had the right ingredients. It's the same thing as a chef deployed in a farmers' market. ● For us, cooking is about putting really good stuff on a plate. It's going to taste different depending on the season. It's going to taste different depending on the chef. But it's the same foundation, the same track, the same note. I think the most interesting thing about "versions" is that maybe one day, let's say, the keyboard player is leading the band, and the next day the bass player is leading the exact same band. When the bassist was in charge, the song completely changed. I think it's the same thing for food. You can give five chefs the exact same ingredients and tell them what dish you want them to create. Every time, each version is going to be completely different, even though everyone is going for the same outcome. Not perfect... but perfect. ● At Yardbird, the music we play has a huge influence on the mood. In the first Yardbird location, I overlooked the acoustic side of things. I knew I was gonna play loud music and play a lot of music I liked. When I first started building the playlists, they were based on the skate videos I watched growing up. I was interested to see if customers would recognize the music from the videos; then we could have those conversations. The guy who does our logos is an old skateboard graphic artist, and it's fun to see people recognize that part of their lives—how it automatically makes them feel comfortable. During dinner service, the music starts lighter; then it goes heavier toward the end of the night. Around 10:00 p.m., we usually turn up the volume and play more '90s hip-hop. ● We invested a lot of money in the sound at the new Yardbird space. We put in a proper acoustic ceiling; we got Funktion-One

Being a chef means being both selfless and super selfish.

speakers. Sound engineering is arguably the most important part of design in a restaurant. Our sound system is pretty much the thing I really care about most. We want to work backward from acoustics. The plain white walls don't bother me. Neither does the lack of pendant lighting. I don't give a fuck. But if the sound sucks, that's going to affect the quality of everything. ● At RŌNIN, we make a menu of about 15 things, and then for music, we just riff off each dish. In the beginning, I would only play dub, session reggae, and ska. That didn't last long... it was kind of nuts, and honestly, dub is not a great musical genre for eating to. But that sensitivity was kind of what we were chasing in the kitchen, as well. It was like, OK, so we're going to do a sardine dish... let's just say, start with tomatoes and eggplant, and then maybe we'll make an eggplant dish with a sardine garnish. I would always be experimenting with a version of a version of a version of a version of a version of a dish! A year later, we still approach things like that, but I guess not as strictly. Still, the very positive thing that came out of that focus: Take your inspiration directly from the things around you. ● My thinking is, music is pretty much always going to be the first thing you experience when you walk into a restaurant. If the music is too loud, tinny, or chaotic, it's probably going to throw you off. It's going to be difficult to relax or take in what's around you because you're so distracted by noise. Don't get me wrong—we don't always find the right line, and people still complain about the music being too loud in my places. But I'm confident in saying, it sounds good. Bad sound quality is something you will feel even if you know nothing about music. People don't necessarily notice how good something sounds, but they will definitely notice how bad it sounds. Like the food—if it's amazing and the service is amazing, details may go unnoticed. People will quietly enjoy themselves, and walk out not even knowing why they're happy or feeling good. The same subconscious thing is true about good sound. It's not necessarily recognition that we're looking for among all the things we want our restaurants to excel in, but I know that we put the effort into it and I know it makes a difference.

EINAT ADMONY

After spending her childhood outside Tel Aviv, Admony served as a cook in the Israeli Army, spent a few months traveling around Germany, and then landed in New York City to begin her culinary career. In 2005, with her husband and business partner Stefan Nafziger, she opened Taïm, a quick-service falafel restaurant in Manhattan's West Village. In 2010, Admony launched an upscale Mediterranean restaurant, Balaboosta, which translates to "perfect house-wife" in Yiddish.

Recipe Inspiration:

Miracle of Love

by The Eurythmics

Around the Globe Playlist ▶ This playlist is a collection of my life in pieces. Each song has its own story, different times and places, different people. Each one reminds me of a situation, a love story, a tragedy, or a happy ending. This list pulls me onto an emotional rollercoaster that makes smile at the end.

1.	**Ziva**	Pollyanna Frank
2.	**O Leãozinho**	Caetano Veloso
3.	**Jerusalem**	Alpha Blondy
4.	**Africa Dream Again**	Youssou N'Dour
5.	**Ve'ech Shelo**	Ariel Zilber
6.	**Why**	Annie Lennox
7.	**Hermetico**	Balkan Beat Box
8.	**Bohemian Rhapsody**	Queen
9.	**Osher**	Idan Amedi
10.	**Where Do the Children Play?**	Cat Stevens
11.	**Me Gustas Tu**	Manu Chao
12.	**Ja Is One**	Mosh Ben Ari
13.	**Trem das Onze**	Demônios da Garoa
14.	**Margish Hashem**	Arkadi Duchin

Tunisian Tuna salad

with Harissa Vinaigrette

BALABOOSTA AND TAïM

2 large or 3 medium russet (baking) potatoes, scrubbed but not peeled

Kosher salt

4 large eggs

1 medium carrot, cut into matchsticks

2 teaspoons fresh lemon juice

3 or 4 preserved lemon wedges

10 oz (285 g) drained solid white tuna packed in oil (use Italian tuna in a jar, if you can find it; you want 10 oz /285 g total meat, so you'll need to buy more than the can weight lists to account for the oil you'll drain)

½ cup (75 g) pitted kalamata olives

½ to ⅔ cup (120 to 160 ml) harissa vinaigrette

¼ red onion, thinly sliced

This song reflects my sense of finding my calling, my destiny, my happiness. The recipe is simple, great for almost every occasion, balanced—and rewarding, as you can use the harissa and the labneh in other dishes. I created this recipe when I first opened Balaboosta in 2010 and it simply reminds me about what I love about cooking.

Serves 4

Put the potatoes in a medium saucepan and add cold water to cover them by a couple of inches. Add 1 teaspoon salt. Bring to a boil over high heat, reduce the heat to medium, and simmer for 20 to 30 minutes, until the potatoes are tender (a fork or knife should go in and out easily). Remove from the heat and set aside to cool.

Have ready a bowl filled with ice and water.

Fill a small saucepan about three-fourths full of water and bring to a boil over high heat. Once boiling, reduce the heat to medium and carefully slide in the eggs. Cook for exactly 12 minutes. Using a slotted spoon, immediately transfer the eggs to the ice bath to stop the cooking. Let the eggs cool completely before peeling. (If not using at once, refrigerate for up to 1 day.)

While the eggs are cooking, in a large bowl, toss the carrot with the lemon juice and a pinch of salt. Let sit for 5 to 10 minutes to pickle the carrots slightly.

Rinse the preserved lemon wedges to remove some of the saltiness. Remove the seeds and most of the flesh, then cut the rinds into thin ribbons; you should end up with 3 or 4 tablespoons. Add to the bowl with the carrots.

Peel the potatoes and cut them crosswise into slices ½ inch (12 mm) thick; add to the bowl with the carrots.

Crumble the tuna slightly and add it to the bowl. Add the olives.

Pour about ½ cup (120 ml) of the vinaigrette into the bowl and gently toss everything together, taking care not to break the potato slices. Taste and add more vinaigrette and salt, if needed. You probably won't need any more salt, as the olives and preserved lemons are both salty.

Transfer the salad to a wide, shallow serving bowl. Peel the hard-boiled eggs, quarter them lengthwise, and arrange on top of the salad. Garnish with the red onion and serve.

For me,

I started cooking when I was very, very young. I didn't have much choice: I grew up Jewish, and while I was never religious myself, my parents got very religious when I was still little, so we always had serious Friday Shabbat dinners. From the time I was about five years old, I was constantly prepping food and cooking with my mom. At the beginning, I didn't like it because it was a chore. On Fridays, I watched all my friends going out to play because school finished early, while I was stuck in the kitchen before Shabbat helping my mom. ● I was born and raised in Israel, so my first interaction with music was Israeli songs. There was never music at Shabbat dinner or the big feast on Friday night; the music happened during the week when we were cooking or preparing for Shabbat or the holidays, and it was always Israeli folk music. My dad would put on Yemenite music, Israeli music… a lot of radio, Israeli radio. ● Over time I have come to learn and understand a lot of different genres of music, but I grew up with that Israeli folk — almost no foreign music at all. I remember how fun it was when we were cooking with the music in the background, which was pretty much all the time. Music added energy to the kitchen and put smiles on people's faces and it was very, very nice. I remember how people moved differently around the table or at the countertop when they were cooking with music on, and I loved it. ● Before I got to the military, which is mandatory for most people who live in Israel, I used to hang out with a lot of crazy criminals, and I had this big street personality. I've always been smart — maybe more street smart than book smart. When I first joined the military, I was working with pilots;

I was their driver and they were intelligent people. They taught me about new music, and it changed everything for me. Music really opened me up a lot. I was tough back

food is

then… very closed up. I definitely didn't share my emotions. I was a pretty crazy kid, but music helped make my heart a little bit softer and helped me connect to others. Back then, my English was even worse than it is now, so I was absorbing a lot of sentences and lyrics I couldn't actually understand; but now I think it's even more interesting to get connected to music without the lyrics. I think those two years totally changed my life and got me where I am today—I'm much more aware of things and willing to explore. I traveled for seven years around the world and did a lot of different things because I had a great capacity for exploration within me. And I think music inspired a lot of that. ● These were the years when I found my style of music. David Bowie's *Ziggy Stardust*, the Smiths, Cat Stevens. A band called Pollyanna Frank was played all the time on Israeli radio. They, along with David Bowie, are among my favorite artists ever. It's funny because the lead singer, Ellyott Eva Ben-Ezzer, is married to one of my best friends in Israel. She's a big LGBT activist in Israel, and now she's one of my closest friends — and I used to adore her when I was seventeen. ● Ellyott singing about the government, about the military, about the soldiers and our kids having to fight at the age of eighteen, giving them guns…in that way, music helped open my eyes. All my traveling opened my mind too, but I think music is the first thing that started changing my brain and the way I was looking at the world. When you start hearing different voices, it opens your mind and you start meeting different people, not just Jewish people. ● After I left the military, I wanted to see more of the world, so I lived in Germany and then Amsterdam. I used to go to a lot of concerts over there. I was a big rave girl as well, so I listened to a lot of trance music. I had a big RV that I drove all over Europe. Once I took DJ Suzuki, one of the biggest Japanese trance DJs in the late '90s and early 2000s, to a festival. The RV was huge, with a proper living room in back, and that was where DJ Suzuki, Dana International's dancers (Dana is one of the biggest performers in the world; she won the Eurovision song contest in 1998 and represented Israel several other times), and about ten other people rode. ● One day, I was driving from Amsterdam to

a tool

Utrecht. I sat behind the wheel and DJ Suzuki was in the back doing a DJ set while I'm driving. It was wild! I was in the front with another Israeli guy and when we pulled up to the festival, I asked everyone to give us a moment of silence because I wanted to hear something Hebrew. My friend in the front took out his guitar and started playing a song by a very famous singer in Israel, Ariel Zilber. The song was "Ve'ech She'lo."

● It's one of my favorite songs and he sang it maybe five times over with his guitar. And I cried. I cried from excitement, because this was a very nice song, a very familiar, very famous song in Israel. I remember that moment, right before we were about to go into a big crazy festival with five thousand people…and I am crying over this beautiful Israeli song. It was so emotional, even though I had the headliner to the festival DJing in my RV. At the end of the day it was the strength and beauty of this song that really struck me, more than any trance music. I think about it still and I still love it. ● All my life—with my parents, when I was in the military, when I lived in my RV—I was cooking everywhere I went. I fed people. When I talk about inspiration for my creativity in the kitchen, I know the process springs from a million different things and a lot of memories, many of which are tied to music. It's funny; there are recipes that I haven't changed for ten years, but then I will listen to a song and it reminds me of something else and then I suddenly tweak that recipe because of the memory it brings up. For chefs as in all realms of art, inspiration and creativity come from so many different associations. ● For me, food is a tool of communication. It makes it easier for me to tell people I love them. That has always been hard for me to express in words, and when I was younger, it was even harder. Music and food both make my heart a little bit spongy, a little softer. Because I don't play music, food is my way to get close to people. Sometimes even a smell will remind you of a whole story, something that opens your heart, making you a child again. I love that.

of
communication.

DOMINIQUE ANSEL

James Beard Award–winning Pastry Chef Dominique Ansel has shaken up the pastry world. He opened his first shop in 2011 in NYC with just four employees. As Chef/Owner of eponymous bakeries in New York, London, and Los Angeles, and a restaurant in Los Angeles, Dominique has created some of the world's most fêted pastries. For his prolific creativity, he was named the World's Best Pastry Chef by the World's 50 Best Restaurants awards in 2017.

Dinner and Dessert Playlist ▶ For me, cooking and baking is about connecting with people and sharing what you've put your heart into with the people you love. In that moment, when you see someone take a bite of something you've just made and they smile, you know you've done your job. So this playlist represents that — what I would play if I were cooking or baking for the people I care about most. Whether it's sitting around the dinner table, enjoying cookies that just came out of the oven, or sharing madeleines that are still warm when you take a bite.

1.	My Baby Just Cares for Me	Nina Simone
2.	Come Fly with Me	Frank Sinatra
3.	Why	Annie Lennox
4.	Take the "A" Train	Ella Fitzgerald, Duke Ellington
5.	Let's Face the Music and Dance	Nat King Cole
6.	Mack the Knife	Bobby Darin
7.	Hard Place	H.E.R.
8.	Love and Happiness	Al Green
9.	Misty Blue	Dorothy Moore
10.	You Send Me	Aretha Franklin
11.	River	Leon Bridges
12.	Tears Dry on Their Own	Amy Winehouse
13.	Tennessee Whiskey	Chris Stapleton
14.	Airmail Special (Live at Zardi's 1956)	Ella Fitzgerald
1.	Orange Colored Sky	Natalie Cole

EXTRA-SILKY PUMPKIN PIE

I didn't grow up eating pumpkin pie or even knowing what a pumpkin pie was, for that matter. I learned about the American traditions of pie when I came to the U.S. and people told me how during the fall and holiday season, you bake and eat pie with your family and friends—whether it's an apple pie during harvest season or a pumpkin pie for Thanksgiving. Now, each fall, we hold our annual Pie Nights with all different kinds of pie, both savory and sweet, and for Thanksgiving each year we make hundreds and hundreds of this Extra-Silky Pumpkin Pie—it has become a tradition of ours and for our guests to celebrate the holiday together. We triple-strain the pumpkin filling so it becomes silky smooth and custardlike, and it goes perfectly with the gingerbread-spiced piecrust with fresh-whipped Chantilly on top.

Makes one 10-inch (25-cm) and an extra crust for another time.

Recipe Inspiration:

FOR ONCE IN MY LIFE

by
Stevie Wonder

■ For the pie dough:

1 stick butter, at room temperature

125 g light brown sugar

2 ¼ tablespoons fresh lemon juice

1 tablespoon milk

1 vanilla bean, seeds scraped

220 g all-purpose flour

2 tablespoons cornstarch (cornflour)

¼ teaspoon baking soda (bicarbonate of soda)

Pinch of Maldon sea salt

1 teaspoon ground ginger

2 tablespoons fresh ginger, finely grated

1 teaspoon ground cinnamon

Pinch of ground nutmeg

■ For the pumpkin custard:

380 g pumpkin purée

380 g cream

121 g egg yolks

114 g granulated sugar

1 ½ teaspoons ground cinnamon

1 teaspoon ground nutmeg

■ **Whipped cream,** for serving

▶️

To make the dough, in a stand mixer fitted with a paddle, cream together the butter and brown sugar on medium-low speed until light and fluffy, about 3 minutes. While continuing to mix, stream in the lemon juice, followed by the milk and vanilla, and beat until evenly combined.

In a bowl, whisk together the flour, cornstarch (cornflour), baking soda (bicarbonate of soda), salt, ground ginger, grated ginger, cinnamon, and nutmeg until combined. With the mixer on medium-low speed, add in one-third of the dry ingredients until combined. Repeat with the next third, then the final third.

Scrape down the sides of the bowl and transfer the dough to a sheet of plastic wrap (cling film). Form the dough into a rectangle no more than ½ inch (12 mm) thick, wrap in the plastic, and chill in the refrigerator for at least 1 to 2 hours.

Remove the dough from the fridge. Divide in half. (This recipe makes 2 pie crusts, so you can keep one half wrapped in plastic in the fridge for up to 3 days or freeze for up to 3 months.) On a lightly floured surface, roll out the dough into a 14-inch (35-cm) round. Transfer to a pie plate, gently pressing down into the corners and up the sides. Trim away the excess dough using a paring knife, leaving a 1-inch (2.5-cm) overhang around the edge. Fold the edges under, then form a fluted edge around the rim with your fingers. Lightly pierce the bottom surface of the dough with a fork. Chill or freeze the pie shell in the pie pan until ready to bake.

Preheat the oven to 350°F (180°C).

Line the pie shell with a coffee filter and fill with rice or dried beans to blind-bake the crust. Bake for 14 to 16 minutes, until the bottom is just lightly baked. Remove from the oven and discard the coffee filter and rice or beans. Return the crust to the oven and bake until golden brown, about 4 more minutes. Remove from the oven and let cool. Reduce the oven temperature to 325°F (160°C).

To make the pumpkin custard, in a large mixing bowl, combine all the ingredients. Blend with an immersion blender until smooth and creamy. (You're looking for an even, smooth custardlike filling without any lumps. We triple-strain ours.)

To assemble the pie, pour the custard into the already-baked and cooled pie crust and fill to just below the top.

Bake for 20 to 35 minutes. Check for doneness after 20 minutes; the pie is done baking when a paring knife inserted into the center of the pie comes out clean.

Let cool on a wire rack, then chill in the fridge until ready to serve.

Serve with a dollop of fresh whipped cream on top.

Music also introduced me to a larger world

Some of the first English words I learned were from listening to American songs

Songs tell a story, and for good chefs, so does their food. For me, baking is about creating memories and emotions—playing on what people think about when they eat dessert. It's most often to celebrate something special, from birthdays to wedding days to spending time around the table with the people you love the most. It's why our Cookie Shot makes you think back to childhood days drinking cookies and milk, or why the Frozen S'mores bring you back to summer days around the campfire. ● When I was growing up, I actually ate poorly and had pretty bad food—oftentimes, not enough food, as my family was very poor. I found cooking as I was looking for a job to make some money to help support the family. It opened up the whole world for me. ● Music also introduced me to a larger world. Some of the first English words I learned were from listening to American songs growing up, everything from soul and rock 'n' roll from the '70s like Marvin Gaye to '80s and '90s pop music. Since I grew up outside of the U.S., the American songs I remember hearing were always several years delayed from what was actually current on the radio there. Most of the time, I knew the lyrics in English before I knew what they actually meant. I've liked a lot of bands and artists, and ultimately, for me it was all about the oldies. Charles Aznavour was always playing in my house. Back when I was working at Daniel, Marvin Gaye was always on the stereo. I used to trade cassettes and CDs with friends, which allowed for a sharing of ideas and creative thoughts.

● When it comes to music and food, it's all about taste. Of course, music together with food is such a sensory and sensual experience. Music is an instant mood-changer and figuratively and literally sets the tone for the meal. You'd be surprised how much our bakeries and restaurants pay attention to their playlists. During the height of the Cronut, when I was working twenty hours a day, there was a line of 150 people around the block, and life never felt harder. My girlfriend got me a vinyl copy of "What a Wonderful World" by Louis Armstrong. I remember just sitting there, after an entire day and night on my feet, listening to it play and feeling instantly better. ● At U.P., our tasting table upstairs at Dominique Ansel Kitchen in the West Village, we have a dedicated playlist for every menu we create. The menu changes once or twice a year, from a menu all about one's earliest memories in life to one that traces through different American dreams in history. We even have one that's all about cheese on our little dairy farm here, and the playlists are inspired by the dishes. It's that final piece to making a complete experience.

NYESHA ARRINGTON

A Southern California native, Chef Nyesha Arrington was introduced at a young age to diverse foods such as bulgogi, octopus, and homemade kimchi. These culinary experiences infinitely shaped her palate development and her ideas about cooking by culture. Nyesha cut her teeth working with legendary chefs Joel Robuchon, Claude Le Tohic, and Josiah Citrin. The late *Los Angeles Times* restaurant critic Jonathan Gold selected both of her restaurants for the Best 101 of Los Angeles, and wrote of Nyesha's cooking, "Her food tastes like L.A."

Song: California Soul by Marlena Shaw

When I think of home, I think about warm, sunny days, skateboarding by the beach, and brunch. My huevos rancheros dish captures the vibe of "California Soul" adapting from Latin flavors and intermingling seasonal produce.

Serves 6

Mise en Place Playlist ▶ I created this playlist to use when I am on the road. I love cooking with music on to create the perfect vibes!

1.	**Strawberry Letter 23**	The Brothers Johnson
2.	**Passin' Me By**	The Pharcyde
3.	**If I Ruled the World (Imagine That)**	Nas featuring Lauryn Hill
4.	**Devil's Pie**	D'Angelo
5.	**California Love**	2Pac featuring Dr. Dre
6.	**I Turn My Camera On**	Spoon
7.	**Bam Bam**	Sister Nancy
8.	**Redbone**	Childish Gambino
9.	**No Ordinary Love**	Sade
10.	**I Love My Life**	Demarco

Recipe Inspiration:

California Soul
by Marlena Shaw

Cali Huevos Rancheros

▼ Nyesha Arrington

■ For the roasted tomatillo salsa:

6 tomatillos, husked and rinsed

1 small jalapeño chile

1 small serrano chile

2 peeled garlic cloves

½ cup chicken or vegetable stock

1 yellow onion, chopped

¼ cup chopped cilantro (coriander) leaves and tender stems

½ cup spinach

1 tablespoon fresh lime juice

½ teaspoon salt

■ For the lentils:

3 tablespoons coconut oil

½ cup chopped yellow onion

1 tablespoon chopped garlic

2 cups cooked lentils

Ground coriander and cumin, for seasoning

Lime juice, for seasoning

Salt and freshly ground black pepper

■ **6 corn tortillas**

1 tablespoon coconut oil

6 eggs

Salt and Korean chile flakes, for seasoning

¼ red onion, sliced crosswise

Cilantro (coriander) leaves, for garnish

Queso fresco, crumbled, for serving

1 or 2 limes, cut into wedges

1 avocado, sliced

To make the salsa, preheat the broiler with a rack about 4 inches below the heat source. Place the tomatillos, jalapeño, serrano, and garlic in a lightly oiled baking dish. Broil, turning occasionally, until they're blackened in spots, 10 to 12 minutes. Remove the baking dish from the oven and add the chicken stock. Use a wooden spoon to scrape any bits stuck to the bottom. Set the tomatillos, chiles, and garlic aside to cool, reserving the stock.

When they are cool enough to handle, peel most of the skins from the chiles and remove the seeds. For a spicier salsa,

leave in some or all of the seeds. Remove the softened garlic from the peels. Put the roasted tomatillos, chiles, garlic flesh, onion, cilantro (coriander), spinach, lime juice, and salt in a food processor.

Add about half of the liquid from the baking dish to the food processor and pulse 3 or 4 times, or until the salsa is mostly smooth and no big chunks of tomatillo remain, scraping down the sides as necessary. Adjust with more liquid, lime juice, or salt, based on consistency and taste. Transfer to a small serving bowl and set aside.

To make the lentils, in a medium skillet over medium heat, melt the 3 tablespoons coconut oil and heat until warmed through. Add the onion and garlic and sauté until the onion is translucent, about 5 minutes. Add the cooked lentils and season with the coriander, cumin, lime juice, salt, and pepper to taste.

Continue to cook for about 5 minutes, stirring constantly. Remove the lentils from the heat. Set aside and keep warm.

To fry the tortillas, heat a large nonstick or cast-iron skillet over medium-high heat until hot. Working with 1 or 2 at a time, dip the tortillas a bowl of cold water, place in the skillet, and cook without moving until lightly charred on the first side, about 1 minute. Flip and cook on the second side for 30 seconds. Transfer to a clean towel placed on top of a plate and fold the towel around the tortilla. Repeat with the remaining tortillas, stacking them in the towel.

When ready to serve, place the tortillas on a warm serving platter or individual plates. Spread each tortilla with the lentils. Add the 1 tablespoon coconut oil to the skillet and heat until shimmering. Add the eggs and cook without moving until the whites are set but the yolks are still runny, about 3 minutes. Season to taste with salt and chile flakes. Transfer 1 egg to each tortilla and dollop with the salsa. Sprinkle with the onion slices, cilantro (coriander), and queso fresco.

Add the lime wedges and avocado slices to the platter or plates and serve immediately.

I have been surrounded by music my entire life. My dad is a musician, and he was in the '70s funk band called Phase, who is really well known for their slap funky bass style. My dad loved Sade, and he would play "Smooth Operator" for us as kids. Listening to Sade growing up, I felt her soulful voice was so timeless, and her classy elegance resonated with me as a young female. I thought she was a perfect human who had a spiritual aura. That immersion translated into my adulthood; back then, we always had music playing in our house during weekend cleanup, and now in my house we always have awesome music playing while doing housework. I have fond memories of making those kinds of chores fun and inclusive with the family, and could feel it was character building as well. ● When I was seven or eight, my next-door neighbor's little brother had an electric guitar he would try to play. I had a crush on him and thought we should start a band. My dad tried to appease us by giving us lots of advice. I tried to learn how to play my dad's bass, but it was gigantic and heavy, so my tiny fingers couldn't pluck it. Still, in my mind, even trying was like I was onstage, and I loved it. Those are the kinds of things that really shaped me as a human, being able to connect with people and just having fun. We tried to start a rock band, which was super cute, trying to get out there and do it myself. ● The parallels of my life are rooted in music and food. In my house growing up, those were two things that were always around. My mom made us sit at the dinner table every single night and finish our dinner. Even if it put me in tears because I didn't like it at the time, I'd have to finish my dinner. We'd come together as a community for the ritual from beginning to end, eating, doing the dishes together, and listening to music. ● Years later, I was Stevie Wonder's private chef during his *Songs in the Key of Life* tour. The best part was that I was able to bring my dad. My dad thought Stevie was the Eighth Wonder of the World and an amazing, impeccable human. When I sat next to my dad while he watched Stevie play, he nudged or elbowed me every thirty seconds. He was so moved, tears fell from his eyes. I love giving my parents these experiences because my life

is a lot different from theirs. They're blue collar people who worked really hard to enable great opportunities for me, and also provided me with a skillset for living, like a full tool belt. I worked hard to give them something back, and that time with Stevie was epic for me. ● During the tour, I felt kind of like a vagabond, cooking all over the world for Stevie. He is the best person I've ever cooked for. I really found inspiration cooking for someone who couldn't see my food. I adored every moment I got to share with that man. While blind, he is amazingly aware of his surroundings and requires little help to get around. He's incredibly strong. His words are articulate and thoughtful. I had phenomenal and stimulating conversations with that man. ● As I got older, I tapped further into my parental roots, which grew organically and naturally within me. They taught me to just be a better version of myself every day. I've refined this simple philosophy in different ways throughout different eras in my life. Being able to share with my team the life lessons from my dad about being a musician allows me to build an intangible essence and spirit around us— the idea of sharing food through the love of music. One huge parallel is the difference between a solo artist and a band. Everyone is championing their own lane, whether it's guitarists or the bassist, vocalists or putting visuals behind the live show, but everyone is working together. I communicate best using music to make these two elements intersect in my cooking world. Over time, my musical range has grown and changed with what's going on in the kitchen. I listen to more classical music and softer music these days. I listen to pop culture music, just to stay hip (not that I'm like, super old!). As with music, my taste in food is refining as well. I continue to search for meaning and rooting and authenticity and purpose, and tap different people with different backgrounds all the time, to keep growing. ● People are looking for authenticity. They're looking for something that makes them feel. Our society today is so often about instant gratification, subjects or ideas that can be very fleeting. A lot of our culture is about trying to do the next big thing or outdo each other. With food, you can't really fake the funk on that. When you can articulate a message through food that's a family legacy, a cultural legacy, that's celebrating the terroir of both a spiritual and geographical location. It's a creation, involving today's artisans of all kinds. It's inspiring to see all the different styles of festivals around the world, merging their energy and incorporating an immersive experience with storytelling, food, and music that is porous and open and celebrates our coexistence. ● When I set out to create a restaurant, a dinner experience, or a dish, I want people to feel something. I am a person of intention, maybe sometimes to my detriment. I think a lot and I like to be light, open, and go with the wind. My music influences work for me in the same way. If I am in a Rage Against the Machine mood today, we try to rally right before service, and everybody is pumped. If it's a classical music day, creating an elegant soigné ravioli dish is like we're doing ballet. If it's a pulse electronic vibe, then everyone is crushing it. When you're trying to translate that spirit through a plate, you're hitting the same notes, whether elegance or aggression. ● One of the best examples of how music affects my cooking is the influence of Kendrick Lamar's song "Humble." The lyrics are about growing up in the hood, not having money for food and eating syrup sandwiches. I remember my mom doing that—Wonder Bread and syrup, and actually, it sure was delicious. I had totally forgotten about those sandwiches, and his song brought back a lot of memories. The *DAMN.* album came out two weeks before I cooked at Coachella, and it was so fire. His performance that year at the festival blew me away. ● When I opened Native, I was planning a brunch menu and decided to make a play on syrup sandwiches. I elevated it with milk bread, six two-inch pieces, which I seared and injected with creamy syrup, then covered the sandwich with maple dust. Originally I wanted it to look like the classic bread-slice square, but six two-inch pieces of bread worked better for the injection. It took a couple of iterations to get it right and became one of our best-selling dishes. I still get e-mails from people pissed off that we closed brunch and stopped making it. ● In a kind of bookend, right before we closed Native,

I had one of the most powerful cooking-and-musical moments that I've shared with my team. Late in service, I was washing dishes. I decided to move the woman who was doing hot apps and put her on the pass so she could run service. I jumped in on the line when I needed to. It was such a graceful moment because everyone was cross-training, and everybody knew what everyone was doing. Then there came a moment where I was plating our spicy beef ramen and wonton dish, and I didn't realize that Beyoncé's "Halo" was on. To my left, the meat station guy starts singing the song; to his left, our hot apps dude starts singing; and then the woman at the pass starts singing. I loved that energy of people doing their best, being passionate, and getting it done in a good environment. I teared up because we knew it was the end of something, we were cooking in a professional environment, and our hearts were open because of the music.

When you can articulate a message through food that's a family legacy, a cultural legacy, that's celebrating the terroir of both a spiritual and geographical location.

SELASSIE ATADIKA

From a young age, Selassie Atadika could be found in the kitchen, grinding pepe not too far from her mother's apron strings. This early culinary interest has evolved from her Ghanaian roots through time spent and meals sampled in the U.S., Europe, and countless countries in all corners of Africa. She brought her innovative approach to African cuisine — what she calls new African Cuisine — to Ghana at Midunu, a nomadic dining concept.

This is Africa! Playlist ▶ These playlists cover two moods: "Inspiration" is upbeat and is the music that fuels my inspiration in the kitchen — the music I listen to while developing a menu or pre-service to get myself and my team energized. "Experience" is more mellow, perfectly suited to accompanying the dining experience. This is the music you will hear while eating at Midunu and the music I listen to while dining with family and friends.

▶ Inspiration

1.	Aben Wo Aha	Daddy Lumba
2.	Africa	Salif Keita
3.	Munt'Omnyama	Mafikizolo featuring Jahseed and Stoan
4.	Jailer	Asa
5.	Vuli Ndlela	Brenda Fassie
6.	1er Gaou	Magic System
7.	Sweet Mother	Prince Nico Mbarga and Rocafil Jazz International

▶ Experience

1.	African Dream	Wasis Diop and Lena Fiagbe
2.	Odo Carpenter	Bisa Kdei
3.	Indépendence Cha Cha	Le Grand Kallé and L'African Jazz
4.	Chileshe	Hugh Masekela
5.	Into Yam	Ringo Madlingozi
6.	Tadieu Bone	Ismaël Lô
7.	Meet Me at the River	Miriam Makeba
8.	Never Far Away	Lagbaja

▲ GHANA

▼ Selassie Atadika

I fell in love with this dish as it highlights some of the wonderful places on the African continent and its amazing food culture. The sauce is traditionally prepared as a soup in northern Ghana and served with *tuozafi*, fermented and cooked millet. Sibre mushrooms are a rare, foraged local mushroom with an amazing flavor.

Serves 4

MUSHROOMS
with
WREWRE SAUCE

■ For the mushrooms:

8 cups sibre mushrooms or other wild mushrooms, cut into thick (2-inch/5-cm) pieces

1½ cups peanut (groundnut) oil

16 garlic cloves, smashed

Salt and freshly ground black pepper

8 skewers (5 to 7 inches/13 to 18 cm each)

■ For the sauce:

1 cup wrewre seeds (wild melon gourd seeds)

1 medium onion, chopped

2 medium fresh tomatoes

1 long red chile, or to taste

5 g dawadawa (fermented locust beans)

½ teaspoon salt

2 cups warm water

Toasted benne seeds, for garnish

Preheat the oven to 350°F (180°C).

To make the mushrooms, in a bowl, stir together the mushrooms, oil, and salt and pepper to taste. Transfer to a baking dish and roast for 20 to 30 minutes, stirring once or twice, until the mushrooms have released their water but are not yet dry.

Remove the mushrooms and let rest until cool enough to handle. Carefully thread them onto the skewers. Arrange the skewers on a baking sheet and set aside.

To make the sauce, in a hot, dry saucepan, toast the wrewre seeds for about 5 minutes, until golden brown. Remove from the pan and let cool slightly.

Meanwhile, in a blender, combine the onion, tomatoes, chile, dawadawa, and salt and blend until smooth, then add the mixture to the saucepan.

Blend the toasted wrewre seeds with the warm water until smooth. Strain the mixture to remove the husks and add it to the saucepan. Place over high heat until it boils, then reduce to medium-low heat and simmer. Stir frequently to prevent the mixture from settling on the bottom of the pot. You will notice a slight oil separation on the top of the sauce, and a deepening of flavor when the sauce is done, 30 to 40 minutes. For an added creamy texture, blend the finished sauce at high speed just before service.

When ready to serve, preheat the broiler. Slip the mushroom skewers under the broiler for a few minutes to get some crispy edges.

Serve the skewers drizzled with the wrewre sauce and sprinkled with toasted benne seeds.

Recipe Inspiration:

RICA **by Salif Keita**

MUSIC BECAME MY COMPANION IN THE KITCHEN

●

I believe everyone has a personal soundtrack. When you meet them, you get to experience some of their favorite music or musical influences while adding to each other's playlists through exchanges of music. For example, I found out what my friends from school's songs were. We began to share our individual music with each other. Then as we spent time together, we would hear a song on the radio, and that could soon become a shared song from that experience. I'm from the generation when you would make friends mixtapes, and the mixtapes we shared were soundtracks of that relationship.

●

I have an eclectic collection of music that spans classical to jazz, pop, hip-hop, R&B, African traditional, afro-jazz, afro-pop, afrobeat, highlife, hip life, and on and on. My collection and musical influence have a lot to do with where I have traveled. My teenage and college years were heavily influenced by where I was and whom I was with, so American pop, R&B, and hip-hop featured greatly.

The first music I fell in love with was what my parents listened to, which was highlife. Highlife music originated in Ghana, and is the backbone of traditional Akan music, but played with western instruments. I didn't do it consciously, but at some point I realized that my food philosophy is similar, in that New African Cuisine is based on the lessons I've learned from the traditional African kitchen and now I'm applying them to the current food landscape to create a new form.

●

Growing up in New York, my father listened to a lot of diverse tunes from all over the world, but there was one song by a Ghanaian artist that was in particularly heavy rotation, "Aben Wo Aha." When he played it, he invariably started dancing. I would be bopping along trying to keep up with him while he was jamming. My younger brother was into rap and hip-hop music at the time, so I wasn't sure he took notice. But when he got married in 2010, as the MC introduced the wedding party, the song my brother chose was Daddy Lumba's "Aben Wo Aha," as my parents walked out. At age seventy, my father still broke out and danced his way through the crowd.

●

And so inevitably music became my companion in the kitchen. It kept me company while I was baking. After many years of traveling throughout the African continent and enjoying different culinary experiences, the music of those experiences and cultures have become part of me and my food. My cooking pulls from and is inspired both by those various cuisines and by the music from those experiences and cultures.

●

My musical guilty pleasure has been to get CDs from a few key musicians from every African country I visit. With the move to digital, it has become a little challenging, but I can still find them. Music says so much about a people and their culture. Some of the artists I love are Lira (South Africa), Freshlyground (South Africa), Yvonne Chaka Chaka (South Africa), Jimmy Dludlu (Mozambique), Kayode Olajide (Nigeria), and Fela Kuti (Nigeria).

●

I have made a deliberate effort to reflect a variety of cultures at Midunu, from the preparation to the music to the dining experience for my clients. During our themed dinners, where music is played in both the front and back, I use it as an opportunity to share the music of the African region where some of the dishes are from. So, if the dinner is predominantly Ghanaian cuisine, I match it with a playlist spanning several decades and genres of Ghanaian musicians and artists. I find the pairing enhances the meal, educates the guests, and brings depth to the experience that the food alone could not do. In a way, my work and life are inspired by the music of my terroir.

ALEX ATALA

In 2015, Alex Atala became the first Brazilian chef to have a two-star restaurant in the Michelin Guide. His main restaurant, D.O.M., was the one to receive that honor and has retained it ever since.

Also established by the chef, ATÁ Institute is an initiative created with the mission of bringing together knowledge and eating, eating and cooking, cooking and producing, and producing and nature.

Recipe Inspiration:

Into

My

Arms

by Nick Cave and the Bad Seeds

1.	**Alegre Menina**	Dorival Caymmi
2.	**Palhaço**	Egberto Gismonti
3.	**Bachianas Brasileiras**	Heitor Villa-Lobos
4.	**Xiquexique**	Tom Zé
5.	**Don't Be Cruel**	Elvis Presley
6.	**Alternative Ulster**	Stiff Little Fingers
7.	**Hangin' Round**	Lou Reed
8.	**Into My Arms**	Nick Cave & The Bad Seeds
9.	**Sheena Is a Punk Rocker**	Ramones
10.	**Misguided Angel**	Cowboy Junkies
11.	**Real Wild Child (Wild One)**	Iggy Pop
12.	**Joe's Garage**	Frank Zappa
13.	**I Walk the Line**	Johnny Cash
14.	**Hold On**	Tom Waits
15.	**Father and Son**	Johnny Cash
16.	**Victime de la Mode**	MC Solaar
17.	**If Tomorrow Never Comes**	Kent Blazy, Garth Brooks
18.	**Nothing Else Matters**	Metallica
19.	**Cum On Feel the Noise**	Slade
20.	**48 Crash**	Suzi Quatro
21.	**Ace of Spades**	Motörhead
22.	**Last Caress**	Misfits
23.	**Oi! Oi! Oi!**	Cockney Rejects
24.	**Jimmy Jazz**	The Clash

My Life Playlist
▶ This playlist is an attempt to bring together some of the things, moments, and stories that shaped who I am. There is a bit of punk rock, as there has to be. Some of these are tunes that were present at a moment in my life with family and friends who have inspired me professionally and shown me that the way I was going was the correct one.

▲ Alex Atala

BRAZIL

Scallops, Cashew and Marrow with Rôti

D.O.M.

Nick Cave's music has had a great influence upon the cuisine that I make today, and this song speaks to me a lot, especially in the present moment of my life. I believe the main mission we have right now is to keep nature in its natural flow. If an interventionist God is not to be believed in, neither should we be interventionist.

Note: Allow 5 days to prepare the rôti sauce. You will need a waffle iron to make the *beiju* tile.

Serves 10

■ For the vegetable stock:

½ carrot

½ onion

2 celery stalks

½ Brazilian zucchini (courgette)

200 ml dry white wine

750 ml water

2 sprigs rosemary

1 sprig thyme

2 bay leaves

■ For the rôti sauce:

1 carrot

1 leek, thoroughly washed

1 celery stalk

1 tomato

1 onion

3 garlic cloves (or ⅓ of the garlic bulb)

4 g coriander seeds

4 g black peppercorns

9 ml corn oil

130 g bovine bones

1 kg *mocotó* (see headnote)

250 ml dry red wine

125 ml *izidro*

1.3 liters water, at room temperature

■ For the marrow sauce:

375 g marrow, about 5 pieces, each about 4 inches (10 cm) long

1 onion, cut into small cubes

Olive oil, as needed

2 tablespoons (90 ml) rôti sauce (see above)

2 ½ cups (250 ml) vegetable stock (see above)

■ For the *beiju* tile:

3 ½ cups (350 g) *puba* flour (fermented manioc flour)

350 ml alkaline water

1 tablespoon salt

1 cup tapioca

■ For assembly:

All-purpose flour, for dredging

10 slices marrow, about the size of the scallops

Fleur de sel and freshly ground black pepper

Butter

20 slices cashew

20 sea scallops

Olive oil

Chervil leaves, for garnish

To make the rôti sauce, thinly slice all the vegetables except the onion and garlic. Set aside.

Put the coriander seeds and black peppercorns inside a bag or cloth and hammer them until they break (but don't let them turn to dust). Pour the crushed spices from the bag into a preheated frying pan over low fire and leave them there until they start to smoke.

At this point, add the corn oil to the pan. When it is hot, place the garlic cloves (still with skin) face down in the pan. Brown them on all sides, but (very important) don't let them burn. ▶❘

Stir in the carrot and simmer slowly, stewing always on the low fire. When the carrot is almost dissolving, add the onion (with skin) and keep stewing. You should have been cooking slowly for about 2 hours by now. When the mixture is the consistency of gravy and all the ingredients in it are dissolved, throw the leek and celery in.

At this point, start roasting the bovine bones: Preheat the oven to 400°F (200°C). Place the bones directly on the oven rack without piling them and roast for about 1 hour and 25 minutes. (Place a pan under the rack so the oil from the bones doesn't spill in the oven.) Leave them roasting and get back to the rôti.

Add the tomato to the pan that is already on the fire and keep stirring until everything dissolves and turns into a well-blended mirepoix, about 50 minutes.

In a large pot, spread the mocotó so it covers the bottom. Add the mirepoix (the stock from the first pan) over the mocotó, and above that, arrange the roasted bones. Add the red wine, the izidro, and the water. Increase the fire until the mixture starts boiling. The moment it begins to boil, lower the fire to the minimum and leave it simmering for 24 hours.

After 24 hours, strain the mixture into a clean pot. Throw away everything that is still solid. Put the stock back over a low fire and simmer very slowly for 5 days. Every day, four times a day, check it and, with a scoop, remove any oil that pools on top. After the 5 days, the result should be a thick sauce. To test for doneness, dip a spoon in the sauce and then clean a part of the spoon with your fingertip. No sauce should drain through the cleaned part and the sauce should form a thin, translucent layer.

Strain the sauce through a thin chinois (or sieve lined with a coffee filter) into a glass measuring cup or heatproof bowl. You can store in the fridge for up to 24 hours.

To make the vegetable stock, chop all the vegetables into small cubes and place them in a deep pan over medium fire along with the wine and water. Add all of the herbs. Stir well and simmer for about 10 minutes, until somewhat reduced and the broth gains flavor and aroma. Strain and set aside. You should have about 2½ cups (250 ml).

To make the marrow sauce, in a deep pan, melt half of the marrow over medium fire until it turns into oil. Meanwhile, blend the onion in a blender with just enough olive oil to make a smooth purée. Add the onion purée to the hot marrow oil and stir until it browns. Add the 2 tablespoons rôti sauce and the other half of the marrow and let the marrow melt. Add the vegetable stock, warm it up, and then remove the pan from the fire. Push it all through a thin chinois into a clean pot and set aside.

To make the beiju tile, place the puba flour in a bowl with the water and salt and stir briefly. Let the mixture rest for 5 minutes. After it has rested, loosen any flour lumps that have formed. Push the tapioca through a sieve into the hydrated beiju flour and stir to mix.

Pour a thin layer of the batter on the waffle machine. Leave it there until the tile is firm and crunchy.

When ready to serve, in a small pan, warm up the marrow sauce over medium fire and keep hot for serving.

Preheat a large, dry (no oil) frying pan over high heat. Dredge the marrow slices in flour and throw them into the hot, dry frying pan for a few minutes, turning once, until nicely browned on both sides. As soon as the marrow is browned, retrieve it from the fire and season with fleur de sel and black pepper. Set aside.

Wipe the frying pan clean and return to high heat. Melt a little butter in the pan. Add the slices of cashew and sear on both sides until nicely browned. Retrieve from the fire and season with fleur de sel.

Season the scallops with fleur de sel and pepper. Heat a bit of olive oil in a clean frying pan over high heat. Sear the scallops on both sides.

To serve, in each of 10 deep plates, place 2 spoonfuls of the marrow sauce, 2 of the seared scallops, 2 of the cashew slices, and a hot marrow slice. Garnish with a beiju tile and a sprinkling of chervil and serve immediately.

Like going to heaven to have a word with God

● Music has always been a big part of my life. When I was young, I had a lot of energy, and most of the time I didn't know what to do with it. Music was the first thing that showed me a way to express that energy, and certain songs have made up the soundtrack of my life. ● Music was also what led me to find my true calling, the one thing I would devote my life's energy to: the kitchen. ● I first went to Europe at eighteen to live the dream of making music by becoming a DJ. I painted walls to pay the bills, but to get a permanent visa, I had to enroll in a school of some kind. A friend in the same situation as I was in a cooking course, so I went with him and enrolled in the Hospitality School of Namur, in Belgium. In the beginning, it was quite frightening. I started out as a helper, peeling potatoes and washing dishes. I couldn't see myself as a gear in such a synchronized machine as that, so I almost gave up. But, when I first got to touch the fish and fresh vegetables, and then when I got to use truffles and mushrooms that were in season, that's when I felt my life references and direction taking shape. ● However, I was still searching for part of my identity through music. In between listening to Led Zeppelin, the Stooges, and so many others, I had the great fortune of hearing a Brazilian musician. Brazilian music wasn't very popular outside of its native country at the time, and when I heard him, I found a reference to my life in Egberto Gismonti's "Palhaço," which is now part of my personal soundtrack. It is a long instrumental track about his work in the circus. In the middle of it, he sampled the sounds of children laughing and a few other things that portray the joy and melancholy of a clown and how he surrenders his life to make those children smile. ● One of my biggest idols is Nick Cave. He lived in Brazil in the late '80s and was married to a friend of

mine, so I got to meet him when I moved back to the country. To be impressed by his music one day and then be sitting in a bar having a beer with him on the next was like going to heaven to have a word with God. That might seem silly for some people, but keep in mind that back in those days, not even mainstream artists would come to play in Brazil, never mind an alternative one like Nick. And then, out of the blue, I was sharing a table with him. It was amazing! ● I can't speak of my life and its transformations without recognizing "Alternative Ulster" by Stiff Little Fingers. Searching for an alternative way to live was something I realized I'd always have to do. I couldn't simply take the usual path as a suburban boy, cook, Brazilian, or father. I knew the traditional ways weren't made for me, and as my cooking skills grew, I knew I wanted to cook something different. My identification with punk rock during my teenage years came from that suppressed inner energy. From the moment I was able to channel that energy into my work and express it in the results, it became my ace in the hole. ● One of the most amazing things about growing old is starting to appreciate other flavors as time goes by. Music and the palate are quite similar in that way. When I was a boy, I only liked rock 'n' roll and wouldn't eat that many things. As I got older, both my ears and my mouth developed and I like almost everything. Very early on, I used to listen to Brazilian classical composer Heitor Villa-Lobos, but only as I got older did I begin to understand the depth of this man's work. He has a masterpiece called "Bachianas Brasileiras" (Brazilian Bachianas), a reference to Brazil and to Bach. I fell in love with this theme and it occurred to me that what Brazilian cuisine lacked was someone who was as passionate for it as Villa-Lobos was for our music. The title of one of my cookbooks is *Escoffianas Brasileiras* because, like Villa-Lobos, who brought together his pride and joy (Brazilian music) and his lifelong reference (Bach), I joined Brazilian cuisine and my greatest reference in gastronomy, Auguste Escoffier. ● Food is culture. The moment we start understanding that is the moment we will start to see food for what it really is: a form of expressing emotions, which changes

depending on who is cooking and where that person came from and grew up. It is funny that we have no problem seeing music as a form of expression but we have trouble seeing food that way. My goal has long been to put Brazilian cuisine and ingredients on a pedestal. The energy I've always had and that punk rock aesthetic was the engine that pushed me to try to achieve something I saw in a completely different type of music, classical, springing from my love of Villa-Lobos. I opened D.O.M. because I decided it was time to have an authorial restaurant that unraveled the flavors and mysteries of Brazilian cuisine and its ingredients. I wanted to offer dishes made out of the classical components we learn in cooking school, but also full of Brazil. At that time, the end of 1999, many people didn't know what açaí, pupunha, or cupuaçu were. It worked! ● In 2019, I had the pleasure of watching Nick Cave play live in São Paulo (he and his band were outstandingly good), but the greatest pleasure came the next day when I found him having lunch at my restaurant. I thought he wouldn't remember me, but he did. We had a word about the '80s, and it was really nice. His song "Into My Arms" has great importance in my life and resonates deeply with me in my relationship with Márcia, the mother of my twins. I'm a father as well as a cook, and I also relate music to that role. For every child, I have a different soundtrack. Pedro is my oldest son and I always think of "Numb" by Linkin Park when I think of him because he loves that song. Tomás is the middle child and perhaps the most energetic one. I'll never forget him explaining to me the difference between Rise Against and Rage Against the Machine, and us listening to those bands together. Joana is the girl of the house. Last summer she learned how to play a beautiful song by Alceu Valença called "La Belle de Jour," and listening to her play made it even more beautiful. ● The story of me becoming a cook is also truly a story about my relationship with music. My training as a cook in Europe wasn't something I had planned. I went there to be a DJ, but found cooking school as a way to guarantee my visa. I didn't find the DJ job but I found music, and music showed me the kitchen, and it's been a three-way love story ever since.

DAVE BERAN

Dave Beran's culinary career began at MK in Chicago, followed by a position at Tru. He then joined the Alinea team and was promoted to chef de cuisine before assuming the opening executive chef position at NEXT in 2011.

In 2017, Beran moved west to Los Angeles to open Dialogue, an intimate, Michelin-starred restaurant serving a seasonally changing multicourse tasting menu. He is also the chef and owner of Pasjoli, an elevated French bistro in Santa Monica.

Albums to Eat To Playlist ▶

Conceptually, right now I am not good at playlists. I've been deep-diving so hard into the notion of the complete thought or storyline that I've felt conflicted about the entire idea of a playlist. Who am I to take an artist's work apart and reconstruct it as my own work—it's a selfish viewpoint, but one that has been my latest focus within music. So rather than writing a playlist, I would prefer to suggest five albums that should be listened to straight through, in order. The notion of songs not being singles, but instead parts of a bigger idea, has really motivated me to rethink how I look at music, food, and storylines as a whole. All brilliant albums have a layering of themes and musical connections, and the general concept at work of tracks supporting each other to create a bigger idea. We all know songs off of these albums, but take the time to listen to them, in order, the way they were intended, without interruption.

Since I have no of understanding of music theory, I will just say that to my ears, this composition begins very conflicted—almost as though it was written as two separate conversations. There is tension and then buildup in the middle, before resolution arrives between the two and the piece ends in a clean and serene melody. This dish reflects the same concept, things that seem to conflict but, balanced properly, blend together in a harmonious fashion.

Makes 25 portions

1.	**What's Going On?**	Marvin Gaye
2.	**To Pimp a Butterfly**	Kendrick Lamar
3.	**OK Computer**	Radiohead
4.	**Igor**	Tyler the Creator
5.	**Blonde**	Frank Ocean

Golden Osetra Caviar with Coffee and Hazelnuts

Recipe Inspiration:

Étude #2 from Études for a Piano Vol. 1

by Philip Glass

Golden Osetra Caviar with Coffee and Hazelnuts

Recipe Inspiration:

Étude #2 from Études for a Piano Vol. 1

by Philip Glass

■ The components:

Golden osetra caviar

Coffee anglaise

Toasted hazelnuts

Lapsang Souchong tea oil

Freshly ground black pepper

Alyssum flowers

■ For the coffee anglaise:

25 g ground coffee

150 g milk, plus more as needed

150 g cream

35 g sugar, plus more as needed

4 egg yolks

5 g cornstarch (cornflour)

5 g salt, plus more as needed

Seeds of 1 vanilla bean

Salt (optional)

■ For the Lapsang Souchong oil:

50 g Lapsang Souchong tea

25 g water

100 g grapeseed oil

■ 75 g hazelnuts

To make the coffee anglaise, in a bowl, whisk together the coffee, milk, and cream. Infuse in the refrigerator for 48 hours, then strain the solids out of the coffee cream.

In a heatproof bowl, combine the sugar, egg yolks, and cornstarch (cornflour) and whisk together.

In a saucepan, whisk together the coffee cream, salt, and scraped vanilla bean and bring to a simmer over medium heat. Temper the hot cream mixture into the egg mixture.

Return everything to the saucepan and bring to a simmer. Strain the anglaise into a mixing bowl nested over an ice bath and whisk until cool. If necessary, balance the flavor with salt and/or sugar. If it seems too thick, add a minimal amount of milk. Set aside.

To make the Lapsang Souchong oil, combine all the ingredients in a pot, bring to a simmer, and cook until all the water has evaporated. Strain the oil and discard the tea. Set aside.

Preheat the oven to 325°F (165°C). Spread the hazelnuts on a baking sheet and toast until golden brown, about 15 minutes. Let cool, then crush into small pieces.

For the build (in a serving bowl from bottom to top):
1. Toasted hazelnuts (3 g per portion)
2. Black pepper (1 crack from a pepper mill)
3. Lapsang souchong tea oil (1.5 g per portion)
4. Coffee anglaise (5 g per portion)
5. Golden osetra caviar (10 g per portion)
6. Alyssum flowers (10 flowers per portion)

Music has always had a tremendous influence on what I do at the restaurants where I've worked. It has shaped my entire thought process of menu structure, adding to hidden meanings, layering of thoughts, and development of dishes. Lately much of my R&D time on food overlaps with trying to understand music theory as a secondary form of creative inspiration. As a chef, I am always trying to understand the creative process in other mediums in order to evolve my own. Music helps to put me in a specific mindset. I've always used music as the backdrop for inspiring creativity—sometimes as the impetus, sometimes just as the soundtrack for being in a creative scenario. Often on R&D days at the restaurant I will work alone, keep the lights lower, play some piano music or just something calming and focused, without words—lots of Philip Glass—and put myself into the mindset of creating. ● When I worked at Next, we went to Spain on an R&D trip for our tapas menu. At that point, I was marathon training. Running was the best way for me to stay focused on work trips, and also a great way to explore new cities. I would throw on my headphones and run. At some point during the run, I would open maps on my phone, figure out where I was, and find a new route home. On one of my runs, I got caught in a rainstorm. I was probably three miles into my run, listening to my typical running playlist, when I decided it was time to go back. I pulled out my wet phone, and in an effort to open maps to find a route home I accidentally changed the music I was listening to—at the time—my least favorite Roots album, ...and Then You Shoot Your Cousin. My phone flaked out, I couldn't change the album, I couldn't use the maps. So I just ran. Seven miles and three cycles through the album later, I was in love with Barcelona and the record—an album that would eventually shape the menu structure of Dialogue. ● The Roots are one of the bands that have had the most influence on what I do. There was a moment before Dialogue opened, as I was trying to understand our menu structure and storyline, that I fell in love with the notion of the "full album." I was asking the question of how we would structure the menu, how the courses would

relate, and simultaneously started to notice the effect of playing a full album straight through, rather than listening to individual songs the way most of us do now. I fell in love with the thought process, the connection, the way track 5 needed tracks 4 and 6 to complete a thought. This notion of a larger story and feeling the sense of purpose in a collection of songs was something I hadn't really considered. ● We don't pair songs with food—mainly because we stagger our seating, so everyone is on a different course. But at our restaurant, we play albums that parallel the tasting menu. Our menu structure is deeply inspired by the idea of a full album. These albums are typically jazz influenced, as both the premise of our restaurant and the flow of a jazz composition are framed around the idea of forward progress. Our menus are all about getting from point A to point B. ● For recordings with vocals, typically we lean toward hip-hop, for two reasons: First, our restaurant is very small, so we need energy. With classical music, we found that the restaurant feels very stuffy and pretentious. With hip-hop, it feels more energetic, fun, and light-hearted. Second, hip-hop vocals are essentially rhythmic storytelling/talking in a cadence. When you play this in a dining room, it gets people talking, also in a cadence, which keeps the dining room moving at a specific pace. We use the music to build the energy in the room, gently pushing the volume and energy of the music as the evening progresses. We don't pair the food with the music; the music frames the pace and energy of the evening. ● Much like a song in an album, our courses rely on each other to complete the idea—things that have to be seen and understood in the order they are presented. If you have a course out of context, it may not make sense, in the same way that hearing a song out of order may not really complete the idea. With great music, you find layers of thought. There is the obvious—what you find at face value—and then there's the theory, the structure, the deeper interpretation. The same is true with great food, it is more than just the flavor, it's the whole package, it's a story. ● Food and music also both have strong nostalgic triggers. Anything that can transport someone back to the mindset of a time or place is impactful. As children, we begin building food and scent memories at a very young age. Moments of nostalgia and connection can often be triggered by the smell of cookies baking, or a roast in the oven—the same way that a Motown record will always remind me of working on a '51 Chevy pickup with my dad. Perhaps it's that desire that leads to this recent intrigue in the pop culture status of food. It is something that people can connect with, something that is familiar enough, but also a form of expression that can still remain individual, one that is always open to interpretation. ● When I was seven, my father, stepmother, and I went to see my grandparents in northern lower Michigan. It was my grandfather's birthday. We typically took the trip up to their cabin every year around that time and would spend a week or so. We would always have dinner at the Douglas Fir Inn. It was a small restaurant on a lake, with a lovely view of the water. We would sit at the round table by the window. We would have dinner, my aunt, my uncle and his wife, my dad...that was the family. There were always lots of stories about when everyone was young and the pranks they would all play on my Aunt Susie. My grandfather would always tell fish stories, although they were usually about the fish my grandmother caught. ● We would always give my grandfather a birthday hat to wear before the cake came out. That year the string on his hat broke. Immediately my grandmother pulled transparent tape from her purse and taped his hat to his head. He was bald; she was prepared. Keeping in stride, he blew out the candles. It took a few tries, and his hat continued to fall off. ● We ultimately ended up at a little lakefront bar down the street like we always did. There was a jukebox in this bar, older 45s mostly. Toward the end of the night, most of the family had consumed a few drinks and were pretty loosened up. My grandmother would dance with me, with everyone. At the end of this particular evening, I remember coming back from playing pinball by the door, looking out the back of the bar, and seeing my grandmother and grandfather slow-dancing in front of the window, the lake in the background reflecting the moon and stars above. The song "Harvest Moon" by Neil Young was playing. I remember just sitting and watching the two of them dance together to that song. There might have been thirty people in that bar, but the way I remember it, they were the only two. It was like a scene from a movie. ● My grandfather passed away the following year. Dancing in front of that window, the reflection of the sky off the lake behind him, arm in arm with my grandmother as they had been for the last forty or so years...that's how I will always remember my grandfather. And "Harvest Moon" will forever be one of my favorite songs.

We use the music to build the energy in the room... We don't pair the food with the music; the music frames the pace and energy of the evening.

JAMIE BISSONNETTE

Jamie Bissonnette is the James Beard Award–winning chef and partner of Boston favorites Toro, a Barcelona-style tapas bar, and sister restaurant Coppa, an Italian enoteca located in the South End. Toro also has homes in New York City, Bangkok, and Dubai. Bissonnette was awarded the inaugural People's Choice: Best New Chef award by *Food & Wine* magazine. In May 2014, he was honored with the James Beard Award Best Chef: Northeast.

More Noise and Other Disturbances Playlist ▶
I like a pretty big variety of music. This playlist is for me to keep my head clear. I love the variety, but also the progression from energy to more relaxing. But it can also be played on random and surprise you with some sweet, sweet tunes.

Song: Beef Bologra by Fear

1.	Bell Bottoms	The Jon Spencer Blues Explosion
2.	Big Take Over	Bad Brains
3.	Miuzi Weighs a Ton	Public Enemy
4.	21st Century Schizoid Man	King Crimson
5.	Am I Evil?	Played by Metallica
6.	Waterfalls	TLC
7.	Beef Bologna	Fear
8.	…Shall be Judged	Burn
9.	Running into Walls	Into Another
10.	Lonely	Rollins Band
11.	Devil's Night Out	The Mighty Mighty Bosstones
12.	Black and Blue	The Selecter
13.	It's Not Funny Anymore	Hüsker Dü
14.	Sweet Leaf	Black Sabbath
15.	Motorhead	Hawkwind
16.	The Party's Over	Willie Nelson
17.	Shadowboxin'	GZA
18.	Dance Wid' Me	Hepcat
19.	Take Five	The Dave Brubeck Quartet
20.	Engine	Supertouch
21.	Fat Man	Derrick Morgan

Beef

USA, DUBAI, UAE BANGKOK, THAILAND

Beef Beef Beef,

I love this song. I thought it would be a great thing to make, as I listen to Fear a lot when I butcher.

Makes about 2.2 pounds (1 kg) beef bologna; serves 15 to 20 people as charcuterie or could make 10 sandwiches

Beef Bologna

Recipe Inspiration:

Bologna by Fear

1,100 g beef top round (topside)

180 g pebbled or crushed ice

75 g palm sugar

15 g salt

8 g freshly ground black pepper

6 g garlic powder

1 g pink salt

1 Thai chile

120 g fish sauce

½ teaspoon olive oil

1 package banana leaves

Cut the beef into ½-inch (12 mm) cubes and chill.

Using a meat grinder, grind the beef with the small (⅛ inch/3 mm) disk. Grind 2 more times while slowly incorporating the ice.

In a large bowl, mix half of the ground meat with all of the other ingredients except the olive oil and banana leaves.

Grind the seasoned mixture one more time, then transfer to a stand mixer. Add the remaining half of the beef and paddle for 5 minutes.

Heat the olive oil in a small frying pan. Pinch off about 1 ounce of the beef and fry to medium-rare. Taste and adjust the seasoning.

Using your hands, gently mold the beef into a roast shape, roll up in banana leaves, and truss like a roast. Hang overnight.

Put the rolled beef in a large pot and add water just to cover. Bring to a boil over medium heat, then lower the heat and simmer gently until the internal temperature is 165°F (74°C).

Cool in an ice bath, then let sit for 1 or 2 days in the fridge, to ripen. Peel the banana leaves off and slice to the desired thickness.

Serve hot or cold!

Music has always been a part of my life, even before I was cognizant, because my father was a jazz musician and we always had music around. There are two artists that are the most important to me. I can't say which one matters more, so I have to stick with two: Dave Brubeck, either the Dave Brubeck Quartet or the Dave Brubeck Trio, depending upon which record. That style of jazz, late '50s, big jazz bands made me realize that music was really, really, really important to me. Hearing my dad's band play those records and those songs and listening to it at home and understanding how music could move me changed my life. ● Next was a band called Judge, a straight-edge hardcore band from New York that I got into when I was in junior or senior high school. They had anger, and a message that talked about being different than everybody else in society. Yet, they were still in a subculture that had its own kind of society. Their music really motivated me to be more DIY, because that's what got them to where they were: part of a DIY, but group, hardcore. ● When I was a kid, I felt like I didn't belong, but when I started to fall in love with music like punk and hardcore, I really developed an identity. It made me realize that I could be part of something that wasn't like everybody else, and that's very much what this music spoke for. I became straight-edge; I was a vegetarian and then vegan. I fell in love with this world of music because it was so much more than the music. I got into hardcore because I wanted to be different. We got tattooed in the early '90s on our hands, necks, and arms, which is really common nowadays, but back then that was our way of saying, "Hey, we're not like everybody else." We wore different clothes because if we were on the bus or the subway, we wanted people to look at us and see we were definitely not mainstream. We didn't do this *just* to be different; we did it because we didn't agree with what was going on in the mainstream. It was like a badge of honor as a hardcore kid to hate classic rock, because you liked the Misfits or Black Flag and that was that. ● The thing I was realizing about music was that I could use it to bring people together. I'm a pretty socially awkward person sometimes, and if left talking to a bunch of strangers, especially when I was younger, I didn't know what to talk about. But if I could say, "Oh what kind of music do you like?" I could immediately start a connection with people. ● I didn't get to see my dad a lot when I growing up because he was a workaholic (which is probably where I get it from). His band would play a lot at this local bar. They're a jazz quartet called Legacy—they still play now. Going there with my mom to sit in a bar as a nine- and ten-year-old, watching my dad play and watching everybody enjoy it, really made me understand how important it is to be engaged, and engaging. My father's band was gregarious and reached out to the audience. I thought even at that time, *This is so important.* I loved it. I also really loved being in a restaurant at a young age, because we almost never went out to eat. Being able to hang out in a restaurant gave me that desire to be surrounded by people and to be social, which is surely a big reason why I love having restaurants today. ● Much like the way music dawned in my life, food was the most important thing in my life before I could vocalize it. I was getting into playing music, but we also did something related to eating before band practice or starting a tour or before a show. We'd play at a venue, and then afterward it was very food-centric, whether we were talking about animal rights or being vegetarian. We fell into studying different kinds of religions that were based on the music we liked from bands like Shelter, the Cro-Mags, and 108. We started going to Krishna temples because the best thing about praying at a Krishna temple was the vegan buffet—aside from the spirituality, of course. I learned all about dosa and how to make different daal, and to this day I still love Indian food. I remember those days vividly when I cook Indian food at home. ●

My interest in food grew so strong that when I wasn't touring, I stopped practicing and spent more time exploring different foods. I got kicked out of the band because I couldn't remember some of the music— I was too busy trying to figure out what we were going to eat. I was also cooking for us, and that's why when I was seventeen, I decided that culinary school was the route for me rather than, you know, being the next big musician. ● I started traveling and cooking.

> I got kicked out of the band because I couldn't remember some of the music— I was too busy trying to figure out what we were going to eat.

I got a job in Paris. One day, the chef told me that I was a good cook, but I wasn't great. He said I would never be great because I wasn't able to eat the food that we were cooking. (I would taste things and spit it out, because of being a vegetarian, so I was kind of rebelling against the fine-dining industry.) He told me this over and over again until one day he said, "Listen, I know you love music. Think of it like this: Imagine that you're the best musician that you can be when you practice, but you never play with a band. You'll never be as

successful as a musician if you can only play for yourself. That's what you're going to do as a cook who doesn't eat the things that you want to cook. Unless you want to be a chef specializing in vegetarian food only, you have to start eating meat, and then you can understand how to play with the band." That was a very important lesson for me. ● I see a lot of comparisons between music and cooking. You can go to Berklee and you can learn all of the theory behind music, but until you play it and practice and get that rote learning, so it's part of your DNA, you really aren't in command of your instrument. It is the same with cooking. You really need to do it over and over and over again to make it your own. Playing the same song over and over and over again and cooking the same dish over and over and over again are parallel experiences. I tell young chefs that Metallica still plays "Whiplash" and the Who still play "My Generation" and they just get better and better. You're never going to see a great band stop playing a hit off their first record just because they wrote a new record. Making something new doesn't mean that they can't do everything from before or ignore the classics; it's just not how it works. ● Take, for example, Oscar Peterson playing a Dave Brubeck song. The first time he plays it, he's going to play it exactly the way it was written

and that might be by himself. Then he practices and he gets to know the song. The more he plays somebody else's song, the more Oscar Peterson's style infiltrates. Oscar's heavier left hand is going to dominate that song and he's going to turn that song into his own song. And I think that cooks don't realize that. They all are so interested in writing a new hit song that they forget that you need to have a base to start. ● The influence of the music that I love on the food that I make is definitely that I want it to be different. We want to challenge people. We want to set ourselves apart, like jazz in the '50s, like punk rock in the later decades. I've always been drawn to more rebellious music. That's the way we cook and the way we run our restaurants. ● When I hear Black Sabbath playing in one of our restaurants, I feel like it's a personal fucking victory. To hear, and to play for our customers, a band that was so controversial, so different, and so involved in their style of music. They're such a talented band, with all the blues progressions and blues skills, it's amazing. When I was a kid, if I played Sabbath in the car, my parents and their friends were like, "This is noise. You can't play this!" Now we have it in the restaurant, and if people think, "Oh yeah, this is great, I like *Paranoid*," that is so cool. That is pretty remarkable to me.

SEAN BROCK

Sean Brock focuses on the past, present, and future of Southern Appalachian culture. He spent over a decade in Charleston, South Carolina, where he explored the possibilities of modern Low-Country foodways. Raised in rural Virginia, he has been involved in the repatriation of the Southern pantry and cuisine for the past 20 years. Chef Brock recently began a lifelong project entitled "Before It's Too Late" dedicated to recording the cultural and culinary wisdom of the South. Brock is James Beard Award winner and author of the *New York Times* best-selling cookbook *Heritage*.

When I think of the birth of jazz and the blues in the South, I imagine the rhythms that are born in the field, especially harvesting rice. This is the dish that always pops up for me, as it's one of my favorite recipes.

Serves 6

Goin' Down South Playlist ▶
Whenever I want to talk to people about where I live, I crank this playlist. Southern music, like Southern food, does an amazing job of imparting what it feels like to live in the American South. This is also the playlist I enjoy on long road trips through the South, looking for the next old-timer that I can hang with and capture their story.

1.	**Poor Black Mattie**	R.L. Burnside
2.	**Goin' Down South**	R.L. Burnside
3.	**Cover Me Up**	Jason Isbell
4.	**Live Oak**	Jason Isbell
5.	**Ladies Love Outlaws**	Waylon Jennings
6.	**Lonesome, On'ry and Mean**	Waylon Jennings
7.	**All Night Long**	Junior Kimbrough
8.	**You Better Run**	Junior Kimbrough
9.	**Goin' Down Slow**	Duane Allman
10.	**Outfit**	Drive-By Truckers
11.	**Decoration Day**	Drive-By Truckers
12.	**The Bottle Let Me Down**	Merle Haggard
13.	**Mama Tried**	Merle Haggard

Recipe Inspiration:

ALL NIGHT LONG

by Junior Kimbrough

LOW-COUNTRY CRAB RICE

■ For the base:

¼ cup small-dice bacon (streaky), preferably Benton's bacon

⅓ cup dried shrimp (prawns)

1¼ cups very finely diced sweet onion

1 cup very finely diced celery

1 cup very finely diced red bell pepper

2 teaspoons minced garlic

1 tablespoon kosher salt

■ For the tomato jam:

2 cups cider vinegar

1 cup brown sugar

3 ripe heirloom tomatoes (blanched, peeled, deseeded and chopped)

½ cup Worcestershire sauce

Whole nutmeg

Whole cardamom

½ cup extra virgin olive oil

Salt

■ For the rice:

4 cups water

1 tablespoon kosher salt

¼ teaspoon freshly ground white pepper

1 fresh bay leaf

1¼ cups Anson Mills Carolina Gold Rice

4 tablespoons unsalted butter, diced

■ 3 tablespoons unsalted butter

1 pound lump blue crabmeat, picked over for shells and cartilage

1 tablespoon fresh lemon juice

2 tablespoons finely chopped chives

2 tablespoons grated crab roe bottarga (mullet bottarga works as a substitute)

To make the base, put the bacon in a large skillet and cook over medium heat until the bacon starts to soften and the fat renders, about 1 minute. Add the dried shrimp (prawns) and stir for 1 minute. Add the onion, celery, bell pepper, garlic, and salt and cook, stirring occasionally, until the vegetables are softened, about 6 minutes. Remove from the stove and set aside.

To make the tomato jam, add the vinegar and sugar to a large nonreactive saucepan over high heat. Bring to a boil and reduce by half, about 7 minutes. Add the tomatoes and Worcestershire then bring back to a boil. Simmer the mixture until very dry, stirring occasionally, about 40 minutes. The mixture should be a very dark brown color and very thick.

Add the mixture to a blender with the olive oil and blend until smooth, about 2 minutes. Season with salt and one or two runs of the nutmeg with a microplane. Season with cardamom.

To make the rice, combine the water, salt, pepper, and bay leaf in a medium saucepan. Bring to a boil over medium-high heat, and stir to be sure the salt has dissolved completely. Reduce the heat to medium, add the rice, stir once, and bring to a simmer. Simmer gently, uncovered, stirring occasionally, until the rice is al dente, about 10 minutes. Drain. Transfer to a clean medium saucepan, stir in the 4 tablespoons dicedbutter, remove from the stove, and cover to keep warm.

To finish the dish, in a large skillet over high heat, melt the 3 tablespoons butter and cook until foamy. Add the base and the crabmeat and cook, gently without stirring, until the butter begins to brown and the crab is hot and crispy, about 4 minutes. Lightly fold in the lemon juice. Divide the rice among the plates, placing it on top of the jam, and sprinkle it with chives. Spoon the crab on top and finish by sprinkling with the bottarga. Serve immediately.

Music has always been around me, it is tied to where I'm from. Southwest Virginia is the birthplace of country music; it's where all the amazing bluegrass musicians are from and the music is just such a big part of life there. Looking back and realizing how art, food, and music combine to make an incredible contribution to culture, that's when I get so excited. My first memories of music are definitely my grandmother singing to me; she would sing these old church hymns that I can still hear. There's one that I remember the most—I don't know the name of it, but the chorus was, "Oh wife, I've found a modern church, I worshiped there today." I've looked and looked and looked and looked and can't find it anywhere. I would just love to be able to play that thing on repeat. I can clearly hear my grandmother's voice singing, and it gives me goosebumps.

●

My earliest memories of music are what my father listened to. Thinking of him listening to his music strikes a huge chord of nostalgia in me; it was really special. The music embodied his personality, his look, his dialect, his work ethic, his overall being. If I were to pick three of the bands that really represent him, it would be Creedence Clearwater Revival, ZZ Top, and AC/DC. Those artists were the soundtrack of my childhood. My dad also bought me—well, he didn't buy it, technically; he traded a shotgun for it—a 1977 Les Paul copy, silver-faced with Fender chart amplifiers. I was probably ten and I made all kinds of ruckus on that thing.

●

When I listen to music today, it still takes me back to my childhood. I remember seeing how much my dad loved music because if he was there, there was music playing. In his car, in his garage, where his business was…I mean, it was just nonstop music. And I inherited his habit. When I wake up in the morning, the first thing I do is put music on, and then I play music all day—different stuff based on how I'm feeling that day, on how I need to feel. That creates the daily soundtrack that to me just, I don't know how else to put it, fuels my tank.

I grew up in a very rural part of the American South, in the coalfields of Virginia and Kentucky Downs, and there were very few places to see live music. The only opportunity we had to see bigger acts was once a year at the fairgrounds. My first big concert was Willie Nelson at the West Virginia State Fair. It was around '90, '91, whenever the IRS tour was, and he was out touring to raise funds to pay his taxes. I went with my mother, my little brother, and my grandmother. We had just moved to West Virginia and my grandmother had moved with us to act as a nanny while my mother worked, because my father had just died. I remember the excitement of seeing my first big concert and it being Willie Nelson. It was just amazing. I loved Willie Nelson as a kid because my grandma loved him, my mom loved him, my dad loved him. I remember sitting there, taking in my first experience of music, live and loud, how it felt traveling through my body, how hypnotic it was, how kind of subversive it was, and how emotional it was during that show. That was where I truly discovered what music can do on an emotional level. He started singing "Blue Eyes Crying in the Rain," with those beautiful lyrics, and my grandmother and mother choked up and started sobbing, thinking about my father. I'm sitting there in the crowd watching my mother and my grandmother bawling over this song…it was the first time I'd seen music touch someone like that. Most importantly, it was my first time experiencing how music can nurture and heal the soul and the importance of that, how important it is in our lives to be able to have music to help heal.

●

Music also helped me heal when I got sober. There's no music in rehab, no computers, no phones, there's no nothing and so I was just really missing my music. I remember going to the nurse's station and asking them to print out the lyrics to Jason Isbell's "Cover Me Up." That's all I had, just my memory of hearing him play that song and those words printed on a sheet of paper. But it was huge because I knew that if I did the work to become sober, I would have the opportunity to become a higher version of myself as well. So, Jason, that song, and that album are a big, big, big inspiration in where my life is today.

●

I met Jason back in the early 2000s, the same year he first joined the Drive-By Truckers; but I really like a lot of his solo work as well. He was very, very young when we met. I happened to meet him early on in Athens, Georgia, and I followed his career from then on. He kind of disappeared and then emerged with this new sound. There was a new depth in his songwriting, full of soul and emotion. I'd never heard anything like it before, it was just extraordinary. I remember going to see him play in Charleston, and it blew me away. We got to catch up and he invited me to his and Amanda's wedding. And I was like, "Wow, that's frickin' crazy," and when I asked him if he was sure, the only thing he said was, "You have to promise not to make fun of the food." I asked him, "Who's cooking?" and he said, "We don't really have anyone." So I said, "Well, I'll be cooking for you two." So sure enough, I cooked for their wedding. I asked a couple of my friends to help me, some Nashville chefs.

●

Around this time, his fame had started to rise, and his story was about sobriety. He hit rock bottom and ended up going to rehab. When he came out of rehab, he wrote what I think is the most beautiful album ever written in the history of music, called *Southeastern*. I think he is the best songwriter of our generation. He sings about sobriety in an amazing way. When that album came out, I was still drinking heavily, and hearing him sing about sobriety made me think about how it completely transformed him into a much higher version of himself. That was inspiring to me and I knew that someday, I would be able to talk sobriety with him. It was inevitable. "Cover Me Up," which he wrote right out of rehab, maybe the first song he wrote afterward, that might be my favorite song of all time. It's a full-on tearjerker, chills and goosebumps, entire-body emotional responses, something that shows the true power of music. There's a line in it that

blows me away: "I swore off that stuff forever this time." When he plays it, people go crazy because they're so frickin' happy for him! Sobriety changed the trajectory of his career and life, and his music and the inspiration I took from it changed mine.

●

One could also use the example of eating whole-hog barbecue while listening to Junior Kimbrough and drinking cheap American beer. They all fit together, they all belong together. I have a theory that drives a lot of my thinking when it comes to what my cuisine needs to be, where it needs to come from, and music and art have a lot to do with that. My favorite forms of all those things come from a very similar place, a very specific place. A place where not much is available, and a lot is needed to nurture for something to show up. Soul food certainly does that, country cooking certainly does that, the idea of gathering humble, simple, and unassuming ingredients, then through the need for nurturing and to nurture others, you create something extraordinary—starting with simplicity and making something extraordinary.

MUSIC CAN NURTURE AND HEAL THE SOUL

ERIK BRUNER-YANG

An agent of innovation, Erik Bruner-Yang creates space. Through his D.C.-based concept-development company, Foreign National, he offers an alternative: food and space as commons. His restaurants are instinctual; contemporary yet habitual. Bruner-Yang is a James Beard Award finalist and was named StarChefs' D.C.-Chesapeake Rising Star 2018 Restaurateur.

Recipe Inspiration:

I'M SIXTEEN

by
Dengue Fever

The Old Me, the New Me Playlist ▶ This playlist is a collection of bands and songs that I loved as a teenager and in my early twenties. All were influential for me, and are songs that I can still listen to and feel excited. I've also included a couple of new songs that I've been into recently. I consider a lot of these bands and musicians as pioneers of music.

1.	The Ice of Boston	Dismemberment Plan
2.	End the Washington Monument (Blinks Goodnight)	Q and Not U
3.	Chase the Money	E-40 featuring Quavo, Roddy Ricch, A$AP Ferg, ScHoolboy Q
4.	Essentially	Japanese Breakfast
5.	The Ghost of Genova Heights	Stars
6.	Handle with Care	Traveling Wilburys
7.	A Shot in the Arm	Wilco
8.	Digital Bath	Deftones
9.	Will You Smile Again for Me	…And You Will Know Us by the Trail of Dead
10.	Reprobate's Resume	Les Savy Fav
11.	Leflaur Leflah Eshkoshka	Heltah Skeltah
12.	They Live By Night	The Make-Up

Cambodian Crispy Shrimp Fritters

WITH LIME & BLACK PEPPER SAUCE

▼ Erik Bruner-Yang

Dengue Fever is one of the coolest bands in America — they incorporate the classic Cambodian rock 'n' roll sound with the contemporary, all while paying homage to those that inspire them. Much like my cooking style.

Makes 60 fritters

■ For the fritters:

300 g fresh baby shrimp (prawns) (small-body shrimp, fresh water shrimp, or saltwater shrimp is fine)

50 g chopped scallions (spring onions)

50 g julienned carrots

5 g ground turmeric

125 g rice flour

½ teaspoon baking soda (bicarbonate of soda)

½ teaspoon salt

50 ml water

50 ml coconut water

■ For the dipping sauce:

2 teaspoons salt

1 teaspoon MSG

1 teaspoon sugar

1 teaspoon freshly ground white pepper

1 teaspoon freshly ground black pepper

1 teaspoon freshly ground green pepper

2 chopped Thai chiles

Juice of 4 limes

■ **200 ml vegetable oil**, for frying

Salt, for sprinkling

To make the fritters, in a medium mixing bowl, stir together all the ingredients until everything is distributed uniformly and the batter has as few lumps as possible.

To make the dipping sauce, whisk together all the ingredients in a bowl. Set aside.

Use a 2-ounce ice cream scooper to shape the fritters.

Pour the vegetable oil into a nonstick frying pan. We will be doing a shallow fry on these fritters. Arrange in the pan and sear on each side evenly until crispy. Transfer to paper towels to help drain the oil. Sprinkle lightly with salt.

Serve hot, and don't forget to dip the fritters in the sauce for that extra flavor! Offer diners their own small dipping bowls, if you like.

WASHINGTON, D.C.

My mother always kept me busy when I was growing up. We moved a lot because my dad was in the military and to help me make friends, she always signed me up for a million different activities. It was important to my mom that I become well rounded in life. By the time I was in high school I was playing piano, trumpet, and guitar. My first real dream in life was to be in a famous band. I was obsessed with the Deftones and Incubus in high school; being in a cool band that successful was all I ever wanted for the longest time. ● All those activities really opened me up to figuring out different parts of myself. As I started taking piano more seriously, I found a natural talent and started participating in more competitions. My mom always gave me a really hard time about practicing, and I got so tired of her badgering me about it that I began paying for my own lessons. I believed she had no right to tell me what to do if I paid for the lessons on my own. I started working in the restaurant industry at fifteen because I wanted my own financial freedom, but also because I loved playing piano so much and wanted to support that passion. At the time I was gigging a lot; I played the keyboard and needed to buy my own equipment. I was also active in the regional classical piano competition circuit. ● It was at my first restaurant job that I discovered modern music. Up until then I had been playing strictly classical music at my piano recitals. Working at Mrs. Tindell's Popcorn Factory, making caramel popcorn, introduced me to more rock 'n' roll, R&B, and rap. I remember being so into music—staying up late every night and listening to DC 101. I'd record music off the radio, making these little mixtapes that I would listen to all the time. I wanted to make some friends so I could be in a band. When I was sixteen, I met some seniors in high school and joined their band, called Temporary Basement, as a piano player. And that's what I did from the age of sixteen until I was about twenty-seven. ● This period was a weird journey of trying to figure myself out and learning to express all of the creative emotions within me that had had no outlet. I remember so many nights where I thought I was the coolest person in the world—all alone late at night, doing drugs and listening to music. Two bands that I always listened to when I was super high were Stars and Wilco. I always had an emotional connection to the music and lyrics of those bands. ● My main band was called Pash, which formed in 2002. We truly dedicated ourselves and agreed that we were really going to try to make it; however, like so many bands, we didn't, and we broke up in 2008. During the spring and summer of that year, we had a huge tour lined up that was our "Make It or Break It" tour, ending with SXSW. At the end of the festival, we joined another tour of a band from Canada called Stars for one more leg. We figured that if nothing happened after the SXSW or Star's tour, we would break up. Our last show was in Alabama, and it really felt like it was the end of an era and the end of our band. I was going to go back to D.C. to revisit some solid chef opportunities that I had put on the back burner. I remember listening and watching Stars play that night, just after we had played our last show with them. I cried, knowing that a chapter of my life was officially coming to a close. ● It's strange…once I started really focusing on being a professional in the culinary world, everything from my previous life as a musician came to a halt. There are so many friends of mine that knew me only as a musician, and there are many friends of mine now that only know me as a chef and entrepreneur. Even my wife, whom I met in 2011, has never seen me play live music. I think she's only ever seen me pick

STRUCTURES ARE MEANT

TO BE BROKEN

up a guitar once or twice at a family barbecue. ● Something that defined me for twenty years now plays a minimal role in the most recent ten. But I'm still defined by the emotional energy that was required for me to dive into music—I put 100 percent of it now into being a father, being an employer, and being a chef. However, music still plays a big part in the energy and the experience of our restaurants. I didn't realize how all-consuming music had been in my life until I fully committed to be a chef and restaurateur. Since I made that transition, I haven't touched a musical instrument. I've become obsessed and goal driven and no longer have the creative energy to switch back and forth between my culinary and music worlds. I have only been to one concert since 2012. I used to go to concerts all the time and was playing almost 150 shows a year when I was in a band. Being around music and playing music was how I defined myself for a large chunk of my life. And now my life is so different. ● At our restaurants, we always strive to make sure that we have great playlists that encapsulate the identity of the space and our city. But for me personally, I do not have room emotionally for the existential experience of music since I decided to stop playing and start figuring out what the next phase of my life was going to be. One thing I noticed after I opened Toki Underground, which was my first step into the independent "cool food" world, was this really odd expectation that if you are a second-generation, modern Asian-American chef offering a unique spin on your cuisine, you'll be playing '90s hip-hop. The "hip" sushi and ramen experience nearly always had Tupac and Notorious B.I.G. playing in the background. ● Hip-hop does make the dynamic of a restaurant interesting, but I still found it really strange. The more I traveled, the more I saw other spaces replicating that experience. It felt disingenuous and watered down. I came to resent that "cool Asian restaurants" are inexplicably tied to the '90s hip-hop. It became something that we actively avoided at Toki and Maketto. ● Maketto was part of the wave of gentrification in the Northeast D.C. neighborhood, the changes rendered by which have their pros and cons. We embrace this clash of cultures with our music. Some people might feel offended by something that isn't natural to their point of view. Maketto tackles this discomfort head-on and I think we've done a pretty good job. ● Toki Underground and Maketto are next door to the Rock & Roll Hotel, which is a pretty cool mid-size independent rock music venue. The first couple of years we were open, we were consistently in tune with what bands were coming through. We made sure they knew to come hang out and would give them a discount. At the time, there wasn't much for these bands to do in that area when they'd pull into the club. Almost everything on that strip, except for our places, were only open at night. I remember during my touring days getting into a new town and wondering where to go. Without the Internet like it is today, you'd just sit in your van or a dark venue until it was time to play or find something to eat. With artists and bands like Cibo Matto, the Kills, or El-P coming through Northeast D.C., we always made sure to actively reach out and let them know they could come and hang at our places in their downtime. ● I will always have that punk-rock DIY spirit in me. It is so deeply ingrained into my life and how I function on a daily basis. I'm still governed by the attitude that rules and structures are meant to be broken to find true art!

MANU BUFFARA

Manu Buffara is the executive chef and owner of Manu, located in Curitiba, Brazil, which has received critical acclaim for its tasting menu and been recognized by the World's 50 Best Restaurants. Manu found her passion for cooking, realizing her way of communicating was not through words but taste. Inspired by her family and background, Manu learned the value of land and animals growing up in the countryside and incorporates this in her everyday technique. Manu's devotion to sustainability continues through her work with local communities to transform abandoned sites into urban gardens and educating locals on how to care for the gardens and feed themselves.

Restaurante Manu Playlist
▶ We play this list at the Manu restaurant, and it includes all of our team's favorite songs. All the songs are Brazilian, and some of them have an important connection with a phase or event of my life or my career in the kitchen.

1.	Ex-amor	Ney Matogrosso
2.	Amanhã é Sábado	Roberta Sá e Martinho da Vila
3.	Varanda Suspensa	Céu
4.	Sonho Meu	Dona Ivone Lara
5.	Carinhoso	Paulinho da Viola e Marisa Monte
6.	Samba da Benção	Maria Bethânia
7.	Só Tinha de Ser com Você	Nana Caymmi e Danilo Caymmi
8.	Cuidando de Longe	Gal Costa e Marília Mendonça
9.	Água de Beber	Astrud Gilberto e Antônio Carlos Jobim
10.	Preciso Me Encontrar	Cartola

FEIJOADA

Feijoada is one of the most popular dishes of Brazilian cuisine. The recipe was created by the African slaves who came to Brazil. The dish is traditionally consumed on Saturdays and at celebratory lunches. This song by Chico Buarque, who is one of the biggest names in Brazilian popular music, describes the feijoada recipe with its ingredients, typically Brazilian.

Serves 10

2 kg dried black beans, soaked overnight	20 g chopped cilantro (coriander)
1 orange	2 ladyfinger chiles
300 g unsalted jerked beef, cut into large cubes	350 g paio (smoked pork sausage), cut into pieces
2 unsalted pig's ears, cut into thirds	400 g spicy pork sausage, cut into pieces
2 unsalted pig's tails	250 g smoked pork loin, cut into large pieces
2 unsalted pig's feet	
2 smoked ham hocks	100 ml cachaça
400 g smoked pork ribs	Salt and freshly ground black pepper, if needed
1 teaspoon olive oil	
250 g bacon (streaky), diced	Steamed white rice for serving
200 g onion, chopped	
50 g chopped garlic	■ Traditional garnishes:
4 bay leaves	Sautéed kale, farofa, fried cassava, and orange slices
30 g spring onions, chopped	

Recipe Inspiration:

FEIJOADA COMPLETA
by Chico Buarque

Drain the beans and put them in a large saucepan. Cover the beans with plenty of water and bring to a boil over high heat. After boiling, lower the heat to maintain a simmer and add the whole orange (with peel), the jerked beef, and the pig's ears, tails, and feet. After 30 minutes, add the ham hocks and the pork ribs.

After another 30 minutes, remove the orange.

Heat the olive oil in a large frying pan over medium-low heat. Add the bacon and fry well, about 10 minutes.

Add the onion and the garlic to the frying pan and cook for another minute. Add the bay leaves, spring onions, cilantro (coriander), and chiles and stir well.

Transfer a ladleful of beans without broth to the frying pan. Stir well and mash with a fork. If necessary, add a bit of broth to help everything blend.

Transfer the mashed mixture to the pot with the beans. Add both sausages, the pork loin, and the cachaça.

Cook for another 30 minutes. Taste the stew to see if you need salt and pepper.

Serve over white rice, garnished with kale, farofa, fried cassava, and orange slices.

There is an artist that I like named Roberta Sá. She plays a new type of contemporary music, called Amanhã é Sábado. I love the sound, I love her style. It inspires the way I'm treating my kitchen and my restaurant right now. She's a new generation of female singer in Brazil. She used to be a journalist and then she became a singer. I started as a journalist and then I started cooking. Her story and life influenced my thoughts and my journey into restaurants. I have a lot of her music on our playlists at Manu and I really like the way she thinks about music, which ties directly into my food.

I think Musicians express their feelings through music, and they embed ideas that are bigger than life into their songs. Their music can create moments that stay with you for your entire life and give you a way to express your own feelings in the same way. Food is the same thing for me as I express my thoughts and feelings through my menu, my cooking, and my presentation, as I think about the world on a plate. Through this strong connection, music gave me my identity and made me who I am today.

Music can transport you to another place or another part of your life. The music I really remember was when I married my husband. We have been together for fifteen years, since I was twenty years old, and married for five. When we got married, we chose the music. Our wedding song was "Pra Sonhar" from Marcelo Jeneci, a Brazilian singer. When you get married in Brazil, you always want to play a type of *marcha nupcial* (wedding music), so we choose a Brazilian style. We wanted to use music that would express how we felt during those ten years of dating, living together and being in love before we got married. **about**

Food is art and when we create a dish we have to think that way about the ingredients. More and more, people are recognizing food as a piece of art. You are not just eating; you are having an experience, and these experiences gather into a story. When you create music, you have to think about the notes, what instrument you're going to use before you while transforming those ingredients into your art. For artists, musicians, and chefs, there is no separation during the creative process; everything comes together.

When I create something in the kitchen, I always think about the vegetables in the garden. I always think about the freshest produce first and then the other ingredients follow. My process is connected to an older style—it's like bossa nova, the old style of music in Brazil that I think is very sweet. My food is connected to the garden and to that genre of music. When I choose the music to play for the people in Manu, it has the same thoughtfulness and style as the food I am cooking. The music experience should connect directly to a dish you created.

the
world

During prep, we don't have music in the kitchen, because I love to hear the sounds of the pans everywhere. Arguably the best thing about working with food and being in the kitchen is the quality time you get to spend with ingredients. Just like any artist, if there's too much noise when you are cooking and thinking, it can affect the final dish. During the service, in the kitchen and the main dining room, the music is quiet and the same in the dining room as in the kitchen; we want guests to be into the food and everything in sync. Most of who we play are Brazilian singers like Roberta Sá, Céu, and Tulipa Ruiz and classics like Cartola, Maria Bethânia, and Gal Costa.

When we finish service at the end of the night, we don't have music for guests. It's like when you finish a show: you want to leave the guests alone with their thoughts. It's the same for the kitchen; we start to think about the show we put on that night, but then we start thinking about tomorrow night's show and think, what can we do to make tomorrow night's show even better.

Three years ago, a friend of mine told me, "I think both of your restaurants are amazing, but you need to change the soundtrack because it's not the same vibe as you and your food." He knew me as a friend, and he knew it was not my style of music. He told me that I needed to choose the music with the same insight that I put into the ingredients that I love in the kitchen. Once we changed the music, the whole experience changed, and I think that was because of finding the right mix of music and food. Now we keep changing the music as we change the food, so that the playlist and menu evolve as one. So, when we start the service, for example, we like to listen to

on
a
plate

light songs, mainly bossa nova like João Gilberto and Tom Jobim. It helps us concentrate all night long. In the middle of the service, when we're running the kitchen and the restaurant is full, music like samba and samba rock is the perfect match and makes us faster and excited. At the moment, I also prefer listening to some contemporary artists like Céu and Criolo in addition to Roberta Sá.

At the end of the night, when the guests are almost done, and thinking about the dinner experience, we play some Brazilian pop music. Romantic ones, like Marisa Monte, Adriana Calcanhotto, and Caetano Veloso, are my favorites to relax with and say goodbye to the kitchen.

CÁMARA

GABRIELA

Gabriela Cámara is the restaurateur, chef, and cookbook author behind renowned seafood restaurant Contramar in Mexico City, Cala in San Francisco, and Onda, in partnership with Jessica Koslow, in Santa Monica. inspired by the confluence of food, art and culture, Cala offers local, sustainable seafood and Bay Area ingredients, while Contramar continues to win accolades and recognition as one of the top restaurants in Mexico. A James Beard semifinalist, Gabriela continues to pioneer sustainability practices and cultivate equitable restaurant environments at her restaurants, while highlighting modern Mexican cuisine.

Song: Chan Chan by Eliades Ochoa y El Quarteto Patria

Contra Playlist ▶ This is some of the music we play in the kitchen while cooking at Cala.

1.	**Shoop**	Salt-N-Pepa
2.	**Mi Historia Entre Tus Dedos**	Los Llayras
3.	**El Verde De Tus Ojos**	Los Yes Yes
4.	**Oye Mujer**	Raymix featuring Juanes
5.	**Los Caminos De La Vida**	La Tropa Vallenata
6.	**Perfecta**	Miranda! featuring Julieta Venegas
7.	**Crawfish**	Elvis Presley
8.	**I Like It**	Cardi B, Bad Bunny, and Jay Balvin
9.	**Criminal**	Natti Natasha x Ozuna featuring Mentes Criminales
10.	**Fuego**	Bomba Éstereo
11.	**Callaita**	Bad Bunny featuring Tainy
12.	**I'm Still in Love with You**	Sean Paul featuring Sasha

This recipe is tied to the song for me because it's on a playlist we've been listening to at Contramar from the very beginning. It feels a little bit festive, fresh, exciting, and this is how I feel when I am making an *aguachile*.

Serves 4 to 6

TROUT
AND
PISTACHIO
AGUACHILE

Recipe Inspiration:

CHAN CHAN

by
Eliades Ochoa
y
El Quarteto Patria

---

500 g fresh trout, cut in sashimi-style fillets

2 teaspoons sea salt

½ red onion, thinly sliced lengthwise

1 cup cilantro (coriander) leaves

½ cup freshly squeezed lime juice

½ cup freshly squeezed orange juice

1 serrano chile, without the stem

50 g clean chopped pistachios

2 tablespoons fresh cold-pressed olive oil

Maldon sea salt or other finishing salt

Arrange the trout fillets on a serving platter. Sprinkle 1 teaspoon of the sea salt over it all.

In a small bowl, sprinkle ½ teaspoon of the sea salt over the onion.

In the jar of a blender, combine the cilantro (coriander), lime and orange juices, chile, and remaining ½ teaspoon salt and blend to liquefy. If it's frothy, let it sit for about 5 minutes so it settles. Pour the contents of the blender over the trout and distribute the chopped pistachios evenly over everything.

Scatter the onion slices over the top. Drizzle with the olive oil and sprinkle with the finishing salt. Serve immediately.

I don't remember life without food and I don't remember life without music. ● I come from musical families, especially my Italian family, so music has always been a part of my life. My grandfather was a singer in the opera. My great-grandfather was a musician. Listening to Puccini operas has also richly influenced my life. What we listen to, what we read, is a huge part of what shapes us. There are things that will remain with us forever—for me, the Greek tragedies are another—and influence how you think. ● In both Mexican and Italian cultures, food is traditionally always accompanied by music. There is truth in those cheesy movies of Italian Mafia New York, the scenes in restaurants where there is always a background of Italian or Neapolitan love songs. Sharing food is a time of joy, sharing, and socializing in both the cultures I come from. ● The music I first heard, of course, was that of my parents. I grew up listening to the Beatles, Bob Dylan, and son jarochos. I was raised in a progressive, socially aware environment and the music was fitting. The music and message of those artists definitely played a part in making me who I am now. It wasn't by design by my parents, but their music represented who they were and the teachings of both led me down the path to the life I chose. ● I got my first Sony Walkman when I was eleven. My father brought it back to me from a trip to the United States. He handed me this amazing new thing; it was like a little purse, but with magical powers. I started listening to cassettes every day, all the time. I felt like I was the coolest kid and like I had access to something rare. And it was different then than it is now. These days, every kid, from anywhere, can have access to everything. Back then, it was special. Finding your music was a great adventure, and what you ended up listening to became who you were, in a way—your identity. You had to look for new things or things new to you, and actually become knowledgeable about them. It was a great pleasure and I am very fortunate to have always lived in a culture, both local and wider, where music was deeply interwoven. ●

**What
you ended up
listening to
became who
you were**

This dynamic has been a constant throughout my life. Sharing music from the late '80s and early '90s in my early teens in Italy created a common ground with people and as a result, I am still friends with them. Music is a starting point for sharing values and knowledge and tastes and points of view—listening to the same music is like growing up with somebody. In a way, it seems like this is an experience that nothing but music can give you. Songs so often register as permanent memories; a vivid one for me is going to listen to jazz in small places in New York as a teenager. That concreteness and connection is something I value very much with friends and my work and my food and my life. ● There are so many bands that I love and which have influenced my work, because they have been there since I started working more formally in food. One singer that has always accompanied me is Caetano Veloso. Music is really an accompaniment to life, to moods, the state of being and existing. In the case of Caetano Veloso, it has been comforting to have his voice in the room at points in my career, to have his music. Caetano has been an inspiration in terms of what he represents as a Latin American progressive protest singer. ● When we opened Contramar, we knew we wanted Latin-sounding background music, but we didn't want it to be the center of the restaurant. A new record, *El Mundo se va a Acabar*, by Mono Blanco, had just come out and we received a copy the night that we opened for friends and family. The group is from Veracruz and is influenced by folkloric Cuban music. I loved how perfectly the music matched the tone of the food that we serve at Contramar. Even if they are from a different coast of Mexico, the spirit is very intimately related. I think that the music from Veracruz, which is very melodic, is culturally linked to the food and style of cooking that Contramar specializes in—fresh, good, nourishing, delicious, exciting, brilliant, bright, acidic, and savory. The Afro, Caribbean, Latin beats are that food for me. ● Growing up in different parts of the world, having music as a common denominator and as a cultural bond with certain groups of people has also been important in my life. Coming to Mexico City, establishing the restaurant and being able to relate to music like *cumbia* and *banda*, popular types of music in Mexico, was an important way of connecting with many of the people who are a part of Contramar, both those who work there and the guests who spend time with us. The timeless interplay between food and music becomes partying and making noise. That's something I think about when setting the right balance with the music in our restaurants.

ANDREA CARLSON

For over a decade,
Chef Andrea Carlson has
left a resounding legacy
on Vancouver's dining scene.
Her commitment to home-
grown ingredients and active
support of local food systems
has led to strong relationships
forged with farmers and
growers who have now caught
the attention of chefs city-
wide. Her signature style
of cooking — delicate, earthy,
and vibrant — captures
the essence of farm-to-table
dining and is a tangible
reminder of her lasting impact
and leadership within the
culinary community.

Chubby Toes and Warm Nose Playlist ▶ Just the things that came to mind for this moment of this day. Tomorrow will be a whole new experience.

1.	**Yèkèrmo Sèw**	Mulatu Astatke
2.	**My Funny Valentine**	Chet Baker
3.	**Only You**	Steve Monite
4.	**'97 Bonnie & Clyde**	Tori Amos
5.	**Colourful Environment**	Gboyega Adelaja
6.	**Wondering Where the Lions Are**	Bruce Cockburn
7.	**I Never Talk to Strangers**	Tom Waits with Bette Midler
8.	**Conversation 16**	The National
9.	**Madame George**	Van Morrison
10.	**Everybody Loves the Sunshine**	Seu Jorge & Almaz

CANADA

This song feels deeply contemplative and restorative. Perfectly paired with a simple and nourishing broth to soothe body and mind.

Makes 6 cups (1.5 liters)

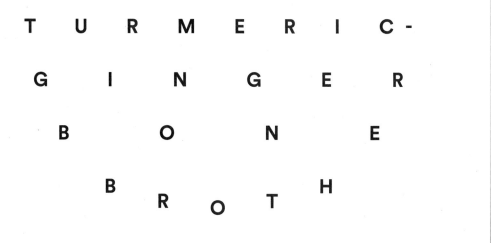

TURMERIC-GINGER BONE BROTH

5 lb organic chicken bones

2 tablespoons white wine vinegar

1 onion, chopped

4 inches fresh ginger, peeled and sliced

Salt

2 teaspoons freshly grated turmeric root

Recipe Inspiration:

WIND AND SNOW

by Grouper

Place the bones and vinegar in a large pot and cover with cold water. (Vinegar helps draw out all the nutrients from the bones.)

Bring to a simmer and skim any foam off the surface.

Keep cooking at a low simmer for 48 hours, topping up the water as needed and keeping the pot partially covered to avoid losing too much water.

Add the onion and ginger when you have 6 hours of cooking left. Cook for the remaining 6 hours.

Strain the broth and discard the bones. Season the broth with salt to taste.

If using immediately, add all of the turmeric, or heat up a cup at a time as desired and finish with a pinch of turmeric.

MUSIC HAS

BEEN A STRONG MO

AND BONDING IN

IN THE KITCH

BEEN IN . . . IT

INCREDIBLE

IN NOT FALLI

THE TRADITIONA

STRUGGLES, IN T

SEXISM, THAT

MORE PREVAL

KITCHENS BACK IN

Song: Wind and Snow by Grouper

▲ Andrea Carlson

W A Y S

V A T O R

U E N C E

S I ' V E

S A N

E S S O N

I N T O

P O W E R

S C A S E

W E R E

T I N

H E   D A Y .

Music was not allowed in the religiously oppressive household of my youth. Consequently, I was alienated from my peers in this department. I developed a goth music interest in my mid-teens through my fellow social outcasts and started listening to The Cure, Depeche Mode, Joy Division, etc.

My first concert was while visiting my grandmother in Vancouver, away from my anti-music stepfather. My mom surreptitiously took me to the David Bowie *Glass Spider Tour*. It made quite an impression.

When I came to the Canadian west coast in my late teens, I discovered old Rolling Stones and '70s folk music through a friend's mom's record collection. I also took an interest in Andy Warhol and other modern artists, which really took hold of me, as did the music of Lou Reed and the Velvet Underground. I embraced all genres of music — clearly making up for lost time. Friends and I had the opportunity to see indie bands rolling through Vancouver in the '90s, like Blur and Soundgarden, and I would go to the annual Vancouver Folk Music Festival, held for a three-day period and featuring musicians from around the world.

Music has always been a strong motivator and bonding influence in the kitchens I've been in. It can, however, also have a polarizing effect, if you're not careful. When I first got into restaurant kitchens, I was listening to Ani Difranco — it set a strong tone in the kitchen and without me realizing it at the time, it was an incredible lesson in not falling into the traditional power struggles, in this case sexism, that were more prevalent in kitchens back in the day. One chef even warned me against listening to Ani's music (as well as me volunteering at groups like Rape Relief and Women Against Violence Against Women), claiming it sent the wrong message or something like that… but obviously, I ignored them.

SANDIA CHANG

Trained at the internationally recognized Culinary Institute of America in New York, Sandia is the sommelier at both bubbledogs and the Michelin-starred Kitchen Table. She prides herself in knowing all her suppliers personally, making regular visits to the small-batch producers in Champagne to research and curate the restaurants' wine lists. In 2018, Sandia was awarded the Best Front of House award at the *GQ* Food and Drink Awards, as well as the Welcome and Service Award by Michelin.

Song: Jump by Kriss Kross

It's My Eclectic Life Playlist ▶ Songs that bring back memories of certain times of my life.

1.	**Blue Monday**	New Order
2.	**Where Is the Love?**	Black Eyed Peas
3.	**Go West**	Pet Shop Boys
4.	**Under Pressure**	Queen and David Bowie
5.	**Pandora's Box**	Orchestral Manoeuvres in the Dark (OMD)
6.	**Lightning Crashes**	Live
7.	**Friday I'm in Love**	The Cure
8.	**Country Grammar**	Nelly
9.	**Volare (Nel Blu di Pinto di Blu)**	Gipsy Kings
10.	**Just Can't Get Enough**	Depeche Mode
11.	**A Little Respect**	Erasure
12.	**Roses**	OutKast

▲ Sandia Chang

Daddy HOT DOG

This is the Mac Daddy of all hot dogs, and it'll make ya Jump Jump.

Serves 6

80 g butter

115 g all-purpose flour

500 g water

500 g milk

5 g salt

530 g grated Red Leicester cheese

Freshly ground black pepper

500 g cooked macaroni
(your favorite mac and cheese pasta)

6 good-quality hot dogs and buns

Crispy bacon (streaky) crumbles, crispy bread crumbs, and crispy onions for toppings (optional)

Melt the butter in a saucepan over medium heat, then add the flour. Cook for 1 minute, whisking constantly.

Add the water, whisking constantly and vigorously, then add the milk in the same way.

Season with the salt and keep on whisking so the sauce does not catch to the pan. Cook until the sauce starts to thicken, about 10 minutes.

Add the cheese in 3 parts, whisking constantly after each addition.

Season with pepper to taste and remove from the heat.

If not using right away, transfer the sauce to a container and cover with plastic wrap (cling film), pressing it on the surface of the sauce. Set aside and let cool, then refrigerate until ready to use.

When you're ready to serve, reheat the sauce gently in a saucepan over low heat. Add the macaroni and stir to coat evenly.

To serve, put a hot dog on a roll and add some macaroni and cheese on top, covering most of the frank but letting both ends show. Sprinkle with bacon and bread crumbs and top with crispy onions, if you like. Repeat!

Recipe Inspiration:

Jump

by Kriss Kross
by Kriss Kross

Being a part of a band or orchestra really teaches you about harmony with

I've always had this philosophy: drink what you like, eat what you like, and be with who you like and you'll never go wrong. With music, it's the same. I listen to the music I like and do what I enjoy, and I believe the results are full-heartedly and passionately good. ● Growing up in Saudi Arabia, my only connection with popular music was what my brother, who is six years older than I, exposed me to. He was going to high school in the U.S., and whatever he brought home when he came to visit me during the summers, I fell in love with. I am a huge fan of the Pet Shop Boys because of that—when I hear them, it always reminds me of the bond between me and brother. ● I first came to England in 2008. My husband and I had been going through a hard time, living apart while I was in America and he was working in England. Then there came an opportunity to see the Pet Shop Boys play live in his hometown of Newmarket, England. He got tickets, and it was a really special moment when I finally got to England. It was a good time to be together, and on top of that, we were listening to my favorite band in his hometown. ● Sharing the '90s British

▲ Sandia Chang

New Wave music my brother introduced me to may be the only common ground he and I had between the two of us, but music has always been a very strong bond for my family. Growing up, we were never allowed TV during dinnertime. Instead, my father always played records while we ate together as a family. My father is a great singer and plays the guitar. He loved listening to Perry Como and Louis Armstrong; "What a Wonderful World" is probably the first song I fell in love with. Music had a positive influence throughout my childhood and beyond, and my dad helped forge this lifelong love affair with music. ● I did the thing so many kids do and joined a band when I was thirteen years old. Being a part of a band or orchestra really teaches you about harmony with others and teamwork, of working toward something bigger than you. It shows you how a lot of people can come together to create something beautiful, as long as everyone does what they are meant to do correctly and sensitively. These lessons carried through to the building of my restaurants and putting the teams together. Same ideals, different artistic form.

others and teamwork, of working toward something bigger than you.

MAY CHOW

May Chow burst onto Hong Kong's foodie scene in 2013 with Little Bao, serving inimitable Chinese burgers. With a reputation for creating unexpected flavor twists, and mixing fine-dining techniques and traditional ingredients, Chow has garnered a loyal following of diners as well as critical acclaim; she was named Asia's Best Female Chef 2017. Chow's success is due to more than her style and creativity; her work is underwritten by dynamic cross-cultural knowhow. Her popularity stems from skill as an innovator and her understanding of what makes diners really tick.

Happy Paradisio Playlist
▶ These Happy Paradise anthems are a mashup of Cantopop, canto disco, disco, funk, hip-hop, female power voices. I generally lean to more female music as well. I think this list embodies the spirit of all the years of music compilation and creating something fun, unique, and original to Happy Paradise. We want everything here to reflect how I feel about Hong Kong and how I feel about myself.

1.	Hot Stuff	Donna Summer
2.	Bad Girl	Anita Mui
3.	Stand on the Word (Larry Levan Mix)	The Joubert Singers (Unabombers Edit)
4.	Rock Me Again & Again & Again & Again & Again & Again	Lyn Collins
5.	Electric Relaxation	A Tribe Called Quest
6.	Creep	TLC
7.	Smooth Operator	Sade
8.	Dance Wit Me	Rufus & Chaka Khan
9.	Young Hearts Run Free	Candi Staton
10.	Part Time Lover	The PB Underground
11.	Cook It	Cookin' on 3 Burners featuring Fallon Williams
12.	Heart of Glass	Blondie
13.	Monica	Leslie Cheung
14.	Hey Ya!	Outkast
15.	Whatta Man	Salt-N-Pepa featuring En Vogue

Recipe Inspiration:

THE SEED (2.0)

by The Roots Ft. Cody Chesnutt

SZECHUAN FRIED CHICKEN

Questlove loved fried chicken so much, at one point he even opened his own chicken joint. I love his style and he inspired this recipe.

Serves 4

LITTLE BAO AND HAPPY PARADISE

Recipe: Szechuan Fried Chicken

60 g kosher salt

2 liters hot water

1 whole chicken, cut into 10 bone-in serving pieces

■ For the Szechuan spice mix:

10 g garlic powder

10 g freshly ground black pepper

10 g paprika

10 g sugar

10 g red chile powder

10 g ground cumin

5 g white sesame seeds

■ For the peppercorn chile oil:

50 g Chinese chile oil

50 g Szechuan peppercorn oil (store-bought is better)

■ 50 g flour

50 g cornstarch (cornflour)

5 litres frying oil such as canola oil or soybean oil

In a bowl or pot large enough to hold all the chicken, stir the salt into the hot water. Let cool.

Add the chicken to the brine and let brine in the fridge for at least 4 hours.

Meanwhile, make the spice mix: In a bowl, mix all the ingredients together.

To make the peppercorn chile oil, whisk together the two oils in a bowl.

(You will have leftover spice mix and peppercorn chile oil—save them for future frying!)

Drain the chicken from the brine and pat dry.

In a large bowl, whisk together the flour and corn-starch (cornflour). Dredge the chicken in the flour mixture until fully coated and let sit in the bowl with the coating clinging in the fridge for about 30 minutes, until the coating becomes adhered and sticky.

Meanwhile, heat the frying oil in a deep pot to 190°C (375°F).

Dredge the chicken pieces in the flour mix again until well coated. Shake off any excess.

Carefully add the chicken pieces to the hot oil and fry for 3 minutes. Remove and let rest for 3 minutes. Fry again for 3 minutes. Remove and arrange on a cooling rack. Transfer to a large clean mixing bowl.

Drizzle 30 g of the pepper-corn chile oil evenly over the chicken, sprinkle with 30 g of the Szechuan spice mix, and toss to coat.

Serve hot.

I bloomed much later in life and I think my music preferences at the time reflected that. When I was young, I was influenced by what my peers listened to. I wasn't comfortable with my lifestyle and I felt like the music I listened to wasn't me either. The only music I listened to was popular, mainstream pop music, which wasn't just about the music, but the behavior around it. Bands like New Kids on the Block or this local artist Sammi Cheng were all about appearance and only talking about popular trends. I used to follow them, but I felt a real disconnect from them and my own personal life. I enjoyed it at that moment, but I feel like I really didn't have a strong connection with what they were saying. ● It wasn't until I went to the U.S. and studied more English that I connected with the lyrics more. I also started listening to different types of music. I went to a very hippie boarding school and all the kids listened to Tracy Chapman. Then I went to college and I hung out with a bunch of artists; I never had artist friends before, and they were much more adventurous in their music selection. We would go to this club night called Heartthrobs, and I believe the DJ who used to spin, DJ Redfoxx, is now doing mixes for Beyoncé. I felt so lucky to be nineteen and listening to such great music. My appreciation of music is something I am now very comfortable with, and now I know how to choose the right music to fit my mood. That has to do with my growth as a person, as well. ● Like I said, I really was a late bloomer. I fell in love at the age of nineteen and I came out at that time, as well, so I was listening to Scissor Sisters, Kate Nash, and Lykke Li. I can see the influences of music on the changes in my life, both in where I was living and how I saw myself. I was confused when I was young, and I didn't really think about music on a deeper level because I was mainly listening to pop music. Slowly, as I became more aware of what music could be, I began to understand it within a larger context. Now my appreciation for great music runs very deep, even though I didn't grow up with it. As I was figuring out who I was, I was also figuring out what I loved and what represented me. I would say this is the time of my awakening. I started to go to indie concerts, going to see small bands like Aqualung and MIKA, going to a lot of different clubs. I really loved and related to MIKA. He has an interesting background because he is an immigrant and he is gay, and I loved that he is cheerful about life. His music has a positive sound, but he dives into really deep issues and I related to that. I felt liberated, finally going toward my path to being a person with a clear identity. ● I remember my first breakup, listening over and over to Adele and MIKA, which was a little self-indulgent, but it helped me get through the rough patch. I feel there are three types of songs I really like: those about the pursuit of happiness, the search for love, and enjoying freedom—three things I really connect with. Whether those subjects are in the lyrics or in the beats, that's what I'm always looking for. ● In the two

I had to adjust the volume and the seasoning to make sure they were balanced.

▲ May Chow

restaurants I opened, Little Bao and Happy Paradise, I use music just as much as the food to connect with people. Little Bao focuses on fun, so our playlist includes a lot of '90s hip-hop and indie music. At Happy Paradise, which is a progressive celebration of Chinese and Cantonese food, we define the music as a "polysexual heaven," and it is the soundtrack for our take on an artistic approach toward a modern Chinese dining experience. Expect Balearic tropical jams, power female voices (think Chaka Khan, Madonna, Whitney, Donna Summer), disco, and '70s to '90s Cantopop, with a hit of hip-hop, indie, and everything in between. It sounds insane, but it works. I don't think people ever thought about listening to this mix of music while eating Chinese food. It's not common, but it's something that I really appreciate. ● For awhile I worked along-side a DJ called DJ Fabsabs. The story of our first meeting is funny: I wanted to find a DJ who was not only able to play Chinese music, but also able to play around with it, deliver different beats and different vibes, so we could curate a music playlist specific to Happy Paradise. One of my colleagues told me that they had found the perfect person for me. That was a clear moment when I realized this job isn't about just doing it by myself, but instead about finding like-minded people already doing similar things who I could collaborate with. ● I called him on the phone and he spoke to me in perfect Cantonese. Then I met him — and he's a white guy! I'm like, "What?!" This Chinese music expert is a white guy, but he speaks terrific Cantonese. Turns out he had grown up in Hong Kong, and he'd been collecting Cantopop vinyl for decades. He has this massive collection, totally under-stood what I wanted, and he is also gay. We started putting queer power anthems against Canto music, playing Power Voices from China versus things like Madonna and Chaka Khan. It was such a fun experience to curate with him. That's a perfect exam-ple of how we connect our food with our music at Happy Paradise. ● Ultimately there is no one type of good music; there are only different rhythms and different beats in many different genres. Food plays in the same way, because there are only different ingredients and different flavors. When we

talk about the restaurants that we celebrate now, it's not just about the food — we talk about their vibe. We talk about their lighting. We talk about their music. Many authentic restaurants are able to achieve this total experience because they are derived from someone's clear vision. Having the "right" music is key, as it affects all senses. I remem-ber during the early days of Happy Paradise, we had the music super loud. Meanwhile, guests mentioned to me that the food was under-seasoned and too subtle. I had to adjust the volume and the seasoning to make sure they were balanced. ● I spe-cifically had a vision to explore Chinese culture and to showcase it to an interna-tional audience. In retrospect, I've always wanted to find my personal expression of how to do the music, so that it enhances what I am cooking. When we looked at the music options, we weren't just simply say-ing, "We're going to do traditional Chinese food and then we're going to play some tra-ditional Chinese music. This is the Chinese music, and this is the Chinese food." I had to ask the question, "What is May Chow going to do with it?" I had to adjust the volume and the seasoning to make sure they were balanced. For example, I thought of Miley Cyrus, who went from being a Disney child star to doing her own type of music. She had to prove the point to her fans that she was not one-dimensional, not two-dimensional, or even three-dimensional. Sometimes when people perceive you from one angle that they love you for, they can't necessar-ily see you from any other. For example, people said Rihanna can't do Adele-type music, because people don't want to see Rihanna doing Adele music — even though her ballads are quality music, they just want her to do "Umbrella." But she didn't take no for an answer, she made the music she wanted to make. I had to adjust the volume and the seasoning to make sure they were balanced. What I learned from all of these artists is that you need to work very hard to prove that you can be true to your art and take it in different directions. While it's much harder to start out doing one style and then expanding, I applied the insight from the people who inspired me to what has happened in my restaurants when I was creating dishes, and have found success.

SHIRLEY CHUNG

A native of Beijing and a proud Chinese-American, Chef Shirley Chung brings a playfulness and refinement of flavors to her culinary creations. Shirley emigrated to America at age seventeen for college, and worked in Silicon Valley before following her passion for food. She attended the California Culinary Academy in San Francisco, and trained with Thomas Keller at Bouchon, Guy Savoy, and Jose Andres at China Poblano.

I Am Chinese-American Playlist
▶ Growing up in Beijing, I always knew my family was different from my friends' families. We had coffee and milk at breakfast time instead of soybean milk and congee. My grandma and my parents secretly listened to Western classical music and English songs from old records and a short-wave radio station called "Sound of America" behind closed doors. After my grandma passed, my father told me we were moving back to California. The Chung family has been in Southern California for five generations, since 1900. I grew up with songs and music from both cultures, so this is who I am. I embrace and love being Chinese-American.

1.	Never Regret	Beyond
2.	He Ri Jun Zai Lai	Zhou Xuan
3.	Bohemian Rhapsody	Queen
4.	The Great Wall	Beyond
5.	Wake Me Up When September Ends	Green Day
6.	18th Floor Balcony	Blue October
7.	Half Dreaming But Half Awake	Alan Tam
8.	From the Bottom of My Broken Heart	Britney Spears
9.	Sky	Faye Wong
10.	Surge of Red Dust	Sarah Chen
11.	Heaven	Bryan Adams and DJ Sammy
12.	Love Me Tender	Elvis Presley
13.	Santeria	Sublime
14.	Hard Headed Woman	Cat Stevens
15.	Girl on Fire	Alicia Keys

Song: Surge of Red Dust by Sarah Chen

▲ Shirley Chung

Surge of Red Dust by Sarah Chen

USA

MS CHI CAFE

Surge of Red Dust

"Surge of Red Dust" is about a love story during WWII, and love didn't win. It reminds me of a similar story in my family. Grandpa was second-generation Chinese-American and grew up in L.A. His father sent him back to Beijing for medical school, and that's where he met my grandma. Over the next fifty years, they circular migrated between the U.S. and China. They fell in love over their common political goals, as some of the first who joined the Communist party. In the end, the same political party tore them apart. Grandpa escaped back to the U.S. in 1975, and Grandma never forgave or spoke of him again.

This soup is savory, earthy, a little spicy, and slightly bitter from the angelica root. The base flavor is Chinese herbal medicine, very complex and bold, and it finishes sweet because of the goji berries. Just like the love story of my grandparents, life is hard, love is not perfect, and there are heartbreaks, sprinkled with happiness. Grandma was stubborn — her bedroom window was held together with a green wire that Grandpa put on as a temporary fix and she left it there for fifteen years. Right before Grandpa passed away in San Francisco, he stared at me and thought I was Grandma. "Siyi, don't forget your sweater, wait for me, I am about to get on the train." I believed they still loved each other...and that their love lives on in this bowl of soup.

Serves 6 to 8

2 lb (900 g) pork neck bones	
2 lb (900 g) pork spareribs	
1 teaspoon canola oil	
4 cloves garlic, peeled but left whole	
¼ cup (40 g) black peppercorns	
¼ cup (40 g) white peppercorns	
3 tablespoons (18 g) whole cumin seeds	
3 star anise	
2 oz (56 g) angelica root	
2 oz (56 g) American ginseng	
1 cinnamon stick	
3 tablespoons (45 ml) soy sauce	
2 tablespoons (30 ml) dark soy sauce	
4 dried shiitake mushrooms	
2 tablespoons (14 g) goji berries	
Salt	

Put the pork neck bones and spareribs in an 8- to 10-quart stockpot, fill with water, and place over medium heat. When the water starts to bubble but not quite boil, turn off the heat and let rest for 10 minutes. You will see blood start to coagulate at the ends of the bones. Wipe them off and place all of the bones in a clean large stockpot to make the soup. Fill with water to barely cover the bones.

Heat the oil in a small sauté pan over medium heat. Fry the garlic in the oil until golden. Remove from the heat and set aside.

Put the black peppercorns, white peppercorns, cumin seeds, and star anise in a soup spice pouch and add it to the stockpot. Add the fried garlic, angelica root, ginseng, cinnamon stick, soy sauce, dark soy, and dried shiitake. Simmer over low heat for 3 hours. Add the goji berries during the last 5 minutes of cooking. Salt to taste and serve hot.

▲ Shirley Chung

Music plays a very big part in Chinese culture. We had our own instruments and our own style of composition, and it stayed that way into the '80s. Then Chinese people started to absorb global pop culture and started translating Western music into Chinese. We also started to have our own pop music. ● Just like with music, we have a very deep food culture, with five thousand years of our own traditions. Lately, Chinese culture has really opened up to the world, taking in a lot of influence from Western culture as well as modernizing itself, growing as the world grows and spreading its influence across the globe. ● Not too long ago, only Chinese people cooked Chinese food, and there were only eight regions of food from China that were considered authentic. As people grew more interested in Chinese food, and as people in China began to bring more of their food out of the country, people began to see this type of food all over the world from all different regions of China. Dumplings are now one of the most popular foods in America, but that is only a recent trend. ● Food has always had a big influence in my life. Growing up, my family always connected through food, which is how my grandmother raised me. When I was in elementary school, I liked to have parties so I could share food with my friends, but also share music with them. Listening to music

and eating are such joys when you can share these rituals with other people. To this day, I make connections with people through cooking for them and singing with them. Food and music create such close connections because they connect people's emotions without actually having a shared language. They are common languages of love that express your feelings. ● My father introduced me to music. He loved classical music and Western music, but I grew up in Beijing in the late '70s and '80s, a very conservative time, so my dad had to hide it from almost everybody else. It was like a secret we shared. He would always hum "Dance of the Sugarplum Fairies" around the house, so it was the first song I fell in love with. I loved the beat, and the way it connected me with my father. ● Music is often the first thing that connects you with new people. When I first moved to the Bay Area in America, I was seventeen. I was meeting a lot of foreign students and going to ESL classes. We foreign kids were barely speaking English and we didn't share the same language, but what we could do was share the music that we all liked. I remember bringing my Chinese and Cantonese pop music from Hong Kong to share with my friends, and they shared pop music from Korea and Japan with me. That's how we connected with each other. Later on, when I got out of my ESL class,

I was listening to American pop music like Boyz II Men and Kriss Kross. It was the first time that I experienced R&B and hip-hop. This type of music is very unique to American culture, and that is how I first really learned about the culture, through its music. ● My love for both Chinese and American music allowed me to connect with myself and in turn to cook the food that really represents who I am. When I went on *Top Chef* for the second time, I wanted to do better than the first time. I wanted to do something bigger, but I didn't know exactly what that was. I was driving in my car when Alicia Keys's "Girl on Fire" came on, and it clicked in my head how I wanted to represent myself. I am proud of who I am, and part of who I am is what I cook. I'm a Chinese-American, but I never truly cooked 100 percent Chinese-American food. I really wanted to present that on the show and represent the future of Chinese-American culture, too. Filipino-Americans had a food movement, Japanese-Americans had a food movement, a lot of other Asian-American cultures have had a food movement, but Chinese-Americans have not. I was hoping that by cooking 100 percent Chinese-American food, I could help kickstart that movement. "Girl on Fire" inspired me to really cook what I wanted to cook, to embrace who I am, and to represent

Food and music …

my culture on national television. ● The music I love, the food I cook, and the restaurant I created all match the kind of person I am. I'm a very outgoing, happy person in general, and so the music that I listen to is very upbeat with a lot of passion. I also like to listen to rock music that has high energy instead of slow and mellow music. My style of food really reflects that as well, and is always packed with big flavors that play with a lot of texture and really bright colors. ● My restaurant, Ms Chi Cafe, is a very casual, pop-influenced cafe that has really bright colors and food alike. It is very poppy and very inviting, a space that everyone is invited to be a part of. Everything about it is all sort of connected to who I am and that's my life in the world of music— everything comes together. We play a lot of pop songs like Ariana Grande, Britney Spears, and those kinds of fun, teenage happy songs. Sometimes when we are tired in the kitchen and we want to have some fun, I make my line cooks be my backup dancers while I dance and sing to Britney Spears. We can all wake up a little, and music definitely brings a lot of joy to us. We always believe that happy people make food taste better. We are constantly having fun, and much of the time it's because of the music. ● I'm a very emotional cook; I always cook with my heart. A lot of times, music directly affects how

I cook or how the food turns out. It emerges from the way a song affects how I feel at that moment. My Surge of Red Dust soup recipe came about because I wanted to create a dish dedicated to my grandparents. Around the time that my grandfather passed away, I wanted to create a dish that told my family story. When I was thinking about what to cook, I was listening to some of my grandparents' old classical records, from Frank Sinatra to Old Shanghai's Zhong Xuan, and those songs sparked my memory. It made me miss them a lot and I thought about the journey they went through and remembered their love story. It ultimately made me think of how they felt when they ended up breaking up. Their story was not a forever love story, but it was a very good love story that took place around World War II, when they traveled together around the world... only to end in heartbreak. The songs on those old records brought up all of those emotional memories and at that moment, I created this dish. ● My grandfather was a fifth-generation Chinese-American, and his father came to America as a Chinese herbalist. When I thought about all they went through, their heartbreak, and tied into the emotion of their records, I cried. I took all of that and created a bitter Chinese herbal broth, which I ladled into the

bottom of a dish. When I tasted that broth, I felt like I could taste my heart at that time. I also added spice to the broth because of my grandmother. She didn't get to see who I became, but she had always been my role model. She was such a strong woman, and so I made it spicy to make it extremely savory as a counterpoint to the bitterness. I wanted to add in a little sweetness at the end because I wanted to remember the happiness that came from their relationship, so I added goji berries to finish. This dish is very complex because their relationship was complex. And life is not all about sweet, so there's bitterness, there's balance with spiciness, and there's a little brightness. ● I felt like I could taste my heart at that time because I was very proud of who I had become. I really wanted to showcase that moment to my parents and to my grandparents, who I felt were watching me from above. I get very emotional when I think about this dish because it is also tied to that music I was listening to that makes me think about my grandparents. I wanted to be honest about how emotional I can be, that I can be sad because I miss them. Everything about this dish is my emotion. It is not the happiest emotion, but it is a dish I am very proud of.

love

SARAH CICOLINI

Sarah Cicolini was born in 1988 in Guardiagrele, Italy. She moved to Rome to study medicine, but at twenty-two years old, she left university and interned at Roy Caceres's Michelin-starred restaurant, Metamorfosi. During the spring of 2017, Sarah opened SantoPalato in Rome with her friend and co-owner Alberto Bloise. Her dishes are authentic, rooted in the Roman tradition, and based on ingredients she hand-picks during her daily market trips.

Song: DNA. by Kendrick Lamar

Kitchen Vibes Playlist
▶ This playlist sets my personal rhythm.

1.	**Ready or Not**	Fugees
2.	**L'ultima festa**	Cosmo
3.	**Sonnet**	The Verve
4.	**HUMBLE.**	Kendrick Lamar
5.	**Personal Jesus**	Depeche Mode
6.	**The Test**	The Chemical Brothers
7.	**Two against One**	Danger Mouse and Daniele Luppi featuring Jack White
8.	**Crew Love**	Drake featuring The Weeknd
9.	**What Katie Did**	The Libertines
10.	*****Flawless**	Beyoncé featuring Chimamanda Ngozi Adichie
11.	**Mob Ties**	Drake

ITALY

This recipe
shares stories with
my own roots.

SANTOPALATO

Serves 4

SWEETBREADS, MONK'S BEARD, BABY SPINACH

Recipe Inspiration:

DNA.
by
Kendrick
Lamar

■ For the veal jus:

4 kg veal bones

3 yellow onions

2 celery stalks

2 carrots

Extra-virgin olive oil

Salt

■ 600 g veal sweetbreads,
cleaned and outer membrane removed

Salt

80 g salted butter

Vegetable oil

Freshly ground black pepper

Extra-virgin olive oil, fresh lemon juice,
and salt to taste, for dressing the greens

200 g monk's beard,
boiled until tender and drained

50 g baby spinach leaves

To make the jus, roast bones and vegetables in the oven for 30 minutes at 200°C. Transfer the bones and vegetables to a huge pan with the olive oil and salt. Add water and ice and wait for the boiling begin. After 6 hours, strain the liquid and cool down. Take off all the fat on the surface. Put the remaining broth in a pan and boil again for 3 hours. Now the jus is ready.

Put the cleaned sweetbreads in a bowl of salted water.

In a sauté pan over medium heat, melt the butter in the vegetable oil.

Drain the sweetbreads, add to the pan, and cook for 7 minutes on each side. Season with salt and pepper. Turn off the fire and pour in some veal jus to cover the sweetbreads.

To serve, arrange the sweetbreads on plates and brush with a little more jus.

Dress the monk's beard and baby spinach leaves. Place the spinach leaves over the sweetbreads and arrange the monk's beard in honeycombs on each side.
Serve immediately.

Song: DNA. by Kendrick Lamar

Hip-hop really helped me become who I am now. I started listening to hip-hop artists the moment I understood that I wanted to be a cook. I like the American hip-hop scene— N.W.A., Biggie Smalls, Drake, Kanye West. It's a lifestyle and I believe in it fully. Just like the singers dare with rhythm, I dare with flavors in the kitchen while listening to their music. It's my primary creative influence and its deep message of freedom, experimentation, pushing the boundaries is inter- woven into my cooking. I love to freestyle like a rapper, flowing different tastes when I cook.

●

The hip-hop and rap scene in Rome is inspiring and connected to this city. There are so many songs talking about Rome, and since Rome adopted me, all these songs give me a tremendous sense of belonging to the city. Music helped me meet various people in all the places where DJs play in Rome. They are so welcoming and friendly, which helped me with my social relationships and helped me build roots in my adopted home.

●

This music strengthens you up. It fills you with confidence. It gives you solutions to get through your problems. It helped me out during hard times, especially when I quit practicing medicine to become a personal chef. Being a home chef was my first approach to this professional world. I needed music to concentrate, so I used to put my earphones on and listen to my favorite songs while I cooked.

dare with rhythm,

Just like the singers

I dare with flavors

▲ Sarah Cicolini

●

When I worked at Metamorfosi in Rome, Chef Roy Caceres always listened to Latin music during service. Every dish was inspired by and linked to the music and many ingredients he likes to cook with come directly from his cultural roots. He taught me that music plays an enormous role during pre-service too. It is connected to all creative moments in the kitchen, well before opening hours. One change in my restaurant is that I do not listen to music during service, I am pretty busy and fully focused on cooking. Sometimes I can whisper or murmur some Italian refrains, but that's something that I really do not control, it's independent from my mind. It just escapes when inspiration hits me.

in the kitchen while

listening to their music.

●

I frequently think about new dishes when I'm inspired by songs during a specific moment in my life. Inspiration can come while I drive or while I jog in the morning. For example, my famous *pasta fagioli* comes directly from Wu-Tang Clan's song "Protect Ya Neck." The line "watch your step kid" is repeated and repeated and repeated over and over again — it reminds me to create new things without losing my roots. And when it comes to my roots, when I'm cooking and recollecting recipes from family memories, I always feel the beat of "1984" by Salmo, a famous Italian rapper running through me, pulling me home. I had the pleasure of cooking for Salmo, who chose carbonara from our menu, and it was exactly what I would have cooked for him. I wish I could cook for Kendrick Lamar. I would teach him how to perform the perfect *scarpetta* — when you use a piece of bread to slightly clean the sauce from the plate with it, to elongate the pleasure of eating — on a spectacular *trippa alla romana*.

NINA COMPTON

Winner of the James Beard Award Best Chef: South in 2018 and one of *Food & Wine* magazine's Best New Chefs in 2017, Nina Compton is chef/owner of award-winning Compère Lapin and the highly acclaimed Bywater American Bistro (BAB) in New Orleans. A woman of many hats, Nina Compton also serves as the Culinary Ambassador of St. Lucia.

Recipe Inspiration:

THE SEED (2.0)

by The Roots Ft. Cody Chesnutt

Straight Outta Compton Playlist ▶
Every morning, I wake up, I put music on—sometimes even before I tell my husband good morning. It really puts me in a good mood and sets the tone of my day. I have a very stressful job, and sometimes I need to refocus my energy on something more positive.

1.	**Rocking Time**	Dennis Brown
2.	**Young Blood**	The Naked and Famous
3.	**Don't Speak**	No Doubt
4.	**Break You Off**	The Roots featuring Musiq Soulchild
5.	**Award Tour**	A Tribe Called Quest
6.	**I'm Sorry**	Swell featuring Shiloh
7.	**Bitch, Don't Kill My Vibe**	Kendrick Lamar
8.	**Duppy Conqueror**	Bob Marley & The Wailers
9.	**Hey Young World**	Slick Rick
10.	**Waiting in Vain**	Bob Marley & The Wailers
11.	**Ice Cream**	Raekwon
12.	**The Road**	Machel Montano x Ashanti
13.	**2 AM**	Slightly Stoopid
14.	**Desafinado**	Stan Getz and Joao Gilberto
15.	**Night Nurse**	Gregory Isaacs

Jerk Oxtail & SWEET PLANTAIN Gnudi

This song gets me so pumped when I listen to it; it really gets my creative juices rolling. So the dish I created listening to it has to have depth and flavor. You can find jerk meat on any street corner in the islands. Oxtail is a great Southern protein that works beautifully in this tender, succulent dish.

Serves 4 to 6

■ For the jerk spice:

3 tablespoons cayenne pepper

1 tablespoon onion powder

1 tablespoon garlic powder

1 tablespoon ground ginger

1 tablespoon brown sugar

½ tablespoon ground cinnamon

½ tablespoon ground allspice

1 teaspoon paprika

■ **10 lb oxtail**

1 medium onion, cut into ¼-inch dice

1 carrot, cut into ¼-inch dice

2 celery stalks, cut into ¼-inch dice

6 sprigs thyme

6 tablespoons tomato paste

4 cups dry red wine

4 quarts brown chicken stock

■ For the plantain gnudi:

3 cups canola oil, for frying

2 lb ripe plantains, peeled and cut into thick slices

6 egg yolks, beaten

Pinch of salt

3 cups flour

■ For the herbed bread crumbs:

1 cup mint leaves

1 cup parsley leaves

1 cup cilantro (coriander) leaves

2 cups toasted panko bread crumbs

To make the jerk spice, stir together all the ingredients in a small bowl.

Dust the oxtail all over with the jerk spice.

In a large skillet over medium-high heat, sear the oxtail on all sides, then transfer to a plate and set aside.

Lower the heat to medium and cook the onion, carrot, and celery for 5 minutes, stirring often. Stir in the thyme, tomato paste, and red wine and cook for 10 minutes, or until the liquid is reduced by half.

Preheat the oven to 300°F (150°C).

In a large Dutch oven or other oven- and flameproof dish, combine the oxtail, the red wine sauce, and enough chicken stock to cover the oxtail. Braise for about 3 hours, or until fork-tender.

While the oxtail is cooking, make the *gnudi*: In a deep medium sauté pan, heat ▶|

the canola oil to 350°F (180°C). Fry the plantains until golden brown on both sides. Transfer to paper towels to drain.

Put the plantains in a food processor and purée until smooth. Transfer to a large bowl, stir in the egg yolks, and season with a little salt. Fold in the flour until the mixture just comes together. Pinch off dough pieces and roll into ¼-inch balls. Place on a floured baking sheet as you work. Set aside.

Bring a large pot of salted water to a boil over medium-high heat. While the water is coming to a boil, make the herbed bread crumbs: In a frying pan over medium heat, fry the herbs until they stop bubbling.

In a food processor, combine the herbs and bread crumbs and buzz until the crumbs turn green.

Take the meat off the oxtail bones and set aside on a plate. Discard the bones. Strain the liquid and return it to the pot. Over medium-high heat, cook for 5 minutes to reduce the liquid a little, then reduce the heat to low, return the meat to the pot, and simmer for 15 minutes before serving.

Add the *gnudi* to the boiling water and cook for about 2 minutes, then drain in a colander.

Toss the *gnudi* with the jerk oxtail. Serve immediately, topped with the bread crumbs.

● I would have loved to cook for Bob Marley because I'd love to pick his brain about things—because he wasn't just a musician, he was also a social activist. As for the dish, I have this food memory that I will never forget when I was living in Jamaica. I stopped at this little roadside restaurant, and this guy's breakfast menu was fresh juices and plantain porridge, which I turned my nose up at a little bit, thinking it all sounded terrible. Thankfully, my friend made me try it and it was amazing. It has been twenty years, but I still remember that dish because it was just something that was so simple, but so beautiful. I have never seen it anywhere else but in Jamaica. The porridge is plantains cooked down with coconut milk, ginger, and nutmeg, and it all becomes a silky, creamy soup for breakfast. It's just so decadent, just so simple and it's what I would cook for Bob. ● As I was getting older and understanding how the world runs, Bob became a big influence. Growing up, he was one of those people who spoke a lot about social issues in the Caribbean and how the systems are messed up. Bob Marley was such a rebel, and as a teenager, I was trying to follow that same path of doing what I want, what I believed in. He had so many songs that meant so much to me, like the words of "Redemption Song," but he was also romantic, like "Waiting in Vain." That's such a beautiful song and melody. ● I listen to reggae because it represents a sense of me. It puts me in a peaceful place because I believe when people listen to reggae, it puts them in a good mood. When I'm

in the kitchen, whenever I'm making homemade pasta, I put reggae on, because it's like a repetition. It just puts me in this beautiful mindset to make these things with my hands, and you have to be in a good place to make the shapes or strands look more uniform, more beautiful. You don't want to make something that's misshapen or doesn't look right. ● Jamaicans are very proud people: they're proud about their music and they're proud of their food. I was twenty and I remember being in the kitchen at Sandals Resort by myself, without family or friends with me. One of the cooks invited me to this dancehall event to experience the culture of Jamaica. She picked me up wearing a bright green wig with matching leggings. I felt so underdressed; I did not understand the dancehall culture. Everybody had these extravagant outfits on, and it all came down to the music, the certain dance that was for each song, and I felt out of my element. But it was also exhilarating to be a fly on the wall because I was learning how seriously they take music down there. ● Similar to music, eating a dish from your childhood is more than just a taste. Food transports people back to those memories. I think it's special that you know as a chef that you're able to bring people back to a moment in time. ● My early life setting was our house in the Caribbean—we had this beautiful veranda located in Saint Lucia, from which you could see the neighboring island of Martinique. When I was a child, my mom loved to play music when she was in the kitchen.

I was exposed to music at a young age, and it was always the classics. She'd play Julio Iglesias, because she's a big romantic; Abba, if she was in a fun and festive mood; or Aretha Franklin, because she absolutely loved listening to her. My dad likes the classics. He loved Mozart, but mom set the vibe. You'd wake up in the morning and she'd be playing "Dancing Queen." It really set the tone for the household. It was just one of those things…we'd play music and we'd all help set the table together. We would play music and we'd have lunch. ● That was special for me because, for a lot of families, it's not a daily thing to sit down and eat. Lunch is a big thing in the Caribbean, not so much dinnertime; lunch is the biggest meal of the day for us. My dad would come home from work and we'd all have lunch. There'd be music and we'd sit down for two hours and just spend time together. That tradition was one of those things that just rounded out the moments for us. ● Growing up in St. Lucia, you have friends that are African, Indian, English, and all are connected with food and music. It all intersects. There's a French-African type of music called Zouk, and when anyone hears this music in the Caribbean, everybody gets up and dances together. It's a beautiful, harmonious moment where there's no inhibition, just people letting go. ● Every October in St. Lucia, we have this beautiful celebration for an entire month called Jounen Kwéyòl, which focuses on our food and musical heritage. It's a celebration of creation month, and we have a lot of local drummers drumming. We have something called the Shak Shak, which is a little pod that grows on a tree. When it dries out, the seeds create a tambourine kind of sound, which the drummers shake. With the drums, you hear a lot of West African influences come out. People also get dressed up in traditional St. Lucian garb to celebrate. And there are, of course, a lot of traditional St. Lucian dishes. This cuisine has French influences from the Caribbean, and you will see a lot of local ingredients like rum or cocoa on the menu along with dishes like *accra* (salted fish beignets), *paime* (cornmeal dessert), and *souse* (head cheese). ● I always play music from the moment I get up in the morning. I wake up, I check my emails, I listen to music. I'm in the shower, I put on music. It never stops. I think it drives my husband crazy, but it puts me in a good mood. Just like my mom, the right song sets the tone for my day. It's the same thing with food: once I'm energized to go to work, I energize the people around me. I think it affects how they cook, how my day goes, and how excited they get about our food when I'm in a great mental space to create things. I think music and what I cook go hand-in-hand for me. Good food, good music, and good people are the Holy Trinity—if one thing is off, it doesn't make any sense. ● When I get home from the restaurant, I'm really wound up. I put my headphones on and zone out. I'll read a cookbook or browse through something just to get my creative juices flowing. I'll write little notes, like "sea urchin" or "cauliflower," listening to music at the end of the night. Then I'll go back to the restaurant, try the ideas out, and see if anything comes together or not. Listening to somebody like Santigold, who is just very chill but still very upbeat, gets me into a good zone for getting my creative juices flowing. ● My best friend is a chef. Ten years ago, we opened up a restaurant together. Things are never easy, but we became close very quickly because we went through so many hardships to open this restaurant. We had our soundtrack: '90s hip-hop. We would play Eric B. & Rakim and Run-DMC—we were just so hyped up on the music that we would troubleshoot all these ideas and come up with a dish like roasted halibut, mushrooms, and egg yolk sauce. A lot of those dishes were inspired by being energized by the music and just shooting out ideas. We made up some of the best dishes together because we were on the same wavelength. To this day, he sends me a text with just the words "A Tribe Called Quest" and a song title. Immediately, the memories and dishes that we created in the kitchen together come rushing back. It makes my day, makes me smile about the things that we had to go through ten years ago to open that restaurant. And after ten years, we still have a connection through music. ● As a chef, you're always pushing to be creative, to not do the same thing twice. As artists, we strive for that. Having a restaurant, that's your stage, you're showcasing what you love and what you want people to experience.

IT NEVER STOPS

DOMINIQUE CRENN

Dominique Crenn, the chef/owner of three Michelin-starred Atelier Crenn of San Francisco, focuses on cuisine as a craft and the community as an inspiration. In 2011, Crenn opened Atelier Crenn, a deeply personal project, where her heritage and ode to "poetic culinaria" is embodied through the whimsical creations she shares with her guests. An active member of the international culinary community, Crenn promotes innovation, sustainability, and equality through her participation with various panels and summits. Crenn was awarded World's Best Female Chef in 2016 by San Pellegrino's 50 Best Restaurants.

Crenn Jams Playlist ▶ These are songs from my personal journey... songs I grew up with, songs I dance to in my kitchen, songs I associate with my restaurant family.

Nocturne in E Flat Major

by Frédéric Chopin

1.	Non, je ne regrette rien	Édith Piaf
2.	Nocturne in E Flat Major (Op. 9, No. 2)	Frédéric Chopin
3.	L'amour est un oiseau rebelle	Maria Callas
4.	Ain't Got No — I Got Life	Nina Simone
5.	Take a Chance on Me	ABBA
6.	Rock and Roll All Nite	Kiss
7.	All I Want for Christmas Is You	Mariah Carey
8.	Shoop	Salt-N-Pepa
9.	Lady Marmalade	featuring P!nk, Lil' Kim, Missy Elliott, Christina Aguilera
10.	We Are the Champions	Queen

Song: Nocturne in E Flat Major by Frédéric Chopin

▲ Dominique Crenn

USA

Geoduck Tartelette

Recipe Inspiration:

The elegance and mystery in this song influenced this recipe. Mist clears away to reveal flowers and a perfect bite: koshihikari rice tart with local sea urchin poached in brown butter and geoduck from our own coast intertwined with citrus from Sonoma, and finally a mousseline with citrus, lemon grass, and lemon verbena.

Makes 25 tartelettes

■ For the tart pastry

140 g	Cup4Cup gluten-free flour
130 g	koshihikari rice flour
40 g	brown rice flour
10 g	salt
50 g	brown sugar
140 g	butter
2 g	xanthan gum
1 whole egg (45 g)	
60 g	water

Mix all ingredients except egg and water in robot until mixed. Place in bowl and add egg and water. Mix with hands until incorporated. Roll on setting 4.5 in a pasta machine. Punch 25 punches at 2.25 in and 25 punches at 1.5 in. Place the larger holes in the tart mold and the smaller flat on a silpat. Bake at 325 no fan for 8 minutes, spin and finish for 7 minutes.

■ For the pineapple gel

350 g	pineapple vinegar
1 ea	pineapple charred
10 g	garlic
40 g	ginger
50 g	jalapeno
1 ea	lemon grass
3 g	lime zest
40 g	lime juice

Combine all ingredients and smoke. Strain and reserve until ready to use. Set with 1.3% fish gelatin.

■ For the mousseline reduction

200 g	champagne vinegar
300 g	vermouth
300 g	white wine
300 g	shallots
10 g	lemon verbena
10 g	lemon thyme
10 g	tarragon
1	lemon peel
1	mandarin peel
1	lime peel
2	lemongrass stalks, peeled and chopped
200 g	Pineapple vinegar

Reduce all ingredients except for the pineapple vinegar. Add pineapple vinegar when liquid is cooled.

■ For the mousseline base

100 g	Butter
100 g	Egg Yolks
100 g	Mousseline Reduction

Once weighed out, place everything in a vacuum sealed bag and cook at 75C for 30min. Once cooked, place contents in a blender and blend. Reserve warm. ▶︎

■ For the mousseline cream

1100 g heavy (whipping) cream

2 ea lemongrass stalks, peeled and chopped

3 ea lemon zest

2 ea mandarin zest

3 ea lime zest

25 g lemon verbena

salt and shiro to taste.

Vacuum seal all ingredients and steep overnight. Whip slowly until stiff peaks. Hold separately. Vacuum reduction with butter and egg yolks. Cook at 75C for 30 minutes. Blend to bring together and season with lemon and shiro. On pick up fold 70 g whipped citrus cream into 35 g Mousseline base.

■ Citrus Gel

100 g pomelo juice

25 g Orange Juice

25 g lemon Juice

Shiro Dashi TT

Salt TT

UltraTex

Mix the juices together, Season with Shiro Dashi and Salt. Thicken with Ultratex until a this gel is formed.

■ Sea urchin

Poach .25 tray of sea urchin at 55°C in brown butter seasoned with shiro.

■ Geoduck

1 ea Geoduck 2 lb

Remove the shell from the geoduck along with the belly and innards. Leaving only the skin on siphon tip. Blanch one each geoduck in boiling water for 20 seconds and shock immediately. At this point the skin should be easily removed by hand. Cut the geoduck in half lengthwise. Working quickly, clean the geoduck with a partially damp towel until all the sand is removed. Place the geoduck in a container set on top of a container full of ice, making sure the geoduck is cold. Slice the geoduck as thin as possible with a sharp knife. Reserve in a container set over ice.

■ Citrus slices

1 ea pomello

1 ea naval orange

1 ea lemon

1 ea tangerine

1 ea grapefruit

Break down the citrus separately into supremes. Slice ¾ s of the supremes as thin as possible, around the same thickness as the geoduck and place aside.

Reserve the rest for dice.

■ Citrus Dice

Dice the reserved supremes intro 1 cm dice. Poach in brown butter at 55°C for 10 minutes.

To assemble:
Place a small amount of citrus gel on the tart tops. This will act as a binder. Switching between citrus and sliced geoduck, make a rosette. Reserve the complete tart tops until final assembly.

To finalize, place a small amount of poached sea urchin in the bottom shell, along with a small spoonful of the pineapple gel and a small spoonful of poached citrus dice. Top the tart shell with the geoduck rosette. Tableside, place a small spoonful of the mousseline cream on top of the geoduck.

it's

Music is a continuation of human vibration. We are made up of vibrations, so music is a part of us, it's in our DNA. Being surrounded by music growing up, finding artists I loved as I grew older, helped me discover parts of my personality outside of myself. The first time I really felt LOVE for music was with ABBA, and also Kiss! These groups represented freedom to me. Freedom to dress how you want, to be who you want to be. The way they lived, how they performed, the lyrics they sang…it was all so different from everybody else. It inspired

all

me and made me happy. Nina Simone is my favorite artist of all time. I can't put my finger on just what it is that moves me so much when I listen to Nina; I just feel raw with her. Pure emotion. I loved it when my parents listened to Edith Piaf. My house was filled with songs by Edith Piaf and Maria Callas.

●

about

When I started to learn piano and flute, music became a revelation. Not only hearing music, but realizing I could make it as well, that influenced me early on. I also attended classical music concerts with my family when I was very young. That, linked with the fine dining I experienced, provided me a certain kind of education. I learned to appreciate fine things very early on and understood that I could create them as well.

vibration,

●

There's no music in the savory kitchen at Atelier Crenn, but I always pair a "song" with a dish, even if it's silence. That silence is music because the chefs and I like a bit of quiet to really concentrate. Come service time, there are so many people—servers, sommeliers, cooks, guests—rotating in and out that any music would be drowned out. But back in the

it's

pastry kitchen, my pastry chef, Juan Contreras, and his team are always blasting music. Lots of hip-hop, but a mix of everything. For front of house, right now we listen to a lot of music from the '90s. It keeps us happy, it makes the guests feel relaxed, like they're at home.

●

layers

We do play a lot of music when we eat together as a family. The day before Thanksgiving, we all got together to eat a family meal, like we do every day. But on this day the cooks created a Thanksgiving meal for everyone and we decided it was time to celebrate. Someone put on Mariah Carey's Christmas album and we all went crazy listening to "All I Want For Christmas Is You." We were dancing, jumping around, singing at the top of our lungs. It was the week before the Michelin announcement, before everything changed. I'm so glad we were able

of

to have that time together to just chill and have fun together.

●

It's all about connection, it's all about vibration, it's layers of life. Without music, there's silence. Without food, there's hunger. Creating one or the other is a way of providing something nourishing and inspiring for someone else. That idea of creating an experience for someone, even

life

if they are a stranger, inspires me. ●

NICK CURTOLA

Nick Curtola grew up in the San Francisco Bay Area and migrated to New York in 2009. He is heavily inspired by Mediterranean cuisine, as well as the technical skills and dedication of Japan's great chefs. Currently the chef of The Four Horsemen in Brooklyn, NY, he offers a constantly changing menu that's predominantly seafood focused. He marries flavorful, craveable, and precise food with beautiful natural wines from around the world.

Song: Aja by Steely Dan

Recipe Inspiration:

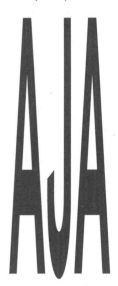

by
Steely
Dan

Blues Masters Playlist ▶ This is just a nice little evolution of blues. Delta and Chicago, and then their influence on some of the greatest rock bands and artists of the '60s and '70s.

1.	Shake it Baby	John Lee Hooker
2.	Dust My Broom	Elmore James
3.	Smokestack Lightnin'	Howlin' Wolf
4.	Crossroads	Cream
5.	When the Levee Breaks	Led Zeppelin
6.	Back Door Man	The Doors
7.	Voodoo Child (Slight Return)	Jimi Hendrix
8.	Magic Bus	The Who (Live at Leeds album)
9.	On the Road Again	Canned Heat
10.	Going Down	Freddie King

Skate Wing

Roasted on the Bone

with

Sungold Tomatoes

and

Aleppo Chili

Ultimate dad rock for cooking quickly while children sleep.

Serves 4

Four 6- to 8-oz skate wings, each 1 to 1½ inches (2.5 to 4 cm) thick, cartilage intact, trimmed of any excess skin

1½ tablespoons kosher salt

3 tablespoons unsalted butter

2 tablespoons extra-virgin olive oil

5 medium cloves garlic, germ removed (if any), thinly sliced

¼ cup vin jaune or dry white wine

2 pints sungold tomatoes

A couple of pinches of Aleppo chile powder

Preheat the oven to 425°F (220°C), convection fan on if you have it.

Season the skate wings with salt on both sides and place in a nonstick ovenproof sauté pan with 2 tablespoons of the butter.

Pop the skate wings into the oven and set a timer for 5 minutes.

Meanwhile, start the tomato sauce by heating up the olive oil over medium heat in another sauté pan. When the oil is warm, add garlic and let it fizzle and cook gently until fragrant and slightly toasted.

When the garlic is nicely toasted (but not browned or burnt), add the wine and let it cook a bit until the aroma of alcohol is cooked off. It should take about a minute or so.

Next add the tomatoes and prick some of them with a little paring knife. Turn the heat down to medium-low. The tomatoes should be just gently bubbling away with a nice amount of liquid from the wine, olive oil, and their juices. While the tomatoes are stewing away (hopefully your 5-minute timer just went off), flip the skate wings and baste them with the butter in the pan. They should be starting to brown slightly and the aroma of toasted milk solids from the butter should be filling your kitchen. Put the fish back in the oven. It should have been in there for about 5 minutes or so at this point. Set a timer for 2 more minutes.

Back to the tomatoes. Add the remaining 1 tablespoon butter to the sauce and move the tomatoes around. You're looking for some of them to be kind of smashed and some to be whole, but cooked and juicy. The smashed ones will leach into ▶|

the butter and wine sauce. Take them to a point that you're happy with and remove them from the heat. The sauce should have a nice sheen from the butter and good acidity from the wine and tomatoes themselves. The fat from the butter and oil should be emulsified and lend balance to the sauce. It shouldn't be broken or too tight.

Check the fish with a cake tester inserted towards the "bone." Do this by placing the cake tester in the fish until you feel the cartilage. Leave the cake tester in there for about 5 seconds, then remove it quickly and carefully bring it to your lower lip. It should feel hot-ish. Beyond warm, but not ripping hot. Skate is best cooked medium. When it's under, it can be a bit tough and chewy and when it's over, it can get mealy and tacky.

When the fish is cooked through, place it on a warm plate. It's okay if it has some butter solids on it. Next, spoon over the warm tomatoes and some of their sauce. Then finish the dish with a good pinch of the chile powder. It will bloom out when it hits the warm sauce. Serve immediately.

● There are so many artists who have influenced my life and work. I'd say someone I especially like is Miles Davis. I know, he's not obscure or anything like that, he's just this badass dude who played trumpet. I mean, not the coolest instrument by any stretch, but he influenced so many artists and was constantly the benchmark for his genre and others. He would reinvent himself often and was not afraid of failure. He knew he had to keep pushing and keep questioning the status quo in order to achieve his unique sound. I always put one of his albums on when I need to focus or just zone out at work. Or when I'm relaxing at home. Especially *Kind of Blue*, *Bitches Brew*, or anything from *The Birth of the Cool* era. Albums with him and Bill Evans are also just phenomenal. He used the trumpet as if it was his voice and he was speaking through it. Something about his sound is just mesmerizing. So smooth and precise…and haunting. He was also a great collaborator, which is something I really like about jazz—and cooking. His innovation and creativity are inspiring and

the right music

stretch beyond the world of music. ● The first artist I really got into was Jimi Hendrix. I loved his voice and his style of guitar. I'd never heard anything like it and it just resonated with me. I remember hearing "Voodoo Child (Slight Return)" and being hooked. I loved the intro and the lyrics. It just stood out to me. Looking back on it, I know it's pop and has been so overplayed over the years, but he's the greatest guitar player who ever lived. I appreciate it even more now because I realize how effortless it sounds and how catchy it is. But if you dig a bit, it's so technical and innovative. He was adding so many layers onto traditional blues riffs while also creating his own unique sound via nontraditional scales. Not to mention experimenting with distortion and taking the electric guitar sound to a level that inspired countless artists. Also, he was just a crazy-talented songwriter—and to think of what he accomplished by the age of just twenty-seven. I think of what I was doing in my twenties…nothing even close to that!! It's easy to just lump him in with all of the hyperbole of rock musicians of his caliber, but he was ahead of his time and we only caught a small glimpse of his potential. In a way, artists like him have inspired me and have created something in me that strives to be different or to challenge myself. ● When I was growing up, my friends and I listened to a lot of Nirvana, Pearl Jam, Soundgarden, Joy Division/New Order, Stone Temple Pilots, etc. We would skateboard around town with our cassette players and swap tapes. It was so fun back then, because you would unfold the cassette notes and learn about these bands. We knew all of the artists' names and all of the lyrics. It was definitely a way we connected. I think it just naturally piqued my interest and curiosity in music. To this day I love to dig around. Maybe see who did a guest spot with so and so, who produced certain tracks, where such and such was recorded. It really puts you in touch with the music, and it's still a way I connect with people. I can't play an instrument to save my life, but I still love the YouTube rabbit hole. One of my cooks plays drums, and I was recently watching a video about Patrick Carney and his recording setup, and then Stewart Copeland and his amazing studio, and then Steve Gadd and his session work. We nerded out for hours during prep talking about all of these great musicians. I love those moments. ● In 2006, I moved to Italy to work in a restaurant. It was really tough for me at first. Wi-Fi had yet to really take off there and smart phones weren't really a thing. These were Internet cafe days! I was in a tiny town and felt really cut off from friends and family. For some reason I had the bright idea to listen to a lot of Radiohead while feeling homesick. It really helped out, though. I would walk around the old medieval towns and take really amazing train rides all over Northern Italy and just zone out to these beautiful and haunting tracks from *Kid A* or *OK Computer*. It was such a cool juxtaposition of contemporary sound with the ancient and peaceful backdrops. It kind of put me in a trance. I would feel like I was in a movie and get a bit lost. It was a really beautiful experience for me. ● Food has had an influence in my life for as long as I can remember. My parents were big fans of the nightly dinner as a family. My mom was an incredibly talented cook and loved trying new dishes each night. We were so lucky, and it's something I strive to do with my daughter. We never watched TV while having dinner, so my dad would pop on some music and we'd sit around and talk about our day. I'm sure that in reality it was like pulling teeth for them at times, but in those memories, we listened to everything from Dire Straits to Igor Stravinsky's *The Firebird*. It really stuck with me over the years. ● Generally speaking, music has set the tone and vibe in every place I've worked. From prep through service. It can also make or break a meal at restaurants. Volume, soundproofing, choice of music for the vibe, etc. Obviously, there were exceptions — St. John restaurant in London, no music — but it's always interesting to see what people are playing. On a personal level, I've learned a lot about music *through* restaurants. In our industry, you find a lot of creative types. They generally have great taste in music and are eager to share the buried treasures they've found over the years. Working at the Four Horsemen has given me a new perspective when it comes to the importance of music in a restaurant. You really notice how much of an afterthought it tends to be and how detrimental it can be to a dining experience. It's made me think specifically about song selection. (We only do full albums, so it's up to our staff to curate the right sound for that day's service.) Then there's the soundproofing that James Murphy, one of the owners, did. It's truly incredible for such an unassuming little restaurant in Brooklyn and was no small feat. I'll hear something at work that sounds absolutely incredible and then quickly head home to hear it without all the noise of the restaurant only to be disappointed that it doesn't have the same depth. I guess a beautiful McIntosh amplifier and one of the best audio guys out there really does make a difference! ● Music plays a huge role in the day-to-day operations of the Four Horsemen. I love prepping to the blues. Legends like Lightnin' Hopkins, John Lee Hooker, Howlin' Wolf, Muddy Waters, and Son House. I love Delta and Chicago Blues. I also love jazz — Grant Green, Herbie Hancock, Art Blakey, Bill Evans, Thelonius Monk, Hank Mobley, etc. I'll put that on when no one is around, when I'm just breaking down some fish. It allows me to be really focused and relaxed at the same time. My favorite way to start service is by listening to something like Arthur Russell. It sets a really positive and fun tone. It's upbeat, funky, and really colorful. He was a genius. It sounds good as the sun is setting and the restaurant is just starting to hum. When we're in peak service, I love *Silent Shout* by the Knife. That opening track gives me chills every time. When it comes on and we're busy, it just feels really great in the dining room. At the end of the night, I really like *Hounds of Love* by Kate Bush. Another incredible opening track, and the rest of the album is haunting and beautiful. Her vocals are amazing, and the record has this eerie vibe that suits late nights. These are just some specific choices, but it shows the detail we take in really matching the right music at the right moment.

at the right moment

LOïC DABLÉ

Loïc Dablé is an Ivorian-French chef serving African Food. Born and trained in France, Dablé is now based in Africa, where he uses his know-how and twenty years of experience for training youth, especially women and local former migrants, at his restaurant Migrations. Migrations offers a contemporary healthy and casual Pan-African menu during the day and private dining experiences at night. Migrations is also a social project that aims at reintegrating local migrants through free vocational training.

Passion Playlist ▶ I chose to call this playlist "Passion" because it appeals to some strong experiences of my life at a point in time. Each title or artist directly connects with a part of me, a feeling I have had in different situations, pleasant or unpleasant.

Song: Mario by Franco & LE TP OK Jazz

1.	**Brigitte Femme de Flic**	Ministère AMER
2.	**Gonna Love Me (Remix)**	Teyana Taylor featuring Ghostface Killah, Method Man, and Raekwon
3.	**Don't Cry**	J Dilla
4.	**200% Zoblazo**	Meiway
5.	**With or Without You**	U2
6.	**Englishman in New York**	Sting
7.	**Dear Mama**	2Pac
8.	**Ziboté**	Ernesto Djédjé
9.	**Famille**	Lokua Kanza featuring Fally Ipupa
10.	**Étoile d'etat**	Koffi Olomidé
11.	**Shalaï**	Extra Musica
12.	**Femme de Feu**	Gadji Celi
13.	**Take Off the Blues**	The Foreign Exchange

SANKARA

▼ Loïc Dablé

This salad is inspired by the late Thomas Sankara, Burkina Faso's president. I created it as I remembered how he valued African culture.

Serves 1

- 15 g *fonio* (African ancient grain)
- 15 g sorghum
- 15 g millet
- 15 g *attiéké* couscous
- 15 g white beans
- 15 g soybeans
- 15 g red beans
- 1 fresh tomato, diced
- 5 g chopped parsley
- 5 g chopped green onion
- 5 g chopped yellow onion
- 5 g combretum micranthum (**kinkéliba**), minced
- 1 tablespoon olive oil
- Salt and freshly ground black pepper

Recipe Inspiration:

MARIO
by Franco & LE TP OK Jazz

■ For the baobab vinaigrette:

- 5 tablespoons coconut oil, melted
- 1 tablespoon vinegar
- 1 teaspoon mustard
- 15 g baobab powder
- Salt and freshly ground black pepper
- A pinch of any spice of your choice

In separate steamers, steam the *fonio*, sorghum, millet, and *attiéké* until tender. Then, in separate pots of boiling water, cook the white beans, soybeans, and red beans until tender.

Drain all the grains and beans, let them cool, then combine everything in a large bowl.

In a medium bowl, combine the tomato, parsley, green onion, yellow onion, and combretum micranthum. Toss with the olive oil, a pinch of salt, and a pinch of pepper.

Add the tomato-onion mixture to the large bowl with the beans and grains. Toss so everything is nicely distributed.

To make the baobab vinaigrette, in a small bowl, whisk together the coconut oil, vinegar, mustard, baobab powder, and a pinch of salt, pepper, and the spice of your choice. Blend well.

Pour the vinaigrette on the salad and toss a bit. Congratulations! Enjoy your SANKARA!

During the peak service, employees may really be stressed; then we play instrumental music with soothing instruments, such as kora, to relieve them. On the other hand, a certain kind of soft music is valued because of the customers; as they are eating, they need to feel relaxed and at ease.

My parents played music almost every day. My mother is Guéré; it is an Ivorian ethnic group. We have a strong presence of music there. The use of African goblet drums is very present during almost any kind of ceremony, whether to praise a mask or to initiate people.

Hip-hop music helped me connect with other people. As a matter of fact, it was during live events like concerts and dance choreographies where I encountered many people with whom I easily got along. Since my youth, I also liked to listen to African music, alongside hip-hop. From the music, I naturally gained in energy and vitality as I was getting older. The first song I fell in love with was "Ziboté" (a great dance song) from an Ivorian singer called Ernesto Djédjé. I do like Bob Marley, even if he is no longer alive. His songs help me feel free and allow me to work freely. His main themes are around freedom, so he helped me understand that I had a choice in choosing what I would like to do or who I wanted to be, without any exterior constraint.

I remember I was motivated by a song by a French rapper called Kery James. The title of the song is "Banlieusards," and is related to people living in the suburbs. The song's title was meant to speak to people living in difficult situations, telling them not to give up, and that poverty is not a fatality. Indeed, I belonged to this part of the French population, so these lyrics encouraged me to fight off poverty by always trying to find an ethical way out.

I started to take cooking courses when I was very young, around fourteen. I do not really remember, but it seems the love for food came with time, as I was cooking. Nowadays, cooking is not just a passion. We have more and more individuals who are interested in the culinary world and are proud to exhibit it as a job. It was not the case before, but with time, food grew in popularity and I think today, being a cook is perceived to be as valuable as being a singer. For me, music and food do overlap, for they give a very trendy and fashionable image and identity to those who have them as their main job.

Music plays a major role during service at Migrations. It directly affects the mood of both the people in the front office and the people in the back office. I think that Fela Kuti's music is one of the best choices for a restaurant. We usually play soft songs, often with no vocals, for the pre-service, to allow the personnel to be focused. During the peak service, employees may really be stressed; then we play instrumental music with soothing instruments, such as kora, to relieve them. On the other hand, a certain kind of soft music is valued because of the customers; as they are eating, they need to feel relaxed and at ease. Therefore, we sometimes play Zulu music with low bass voices. At the end of the night, after customers have left, it is important to speed up employees' moves, to boost their energy so they can clean up quickly. Here selecting hip-hop music or Afro House is the best choice.

When a cook is sensitive to music, like me, it generally has an effect on the way he or she cooks. It is all about the identity we have. As Africans, we want the Pan-African food to fully dwell in its home. In other words, the name of the food, the selected music, and the restaurants themselves all turn around contemporary African culture, most of the time. I once created a dish that I called "Vinaigrette Sumarah à l'encre de sèche" while I was listening to "Killing Me Softly" by the Fugees. Each time I listen to this music, I automatically recall that dish I created and vice versa.

Therefore, we sometimes play Zulu music with low bass voices. At the end of the night, after customers have left, it is important to speed up employees' moves, to boost their energy so they can clean up quickly. Here selecting hip-hop music or Afro House is the best choice.

DÁVILA

DIANA

Diana Dávila is the chef
and owner of Mi Tocaya
Antojería in Chicago, Illinois.
At Mi Tocaya, guests are
invited to enjoy Dávila's takes
on familiar Mexican favorites,
less-known regional special-
ties, and completely new
dishes that are inspired
by her Mexican heritage.

Song: La Cumbia Del Mole by Lila Downs

Khalessi del Barrio Playlist ▶ Dance, perras!
This is a great playlist for dancing, so we
love to listen to it when we're getting
ready for service.

1.	**Magic Spells**	Crystal Castles
2.	**Marciano (I Turned Into A Martian)**	Molotov
3.	**Para Agradecer**	Chicano Batman
4.	**Lose Yourself to Dance**	Daft punk
5.	**Juicy**	The Notorious B.I.G.
6.	**Holiday**	Madonna
7.	**Chantage**	Shakira featuring Maluma
8.	**Nunca Es Suficiente**	Los Ángeles Azules featuring Natalia Lafourcade
9.	**Tus Latidos**	G Flux Ft Sotomayor
10.	**BEBE**	6ix9ine featuring Anuel AA
11.	**Prune, You Talk Funny**	Gus Dapperton

USA

Pipian Negro

One of my favorite things to do is make mole and sauces, and I love this song especially because not only did Lila Downs write it, her style of singing reminds me so much of my style of cooking. It's based on tradition and has a feeling of nostalgia but is new.

Makes 8 quarts (8 liters)

Recipe Inspiration:

La Cumbia Del Mole

by Lila Downs

MI TOCAYA ANTOJERÍA

10 lb blackened poblanos

2 lb blackened serranos

5 lb blackened tomatillos

32 blackened tomatoes

8 blackened onions

6 oz blackened garlic

3 quarts chicken stock, for the spice/nut purée

20 g burnt whole cinnamon stick

6 oz toasted sesame seeds

20 g toasted whole black peppercorns

15 g toasted whole cumin seeds

20 toasted whole cloves

6 oz toasted pepitas

6 oz toasted peanuts

4 oz toasted almonds

4 oz toasted pecans

5 g avocado leaf

8 g dried Mexican oregano

Ash

Sunflower oil

5 quarts chicken stock, to finish the sauce

In a food processor, working in batches, process the chiles, tomatillos, tomatoes, onions, and garlic to a smooth purée. Transfer to a large bowl and set aside.

In a saucepan, combine the 3 quarts chicken stock with all of the spices, herbs, seeds, and nuts and bring to a boil. Remove from the heat and let steep for 10 minutes. Purée in the food processor.

Heat a good drizzle of sunflower oil in a large saucepan over medium heat. Add the spice/nut purée and cook, stirring, until concentrated. Add the vegetable purée and cook to concentrate. Add the 5 quarts chicken stock, bring to a boil, then set the heat to maintain a simmer and cook, stirring occasionally, for 1 hour.

Purée the sauce one more time. Deli up!

▲ Diana Dávila

The creation of food, from the time you begin cooking until you sit down and eat, works very much like a kind of orchestra. You have all of these essentially raw products that have been put together in harmony—not manipulated, but put together to make something beautiful. My grandmother would come up to Chicago every other year to take care of us because both my parents were working parents. Whether I was in Mexico or she was over here, I would walk to the market with her. I would help her peel garlic or pluck hairs from a pig. That's when I started seeing things from the beginning to the end—and seeing people's reactions. When my aunt or grandmother cooked, I got to see the whole process of everything that we needed to do. You are putting your heart and soul into something that is essentially nurturing you and the people you are feeding, in a way that often makes everybody completely fall into a trance. ● It was around this time I first remember seeing people dance, bodies moving to the rhythm. I don't know if it's a Latino thing, but when the dancing part kicks in and you see couples move with the music, it makes me feel the rhythms in a whole different way. There is no specific song, but the image I have is of people dancing to cumbia. ● Those songs were funny, they're always about love: either you're not getting somebody, or someone took them from you, or you are hopeless about one or the other. Love songs are pretty amazing. I've always been obsessed with mariachi music; I find it to be a kind of heart-wrenching music. Putting yourself out there, putting your soul out there, how helpless you are without this person. Pull yourself together, man! It's just so beautiful that you can love or lose in such a grand way...that you can produce something you can feel from the pit of your stomach. ● Mariachi and cumbia music have both always been incredible for me, my favorite genres of Latino music. I especially love dancing to cumbia—it always reminds me of family parties or seeing my parents dance. I don't see that kind of embrace of it happen that much anymore. My parents would go out to dinner and dancing; a date for them would be going to a live show. They would get dressed up, which I always thought was really beautiful. Now I'm a mother, and I like the music that my mom played, usually some banda songs about how some lady did some man wrong. ● Dancing has always allowed me to connect with others. We lived in the inner city when I was young, but then we moved out to the suburbs when I was in eighth grade and there weren't a lot of Latinos there. I always felt different from other people. I'm a relatively social person, but I think one really nice natural thing with Latino music is that when you dance, you dance with somebody. With lots of American dancing, you don't really dance with people— even if you ask someone to dance, you often stay separate. ● With Latino dancing, when you're dancing cumbia, bachata, merengue, you have a partner. You move together, you take someone's hand. That has shaped me, because when you reach out for somebody's hand and you are truly asking for it, it's like what John Lennon sang: "All we are saying is give peace a chance." You're intertwining two different people in a song that you can make into your own. You find somebody else's rhythm and you learn so much from dancing with somebody. You have to be vulnerable. ● In Latino dancing with a partner, by extending that hand, I think it makes the world a better place. You are learning about that other person, and you may not have known who they were before. When you go out to a *baile* and you get asked to dance, it is not a boring dance. Your partner is going to be twirling you around all the rhythms of the song. These are traditional dances that have been around for hundreds of years. ● The power of music is that you can create something that lasts forever, something that makes people feel a certain way. Whether it's a good time or a bad time, music can help us get through something. It makes you feel like you're not alone, because the piece of music holds something. You know that you're alive and that somebody else is feeling the same thing. The power of music to connect people is the same power food has for forging those connections. ● We have stopped looking at food as just as a way of nurturing. These days it's more than that. Chefs can express themselves just like a musician or a painter by using their ingredients consciously to make something that shares and encapsulates their memories. Cooking revolves around our five senses and we can really play with those five senses for our diners. You're not going to always be able to make the same dish, because you may not be in the same mindset as when you created it. It's the same thing with musicians. I've always had the fear that one day food is not going to talk to me anymore and it will say, "Let's ditch this chick." Then I wouldn't be able to cook anymore. Which is a terrible feeling. ● One of the hardest things to do as a musician, I imagine, and in similar ways to a chef, is to continually produce innovative music, the same way we continually try to innovate with our food. There are restaurants that do the same menus over and over again, and that's fine for some people. It's so difficult to challenge yourself to convey different ideas. It's like when you're a painter and there is a gallery show of your new work, but you need to push yourself again right away. That's probably one of the hardest things likewise for musicians and chefs; you come off of having a new album or a new menu and then you have to keep yourself open, to grow, to create new music or recipes, to feel and to get inspired. It's really hard. ● One of my all-time favorites is Madonna, who is the queen of reinvention. I was actually thinking about it the other day, wondering what she's up to right now. I'm sure she is working on something. I do that with my menu, thinking about where I have to point myself after a menu is written and I feel comfortable. You feel good about things that have been happening, but then after some point soon, you have to change. You have to progress, to get into your space again, and ask yourself again, "Who am I?" I feel this is a continuous process.

Cooking revolves around our five senses

POOJA DHINGRA

Pooja Dhingra is the founder of the Le15 chain of patisseries and cafes in Mumbai. Pooja is a hospitality graduate from Cesar Ritz Colleges, Switzerland, and trained in pastry at Le Cordon Bleu, Paris. Featured on the Forbes 30 Under 30 list in both India and Asia, Pooja has won acclaim from critics, the press, and her customers for her extraordinary skills as a pâtissier, as well as for her incredible entrepreneurial journey.

Song: La Vie en Rose by Louis Armstrong

Recipe Inspiration:

La Vie en

A Good Day in the Kitchen Playlist ▶ This is a list of songs I listen to when I have a calm day in the kitchen. It's an instantaneous mood-uplifter and brings me joy. The music I listen to varies depending on my mood and time of day.

1.	**Again**	Lenny Kravitz
2.	**cold/mess**	Prateek Kuhad
3.	**Fly Me to the Moon**	Frank Sinatra
4.	**Banana Pancakes**	Jack Johnson
5.	**Se Eu Nao Te Ass**	Gully Boy
6.	**Sham**	Nikhil D'Souza, Amit Trivedi, Neuman Pinto
7.	**Shallow**	Lady Gaga and Bradley Cooper
8.	**Fallin'**	Alicia Keys
9.	**Drops of Jupiter**	Train
10.	**Tareefan Reprise**	Lisa Mishra

INDIA

Pistachio and Rose Cupcakes by Louis Armstrong

Before I opened my first cafe, I would play this song on repeat while menu testing. I wanted to create a space that felt like a piece of Paris, and this was my song inspiration.

Makes 24 mini cupcakes

110 g salted **butter**, at room temperature

180 g caster (superfine) sugar

2 eggs

80 ml milk

20 g pistachio paste

1 drop of green food coloring

150 g flour

1 teaspoon baking powder

■ For the rose – cream cheese frosting:

100 g **butter**, at room temperature

50 g **cream cheese**, at room temperature

2 teaspoons rose syrup

300 g powdered (icing) sugar, sifted

1 teaspoon light pink food coloring

Preheat the oven to 325°F (165°C). Line your mini cupcake molds with paper liners.

In a bowl, whisk the butter with the caster (superfine) sugar until light and fluffy.

Add the eggs one at time, whisking after each addition.

Add the milk, pistachio paste, and green food coloring and whisk well.

Sift together the flour and baking powder and then fold into the batter.

Pipe the batter into the cupcake molds to about three-fourths full.

Bake for 15 minutes, or until a skewer comes out clean when inserted in the center of a cake. Let cool completely on a wire rack before you frost the cupcakes.

While the cupcakes are baking, make the frosting: In a large bowl, whisk the butter and cream cheese until smooth. Add the rose syrup and beat well. Gradually add the powdered (icing) sugar, whisking continuously until smooth and creamy. Add the pink food coloring and mix until the color is even. Cover and refrigerate the frosting until ready to use.

When the cupcakes are cooled, spread with the frosting and serve.

Song: La Vie en Rose by Louis Armstrong

The Bollywood songs I fell in love with have been loaded with food references for decades — as innuendos, as endearments, and as metaphors.

▲ Pooja Dhingra

Food and music have this thing in common: they both play on memories. I can taste something and immediately be transported to the memory of where I had it for the first time, what it reminds me of, and, most importantly, how it makes me feel. Similarly, with music, I can listen to a song and it takes me right back to a time in my life where the song played an important role. For me, music and food intersect in all parts of my life. ● Early on in my pastry education, during my time in a kitchen in Paris, our sous chef always used to have the radio on. Since then, I can't work without music in the background. Since I mostly work out of a central bakery kitchen, I don't have the stress of pre-service or peak service. So throughout the day, something is always playing in the background. I still remember that even before opening my cafe, creating a playlist was as important to me as my menu! ● The playlist at a restaurant truly elevates the dining experience. Since Le15 is a French-inspired brand, I do listen to a lot of French music. There definitely is synergy between the music I love and the food I make. We curate the playlist to really feel like you are in Paris. While I lived there, I would go to a local cafe near my house, and the thing I remember most, besides the crème brûlée, is their music, which was the same that we play today. My favorites from the list are Edith Piaf and Christophe Mae. ● My father dreamt of being a singer. That never happened, but he used to sing songs to my brother and me to put us to bed every night. Music became something that gave me comfort and has made me feel safe ever since then. I don't remember the exact first song I fell in love with, but it was definitely something from the Hindi Cinema, where I grew up watching movies. Since then, I've always been musically inclined. I wanted to be a dancer. Until I was about ten, the major musical influences in my life were songs from those popular Hindi films. Then suddenly, I remember listening to the Spice Girls and Backstreet Boys and falling in love. ● I've always had a song playing in my head. When I was a kid, I couldn't sit in a car without having the radio turned on. I always carried a mixtape for my Walkman, and then CDs for my portable CD player. I got the first generation of the iPod (which I still have) and it changed my life. Music has always helped pull me through the really tough times. If I fought with my parents, I would slam my door and listen to some Metallica (teenage years are tough!). I would always have something soft and mellow in the background while studying. I needed something in my ears when I would go for a run. I was a creative and imaginative child, and music became my friend and the soundtrack for all the stories I cooked up in my head. ● Music plays a huge role in my culture and heritage. It marks all of our family occasions—weddings, births, funerals—and so much of our entertainment, and food is central to many of these rituals as well. The Bollywood songs I fell in love with have been loaded with food references for decades—as innuendos, as endearments, and as metaphors. Going deeper into authentic Indian music, there's a saying from the *Natyasastra*, a Sanskrit text on the performing arts: "Just as noble-minded persons enjoying delicious food seasoned with different spices relish the taste with delight, so does the knowing audience relish and savor the experience of emotional states in a performance and are moved by them." (*Natyasastra Chapter 6, verses 32–33.*) ● The concept is that both experiences, music and food, are capable of evoking an emotional response from within us. We can also draw similarities between the structure of a raga (the framework for Indian classical music) and the structure of a recipe. The great sarod player Ali Akbar Khan compared the action of his right-hand technique to that of stirring food in a pot. While making a recipe, there are two primary aspects: the ingredients and the method. Similarly, in ragas, the notes and scales are the ingredients, and the realization through artistic performance is the method. Also, there are ragas for times of the day and the season—much like food and its ingredients.

VICTORIA ELÍASDÓTTIR

Victoria Elíasdóttir works at the intersection of food and art. In 2014, she joined her brother, the artist Ólafur Elíasson, in Berlin and helped evolve his Studio Kitchen project, a light-filled canteen in his studio that serves a communal vegetarian lunch to his employees. In the fall of 2018, Elíasdóttir and her brother launched SOE KITCHEN 101, a temporary food and art space in Reykjavík's Marshall House, an arts center housed in a former fish factory. Currently, Elíasdóttir runs her own secret dining space called FOR NOW in the heart of East Berlin.

Replay the Past Playlist ▶ This list contains songs that I have revisited many times throughout my life. Some of them bring back intense feelings, while others comfort me and soothe. For example, "Papa Don't Preach" and "La Isla Bonita" take me back to the times when I was ten years old and spent hours in the garage painting and drawing. Nothing brings back memories and emotions like music and smells, and as I can't share the smell of the acrylic paint with you, I share these emotions and memories in the form of these songs.

1.	**Me and Bobby McGee**	Janis Joplin
2.	**Sultans of Swing**	Dire Straits
3.	**Always Remember Us This Way**	Lady Gaga
4.	**I'd Rather Go Blind**	Etta James
5.	**When I Grow Up**	Fever Ray
6.	**Angel**	Sarah McLachlan
7.	**Symphony**	Clean Bandit featuring Zara Larsson
8.	**Papa Don't Preach**	Madonna
9.	**La Isla Bonita**	Madonna

BRING THE BEET IN

For years, I have had an obsession with beets—and what's more, I've had this slightly weird drive to make people who don't like beets love them. Somehow, I feel a satisfaction in changing people's perceptions about beets. By preparing them in a way that reduces the water content and brings out the natural sugars, one arrives at a condensed, powerful, and flavorful beet.

This song makes me think of the same powerful effect as beets had over me. Listening and watching the music video where Beyoncé brings her strong confidence to the table, the lyrics go on about how "he is the one she wants," but she shows that it's okay to be vulnerable while being proactive and strong. She wears a low-cut bathing suit and proudly takes ownership of her body, showing it off—and if you have worked as hard as she does for a figure like that, I truly understand that you deserve to embrace yourself. And there is no shame in that. I think this sends a great positive message that girls are allowed to take pride in their bodies—without giving anyone permission to come close. I dress up for myself and no one else, as I feel strength and power in embracing my femininity. That's why I identify with this song: We deserve to do what we want to to feel powerful and strong, and if a change has to be made, that is acceptable, too. A good life is hard work, and whether you find power in a great book, motherhood, or a fierce red lipstick, all should be equally acceptable.

This dish goes great with a beautiful burrata, grilled fish, or even a roast. Enjoy the "beat"!

Serves 8

Recipe Inspiration:

LOVE ON TOP
by Beyoncé

2 kg medium lovely organic red beets, with leaves

2 tablespoons acacia honey

1 tablespoon olive oil

■ For the toasted hazelnuts:

200 g hazelnuts

1 tablespoon acacia honey

1 tablespoon fresh chopped rosemary

⅓ teaspoon Maldon salt or any other lovely flaky salt

■ For the beet vinaigrette:

300 ml beet juice, homemade or store-bought

100 g salted butter

2 tablespoons red wine vinegar

3 tablespoons acacia honey

⅓ teaspoon salt

■ **200 g raspberries**

▶❙

Preheat the oven to 200°C (400°F).

Cut off the beet leaves, wash, and set aside. Bake the whole beets for 1 hour on a sheet pan. Let them cool, then remove the skins with a small knife. Try not to peel much of the meat off, only the skin, as the flavor of the slightly burned and caramelized beet brings an important depth to the dish.

Break each beet into roughly 4 parts with a fork to get uneven and naturally shaped pieces. In a bowl, toss the beets with the honey and olive oil. Line a baking sheet with parchment paper, spread the beets on the pan, and bake for 20 minutes at 180°C (350°F). Remove from the oven and set aside. Reduce the oven temperature to 170°C (340°F).

To toast the hazelnuts, place the hazelnuts, honey, rosemary, and salt in a bowl and toss to coat the nuts. Arrange on a baking sheet lined with parchment paper and bake for 8 minutes. Let cool to room temperature and roughly chop. Set aside for serving.

To make the vinaigrette, in a saucepan over medium heat, simmer the beet juice until reduced to 100 ml. Meanwhile, melt the butter in a small frying pan over low heat and cook until it starts to get golden and smell sweet like caramel. Remove from the heat and let cool down a bit. Whisk the butter and the remaining vinaigrette ingredients into the beet reduction and set aside.

Cut the beet greens into irregular shapes and set aside. Chop the stems into sticks about 2 cm (¾ inch) long. In a large bowl, gently mix together the beets, beet greens and stems, vinaigrette, and raspberries. Arrange on a serving tray, sprinkle the hazelnuts on top, and serve.

● ● ●

When my father, Hy, was not cooking on his fishing trawler in Iceland, there was music in our life. Hy would have his guitar on his lap every moment he could. I believe singing and playing was his way of taking a break from daily life. I used to sing with him from the time I was three years old and on — and the first song I mastered was Janis Joplin's "Me and Bobby McGee." We would record on tape and play for my mom when she came back from university. Now, my instruments are the pots and pans in the kitchen — I can play everything from "Itsy Bitsy Spider" to Dire Straits' "Sultans of Swing."

●

From the time I was about eight years old onward, the variety of records in our house continued to expand, from Janis Joplin to things like Guns N' Roses and Madonna. Kris Kristofferson's voice gives me comfort, as it takes me back to simpler times without the self-involved worries of a Northern European adult life. During my first years in the kitchen, we used to take turns doing the "prep playlist," and I always went for my oldies: Bob Dylan, Etta James, Leonard Cohen, Dire Straits, Otis Redding, and of course Janis Joplin. Almost every time, I would get shit from my head chefs because I was slowing down the work tempo in the kitchen with my choice of songs. They were not all wrong — in my first years, I repeatedly struggled to get my mise en place done by service!

●

When I was a teenager, music helped me to not feel alone when I was having a hard time emotionally fitting in. I often used music as my safe space. I felt like music gave me a voice — not necessarily to share my thoughts, but rather to understand them myself. As any teenager when feeling a little lost, music gave me power to push ahead. That's probably why I like musicians who have strong personalities. And in this way, music sometimes created friendships, born of connecting with others through music.

●

My choice of music during my early teenage years is still my go-to music. I used to struggle with the idea that I was born in the wrong era, the '90s. I did not connect much to the music at the time. When I was thirteen years old, my beloved father passed away, and I believe my connection to music from the '60s and '70s became even stronger. It was a way for me to feel my father's presence through the tunes that we used to listen to together. I recall really wishing I had been born during that decade. But with time, I made peace with the fact that 1987 was my year of birth, and through fashion, music, and very liberal and free-minded thinking, I made choices that were not in line with the quite conservative culture of Iceland where I grew up. But it made me feel like I belonged, even if it was only in my own little universe.

●

Without realizing it, I think I often chose artists that have a strong personal presence, providing for me the safety of a time wherein I knew what was to come. This often related to the safe feeling that my father gave me as a child. We would play and sing and for that time being, I knew what was happening—and being quite controlling myself, I must admit that the feeling of knowing the next minute of the song was a relief in itself.

●

Iceland has a strong choir tradition. A house party would not be a real party without the guitar hero who leads the group into "shouting" a folk song together. You only need a few ingredients: guitar, maybe a few beers, and perhaps a shot of Black Death (Brennivin). Both food and music have the power to bring people together at these gatherings—a certain bond that happens at some point during the mix of meal and song. In Iceland, you only need a fresh piece of haddock, some melted butter, and our potatoes, which won't grow larger than the size of a table-tennis ball (even in the longest summers), and you create a celebration.

●

Bottom line: Food and music make people feel so connected! And even though today Iceland has reached the international standard both in gastronomy and music, the Icelandic people still know how to bond over a piece of good fish and a lazy old guitar.

When you eat, you are listening to the story with your mouth

●

Fundamentally, food is about storytelling—a great meal is like reading a great book, or listening to a good album. It's pop culture because everyone loves and can relate to a good story. When you eat, you are listening to the story with your mouth; our palates are so incredibly intelligent. Both eating and listening send messages to the brain, and that's where the feelings and full experiences are formed. Ears to brain or mouth to brain the outcome is very personal.

●

I believe there is much work to be done in Iceland to make food an ingredient in music and music an ingredient in food. On another level, I think that the two fields can be more deeply connected. We often forget, for example, that having food in our mouths makes noise, the sounds from crunchy to gooey that you hear within your skull, something I think is really interesting. I've talked to my brother Ólafur Elíasson about this—to the point that sometimes he only *hears* food and forgets that the taste matters as well!

●

In our secret restaurant, a big part of the experience is the sound of the house. There are many layers of sound: the guests chatting and moving the squeaky chairs, the service staff walking on the old wooden floor, the sounds from outside through the open windows, and so on. The restaurant has its own soundtrack that changes every night, so I choose deliberately not to play music there, as I believe that collectively the guests and we make exactly the right sound to fit diners' experience on any given night. One day I might invite a musician. If I could, I would ask Bob Dylan to come over for a night and add to the soundtrack.

●●●

CIVAN ER

Song: Symphony No. 45 by Franz Joseph Haydn

Civan Er was born and raised in Istanbul. In 2003, he entered the kitchen for the first time while he was doing his MA in International Relations. After only six months, he decided to stay — it had been his passion to cook ever since he was a child. After ten years in his professional cooking career, he started his first restaurant, Yeni Lokanta, in Istanbul. Here he gets ingredients from all around the country, combining them with traditional cooking techniques and his own twist.

Bahtiyar Playlist ▶ These are some of the songs I listened to with my high school mates over a bottle of raki and some meze. We still do these gatherings once a year, converging from our distant residences, and it's more or less the same list, with a few newcomers every time.

1.	**Nilüfer**	Müslüm Gürses
2.	**Yakarım geceleri**	Ahmet Kaya
3.	**Gülmek için Yaratılmış**	Ferdi Özbeğan
4.	**Usta**	Müslüm Gürses
5.	**Sivas Ellerinde Sazım Çalınır**	Selda Bağcan
6.	**Yalan Dünya**	Neşet Ertaş
7.	**Arka Mahalle**	Ahmet Kaya
8.	**Ah Bu Şarkıların Gözü Kör Olsun**	Zeki Müren
9.	**Acılara Tutunmak**	Ahmet Kaya
10.	**Unutamadım - Kaç Kadeh Kırıldı**	Müslüm Gürses

CELERIAC WITH QUINCE

Recipe Inspiration:

SYMPHONY NO. 45 in F# minor, the "Farewell" Symphony by Franz Joseph Haydn

This song comes from a time when I was about to have big changes in my life. I was listening to Haydn's "Farewell Symphony" when making this dish for the first time.

Serves 4

2 teaspoons olive oil, plus 200 ml

1 large Spanish onion, thinly sliced

600 g celeriac (celery root), peeled and thinly sliced with a mandoline or knife

400 g quince, peeled, deseeded, and thinly sliced with a mandoline or knife

150 g feta cheese, crumbled

Juice of 2 lemons

1 dessert spoon hot mustard

2 sprigs thyme

Salt and freshly ground black pepper

Toasted bread and raki for serving

Preheat the oven to 180°C (350°F).

In a frying pan over low heat, heat the 2 teaspoons olive oil. Add the onion and sauté until soft.

In a bowl, combine the onion, the 200 ml olive oil, the celeriac (celery root), quince, feta, lemon juice, mustard, thyme, and salt and pepper to taste.

Transfer the mixture to a baking sheet. Cover and bake for 40 minutes. Check with the tip of a knife. If the celeriac and quince are still firm, cook for 5 more minutes. When done, let cool to room temperature and serve with the toasted bread and raki.

Song: Symphony No. 45 by Franz Joseph Haydn

I
still
make
time
for
myself
to
enjoy
sadness;
it's
a
paradoxically
"unbearable"
pleasure
of
mine.

Looking back, I realize that every chapter in my life has had its own music. When I was nineteen, it was Joe Satriani's "Forgotten." I was in love. (That was during the period of time when I had just started to use the Internet to print out recipes and couldn't stop myself from executing them, day and night. The entire Web became a kind of recipe treasure hunt for me.) In the '90s, I liked hard rock like most people of my generation in Istanbul, especially in my circle. Nothing else in 1993 could have made me wake up voluntarily early in the morning other than a Metallica concert. There would be thousands of fans waiting in the stadium and we all joined together to see them.

●

As I got older, I explored Max Richter's music, and I fell in love with that. I was in a melancholic mood that I couldn't get away from, and I didn't want to. The more I listened to Richter, the less socialized I became and the more I focused on my inner world. I started writing about my feelings, and often this was channeled into coming up with new recipes. I still make time for myself to enjoy sadness; it's a paradoxically "unbearable" pleasure of mine. The music has changed, though; I listen to Ólafur Arnalds, or if I wanna go deeper it is Ahmet Kaya now.

●

In my first kitchen, I used to listen to Bach's *Harpsichord Concertos* early in the morning when there was nobody around; it was motivating and helped me do things more quickly. The kind of music I play or listen to reflects my personal ideas behind the food we are trying to cook: It should look simple, easy to enjoy, but with a lot of thought behind it that you taste when you eat it. Miles Davis, Ahmet Kaya, and Neşet Ertaş are the first ones that come to my mind when I think of my artistic guides. All pure, but charming and timeless at the same time.

PAULINA ESCANES

Mexican born and longtime Puerto Rico resident, Chef Paulina Escanes opened her namesake restaurant in the heart of Condado, offering her unique brand of casual gourmet dishes and desserts in a stylish and sophisticated space. As always, great emphasis is placed on locally sourced organic products and healthy eating. Her menu is complemented by signature cocktails and fine wines, which can be enjoyed in the elegant bar.

Lonchesitos are a perfect comfort food for the day after a big party or when you have a hangover. In México, all the places that offer *tortas ahogadas* or *lonchesitos bañados* are packed by noon with people who need to recover from the previous night. The cure is helped along by the spicy salsa one dips the *lonchesito* into and a very cold beer. People always ask for the coldest beer available as soon as they've ordered. We call it a hangover miracle.

Serves 4 to 6

Mexican Isla Playlist ▶ This playlist is 100 percent me at this moment in my life. I want to sing out loud. I want to dance freely. I want to enjoy every trip with my loved ones. I want to remember my heritage, and would love to share everything I am with the people around me.

Morir De Amor
by Los Ángeles Azules featuring Miguel Bosé

1.	Atrévete-te-te	Calle 13
2.	El Wanabí	Fiel a la Vega
3.	Bieké	Cultura Profética
4.	Nunca es Suficiente	Natalia Lafourcade
5.	Me Gusta Vivir de Noche	Los Tucanes de Tijuana
6.	Entrega de Amor	Los Ángeles Azules featuring Saúl Hernández
7.	Antes Que Al Mio	Los Ángeles Azules featuring Los Claxons
8.	El Dia de Suerte	Héctor Lavoe
9.	La Banda	Héctor Lavoe and Willie Colón
10.	La Rosa Blanca	Hugo Blanco, Willie Colón
11.	La Negra Caderona	Aniceto Molina
12.	La Yerbita	Eliseo Herrera
13.	A la Memoria del Muerto	Fruko Y Sus Tesos, Piper Pimienta

Lonchesitos Bañados

PAULINA ESCANES-GOURMANDIZE

■ For the protein:

1 lb chicken or flank steak, seasoned with salt and pepper

½ white onion

2 garlic cloves

2 bay leaves

1 tablespoon salt

1 tablespoon bouillon paste

■ For the tomato sauce:

4 cups chicken stock

2 tablespoons chipotle paste (from a can)

18 oz tomato paste

8 tomatoes, blanched and skinned

4 bay leaves

2 teaspoons sugar

4 teaspoons salt

■ For the *crema*:

4 cups sour cream

1 cup yellow mustard

2 teaspoons salt

Pinch of freshly ground black pepper

■ **French baguettes**, enough for 4 inches (10 cm) per serving

1 can (15 ½ oz) pinto beans (we like Goya brand)

4 oz unsalted butter

½ teaspoon salt

Coleslaw and sliced radishes and avocado, for serving (optional)

Put the protein of your choice in a pressure cooker. Add the rest of the ingredients and pour in water to cover. Cook for 1 hour. Transfer the meat to a plate to cool, then shred it and set aside.

To make the tomato sauce, combine all of the ingredients in a saucepan and simmer briskly over medium heat, stirring often, until the tomatoes are soft. Drain the mixture thoroughly and discard the bay leaves. Put everything in a blender and purée until smooth. Taste and adjust the seasoning with more salt or chipotle paste, if needed. Return to the saucepan and keep warm until ready to serve.

To make the *crema*, in a bowl, whisk together all the ingredients until thoroughly blended. Set aside.

When almost ready to serve, toast the baguette(s) in the oven until golden but still soft inside. Meanwhile, in a saucepan over medium heat, combine the beans, butter, and ½ teaspoon salt and cook, stirring, until warmed through and the butter is melted. Process in a blender, adding up to ½ cup water as needed to make the sauce silky. Set aside. To serve, cut the toasted baguette crosswise into 4-inch (10-cm) pieces, then split each piece lengthwise evenly through the thickness but leaving each piece attached by a "spine." Spread the *crema* on both cut sides of each piece. Spoon ⅓ cup of the tomato sauce into each serving bowl and arrange a baguette on top of each, with the bread open like a book. Top each with the meat, dividing it evenly, and some of the bean sauce. Garnish with shredded coleslaw and/or sliced radishes or avocado, as you like.

In separate small bowls, serve a cup of the tomato sauce for each diner to dip it in. Enjoy!

P.S. Do have a lot of napkins around.

When I was six, I was in love with the movie *Grease*, so I used to "play" it at any school activity—dressing like Sandy, of course! The first song I fell in love with was "Summer Nights"; of course I know both the Spanish and English versions. Because of that *Grease* obsession, I became very active as a girl. I used to go to contemporary jazz dance classes, and I won a lot of competitions in my hometown. Singing or dancing for me as an adult is a stress relief. I have a dance class with my girlfriends on my rooftop every week just to have fun (and exercise too!), and frequently I do karaoke in my kitchen while cooking or when I have girlfriends over. When I was younger, I was very disciplined and wouldn't miss a dance class. I got very good because of the practice, and I used to compete with older girls, which gave me solid confidence and healthy self-esteem. That discipline stays with me today, especially when I am working in the kitchen.

When I was in college, I had a car, so my musician friends and I would drive to other states and go to amazing concerts. We went to two or three Depeche Mode concerts in a row. I was inspired by music, especially live performances. I learned how jazz music has evolved from classic theory, and that it allows for so many interpretations so that musicians can improvise once they're performing to make it their own musical piece. My friends were brilliant and many of them are successful in the music industry today. Back then, my apartment was the meeting place for all of my friends. We were six girls living together at the time, so you can imagine why my apartment was always packed! I would cook for everyone and they would bring the music and the beers. We had a soundtrack with "those songs" that made our college years so special:

Mr. Brightside	The Killers
Vasos Vacíos	Los Fabulosos Cadillacs
Gimme Tha Power	Molotov
When You're Gone	The Cranberries
Zombie	The Cranberries
Rocket	Smashing Pumpkins
1979	Smashing Pumpkins
I Know It's Over	The Smiths
Creep	Radiohead
Sweet Caroline	Neil Diamond

Chefs have become icons in pop culture because besides just catering or cooking for artists in these past decades, they have become friends and equals. Artists of all kinds appreciate the skills required to achieve a great catering or dining service in the industry—which, if we think about it, requires first a kind of dance or choreography between the front and back of the house to create a wonderful experience for our daily guests.

a kind of dance or choreography between the front and back of the house to create a wonderful experience for our daily guests

I think music without doubt inspires chefs — they cook better when their ambiance is a happy one. As for our guests at the restaurant or at home, music complements their experience as a thing to remember in the whole of it. As I've gotten older and my musical preferences have changed, I see myself cooking out of my comfort zone more often. I'm very curious about unknown spices, ingredients, or techniques, and I do not mind asking around for help or advice for how to use or execute.

As a Mexican, I grew up listening to a lot of American, English, and Irish bands (the Smashing Pumpkins, the Smiths, the Cure, the Cranberries, and U2), but the Latin artists are the ones that I listen to every time I need to reconnect to my culture. They make me feel connected to where I belong: México. I feel more creative when I remember my homeland of Guadalajara, Jalisco. So I always have in my favorite playlists artists like Luis Miguel, Juan Luis Guerra, Timbiriche, Alejandro Sanz, Flans, Fobia, and Aterciopelados. It feels like home listening to them—even though when I was living in Mexico I did not follow them as much—stirring the sentiment of wanting to know and feel where you come from. Most of the Mexican/Latin dishes that we serve at our restaurant were created while listening to Latin music. One example is the song "Entrega de Amor," which inspired our Tacos de Amigo, consisting of corn tortillas, melted cheese, and grilled shrimp with chorizo and beer.

Music has a big effect on the restaurant itself while we're in action, as well. When I'm choosing songs, I can tell the staff becomes more proactive or even cooks better if the music gets them in the right mood. During service, we play mostly reggae songs or something poppy. Some of the songs that get us in the right mood while cooking are:

Redemption Song	Bob Marley
Baja la Tensión	Cultura Profética
Rimas Pa' Seducir	Cultura Profética
Del Tope al Fondo	Cultura Profética
Salimos de Aquí	Fiel a la Vega

The front-of-house playlist has to be trendy, sophisticated, and carefully curated so that every guest will enjoy it. I usually observe the crowd, then decide which playlist we need. For pre-service, it's almost always very Puerto Rican, like reggaeton, classic salsa, or chill vibes like Cultura Profética or Fiel a la Vega. If I open the restaurant by myself before everyone gets in, I play something very Mexican that only I enjoy. For peak service, we mostly put on the playlists "Cafe con Leche" or "Niño Gordo" from Spotify. In between shifts, it's the "Hotel Costes" playlist. For the end of the night, it has to be a fun playlist. It depends on the ambiance of the night and things like if there are more locals or more tourists, but we have magnificent Spotify playlists that friends have shared with us, including "Maria Pascuala Shelter," "Casa Fayette" (2 and 3), "PreCopeo," "Chumbias," "Agusto," and "Hoy se Sale."

We always sing soooo hard when a popular song comes on. Our kitchen is open to our guests, so they can see as well as hear and feel our staff singing out loud, and they really like it. Guests have even clapped for us when we finish singing! One of our most rousing songs is "Atrévete-te-te" by Calle 13.

At the end of the day, the most celebrated dishes at the restaurant are the ones I cook from my household heritage. Guests have told me that these dishes transport them to their own childhoods. Those dishes include La Torta de Elote, a corn soufflé stuffed with charred poblano peppers, cheese, and sour cream; and My Mother's Meatloaf—a mix of pork, bacon, and ground beef wrapped in more bacon and served with a side of a creamy, mustardy coleslaw. I find that it's the same with music, Mexican and otherwise…both food and song take us back to stored memories, mostly happy ones.

MONIQUE FISO

Monique Fiso is one of New Zealand's more formidable chefs. Using traditional Māori cooking techniques and ingredients in combination with her training in some of New York City's top Michelin-starred kitchens, Fiso has taken Māori cuisine to a new level of sophistication. Her restaurant, Hiakai, has been honored with the Innovation in Māori Development award from the New Zealand Innovation Council, and in 2018, Monique was named *Cuisine* magazine's New Zealand Future Food Legend.

Recipe Inspiration:

Rainbows and Pots of Gold

by Stereophonics

MoMo Playlist ▶ These are the first ten songs in exact order taken straight off the playlist I listen to every day while working. I have very eclectic taste in music, and I'm not sure if there is any real theme other than that this whole "MoMo" playlist is music that inspires me to create.

1.	**Immigrant Song**	Led Zeppelin
2.	**Gimme Shelter**	The Rolling Stones
3.	**Hurtin' Me**	Stefflon Don, French Montana
4.	**One of These Nights**	Eagles
5.	**Burnin' for You**	Blue Öyster Cult
6.	**Wonderwall**	Oasis
7.	**Ava Adore**	The Smashing Pumpkins
8.	**Addicted to You**	Avicii
9.	**Ocean**	Martin Garrix featuring Khalid
10.	**One of My Turns**	Pink Floyd

Song: Rainbows and Pots of Gold by Stereophonics

▲ Monique Fiso

NEW ZEALAND

HOKEY POKEY BARS

A dark song involving gold by the Stereophonics; a dark dessert involving gold by Hiakai.

Makes 12 bars

■ For the hokey pokey semifreddo:

150 g caster (superfine) sugar

30 g golden syrup

5 g baking soda (bicarbonate of soda)

550 g heavy (whipping) cream

250 ml sweetened condensed milk

2 g xanthan gum powder

1 g flaky sea salt

300 g 72% dark chocolate, chopped

150 g cocoa butter

Two 24-ct edible gold leaves

To make the semifreddo, line a baking sheet with a silicone mat. Very lightly spray the mat with baking spray and set aside.

Combine the sugar and golden syrup in a heavy-bottomed saucepan and cook over medium heat, stirring constantly, until the mixture is a deep golden caramel color. When you have reached the desired color, remove the syrup from the heat and very quickly whisk in the baking soda (bicarbonate of soda). The hokey pokey will immediately begin to froth. Transfer the mixture to the prepared mat and spread it evenly.

Let the hokey pokey cool completely, about 30 minutes. Once the hokey pokey is cooled, you will need to break it up. The best way is to wear disposable gloves and crunch it into small pieces using your hands. Break it all down into pieces 5 mm (a little less than ¼ inch) or smaller. Set aside.

In a bowl, whip the cream to stiff peaks. Add the sweetened condensed milk, xanthan gum powder, and salt and whip for 20 seconds more, or until the mixture is well incorporated. Be careful not to overwhip.

Fold in all of the hokey pokey that you prepared earlier, including all the crumbs, a.k.a "dust."

Place the semifreddo mixture in a piping bag and pipe into silicone molds of your choosing. At Hiakai, we use an 80 mm L x 35 mm W x 35 mm D half-cylinder silicone mold.

Once they're all piped, place the mold(s) in the freezer overnight.

The next day, prepare your dark chocolate coating: Melt the chocolate along with the cocoa butter in a bain-marie. When the mixture is melted, blend well using a stick blender, then pour into a squeeze bottle. The mixture needs to be warm in order to run well and coat the hokey pokey bars nicely, but do not get the mixture too hot, or it will split.

Unmold your hokey pokey bars straight onto a cooling rack. Glaze the tops with the dark chocolate, working quickly so that the semifreddo doesn't melt sitting out at room temperature. As you glaze each bar, transfer from the rack to a baking sheet using an offset spatula — this will prevent them from getting stuck to the resting rack and making it difficult to remove them after you've finished glazing.

Place the coated hokey pokey bars back in the freezer. When it comes time to serve them, brush them with the gold leaf (you can also place the gold on the hokey pokey bars ahead of time if you wish). Serve immediately.

I first became aware of music at a really young age, around about four years old, for two reasons. First of all, my mother was determined that I would become a ballerina, when clearly I was not cut out for it. Nevertheless, I was listening to classical music and having to do ballet lessons. Secondly, what I really loved was Elvis, because my dad was obsessed with him. The first song I really fell in love with was "Hound Dog." My dad had all of Elvis's records, so I would sneak those and listen to them, but I would always get into trouble and be told I should be listening to my ballet recital music. ● Falling in love with Elvis shaped me as a person. I saw him as quite a rebel—one with interesting eating habits. Elvis ate "fool's gold" sandwiches, consisting of bacon, jam, and peanut butter all rolled up in white bread and then deep fried. It fascinated me because we didn't have United States–style Southern food in New Zealand. I heard about a lot of things out there that he'd eaten or things that he'd done foodwise and I thought, "Oh, that's really fascinating." He influenced me to have an interest in Southern food, which was odd for a child growing up so far away from the American South. As I got older, it got me even more interested in Southern food, and I ended up traveling down to the South quite a bit when I was living in New York City. I was just fascinated by it being so different from where I grew up in New Zealand. Because of my obsession with him, Elvis inspired me to keep my eyes open to that part of America and what was going on foodwise. I just thought he was so rebellious and he had this kind of swagger, and it definitely made me become quite a rebellious child. ● Through Elvis's records, I was able to go and get lost in another world. New Zealand is very, very small and faraway, an island way out in the South Pacific that's the last stop before Antarctica, so we are physically isolated from the rest of the world. It's not like Europe, where you can just get on a train or a plane and you're in another country within a few minutes. Music was a great escape for me because it could take me somewhere else and also tell me about other parts of the world and what was going on. And to me, being quite a curious child, music gave me itchy feet,

making me want to travel. Even at home, music was a great way of just going somewhere else in my head for a while. ● Elvis's entire *Greatest Hits* album has always been a soundtrack playing in the background of my life—I tend to turn to Elvis's music when I'm feeling down. I know all the lyrics to all of his songs, so there's something I find comforting listening to Elvis, as if I'm spending time with an old friend. When I eventually did go to Graceland, I ended up crying at the end of the tour because of what an emotional rollercoaster the experience was. For the kid in me that had been listening to Elvis's music from the age of four, from halfway around the world, it was overwhelming. I had finally made my way all the way to Memphis and was now standing in his house listening to his music. That was quite emotional for me. ● I'm Māori Samoan, and in both cultures, music and food are very intertwined. In Samoan culture, any event or occasion you go to, there's always music, traditional dancing, and then a feast. Māori is very much the same. So in order for you to even be welcomed onto a *marae*, which is a Māori meeting house, first there is the *pōwhiri*, which is when you get called on officially. Then a *waiata*, a song, will be sung, and then the visiting party has to sing a *waiata* in response. After all of that is done, after the songs have been sung, then you're allowed to sit down and eat. So, it's really, really intertwined, which always made me a little self-conscious as a kid because I'm not the greatest singer. Whenever I knew that there was some sort of official ceremony going on in the community where I would have to be involved, I'd always think, "Oh no, there's gonna be songs, and I have the worst voice in the world...Oh God, if I just sing as quietly as possible, maybe it will be okay." I was afraid of going to the event sometimes because I just knew I had a horrible singing voice! ● We have a holiday called White Sunday within Samoan culture, and it always falls around my birthday in October. White Sunday is the kids' day in Samoan culture. I'm not religious, but we used to go to church all the time, mainly the Pacific Island Church. For the most part, all the sermons and songs were always sung in Samoan and I'm not fluent, but I would try my best. Whenever White Sunday was happening, the kids would put on a play full of songs so we'd have to go practice them in advance, usually at my grandma's house. Mum and Dad would drop us off at grandma's house and be like, "You need to practice all the songs that you're going to sing in these plays, so that you don't make a fool of us on Sunday in front of the whole church." ● But being the bad singer that I was, my Sunday school teacher eventually pulled me aside and said, "You know what I think, I think you're just a much better narrator, so you don't have to do the songs and you can just be the narrator of the play. So, when there's a part that requires somebody to stand up and just read out what's going on in the play, that can be your part." And I was like, "Oh, okay, I must sound like a dead cat," and that was the end of my singing career. ● Still, singer or not, as I've said, I have always been deeply inspired by songs. One other songwriter who has been a huge influence on me is Richard Ashcroft. His songs and his albums have affected me as a person and how I do the artistic things I love. He was the lead singer of the Verve, a British band from the '90s. He broke off, started recording solo work, and made one of my favorite songs, "A Song for the Lovers." I still listen to it today. I just really love his songwriting, the way he is able to write beautiful music, and how multi-talented he is — he also played all the instruments. His craft of master songwriting makes his songs stick with you for years. I try to emulate that in the food that I make. I want my dishes to stick with a diner for years in the same way a great song does, so they are still thinking about that moment when they had my dish for the first time. To me, Ashcroft's music is highly emotional, and I've always tried to make food that is quite emotional, too. And not just something that's like, "Oh yeah, that's cool, we're doing this because it's trendy and everyone else is doing it, too." That's more like pop music — not that there's anything wrong with pop music, but I want to cook something with a bit more depth. ● Growing up in New Zealand in the late '80s and '90s, there was a very quiet racism toward my culture. Hiakai has become a vessel to contain my thoughts of, "We're here, I can do our food justice, here's how we're gonna do it, and I'm not going to apologize for it"—the Elvis rebellious spirit, you could say. Sometimes for me the restaurant is about all the emotions on these plates that I'm not even sure people want to deal with. ● At the core of it, when I'm in the artistic decision-making process and contemplating the style of the food that I do and putting together a dish and deciding what makes it onto the plate and what doesn't, I am definitely thinking of my inspirations and influences and roots. I want our food to be artistic, emotional, and unapologetic and at times soul-baring, like Richard Ashcroft. Unique and rebellious like Elvis. And at Hiakai, we're all of those things as we put Māori and Samoan ingredients on the menu and create dishes that hit on the subject points of growing up in New Zealand.

Unique and rebellious like Elvis

MICHAEL FOJTASEK

Michael Fojtasek opened Olamaie in Austin, Texas, in August 2014 as an outlet for his passion for seasonal ingredients and love of Southern cooking and hospitality. Fojtasek and his restaurant have received multiple James Beard Award nominations and have been honored by *Food & Wine* and *Texas Monthly* magazines. Beyond these culinary accolades, Olamaie has served as a touchstone for the community by supporting numerous charities.

Song: The Way It Is by Bruce Hornsby and the Range

Running Playlist ▶ I've been training for the New York Marathon. These are some of the songs that are currently on my playlist while I'm out on the trail. I can't help but get my tempo messed up by the music. But, it's the only time I get just for me, so screw it.

1.	**Run like Hell**	Pink Floyd
2.	**Hallelujah**	Leonard Cohen
3.	**Character Zero**	Phish
4.	**Find Yourself**	Lukas Nelson and Promise of the Real
5.	**Rise Up with Fists!!**	Jenny Lewis and the Watson Twins
6.	**I Am That I Am**	Peter Tosh
7.	**Tom Sawyer**	Rush
8.	**Rush**	Talib Kweli
9.	**You Can Have the Crown**	Sturgill Simpson
10.	**Lay There & Hate Me**	Ben Harper & Relentless7

Recipe Inspiration:

The Way

▲ Michael Fojtasek

USA

Seeing Bruce perform this song at Ashley Christensen's wedding while I was eating her tomato pie: that is one of my most memorable moments of the last decade, so I wanted to make a dish that honored that moment.

Makes one 9-inch (23-cm) pie

OLAMAIE
Tomato Pie

by Bruce Hornsby and the Range

Is it

■ For the pie dough:

177 g butter

150 g all-purpose flour

150 g cake flour

7 g salt

30 g basil purée

62 g cold water

10 g apple cider vinegar

■ For the tomato custard:

6 eggs

124 g milk

124 g cream

300 g mayonnaise

100 g apple cider vinegar

35 g Dijon mustard

20 g salt

200 g onion, any color, chopped

8 g roasted garlic

40 g prepared horseradish, drained

6 g hot-pepper sauce

300 g roasted tomatoes

100 g finely grated cheddar

To make the pie dough, place the butter in the freezer.

Combine the dry ingredients in a food processor and pulse to mix.

Once the butter is chilled, cut into cubes. Add to the food processor with the flour mixture and pulse until the butter bits are pea-sized.

Add the wet ingredients and pulse until the mixture is evenly crumbly. Turn out onto a floured board and finish combining by hand. Pat the dough into a disk. Double-wrap the dough in plastic wrap (cling film) and let rest overnight in the refrigerator.

Preheat the oven to 375°F (190°C).

Remove the dough from the fridge and let soften for a couple of minutes, then roll out on a floured board into a round. Fit into your pie plate, crimp the edges, and fill with pie weights. Blind-bake for 15 minutes. Remove the weights and continue baking for about another 10 minutes, or until the bottom looks cooked. Let cool on a wire rack. Reduce the oven temperature to 275°F (135°C).

To make the custard, combine all of the ingredients in a blender and blend until smooth. Pass the custard through a chinois and set aside.

Scatter the cheese over the bottom of the cooled crust. Press the cheese down gently to make one even layer with very little crust showing through. Gently pour in the custard to just below the edge of crust.

Bake with 1 fan for about 25 minutes. A cake tester should come out clean. Do not shake the pie or you'll get creases. Let cool, cut into wedges, and serve.

When I was growing up, my family always played music while we hung around the house. Cooking was a primary activity on the weekends, so food and music overlapped a lot. My dad likes all kinds of music, so I was listening to Steely Dan followed by Anita Baker and everyone in between as a kid. The first songs I fell in love with were "Bad Bad Leroy Brown" by Jim Croce and "Chattanooga Choo Choo" by Glenn Miller. When I was about six, my first tape came in a cereal box. It meant a lot to me because it was the first music that was mine. I could play it over and over again and completely immerse myself in it. Once I had my own music, I wanted to share the songs I loved with others. ● I used to make mixtapes like everyone else. At first, it was about listening to the local radio's "Top Nine at Nine" and taping those songs. It was fun to share those, but I started to gravitate toward making more personal mixes. Eventually, it was about making a tape that had a good flow and also showed that I was cool enough to listen to all this "great" music. Later, I missed a lot of college classes trying to download the biggest library of songs off Napster onto a huge 6-gigabyte hard drive that I personally installed on my computer. The act of gathering music went beyond a hobby; it was obsession. ● Some of my most memorable music moments are the shows I didn't get to go see. Pearl Jam played in 1993 at a college near my house when I was fourteen. I begged my parents to go and they said no. I'm still a little pissed they didn't allow it. Pearl Jam was everything to me at that point. Two years later, all the kids from all the high schools were going to see Lynyrd Skynyrd at the big amphitheater in Dallas. I'm not upset that I missed that shit...but I do think about it sometimes. ● I can't remember when food didn't have a special meaning for me. Even the Night Hawk TV dinners we ate while watching *Murder She Wrote* with my grandmother stuck with me. As a kid, I liked to fry chicken and make pies. Then I liked to cook for all my friends. It wasn't until much later that I considered it as a career. ● In my twenties, I worked for a record label here in Austin for a short time. During that

▲ Michael Fojtasek

little big
money dreams

job, I attended South by Southwest with a music industry badge that I had bought to explore my newly planned career. At the convention center, I attended a talk given by David Byrne. He said, "If you're not talent, or already established in the record business, get out." It made a huge impact. Soon after, I began cooking. In 2019, I got to cook a dinner in Muscle Shoals Sound Studio. Dave Hood of the Swampers was there and he said that he loved the food. That was the next level for me. ● Music has continued to intersect with food in my professional life. It seems musicians and cooks have so many similarities. I have always listened to all types of music, and that practice seems to have given me the ability to talk to all kinds of people about the music they enjoy. Even if we have nothing else in common, we can talk about a song or an album or lyrics. My tastes have evolved and there have been lots of bands that I have liked over the years. In high school, it was a duo called Jackopierce. In college, it was Yonder Mountain String Band. Post college, it was Wilco. I have traveled all over the world to see all of these bands play and their music has been an inspiration for my creativity and my cooking. ● Musicians are like cooks—we're all craftsmen. I think that anyone, myself included, can pick up a guitar, play three chords, and dream of being a musician. Anyone can cook something and fantasize about running their own restaurant, too. Cooks and musicians have lots in common: little money, big dreams, late nights, and a desire to set yourself apart. Music has influenced my mood while cooking over and over. I've worked in kitchens where there is no music, and those were tougher kitchens to work in, but it made sense. I've finally found the right balance of music during prep, but silence during service. The music I love is of the place that the cuisine I cook comes from. For the first year at Olamaie, I played only songs that were recorded in the South. No one seemed to care about that touch other than myself, but it made a big difference. It was a creative nod to the music that inspired me and the food we cook.

late nights

FOURMONT

CAMILLE

Camille Fourmont is the
founder and proprietor of
La Buvette, one of the
most beloved wine shops
in Paris. In 2014, *Le Fooding*
selected La Buvette as the
best *cave à manger* in Paris.
Fourmont has been invited
to do La Buvette pop-ups
everywhere from New York
to Tokyo.

Good Mood Playlist
▶ This is a playlist for
the moment — play on
shuffle, because it's too
eclectic to decide on an
absolute order.

1.	The Man I Love	Billie Holiday and her Orchestra
2.	Black Water	Timbre Timbre
3.	Rock the Boat	Hues Corporation
4.	Il venait d'avoir 18 ans	Ibrahim Maalouf
5.	Atomic Bomb	William Onyeabor
6.	Wild Woman	Father's Children
7.	Valentine	Tricky
8.	Polaroïd / Roman / Photo	Ruth
9.	Sunset Lover	Petit Biscuit
10.	Prettiest Virgin	Agar Agar
11.	Pas Contente	Vaudou Game
12.	Daa Nyinaa	Ata Kak

Burrata

When I think of Italia—and its dreamy cheeses like this creamy *burrata*—this is always the first song that comes to my mind. It may be really retro, but I keep loving it.

It's often tricky to find some very fresh *burrata* even in Paris. At La Buvette they come twice a week from Puglia, but they're pasteurized; if not, they wouldn't stand the journey. But recently we have some dairy shops that make their own, so you can find a fresh *burrata* from that same day, even in Paris. If you can only find a pasteurized one, just make sure they come from a traditional artisan producer. I use Maldon flakes as much for the evocative taste as for its crunchy consistency.

Serves 2

Recipe Inspiration:

I Wanna Be Your Lover
by La Bionda

1 *burrata* **cheese**, about 125 g

Maldon sea salt flakes

Olive oil (round and fruity, nothing too strong or too bitter in its aftertaste)

Drain the *burrata* gently on paper towels and pat dry to remove the preserving water.

I like to serve *burrata* very simply with olive oil and salt, but sometimes we get more creative. If you have a dehydrator, try dusting it with powdered mandarin zest or a raspberry powder as we do at La Buvette, or sprinkle with a dried aromatic such as ground sage.

Place the cheese on a cutting board or serving platter. Surround with things like fruit and olives. Enjoy.

When I was in my mom's belly, I thought I heard so many songs.
I couldn't tell you which, exactly, but I remember during my whole
life, I would hear something random that hit me like a memory. I feel
a chill when this happens without knowing why. Not that long ago,
I said something to my mother about this, and she said, "Oh my God,
don't tell me about it." It turns out my father had only one record
he was listening to all the time when she was pregnant with me. She
wasn't angry and was kind of kidding about my father's ability to listen
to the same record…and was only slightly worried about any lasting
effects. It was *Harvest Moon* by Neil Young. When I hear it now,
it's weird how it hits me. It's a bit more physical than anything else.

> I started dance classes when I was really young. When my brother
> was born, I was already seven and used to being an only child. I was
> on my own a lot of the time, which was a joyful thing, as far as
> I remember. I would be in my little bubble, in my little safe place. The
> world could fall down around me and I wouldn't admit or know it.

When I was eight or maybe ten, I spent the whole summer with my
mom in the house in Brittany where we went every summer when
I was a kid. My brother was small. I spent all my days in the living room
creating some little choreography to Adios Nonino's *Astor Piazzolla*.
It was accordion music. I loved his music so much and I loved dancing
to it. I was totally in that bubble. Spending afternoons alone creating
my own choreography, dancing to it. Today when I listen to his music,
I feel really emotional every time.

> When you're young, the music you like, you're just a small fan, and
> you're learning to like lots of things. When you're a teen, you adopt
> a precise style of music. It is a socialization thing, you're part of a
> human group. You become a part of one group when you listen to
> Death Metal or you become part of another group when you listen to
> hip-hop. I was more in the hip-hop group. I felt more confident and
> I identified myself as the guy who had to fight to survive.

When I was a teenager, my mother and I started fighting all the time
because I begged her for a pair of Doc Martens shoes. I told her that
everyone had them. Alas, she would not get them for me for that exact
same reason. She wanted me to shape my identity by *not* having the same
thing as everyone else. "This is how you're going to be different, and then
you can assume it, and then you can be proud of it," she would tell me.

> With music, you have some good stuff and some bad stuff, because
> everyone listens to music. Even more so these days, because every-
> one feels like they can make music. You have some great gifted
> talents and you have some commercial nonsense and everything in
> between. Food has transformed that way too, because so many
> people have seen ways to cook and serve through the Internet, but
> without going deep in the knowledge of the food or technique or the
> why. They don't know anything, but they say, "Oh that's a good way
> to serve cause I saw it somewhere." But I do not think it works.

Before creating La Buvette and involving myself more in feeding people,
I learned what worked at three places with three different styles. Each
place always had music. We already hustled pretty hard with moments
of intense rush. Music helped us to keep on track when we were busy.

Even knowing this, I don't play music anymore at La Buvette.
When I worked at my previous job, the restaurant was built out of
marble and mirrors. It was super noisy—that kind of super high-
pitched, painful noise. It ruined my ears. I lost three points of good
hearing in each ear. I was too young to have my ears damaged like
that. I hadn't spent my teenage years going to big concerts. The
doctors couldn't believe what had happened to my hearing.

Today when there is loud music in bad listening conditions, it actually
hurts me. It is physical. I have special plugs for my ears with filters that
make it somewhat more comfortable for me. If I go to a restaurant and
the music is too loud for no reason, I get a bad vibration in my bones.
You know; I can feel it deep inside of my body.

When I found the space for La Buvette, the materials in the interior
were almost exactly the same as they are today! Murals, glass…
I love to listen to music so much, but I knew by then, it must be in
good conditions. Music doesn't make sense if you can't even hear
it, or if it's so loud and you have so much noise that it's not a source
of pleasure anymore. I knew that if I played music people were going
to talk louder, so you play the music louder, so people talk louder.
It's a nightmare idea. People don't enjoy it.

Both my past and the history of the shop contain a silent atmosphere.
When it's quiet during the day, you can hear the little snooze of the
street. The ambient noise and the space is part of the place, its music,
and I love that.

The ambient
noise and the
space is part
of the place,
its music, and
I love that.

MARC-OLIVIER FRAPPIER

Marc-Olivier Frappier is a Montréal-based chef and the co-owner of Mon Lapin. In 2009, Frappier started working at Joe Beef, where he eventually became the head chef. Over the next decade, he came to run all three of the Joe Beef restaurants, and in 2019, he and his wife, Vanya, opened Mon Lapin in Montréal's Little Italy. He deeply loves Vanya, the Montreal Canadiens, and Dairy Queen.

Coniglio Farfalla Playlist ▶
This is an easy-to-listen-to compilation of some of my favorite songs. A lot of them come from testing recipes from my second book. I am most likely to listen to this play-list while being stuck in heavy Montréal construction traffic or shoveling my car from the snow in winter.

1.	The Night They Drove Old Dixie Down	The Band
2.	Baby Bitch	Ween
3.	Juste Une P'tite Nuite	Les Colocs
4.	1990	Jean Leloup
5.	La Poule Aux Œufs Dor	Les Hay Babies
6.	The Suburbs	Arcade Fire
7.	Montreal -40°C	Malajube
8.	Ti-Cul	Les Cowboys Fringants
9.	Brown Baby	Brown Family
10.	Off the Grid	Loud featuring Lary Kidd
11.	Sinsemilla	Black Uhuru
12.	Jazz (We've Got) / Buggin' Out	A Tribe Called Quest
13.	Through the Wire	Kanye West
14.	Johnny	Dead Obies
15.	Lost Ones	Ms. Lauryn Hill

CANADA

SMOKED EEL CARBONARA

Recipe Inspiration:

Je reviendrai à Montréal by Robert Charlebois

I can't exactly recall how we came up with this recipe. Was it when trying to make eel guanciale? Was it by trying to come up with dishes for the fictitious Osteria du Bas-du-Fleuve, also known as the Osteria di Kamouraska, with Alex Landry? Was it simply to try to get Québécois people to eat eel again? The once massively consumed fish has become as difficult to find in households and restaurants in Québec as two Romans agreeing on the proper method to make a "real" carbonara.

Serves 4 hungry people

Salt

75 g grated Parmigiano-Reggiano cheese

75 g *Pecorino Romano* cheese

3 large eggs, plus 3 large yolks

Freshly ground black pepper

30 g pork fat (*strutto*)

160 g smoked eel, cut into cubes about 1 cm by 1 cm (⅜ inch by ⅜ inch)

450 g fresh rye *tonnarelli*

Bring a pot of salted water big enough to hold all the *tonnarelli* to a boil.

In a small bowl, whisk together the cheeses. In a large bowl, whisk together about three-fourths of the mixed cheeses with the eggs, egg yolks, and a good amount of black pepper. Set aside.

In a large, cold, nonstick sauté pan or frying pan, combine the pork fat and the cubed smoked eel. Heat over medium flame until the smoked fish starts to brown slightly the same way bacon would. Remove from the heat.

While the eel and fat mixture is cooling down, drop the *tonnarelli* into the boiling water, stirring once or twice at the beginning to make sure they don't stick together.

Once the pasta is perfectly al dente, strain it, keeping a small measuring jar of the cooking water. Add the pasta to the pan with the eel and place over low heat.

At this point you need to work fast. Add the cheese and egg mixture and a touch of the cooking water to the pan. Cook the carbonara delicately until it thickens, stirring constantly. Make sure it doesn't scramble. When the egg and cheese has thickened and is coating the *tonnarelli*, remove from the heat.

Serve the smoked eel carbonara with the remaining cheese on top and another generous grinding of black pepper. Eat right away (and never reheat!).

I grew up in a French Canadian house in Saint-Hyacinthe, Québec, therefore most music we were listening to at home was French. I didn't necessarily love all the music my parents were playing at home, but I have very clear memories of "L'été Indien" by Joe Dassin on repeat while dusting my room at my dad's place; while at my mom's, it was more the whole Michel Fugain repertoire while putting away toys with my sister, Emilie.

●

Food started to take on a big role in my life at around the age of fourteen. Because of my particular homelife at that age, I was home alone often and had to learn to cook for myself, and sometimes my sister as well. It started with little things like making new toppings for frozen pizzas, but before long that led to making fresh pasta from scratch. I didn't realize it at the time, but my cooking skills kept growing and growing. And significantly, while I wasn't paying close attention, there was always music playing in the background.

I traveled a lot when I was young, doing internships and programs abroad in Italy and the U.S., a summer in Tunisia, etc. The music of Jean Leloup and Les Colocs always brought me back to my roots and helped me explain to others where I came from. I first fell in love with the rebel that is Jean Leloup and his song "I Lost My Baby." It is just amazing—an uncanny mix of tragic lyrics and jovial melody. I was really influenced by this type of music as a young kid. I was transported by the melodies, and then shocked by the lyrics, but somehow all together it showed me that melancholy could be expressed through different moods and lenses.

●

When I moved to Italy at seventeen years old, I didn't speak much Italian at first. I would try to bond with my fellow students by accompanying them to concerts and shows, and at first, I understood nothing. Over time, I really got into the music so I started looking up the lyrics, and that helped me connect with the culture and understand my new friends better. It also helped me learn Italian! I got into Vasco Rossi and J-Ax, some of the really popular Italian music at the time. Today, when I'm cooking Italian food, I just crave this music, and it makes so much sense to listen to it when I'm in that state of mind.

There is a really big culture of music in Québec, and it feels as though this music is quite unknown in the rest of the world. It seems like a very well-kept secret. People know Céline Dion and that's it. There is a huge heritage of incredible and inspirational singer-songwriters like Gilles Vigneault, Les Colocs, Beau Dommage, Robert Charlebois, Jean Leloup, and, one of my favorites, Les Cowboys Fringants. These names are staples in the Québec music scene and have shaped so many recent musicians. What I specifically love about Les Cowboys Fringants is that their lyrics are unbelievably smart and relevant, political at times, and always very strong. Again, these guys are Montréalers, and I love cooking for them at the restaurants on any given occasion. They love food and are real bon vivants.

I really love music made by people I actually know and respect. There is nothing better than connecting with a song made by someone you actually have a relationship with. I have had the real privilege of living in a city that is super dynamic and full of fantastic artists. In the last few years, I've completely been mesmerized by my friend Terrell McLeod-Richardson and his musical career with THe LYONZ. It's a Montréal-based project with real international flavors, and their songs really speak to me. You listen to them and you know they are going to do big things.

●

Most of the restaurants I have worked in are open kitchens. The music of the dining room is part of our reality in the kitchen and it actually helps us get through big nights and periods of intense rush. In pre-service, I like feelgood music like reggae to get everyone happy and on a positive rhythm. I love the playful parallels and puns one can make with musical titles and food. Frederic Morin, of Joe Beef, has really been a huge influence in this, as he is extremely skilled at coming up with puns on the fly. Wu-Tang Clams. Schnitzel My Wizzle. And so forth! I once tried to serve a pink veal tongue (dyed with beet juice) to the Rolling Stones, but I didn't have enough notice and the dish didn't work. I was really bummed out about that.

My favorite nights at the restaurants are when food, music, and the city come together to create something special. We had an amazing friend named John Bil, really one of a kind. He was the world champion oyster shucker and just an exceptional guy. He unfortunately passed away a few years back. He worked with us at Joe Beef and had loads of friends from Prince Edward Island and New Brunswick, all of whom worked in the oyster world. They would show up unannounced with their oysters and fiddles and start playing in the dining room on any given night, fiddling and shucking away—quite usual for Montréal, and just the best.

They would show up unannounced with their oysters and fiddles and start playing in the dining room on any given night, fiddling and shucking away — quite usual for Montréal, and just the best.

GUTIÉRREZ

ALEJANDRO

Alejandro Gutiérrez started his career as a chef at Bogotá restaurant Donostia, with chef Tomás Rueda. He worked in New York City restaurants and in 2010, he returned to Bogotá to become head chef at both Tábula and Donostia. In 2013, he decided to join chef and barista Juan Manuel Ortiz at Salvo Patria for the restaurant's reopening at a new, bigger location. At Salvo Patria, he works on an ever-changing menu focused on fresh, sustainable ingredients from Colombia's stunningly diverse terrain.

Tropi Menu Playlist ▶ I've always joked with a good friend of mine that we should make a menu inspired by tropical songs with food titles. So, what better moment to do it than now. The idea is to read the playlist the way you go through a tasting menu.

1.	**Agüita E' Coco**	Afrosound
2.	**Sopita en botella**	Celia Cruz
3.	**Patacon con Queso**	La-33
4.	**La Malanga**	Eddie Palmieri
5.	**Camaron**	Freddy Fender
6.	**Arroz Con Coco**	Lucho Bermudez y Su Orquesta Sabanera
7.	**Sopa de Caracol**	Banda Blanca
8.	**Arroz con Habichuela**	El Gran Combo De Puerto Rico
9.	**Salchicha con Huevo**	Jimmy Sabater
10.	**El Mondongo**	Los Corraleros de Majagual
11.	**Fried Neck Bones and Some Home Fries**	Willie Bobo
12.	**Moliendo Café**	Ismael Rivera
13.	**Plátano Maduro**	Billo's Caracas Boys
14.	**Melao De Caña**	Oscar D'Leon
15.	**Tabaco y Ron**	Rodolfo Aicardi

COLOMBIA

Grilled Albacore Tuna Belly, Tucupí Chimichurri, Fermented Peppers, Farina

Colombia's Pacific coast is a region full of jungles. Not long ago (in geological time), it was an ecosystem similar to the Amazon, before the Andes formed in between. It is also a place where African slaves settled after fighting for their freedom against the Spanish conquerors.

This recipe is not inspired by a song, but by the music from Colombia's Pacific region itself, where cumbia melts with African rhythms. This kind of music always makes me think of the immense, humid jungle by the ocean. The dish blends ingredients from the Amazon with fish from the Pacific Ocean.
Note, you need a week to ferment these beautiful chiles. Store the unused chiles tightly sealed in their container in the refrigerator.

Serves 4 to 6

■ For the fermented chiles:

1 kg assorted small fresh chiles, a mixture of hot and mild (we use different types from all over Colombia)

35 g fine sea salt

■ For the *chimichurri*:

30 g red onion

100 ml neutral oil

10 g fresh annatto seeds

5 g fresh cilantro (coriander) leaves

5 g fresh purple basil leaves

5 ml rice vinegar

5 g *tucupí*
(savory paste from the Amazon, made with fermented and reduced wild yucca juice; it can be replaced with a mixture of red miso and marmite)

■ For the farina crackers:

100 g farina (coarse-grind wild yucca flour)

1 g salt

400 ml water

1 liter frying oil

■ 500 g fresh albacore tuna belly, trimmed and cut into 100-g pieces

▶❘

To make the fermented chiles, cut the chiles in half lengthwise and place them in a bowl. Mix them with the salt. Pack the salted chiles in a sterilized glass jar that's just big enough to fit them, so there is as little air as possible. Press down to help them release their juices (wear gloves if using your hands). Leave the chiles to ferment for 1 week in a dark, well-ventilated place.

To make the *chimichurri*, cut the onion into small dice. Rinse with cold water and drain well. Put in a bowl and set aside.

In a small frying pan, heat the oil over low heat. Add the annatto seeds, stir to coat in the oil, and infuse for 30 minutes. Remove from the heat and let cool.

Transfer the infused oil and seeds to a blender. Add the rest of the ingredients and blend into a fine paste. Add the paste to the onion and stir well.

To make the farina crackers, in a bowl, whisk together the farina, salt, and water. Place the mixture in a small pot and cook on low heat for 5 minutes, stirring constantly to avoid it sticking to the bottom of the pot.

Scrape the cooked mixture onto a silicone mat and spread it evenly to ½ cm (about ¼ inch) thick. Place in a dehydrator or a very low oven until hard and completely dried.

Meanwhile, in a deep pot, preheat the oil to 190°C (375°F).

Break the crackers into uneven pieces and fry until nice and golden. Drain on paper towels.

Prepare a very hot fire in a charcoal grill.

Rub salt and some of the *chimichurri* oil over the tuna.

Arrange the tuna on the rack and grill just on one side, leaving half the thickness of the tuna belly uncooked.

Cut a scoop of the fermented chiles into small pieces.

Place the tuna on plates. Garnish each with some of the chiles and drizzle with the *chimichurri*. Serve with the farina crackers.

A song is like a dish, a menu is like an album.

Alejandro Gutiérrez

Colombia is a musical country; everyone listens to music all the time. We love to party, we love dancing. Local music in Colombia is diverse, influenced by rhythms that vary from African to indigenous and European music. Colombian music helps us be proud of who we are, of our products. That also happens with our food.

●

The first music I started playing by myself was a few classic rock vinyl records my parents used to have. Even though I listen to lots of salsa, blues, reggae, and jazz right now, I've always had a punk-rock attitude and way of dressing. The Clash influenced me with their take on counterculture and their political and rebel-inspired lyrics. Their style and energy were inspiring for me as a young chef. I was kind of a rebel myself to decide, at a young age, to become a chef fifteen years ago in Bogotá. Nowadays in my restaurant, we have a strongly political way of doing things, we have a voice. I can thank the Clash for that.

●

I remember the first time I listened to Pink Floyd's *The Wall* on vinyl. It was on a sunny afternoon after school, and it blew my mind!! All the effects and sounds, the transitions between songs, the kids' chorus in "Another Brick in the Wall," the art work...everything. A few years later, I saw the movie and it also blew my mind (although I was a bit young for it, so it left me a little traumatized). I still believe the whole album-movie is a masterpiece.

●

Living in Toronto after I graduated from high school, I went to the Warped Tour. At one point during the NOFX gig, a big guy standing next to me threw me over the crowd. I spent a whole song crowd-surfing. I had never felt so happy and so free. I was living far away from home and I wasn't missing anyone or anything. Then, the winter came, and the story was a lot different.

●

Music's not just for joy; it is absolutely necessary when you're heart-broken. When that winter came, I was heartbroken, and I listened to music nonstop. The sadder the song, the better. It helped me get through it until I realized I wasn't missing that person anymore—because I wasn't feeling sad while listening to, for example, "Wild Horses" by the Rolling Stones.

●

As we got older, we leaned on the messages of punk and rock to develop our own voice and rhythm in our restaurant, Salvo Patria. Many of my colleagues and I share the feeling that being in a rush on a kitchen service, all coordinated with your team, is similar to being on stage in a concert. We have an audience, we have a band, we have a sound. A song is like a dish, a menu is like an album. We have a creative job, but we also play those songs again and again. Nowadays, being a musician and a chef are very similar things.

●

Lately I have been listening to a lot of jazz. I love the way it breaks the rules: every sound comes from within, from the soul of the artist. I have been trying to look less to whatever other chefs are doing and let my creative process start the way jazz musicians make their music.

HELOU

ANISSA

Anissa Helou is a chef, food writer, journalist, broadcaster, consultant, and blogger focusing on the cuisines and culinary heritage of the Middle East, Mediterranean, and North Africa. Born and raised between Beirut, Lebanon, and Mashta el-Helou, Syria, she knows the Mediterranean as only a well-traveled native can. Ms. Helou authored numerous award-winning cookbooks, with her latest book, *Feast: Food of the Islamic World*, being the recipient of the James Beard Foundation award in the International category.

From poignant romanticism to social messaging to simply divine music Playlist ▶ My taste in music has changed a lot over the years. I have graduated from pop to folk to classical to world, and I still switch from vocal to instrumental and back. But throughout it all, I have hated what I call "thumping music" (although this didn't really exist in my youth). Instead I have always listened to meaningful music, as it were, either because of the message of the song (women's liberation, social injustice, or civil war, to name a few) or because of its spirituality. I am not religious at all, but I love sacred music. And of course I listen to music just for the sheer beauty of the composition, as in the case of Schubert's trio in my playlist. I first heard it in *Barry Lyndon*, Kubrick's beautiful film, which I absolutely adored at the time, both for its beauty and for its use of Schubert's haunting music, and also for its impossibly sad story.

1.	**O Mio Babbino Caro**	Giacomo Puccini
2.	**Dhun: Misra Kirwani**	Homayun Sakhi & Rahul Sharma
3.	**Blute nur, du liebes Herz**	Johann Sebastian Bach
4.	**Thanks to These Lonesome Vales**	Henry Purcell
5.	**Everybody Knows**	Leonard Cohen
6.	**The Sound of Silence**	Simon & Garfunkel
7.	**el-Hali Ta'bani ya Layla**	Joseph Sakr
8.	**Diamonds and Rust**	Joan Baez
9.	**Laylat Hob**	Umm Kulthum
10.	**Asfur**	Kardes Türküler
11.	**Che gelida manina**	Puccini
12.	**O wär' ich schon mit dir vereint**	Ludwig van Beethoven
13.	**Trio for Violin, Violoncello and Piano No. 2 in E-Flat Major, Op. 100 (D. 929): II. Andante con Moto**	Franz Schubert

L'ham b'Shoufal

LEBANON

Lamb Tagine with Cauliflower

I can't remember the name of the song, but it's Moroccan, and in it, the singer sings about the dishes and food of Morocco. It is an amazing lyric capturing the country's culinary repertoire.

I was walking through Jemaa el-Fnaa when I heard the song coming out of a music stall where the vendor sold cassettes — it was in those days! And even though I don't really understand Moroccan (it's a mix of Arabic and Berber), I could make out names of dishes, which intrigued me. I went to the guy and asked him (in French) about the song, and ended up buying a cassette. I put the cassette in my car once back in London and listened to it obsessively for months. It made me smile to hear the names of the dishes and what the singer was saying about them; that is what I could understand.

Then one summer my car was towed away when I was traveling. (I hadn't seen the sign that the residential bay where I was parked had been suspended.) And to add insult to injury, my car was crushed because I didn't reclaim it in time — and with it the cassette of this song (and lots of other beloved stuff, including my fishing chest waders!).

This recipe is a simple wintery tagine to prepare when cauliflower is in season. In Sicily, where I am now based, cauliflower is officially out of season after Easter. You can use regular cauliflower or any of the colored ones of your choice for a prettier presentation. Just be careful not to overcook it, both at the stage when you parboil it and

also when you add it to the sauce, so that it doesn't become mushy. In the West, people tend to serve tagines with couscous, a total no-no in Morocco, where tagines are always served with bread. The first thing diners do is to dip the bread in the sauce for a taste. Then they use pieces of bread to scoop up the meat and/or vegetables. The norm is to place the tagine (or any other main dish) in the center of the table, which is always round so that those sitting around it can reach it easily — traditionally, diners eat straight from the serving platter, with each keeping to his or her corner.

Serves 4 to 6

3 lb 12 oz lamb fillets, from the neck or shanks

½ cup extra-virgin olive oil

1 teaspoon ground ginger

Big pinch of saffron threads

Sea salt

2 teaspoons all-purpose flour

4 lb 12 oz cauliflower, divided into medium florets

Juice of 2 lemons, or to taste

1 tablespoon paprika

½ teaspoon ground cumin

Peel of 1 preserved lemon, cut into thin julienne, for garnish

Toasted sesame seeds, for sprinkling

Crusty baguette or peasant bread, for serving

▶❙

Put the lamb in a heavy casserole. Barely cover with water and place over medium-high heat. As the water is about to come to a boil, skim any oil or foam on the surface clean. Add the olive oil, ginger, and saffron. Season with salt to taste, reduce the heat to maintain a gentle bubble, and simmer for 1 hour, or until the meat is completely tender and the liquid is reduced.

While the lamb is cooking, bring a large pot of water to a boil over medium-high heat. As the water comes to a boil, add salt to taste and a teaspoon of flour to keep the cauliflower white. Add the cauliflower florets and boil for 2 to 3 minutes, or just long enough for the cauliflower to be al dente. Drain and set aside.

Once the lamb is done, transfer to a large serving platter and cover with plastic wrap (cling film) to keep it hot. Add the lemon juice, paprika, cumin, and remaining 1 teaspoon flour to the braising liquid and stir well. Add the blanched cauliflower and gently stir into the sauce. Let simmer for 5 minutes, or until the cauliflower is just done and the sauce is reduced and silky.

Gather the meat in the middle of the serving platter and arrange the cauliflower and sauce all around it. Wipe the edges clean before scattering the strips of lemon peel and toasted sesame seeds all over the meat and cauliflower. Serve very hot with good bread.

Having hated her before, I loved listening to her in my stoned state.

It's rather difficult to define how music has shaped me, given that my taste has changed so much over the years, from my mother's classical to French pop to English pop to folk with Bob Dylan and Joan Baez, then back to classical and then world music. I guess most of the music I listened to was thoughtful even in my early French pop days. The songs had, if not social messages, personal or melancholy ones. At one stage in my late teens, my friends and family called me *Salut les Copains* after a French magazine that featured all the pop stars I liked, but I outgrew this phase rather quickly. I am not sure if any of them had a lasting influence. This said, I still enjoy listening to Françoise Hardy, for instance, when I am in the kitchen. Then I graduated to the school of folk music sounding meaningful and rebellious messages, like that of Bob Dylan and Joan Baez, who certainly had an influence on making me wish for a more just and open society, unlike the one I lived in in Lebanon. I lived a fairly privileged life there, but not as free as I would have liked it to be. Both my reading of the French existentialists and listening to folk music made me wish to dwell in a wider, freer world as in Europe rather than my restricted one in Lebanon.

Music is ever present in Lebanese and Syrian life, both with musicians playing solo instruments like the oud or the qanun or those singing, like Fayrouz or Umm Kulthum. Music is heard coming out of shops as you walk the streets or in restaurants, or simply in people's gardens. Life without music is unthinkable to most people. It intersects with food when women gather together in the kitchen or in their gardens or terraces to cook or preserve food and start singing together to pass the time — once they stop gossiping!

I used to hate Arabic music when I was young, mainly because we were French-educated and considered all things Western superior to our own culture. I kept this attitude in my first years living in London. But then one year I took a trip to Morocco with my then lover, Donald, who was an interesting, well-read, and fun American man. We went to visit Claudio Bravo, a famous artist in Tangiers, who offered us enormous kif cigarettes. As they all smoked, I decided to join. When we went back to the hotel, Donald put Umm Kulthum on. Having hated her before, I loved listening to her in my stoned state. And from that day on, I started seeking out recordings by her and others; and I think it was from that time that I started taking a serious interest in world music.

While I have been thus open-minded, and in spite of all the music I love, there's one funny thing: as a diner, I cannot stand jazz. I am capable of walking out of a restaurant if jazz music is being played and it's the kind that really grates.

HENDERSON

MARGOT

Margot is from Wellington, New Zealand, and moved to London in the 1980s, where she worked in landmark restaurants. After meeting and marrying Fergus Henderson, they opened their first restaurant together, the French House. Over the last twenty years, Margot and her business partner, Melanie Arnold, have built up an international catering business, based at their restaurant Rochelle Canteen in London's Shoreditch. Margot also contributes to various food publications and has a regular column in *Luncheon* magazine.

Theme Music to *Barry Lyndon* Playlist

▶ These songs capture a moment of all that I love about music. They track a long life, reminding me of many things. They are good old friends and can lift my spirits if needed. While cooking away in the kitchen is probably when I listen to most of them, but also dancing around the kitchen table after a merry dinner. ▶ The hours and hours of dancing to David Bowie, Talking Heads, Joan Armatrading, sweating and filling my soul with their beautiful music, has been a great part of my life. Dancing, driving, cooking…they have all hung in there with me. David Byrne taught us to dance back in the day; he is an incredible mover, crazy moves. ▶ Driving in Scotland along the ocean, kids leaning out the window, listening to Van Morrison, is a great day, it's a great injection of feeling. The senses are heightened. Miriam Makeba takes me back to my days cooking at the Eagle while listening to beautiful music from all over Africa; she can lift the spirits and transport you and give you a great sense of hope. The genius of these wonderful artists, their poetry, takes us from where we are and transforms the moment and we are with them, feeling the memories carrying us.

1.	**Young Americans**	David Bowie
2.	**The Jean Genie**	David Bowie
3.	**Moondance**	Van Morrison
4.	**Me and Bobby McGee**	Janis Joplin
5.	**Take Me to the River**	Talking Heads
6.	**Road to Nowhere**	Talking Heads
7.	**Dreams**	Fleetwood Mac
8.	**A Hard Rain's A-Gonna Fall**	Bob Dylan
9.	**When Doves Cry**	Prince
10.	**Pata Pata**	Miriam Makeba
11.	**Mississippi Goddam**	Nina Simone
12.	**Love and Affection**	Joan Armatrading
13.	**Theme From Zorba the Greek**	Mikis Theodorakis

UNITED KINGDOM

MARINATED CHICKEN

This song always takes me right back to Tiree, an island in Scotland. I'm driving with the window down, this song filling all my senses, and I see the Pictish fort sitting on top of the cliffs. I often drive singing out loud with a terrible voice, my poor kids thinking, what will I cook them all for lunch. We arrive and as a family spill down onto the rocks and start a barbecue on a wood fire. Soon we will dine on an isolated rock with just the ocean below and a few seals coming to say hello.

This recipe for me is the perfect answer to the combination of the lyrics of the song, with their isolated feeling; a hungry tummy; and knowing there is nothing like cooking on driftwood with the wind and the sea around you.

Serves 4 to 6

Recipe Inspiration:

DREAMS

by Fleetwood Mac

■ For the marinade:

500 ml good full-fat yogurt

2 tablespoons harissa

1 tablespoon sumac

Juice of 1 lemon

2 cloves garlic, grated

1 tablespoon thyme (dried is fine)

1 tablespoon oregano

Salt and freshly ground black pepper to taste

■ 1 free-range happy chicken, cut into about 6 serving pieces

To make the marinade, in a bowl, mix all the ingredients together. In the bowl or a large zippered bag, combine the chicken with the marinade and turn to coat well. Let the chicken marinate overnight in the refrigerator.

Find lots of driftwood, or cheat and buy a bag of wood or hardwood charcoal from a local supermarket. Go to the beach. Or your backyard.

Light the fire. Once the flames have dropped and you have an excellent bed of coals, place an oiled grill rack over the fire. Pop the chicken pieces on the grill and cook, turning now and then so the pieces do not burn. But don't be afraid of a little singe.

Make sure the pieces are well cooked, about 35 minutes. No one wants undercooked chicken. Then eat, using your fingers and drinking lots of delicious Pinot Noir. Look out to the sea and dream!

▲ Margot Henderson

For me in those days, listening to music was all about growing up, it was a ticket out of the suburbs to another world.

Growing up can be quite a lonely time of one's life, working out what you want to do, working out if you are any good. This is when strong, beautiful music can speak to you and help you through. Also, for when you want a jolly, where would we be without letting our hair down? I love to dance…James Brown, Kool & the Gang, Commodores…I could go on and on! They have been there to just help me relax and have fun. I also remember being into new wave and bands like Human League, Siouxsie and the Banshees, and Talking Heads. I loved them and we would dance nonstop for hours. Even after finishing work at around midnight, we would head out and dance all night. Keeps one's spirits up in the long hunt for love and affection!

●

Growing up in New Zealand, music was everywhere. We used to sing Māori songs and do *hakas* dances at school, which rooted us in the people of our land. This music filled us with pleasure and love and probably helped me be a better person. I also loved the revolutionary feminist music of my childhood. All those things have brought energy and passion to my work life; I am inspired by these incredible musicians and my love of dancing after work, stretching, letting go after a shit shift, when it all just feels too hard…music takes us to wonderful places. Even if it's sad.

●

Singing in church was always fun, but thinking back, I think I became aware of music at around eight or ten years old, dancing like crazy to *Godspell* and *Cabaret*. I would close the sitting-room doors and put on my grandfather's bowler hat—*Caberet*'s "Money" was a favorite song. The first song I really learned by heart was "I Am Woman" by Helen Reddy. I remember doing my paper route at that time, dying with pain from carrying so many papers and singing it over and over!

We were punks and that was cool; well, we thought we were. For me in those days, listening to music was all about growing up, it was a ticket out of the suburbs to another world. A moment that sticks in my memory is when I was down at the Hutt for late-night shopping on a Thursday with my best mate, William. He said, "Buy the Sex Pistols, buy them!" But I didn't, I bought Ricky Lee Jones instead—which I think might have actually caused a little hiccup in our friendship. Music in Wellington was all about your friendships then. Fantastic bands were coming to our town, everyone read *The Face* magazine and knew what was going on. The Clash, the Boomtown Rats came. We were all together in our love for these bands. It was bonding, fun, and exciting.

Like music, food was always there for me. I was greedy and everyone told me I was good at cooking and I enjoyed it. In so many aspects of working in restaurants, music keeps us going, keeps us moving— a floor is easier to mop with David Bowie singing to you.

●

The scene has changed now. I'm not sure how deeply, but there definitely seems to be a huge desire for fame these days that's influencing things; everyone knows about food, they are all experts—a bit like music has long been. You are no one unless you have a chef as a good friend...just joking! But some people look up to chefs just because they have been on television. It's all crazy. Then again, there are so many incredible chefs now, just like there are musicians. On yet another hand, why are we not celebrating doctors and nurses in the same way? Maybe the explosion of restaurant passion and cookbooks has something to do with the way food has become such an integral part of pop culture, not just culture. Instagram and the like are of course a big part of that—everyone has knowledge at their fingertips and the ability to see behind the scenes at a renowned restaurant, so this sneak-peek love of food culture flourishes.

In a lot of places, music helps define the restaurant or the food on offer, but we don't actually have music in our restaurants. For us, it's the chatter of our guests that is music to our ears. Music during service is just too distracting; everyone goes into their own little world and they forget to engage with each other. But in the past, I have worked in restaurants where the menu never changed, and by God, music helped with the boredom. And it can really bring a kitchen's energy up, spice it and fill it with pleasure, shooing away negative and grumpy feelings and thoughts. After service is another matter; then music powers you through that cleanup.

●

We have served so many wonderful people over the years, but my favorite was a near miss. St. John had just opened and Ruth Rogers called Fergus, my husband and the owner, to say, "Darling, I hope you don't mind, but we need to extend our table to 6." Turned out the additional guests were David Bowie and Iman! They walked in and silenced the room. Then there was a kind of after-roar as everyone was so overly excited that they were in the same room as a legend like David Bowie. Sadly, I missed them by a feather, as I was at the French. I cleaned down as fast as I could, but they were gone in a puff! Legends—great musicians are living legends and when they eat in your restaurants, they inject their passion and glamour.

MEHERWAN IRANI

Meherwan Irani is a chef and restaurateur changing the perception of Indian food in America. His Chai Pani Restaurant Group includes Chai Pani (Asheville, NC; Decatur, GA) MG Road, Botiwalla (Atlanta and Alpharetta, GA), Buxton Hall Barbecue, and Spicewalla. Meherwan is a four-time James Beard Award semifinalist for Best Chef: Southeast, and was deemed a Southerner of the Year by *Southern Living*.

Summer Nights
by Van Halen

Songs I Grew Up to Before I Came to America Playlist ▶ This is not a typical soundtrack for a kid growing up in the '70s and '80s in India. If a smell can instantly transport you back to childhood, then a song has to be the next best thing. The Beatles were my first memory of music; my teenage years in the gym were accompanied by Bruce Springsteen. The Police got me through lying sick for days on a sweaty hospital bed. I picked up the guitar to learn power cords to Scorpions and AC/DC, showed off my newest boom box with INXS, and fell in love to a Peter Gabriel song. U2 was on the radio when I came to the U.S. in 1990, and then everything changed.

1.	I Want to Hold Your Hand	The Beatles
2.	Won't Get Fooled Again	The Who
3.	Born in the U.S.A.	Bruce Springsteen
4.	Walking on the Moon	The Police
5.	Walk Like an Egyptian	The Bangles
6.	Rock You Like a Hurricane	Scorpions
7.	Everybody Wants to Rule the World	Tears for Fears
8.	Never Tear Us Apart	INXS
9.	Faith	George Michael
10.	Hysteria	Def Leppard
11.	Welcome To The Jungle	Guns N' Roses
12.	Free Fallin'	Tom Petty
13.	You Shook Me All Night Long	AC/DC
14.	In Your Eyes	Peter Gabriel
15.	I Still Haven't Found What I'm Looking For	U2

Chai Pani's Aloo Tikki

(spiced potato croquettes)

This dish takes me back to being a teenager in the '80s in India. My parents had left me home alone for the summer, so I hacked the keys for our old Fiat and my friends and I would drive around feeling very cool with our long hair and torn jeans, hanging out in the evenings at the street hawkers outside the bus depot while my ripped Van Halen *5150* cassette squawked out "Summer Nights" on the tinny car speakers.

Summer nights and my radio
Well that's all we need, baby, don'tcha know?
We celebrate when the gang's all here
Ah, hot summer nights, that's my time of the year...

For a seventeen-year-old and his best friends in a dusty town in India, that song kinda summed it up — cheesiness and all!

Serves 2 to 3

6 medium potatoes (any thin-skinned potato like Yukon, Red Bliss, or yellow creamers), scrubbed but skins left on

1¼ cups neutral oil, like canola

½ teaspoon mustard seeds

1 tablespoon finely minced fresh ginger

1 tablespoon ginger-garlic paste

½ teaspoon red chile powder

½ teaspoon ground cumin

½ teaspoon ground coriander

½ teaspoon ground turmeric

Juice of 1 lime

¼ cup finely chopped cilantro (fresh coriander), plus more for serving

1 tablespoon finely chopped hot green chile, such as serrano, plus more for serving

1 tablespoon kosher salt

Chopped onions, for serving

Ketchup, for serving

In a pot over medium-high heat, boil the potatoes until done but still firm. They shouldn't be mushy or soggy, but a fork should easily split one open. Drain and let cool.

Once cooled, in a large bowl, smash the potatoes until smooth. Using a grater or a ricer makes it easier to get the potatoes smooth without any lumps. Set aside.

Heat ¼ cup of the oil in a sauté pan. Once the oil is hot, add the mustard seeds. When the seeds start popping, add the ginger and ginger-garlic paste. Cook until the paste starts to brown, scraping the pan to prevent sticking.

Add the chile powder, cumin, coriander, and turmeric and cook for a minute or two. The mixture will start to clump together. Add the lime juice and scrape the pan bottom to deglaze. Remove from the heat and stir and scrape well until all the mixture is loose. Dump over the potatoes. Add the ¼ cup cilantro (fresh coriander), green chile, and salt and mix everything well together with the potatoes.

Using your hands, divide the mixture into balls slightly larger than a golf ball but smaller than a tennis ball. Pressing gently on the balls, flatten them into disks, or *tikkis*, about palm shaped and 1 to 1½ inches (2.5 to 4 cm) thick. Smooth the edges if they split or crack.

Add the remaining 1 cup oil to a large flat-bottomed pan (nonstick is best) and fry the *tikkis* (as many as can fit without overcrowding the pan) over medium heat, turning once gently to prevent breaking, until golden brown on both sides.

Serve hot with the cilantro, chiles, onions, and ketchup! I like mixing sriracha and ketchup for a spicy sweet dip.

Song: Summer Nights by Van Halen

▲ Meherwan Irani

Music in India is tied to celebration and celebration is tied to music. Not just celebration for the sake of celebration—our celebrations have big religious and cultural and social implications. Take a wedding, for example. Depending on what step of marriage it is, which dance is happening, the music you pick is all tied very closely to things like that. Even if you were to be dropped in out of nowhere, you would know what phase of the wedding you're in by the food that's being served that day and the music that's being played in that particular moment.

● There's another soundtrack that goes with Indian street food—literally the soundtrack of the streets of India. At every street corner not only are there hawkers, there almost always is a boom box playing the latest Bollywood hits or a nostalgic song from the '60s or some Americanized version. Most of India's built-in pop culture revolves around the music of Bollywood, our movie industry. And every Indian movie is still like a musical. You can pick up the mood of the vendor or the hawker or the street corner you are on by the kind of music that's being played. For me, street food is high energy and excitement with just a hint of the exotic. The music's gotta match that. ●

For me personally, the music and the sounds of India influence the way our dishes are put together. Every region has its own dialect, religion, and cultural communities and its own cuisine and specific foods that match. There's no such thing as "Indian food." We're about fifty countries that were brought together, kind of like Europe. Even though people assume it's the same cuisine everywhere in this giant country, it really isn't. For me to eat Bengali food while growing up would be as alien to me as eating Russian food. There is some commonality because many of us come from one region or one subcontinent, so certain ingredients are universal, but still, the way they're treated is completely different. A great example would be, while Spanish food, Italian food, and French food all have a lot in common, at the same time you would recognize one from the other because of culture and preparation and technique.

● Street food is the one cuisine of India that's completely Pan-Indian. It transcends all of those boundaries. The reason being, street vendors are not trying to fit into any particular cultural mold. They're using whatever they have at hand and mashing it up together like a DJ, laying on multiple tracks to create a new sound. The ingredients are familiar, but the end product is constantly evolving and changing. I love that aspect of Indian food because it helps me realize I'm not hidebound by any tradition telling me a dish has to be exactly this way. I can be in America and do whatever I want with "samples," if you will, of all these various "tracks" of Indian food, and put them together in new ways to create new sounds or tastes. I've used that metaphor often to explain to people the difference between the street food of India and any other cuisine. ● I was born in London and I grew up with music as a family business, since my dad was a sound engineer. He was living there at the time with my mom, and just through one of those funny coincidences in the universe, my dad was close friends with Pete Townsend. Yes, the guitar player for the Who. I must've been very young; Pete was writing *Tommy* at the time. He would sometimes come by our apartment because it was quiet, and he'd sit there and write at the table. I don't have any memory of that, but

Street food is the one cuisine of India that's completely Pan-Indian. It transcends all of those boundaries. The reason being, street vendors are

that's just my first music story. By the time I was five, we'd moved to India. Pete came to visit my parents in India, and he gave me my first instrument, which was a guitar. It may have been a ukulele, or some sort of a kid guitar. That was my first memory of music and a musical instrument. Pretty much since then I've always been involved with and interested in music. ● I did eventually learn to play the guitar, so I admire guitar heroes. I've always loved Dire Straits and Mark Knopfler. As I grew older, I learned that he had an unorthodox playing style. He was completely self-taught and never took a guitar lesson in his life. His sound reflects that, just figuring it out on his own. I feel that way as a chef—I have to figure it out on my own. I was never classically trained and even as a musician, I didn't take a single guitar lesson. Growing up in India, it just wasn't accessible to me. My lessons consisted of listening to tapes and rewinding them, back and forth over and over until the tape wore out, trying to figure out how a song was constructed. ● It's easy for me to forget that I grew up in India. My musical influence should be Bollywood, a classic Indian music, but it wasn't. Because my dad grew up in London, even when we moved back to India, his love for Western music dictated what I grew up listening to in the household. I grew up with a real American sensibility. I started connecting with other people who were listening to Western music in my small hometown in the middle of nowhere in India. That wasn't easy. ● The other part of the story is that my parents and my grandmother had a bed-and-breakfast in India, usually filled with Westerners who were coming to a particular ashram near us. So I was also exposed to the music that these guests brought with them. They knew that my dad loved music, so they would always bring us the latest tapes and records from America. There I was, growing up in India in the early and mid '70s, but to a pretty good part living on the cutting edge of Western music, listening to stuff that most of my friends in India would have thought was from Mars. My restaurant Chai Pani is a reflection of that dual-culture childhood. ● Most people think that the bonds that form working in a kitchen are around food and the intensity of getting crushed during service. But truly, so often a big part of the bond in the kitchen is music. One of the first things you find out about somebody you hire is what their taste in music is, and that will actually have an impact on whether you connect with that person or not. Really, people's identities at work are tied up in what kind of music they like, and music determines whether you connect with them on a deeper level or not.
● Each night we have a musical ritual. Pre-service in the front of the house, before people even start their opening duties, there's a twenty-minute discussion about what the soundtrack should be. The opening bell for service, because we have a fixed playlist, is a Bollywood song by Dostana called "Desi Girl." The minute it kicks in, it's almost Pavlovian. Everybody just seems to fall into a rhythm. We made that choice intentionally for opening bell instead of having a random shuffle on the playlist—there's something about the restaurant business that being in rhythm matters, and there's nothing to get you in the rhythm better than having the same opening track every night. It all just kicks in after that. And from there, we just go as one, and it's a beautiful thing.

not trying to fit into any particular cultural mold. They're using whatever they have at hand and mashing it up together like a DJ.

JOHNSON
JJ

JJ Johnson is a James Beard Award–winning chef and author known for cooking the food of the African diaspora. Chef JJ's signature style was inspired by the Caribbean tastes he grew up with, inspiration from his travels, and his signature R&B and hip-hop playlist. JJ published his first cookbook in 2018, *Between Harlem and Heaven: Afro-Asian-American Cooking for Big Nights, Weeknights, and Every Day.*

FIELDTRIP Harlem Playlist ▶ These are a few songs from the fifty-hour playlist we play at the FIELDTRIP. It's all '90s hip-hop and R&B, and it is super nostalgic—everyone in the dining room is singing along to it while they're eating. It inspires happiness and enhances the dining experience.

1.	**Juicy**	The Notorious B.I.G.
2.	**Gin & Juice**	Snoop Dogg
3.	**Killing Me Softly With His Song**	Fugees
4.	**Still Not a Player**	Big Pun featuring Joe
5.	**Love Like This**	Faith Evans
6.	**Where the Party At**	Jagged Edge featuring Nelly
7.	**Jumpin' Jumpin'**	Destiny's Child
8.	**Poison**	Bell Biv DeVoe
9.	**Jenny from the Block (Track Masters Remix)**	Jennifer Lopez featuring Styles P. and Jadakiss
10.	**Dangerous**	Busta Rhymes

CRISPY RICE SUMMER SALAD

6 heads baby bok choy, cleaned and sliced

2 teaspoons olive oil

4 tablespoons coconut oil

1 red bell pepper, seeded and diced

1 shallot, diced

Salt

2 cloves garlic, chopped

2 cups cooked or leftover long-grain white rice

3 tablespoons low-sodium soy sauce

1 tablespoon rice vinegar

1 tablespoon toasted sesame oil

1 tablespoon Thai red chile paste

2 green onions, sliced

3 tablespoons roasted peanuts, chopped

1 bunch parsley, chopped

Lime wedges, for serving

Music sets the creative atmosphere and inspires the overall menu. There's no specific dish influenced by a song. You'll see items on the menu such as "It Was All a Dream," which is the entire menu (including cocktails such as the Big Poppa and Jadakiss).

Serves 4 to 6

Place the bok choy in a large bowl and toss with the olive oil. Set aside.

Heat your saucepan over medium heat. Add 2 tablespoons of the coconut oil and heat until melted. Add the bell pepper and shallot and season with salt. Cook until softened, about 5 minutes. Add the garlic and cook for 1 minute.

Add the remaining 2 tablespoons coconut oil to the pan. Once melted and hot, add the rice and use a flexible spatula to press it into one flat layer. Cover the pan and cook until the rice is heated through and golden and crispy on the bottom, 5 to 6 minutes. Once that side is browned, flip a few large parts of the rice cake and crisp the other side.

Remove the skillet from the heat, keep it covered with the lid, and let sit for 5 minutes.

In a bowl, whisk together the soy sauce, vinegar, sesame oil, and chile paste.

Add the rice to the bowl of bok choy and toss gently to incorporate. Serve the rice on plates and drizzle with the soy sauce mixture. Top with the green onions, peanuts, parsley, and lime wedges.

Music is the bedrock
of the Pan-African
experience. It's indelibly
linked to the transatlantic
slave trade and the
mass forced migration
patterns of millions
or billions of people of
African descent. The
music born out of the
diaspora was created to
inspire hope, to com-
municate, and to build
community. Food has also
been used as an act
of defiance.

● When I was growing up, my Puerto Rican grandmother used to blast salsa music while she was cooking *sofrito* and my Black American grandmother would play Stevie Wonder and Earth, Wind & Fire while she made cherry pies. With those beginnings in the kitchen, music has always been a big part of my life. And being with my grandmothers taught me early on that music is a key ingredient for setting the atmosphere, and that cooking should always be fun.

● Music is the bedrock of the Pan-African experience. It's indelibly linked to the transatlantic slave trade and the mass forced migration patterns of millions or billions of people of African descent. The music born out of the diaspora was created to inspire hope, to communicate, and to build community. Food has also been used as an act of defiance. For a community stripped of its heritage and culture, food offered another opportunity to build and maintain a shared identity. As a result, food and music have always intersected through the desire to preserve tradition, tell stories, and participate in a collective cultural experience.

● Immeasurable creative energy and output have been inspired by the impact of the African diasporic community on the global stage. I love hip-hop and R&B, which was birthed from the same place as the food I make. Centuries of oppression, colonialism, and forced migration created a cultural renaissance across Western civilization. You'd be hard pressed to find a point of cultural significance that hasn't been impacted by the African diaspora. The restaurants I've opened offer diners an opportunity to explore this conversation.

● Music is a feeling. I use it in my dining room at the Henry to bring guests to a specific place. Songs can trigger or encase memories of a specific meal or dish you were eating at another time, or for the first time with us. Even at FIELDTRIP, where the playlist features Harlem-based artists across genres and decades, music works to invoke a feeling of who we are and where we are. My goal in connecting music and food is to inspire a powerful sense of nostalgia.

NAJAT KAANACHE

Born in San Sebastian to Moroccan parents, Najat Kaanache has enjoyed successful careers as both a leading television actress and an award-winning chef across three countries. Her Fez, Morocco, restaurant, Nur, has been named the World's Best Moroccan Restaurant since its 2017 opening. She was the first — and only — Moroccan chef to work at Ferran Adrià's El Bulli restaurant in Spain. A tireless advocate for women's rights, Najat strives to inspire women of all ages to persevere and achieve their dreams.

Mix of Champions Playlist ▶ Music, like food, has the power to reach across all boundaries and touch the soul through the senses. This list represents a sample set of the epic songs that have helped me frame the experiences of my life through their lyrics, rhythms, and energies. They've provided me with a source of renewable motivation, and really transport me into a desired mindset or even back in time to remind me of where I've been and what I've overcome to achieve my dreams. Many of the titles represent my core values, and just thinking about the songs can fill me with creative fuel!

1.	Till I Collapse	Eminem featuring Nate Dogg
2.	Started from the Bottom	Drake
3.	One	U2
4.	Try	P!nk
5.	Angels	Robbie Williams
6.	Sacrifice	Elton John
7.	Girl on Fire	Alicia Keys
8.	Shallow	Lady Gaga and Bradley Cooper
9.	With or Without You	U2
10.	Peace Train	Cat Stevens
11.	Eye of the Tiger	Survivor
12.	We are the Champions	Queen
13.	Clandestino	Manu Chao
14.	Start Me Up	The Rolling Stones
15.	Alors on Danse	Stromae

▲ Najat Kaanache

MOROCCO

MOROCCAN
POACHED LOBSTER

I will speak for my country Morocco "till I collapse"! This recipe celebrates North Africa—its colors, flavors, smells, and heritage—in an artistic way.

Ras el hanout translates to "head of the shop" and is a custom blend all prideful Moroccan cooks create with the best spices from the market. Moroccan citron, because it is low acid, is also known as "sweet citron," and is a form of etrog from the Jewish week-long holiday of Sukkot.

Serves 1

Recipe Inspiration:

TILL
I COLLAPSE

by Eminem
featuring
Nate Dogg

3 cups extra-virgin olive oil

1 large preserved Moroccan citron, sliced (about 2 cups)

1 tablespoon *ras el hanout*

3 or 4 threads saffron

½ tablespoon salt

1 fresh raw lobster, about 2 lb, broken into tail, claws, knuckles, and legs

■ **2 tablespoons salt for each gallon of liquid used to poach**

Combine the olive oil, citron, *ras el hanout*, and saffron in a saucepan and stir to mix. Warm the seasoned oil to 200°F (95°C), then remove from the heat and allow the mixture to infuse the oil for 10 to 15 minutes.

Bring the infused oil to a poaching temperature of 165°F (75°C). Stir in the salt.

Poach the lobster in the following order: tail, claws, knuckles, then legs. Place the parts in the liquid per this timing for best results: The tail will take about 7 minutes to cook, the claws 4 minutes, knuckles 3 minutes, and legs 2 minutes.

The internal temperature of the lobster meat should reach 140°F (60°C). To prevent overcooking the lobster after poaching, you may drain the lobster and place it briefly (2 or 3 seconds) in an ice water bath.

I understand the sounds within my kitchen because I understand music, and without music my heart can't move.

Song: Till I Collapse by Eminem featuring Nate Dogg

▲ Najat Kaanache

If our walls could talk, they would sing with the spirits of the whole Medina having a big party here in Fez. There is an extraordinary movement here because of the power of music, the different artists, the history that has always existed in these winding stalls, the walls, and the magical nine doors. It creates space for the Africans and the music that defines us. ● The most popular music in North Africa is all ours—the type that comes from nature's wires, the sounds created by using the guts of different animals to make instruments. Those sounds are not familiar to many...people usually don't think about the skin or horn or bone or tendons used from the same animals where we get our meat when listening to or creating music. How is it all connected? Food and music show us the parallels within any culture. They cannot be detached, it's how people live and breathe. People recognize music in their hearts and food in their memories, their souls, and their childhoods. ● When I was around eight years old, I was on holiday traveling from San Sebastian all the way through Spain to North Africa. We went to Taza, where you'll find the most magical mountains in Morocco, for a second cousin's wedding. You can find the most amazing mushrooms and olive trees there. It has the best national park and there used to be a culture of living in caves in the area. It's also the home of the first bank in Morocco. When we arrived, we found a huge group of magical human beings full of color, different metals in the tools and jewelry and doors and wheels, and animals that were filling their yards and stalls and the streets with their sounds...all making a music that was new to me. I hadn't heard that type of music in Europe; it was a specific sound. It was brilliant with the mountains, the trees, and the wind. ● I use my cooking tools to create music in my own kitchen. The sound of a fork or a knife or a spatula or a plate or the door of a fridge or the motor of the engine that is running the air conditioner...each one of those sounds brings music to my brain and my senses without even looking. I understand the sounds within my kitchen because I understand music, and without music my heart can't move. I use cooking to create music in our kitchen by leading the way, building our sound with tools and tasks. Again, many human beings do not hear the natural music existing all around us all the time, because you have to pay attention. Even silence offers us a kind of music, most eloquently in a space full of human beings. We play like an orchestra every night, a silent one that has meaning and expresses the culture around us. ● Music helps keep me balanced in moments when I am cooking, experimenting, expressing myself with the physical and sensual qualities of food. Music is the ethereal companion, in the air as a sound, but a sound that is important to creating, to "painting" every dish. I never detach myself from music. When there is no music in the streets, or no party music, we play our own music inside. As we teach young kids, we need to be able to experience music from all sides and hear different rhythms. For those reasons, music is constantly a part of the whole day of work for us, every day. ● We go to work. We have CVs. We have business cards. We have websites—we go out there like animals hunting. In a more sophisticated way, but hunting. In the restaurant world, we try to succeed by the definition that has become us: fine dining, normal dining, rustic, or bistro. This is the way we go out to do our job, to earn a living, to eat. Then there may be money as our reward, and we can buy a bag, shoes, the most expensive things. We hunt, we want to be, have got to be the best, we want to have the best job we can get. ● But in the end, we are animals, with a soul. In the end, we live for food; our creating is for survival, it is for taking care of ourselves on our own, us and our families. It is about time that food

has become the way. We just have to use these changes for good purposes. ● Music taught me how to relate to human beings, and how to understand human beings of different cultures and different languages without even speaking that language. Music helps get us through different tunnels in life, so we can feel happy, harmonious, sad, safe while we are finding our way. I use music to release my soul and to push my soul. Music is like an escape. It's like a tunnel with a big light. ● The music I love, from artists like Eminem, Pink, 50 Cent, Tina Turner, expresses who they are and how they've fought and struggled—who they are and what they have inside. It gives me strength. There's a song by Eminem that we play all the time called "Lose Yourself." We challenge and push ourselves when we hear that song. We put it on for the guys in the kitchen so we can keep going during the day, especially during Ramadan, when no one is eating but we have a full restaurant and we need to make a mise en place on empty stomachs. Music draws a parallel to who I am. Lyrics help me to be me. I don't have anything else. I don't have a hero. Music helps me to survive—actually, more than to survive: to believe.

I use cooking to create music in our kitchen

REEM KASSIS

Reem Kassis is a Palestinian writer and author of the James Beard Award–nominated cookbook *The Palestinian Table*. Reem is based in Philadelphia, where she writes about the evolving and cross-cultural food of the Middle East.

Currently Listening Playlist ▶ This list is a journey from past to present, with some singers long gone and others recently emerged. Some songs are very old, and others are entirely modern renditions of classic hits. The songs resonate with me because they remind me of the two worlds I constantly try to balance and straddle: the old one that shaped me and gave me roots and the new one that opened my eyes to possibility and gave me wings. I listen to these songs most often while driving or if I'm home cooking or dancing with my two little girls.

Recipe Inspiration:

AL QUDS

1.	**Nassam Alayna El Hawa**	Fairuz
2.	**Ommi**	Marcel Khalife
3.	**Dalili Ehtar**	Om Kalthoum
4.	**Shukran Al Azimi**	Adonis
5.	**Marrat**	Noel Kharman
6.	**A Whole New World**	Mena Massoud and Naomi Scott (I have two toddler girls who are way too into Disney movies and now it's *Aladdin*!)
7.	**Nawwar**	Le Trio Joubran
8.	**Ma Betmannalak**	Adonis
9.	**Ya Tayr**	Talia
10.	**Ma Wahashnak**	Mohammed Assaf

Jerusalem Mtabaq

No trip to the Old City of Jerusalem with my mother was complete without a stop at the Zalatimo *mtabaq* shop. This is an easier homemade version of that famous Jerusalem dessert. You can use either a cheese or walnut filling; both options are provided below.

Serves 4

EL ATIQA by Fairuz

■ For the sugar syrup:

1 cup (7 oz/200 g) superfine (caster) sugar

Squeeze of lemon juice

¼ teaspoon orange blossom water

¼ teaspoon rosewater

■ For the walnut filling:

9 oz (250 g) lightly toasted walnuts, coarsely ground

1 tablespoon sugar

½ teaspoon ground cinnamon

■ For the cheese filling:

9 oz (250 g) sweet Arabic cheese (can be found at any Middle Eastern grocery store; if unavailable, substitute mozzarella), coarsely chopped or grated

¼ teaspoon rosewater or orange blossom water

■ 9 oz (250 g) phyllo (filo) dough sheets (12 to 16 sheets, each 13 by 18 inches / 33 by 45 cm), thawed if frozen

⅓ cup (2 ½ oz / 75 g) melted ghee or clarified butter

To make the sugar syrup, combine the sugar, ¾ cup (6 fl oz /175 ml) water, and the lemon juice in a small, heavy pan and bring to a boil over medium-high heat. Simmer until slightly thickened, 2 to 3 minutes. Remove from the heat and add the flavorings. Set aside to cool. (You can store unused syrup in an airtight container in the refrigerator for up to 2 months.)

Preheat the oven to 425°F (220°C) and line a large baking sheet with parchment paper. Choose the filling you will use and prepare by stirring together the ingredients in a bowl. Set aside.

Unroll the phyllo dough and cover with a towel to prevent from drying out as you work. Take a sheet of dough and brush it all over with melted ghee. Top with another sheet of phyllo and brush with melted ghee. Repeat until you have used one-fourth of the sheets. Fold in the sides of the filo dough to give yourself a square of about 12 by 12 inches (30 by 30 cm). It doesn't matter if you are a little off, as long as you have a square shape.

Take one-fourth of your chosen filling (walnut or cheese) and place an equal-size portion in each of the 4 quadrants of the dough square without getting too close to the edges. Take one corner of dough and fold it up and over a portion of filling, lining the point up with the center point. Repeat with the remaining 3 corners. You will end up with an envelope-like square of about 8 by 8 inches (20 by 20 cm). Press gently to hold everything in. Brush with melted ghee and transfer to a baking sheet. Repeat until you have completed all 4 envelopes.

Bake for 15 to 20 minutes, until golden brown on top. Remove from the oven and pour the cooled syrup on top. Serve immediately. This dessert is best enjoyed eaten by hand just as it is in the Old City of Jerusalem.

Family, history, nation, and love. The same themes that abound in Palestinian music are also found throughout my writing and cooking. I cook dishes to remember where I came from and to pass that connection onto my children and others who are outside our land by choice or circumstance. The meals I cook tell the story of a family, its loves and losses, its history, and its day-to-day activities. Our music does the same. They are two sides of the same coin.

●

Like most other cultures, music is a big part of Palestinian and Middle Eastern heritage, addressing themes of nationalism, history, and love. But I think its intersection with food is a unique aspect, because food is so pervasive in Arab cultures. Many kinds of music, like *zajal*, *ataaba*, and *taqasim*, are performed at every gathering or family dinner with relatives, and of course weddings and celebrations. The food is the unifying factor of all these events and often features in the songs themselves. This (translated) excerpt from a Palestinian folk song reminisces about the good old days, and food is a big part of it:

Oh how we long for the good old days,
　　when life was simple and God was praised
Oh how we long for our local foods
　　from gundelia and za'tar to yogurt and split lentil soup
Oh how we long for our playing fields and sitting
　　in the shade of the sycamore tree
Eating meat fried with tomato and a bowl of bulgur
　　alongside a stew of mallow

One of the most beautiful and heartbreaking songs I love, and one of the most widely recognized by most Levantine Middle Easterners, is a poem by Mahmoud Darwish sung by Marcel Khalife called "Ommi." It tells the story of a young man in political exile yearning for his mother's bread, coffee, and tender touch. Bread is the first thing my mother cooked with my daughters,

the first thing I think of when I hear that song is my mother's bread

it's the first thing my girls ask her to make when she visits, and it's the dish that connects me most to her when I make it. The first thought that enters my mind every time I pour flour into a bowl is the first line of that song, and the first thing I think of when I hear that song is my mother's bread.

I had an interesting experience growing up, because my family is Palestinian, so Arabic music was what we heard in the car, where Fairuz and Umm Kulthum were always on, and emitting from my father's old stereo in our first apartment, on which we played children's songs, to the sounds of several of my relatives playing the oud (a precursor to the lute) at gatherings and holidays, and of course at weddings and on TV. However, I also went to an American school, where I was exposed to English nursery rhymes and children's songs, and later on, Western musicians. I dwelled in a gorge between two cultures, at times desiring to shun my own so I could adopt the Western one I encountered at school.

Oddly, music created a divide for me when I was young because the music I listened to at home, the songs I enjoyed on family vacations in the car or at outings and gatherings, was not the music my peers were listening to. I felt almost embarrassed to admit that those were the tunes I enjoyed, and so I started listening to different genres—Arabic and English hip-hop and pop, R&B, rap, etc.— to connect with peers at my American school. I enjoyed many of those songs and I continue to listen to different genres today, but there is a sense of connection I feel with the lyrics and tunes of the classical Arabic songs that I cannot find with other genres. This experience is, I think, what ended up making me someone proud of her culture and adamant about sharing it with the world.

And so, it is Arabic music that ended up being, and continues to be, the most influential in my work and life. Fairuz is a particular favorite, not only because her voice and lyrics remain unparalleled, but because it was her music that I heard on family trips, at gatherings, and at weddings and which evokes so many feelings and memories every time I listen to it. As any Arab family will tell you, almost all of our gatherings involve both food and cooking, so the music I heard at those events is very closely tied to the food I make.

When I moved away from home at a very early age, I desperately grasped at anything that could provide me with a sense of connection to my roots. Food was ultimately how I have nurtured that connection and passed it onto my children—but the music is what nourishes my soul as I do it. Before I wrote *The Palestinian Table*, I never used measurements while cooking. I cooked by instinct, usually with music in the background. When I started testing, I became a bit more clinical, but I found my food was not coming out the same, so eventually I went back to playing music while I cooked (but using tablespoons and cups and a kitchen scale instead of my fingers and eyes for everything!), and that touch, or *nafas*, as we call it in Arabic, came back. Somehow the music helped me feel back at home, transported me to the late summer evenings of tables laden with mezze, and *arak* glasses clanking, and oud tunes floating on the breeze. My cooking, while thousands of miles away, contains the spirit of those memories.

my cooking, while thousands of miles away, contains the spirit of those memories

ASMA KHAN

Born in Calcutta, Asma moved to Cambridge, England, in 1991 to join her academic husband at the University of Cambridge. Asma studied law at Cambridge, and then went on to do a PhD in law at King's College London. But cooking was her passion, and so, in 2012, she began a supper club in her home. She never looked back. In 2015, she opened a pop-up in a Soho pub and her brick-and-mortar restaurant Darjeeling Express opened its doors in June 2017.

After 9 p.m. Playlist ▶ These songs are on my playlist when it's late at night, after dinner. I like to make the dough for the *paratha* or *chapati* the night before it is cooked and served. It's so much easier to roll if the dough has rested for a bit. So this is the music I play when I knead the dough. Often, I wash and soak red kidney beans, black chickpeas, or lentils before sleeping. I do not wash up. I soak the pots in hot water and detergent. I guess the playlist reflects my roots: I am a Londoner with a distinct Indian accent. I am from both the East and the West, and the playlist reflects that.

1.	**Son Of A Preacher Man**	Dusty Springfield
2.	**Don't Let The Sun Go Down On Me**	Elton John
3.	**Volare**	Gipsy Kings
4.	**Hotel California**	Eagles
5.	**Man Kunto Maula**	Nusrat Fateh Ali Khan
6.	**Wada Karo**	Kishore Kumar & Lata Mangeshkar
7.	**Chingari Koi Bhadke**	Kishore Kumar
8.	**Wonderful Tonight**	Eric Clapton
9.	**Yeh Sham Mastani**	Kishore Kumar
10.	**Gaata Rahe Mera Dil**	Lata Mangeshkar & Kishore Kumar

UNITED KINGDOM

Dum Ki Machi

(Steamed Fish in Green Herbs)

This dish always reminds me of a Parsee fish dish called *patra ni machi*, where the fish is wrapped in banana leaves and steamed. The Parsees were a religious minority group that fled to India from Persia to escape prosecution in the eighth century. I used to call this my "Freddie Mercury" dish, because Freddie was Parsee. The traditional Parsee dish is prepared differently; this recipe is a variation. As banana leaves are not always at hand, I steam the fish in foil. This is the "Bohemian Rhapsody" of fish!

Serves 6

6 pieces haddock fillet, 4–6 oz each

6 tablespoons white vinegar

5 tablespoons chopped cashew nuts

3 tablespoons chopped cilantro (fresh coriander)

2 tablespoons chopped mint

3 or 4 green chiles, stemmed and seeded (or keep the seeds; the more seeds, the hotter the paste will be)

2 teaspoons sugar

1 teaspoon salt

Lime slices, for garnish

Put the fish in a bowl and set aside.

Place a steamer over but not touching a pan of water and bring the water to a simmer.

In a blender, process all the remaining ingredients except the lime slices to a smooth paste. Smear the paste over the fish, making sure each piece is well covered.

Seal each fish fillet securely in a piece of aluminum foil.

Place the fish parcels in the steamer over the simmering water. Cover and cook for 20 minutes, or until the fish is opaque throughout when you open a packet and peek. Keep an eye on the parcels to ensure that none of them open up.

Remove from the heat and let cool slightly, then open each packet and turn out the contents on a serving plate. Serve immediately, garnished with lime slices.

Recipe Inspiration:

BOHEMIAN RHAPSODY

by **Queen**

▲ Asma Khan

Every celebration, gathering, or even a small family meeting is accompanied by food

One of my favorite songs as a child was an Indian film song, a Hindi song, "Jalte Hain Jiske Liye" by Talat Mahmood, and it was sung by a friend of my grandfather's. I didn't understand the words, but what I picked up was an emotion of yearning—the yearning to love someone who you cannot have. The passion in his voice and longing for this person that he could not have was something that deeply affected me. ● When I learned to play the guitar, it was the first time I realized that my parents were willing to let me do things that I hadn't seen other siblings or cousins be allowed to do. My mom took me to a guitar shop and bought me a guitar and a book with the lyrics to different singers' songs. I realized that she was actually so happy that I was excited about something, and I remember feeling quite overwhelmed emotionally. I had thought my family would never allow this, but I realized that my mother would stand by everything that I wanted to do. ● The music I've loved the most is old Bollywood music. I used to sit on the bed with my mother and listen to the radio, as there was no other way to listen in the '80s. My mother would listen to old Hindi music on the radio and I would listen with her in silence. I play those songs in my restaurant and sometimes I stop and stand motionless while they take me back to those moments of quietly listening with my mother.

My grandfather used to have these old reel-to-reel recordings. When I was young, I always heard him playing them. He was an expert in music, with a great love of Indian classical music in particular. I must have been about four years old when my grandfather told me that everything my parents had told me about heaven was untrue. He said that heaven is a place where your favorite singer sits and sings in front of you. Everyone was really upset because he was confusing a young child. It is something that I'll never forget, and now I understand.

Music plays a very big part in the life and culture of South Asia. Times of joy, sadness, celebration, weddings, even a train or bus journey is not complete without someone singing or listening to music. Every celebration, gathering, or even a small family meeting is accompanied by food in South Asian culture, and that is followed very closely by music. You see this interplay of food and music at weddings, when there are different kinds of songs for every occasion. In my family, comical songs that insult the bride or groom are written for weddings, followed by more traditional wedding music. Then comes the most painful of all, the bridal song of lament as she leaves home. This is often sung in tears by older women in the house as the girl leaves home. Still today I cannot hear the song that was sung as I left my home the night of my wedding without weeping; music is the heartbeat of every family ritual in my culture. ● We often had very long power outages or cuts in those days in India. We would sit in a huge circle—friends, neighbors, cousins—and sing, as we could do nothing else. As soon as summer holiday started, there were long power cuts followed by monsoons. At that time it didn't seem like a horrible inconvenience to us; it felt like an opportunity for us to get together and sing. When I look back, I realize no one complained, even though everyone was hot. It showed us, and shows me, that if you're all doing something together, in a rhythm, you forget the discomfort that you're in. ● Now, in the kitchen, we sing when things start getting difficult. It helps to erase the stresses of the moment. It doesn't matter if you sing well or badly. That's the beauty of music. You lose fear when you're in a group, when you're not the only one. When we've had people who are not South Asian work with us, they nonetheless start singing the songs with us; the team has even asked some of these people if they actually are South Asian, because they're singing the lyrics. ● Pre-service we do not have music, as that is the time when we have our meeting; also, many of our kitchen team call home during that interval because of the time difference. Peak service, we have retro Bollywood music, because the room is buzzing, it's noisy, it's hot and busy—calling for music of the '70s and '80s. End of the night, we have classical beats or spiritual Sufi music, as once again everyone is winding down, it's quieter, and we lower the lights. ● Outside of the kitchen, music was always an anchor in my life. I had an arranged marriage. I moved to Cambridge in 1991, and I carried with me the CDs of old film songs that I loved. Apart from food, this was the only other thing that reminded me of home. I could not cook, until finally I taught myself to cook. I played my songs, and for that moment I was transported to my home.

very closely by

in South Asian culture,

and that is followed

music.

JAMES KNAPPETT

James Knappett is head chef and co-owner of bubbledogs, where he and his wife and sommelier, Sandia Chang, serve grower champagne and sparkling wine alongside signature hot dogs. Hidden from sight behind a curtain at the back of bubbledogs is Kitchen Table, a twenty-seat "chef's table" where James and his team host intimate dinners with a daily-changing twelve-course menu made up of meticulously sourced and foraged British ingredients. In 2018, Kitchen Table was awarded a coveted second Michelin star.

Song: Hold My Girl by George Ezra

Recipe Inspiration:

Hold

James's Song for His Wife and Daughter Playlist ▶ There is a mixture of songs here — songs I enjoy cooking to and songs that remind me of my wife and daughter.

1.	Hold My Girl	George Ezra
2.	Bitter Sweet Symphony	The Verve
3.	I Dreamed a Dream	Susan Boyle
4.	Californication	Red Hot Chili Peppers
5.	Chinatown	Liam Gallagher
6.	This Is Me	Keala Settle and The Greatest Showman
7.	You're Beautiful	James Blunt
8.	Ecuador	Sash!
9.	In the Morning	Razorlight
10.	The Prayer	Jonathan and Charlotte

UNITED KINGDOM

Cornish Lobster Tail, with Tahitian Vanilla Brown Butter, Red Currants, Chervil, and Wild Juniper

My lobster recipe was created on the day "my girl" Shea was born.

Serves 1

250 g unsalted butter	
2 Tahitian vanilla beans, split	
1 lobster	
2 small wild juniper branches	
1 bunch red currants, about 250 g	
1 bunch chervil, picked into small sprigs	
Maldon sea salt, for garnish	

Place the butter in a heavy-bottomed saucepan and melt over very low heat. Cook gently, whisking every so often, until the butter is browned, 2 to 3 hours.

Once browned, divide the butter between 2 small bowls. Scrape the seeds from the vanilla beans into one bowl of butter and whisk to mix. Tuck in the empty vanilla pods. Set both bowls aside.

Prepare the lobster by putting the tip of a knife down through the natural cross on the top of its head and rocking the knife through to the front. This will kill the lobster instantly. Twist the claws and the tail off the body. Using fish pliers, enter the small hole on the underside of the tail at the bottom and grasp the intestine/waste pipe. Remove and discard the intestine.

Blast-freeze the lobster to −20°C (−4°F) until fully frozen. Thaw the lobster tail, then crack and peel. (Freezing the tail allows you to remove the shell while keeping the raw meat intact.) Let the lobster tail come up to room temperature, then brush with the plain brown butter.

Make a hot fire in a charcoal grill. Place a wire rack directly over the fire. Once hot, place the lobster tail on the rack and grill quickly until the top side is nicely colored, around 1 minute. Turn the lobster tail over and lightly color the underside for 30 seconds.

Remove the lobster tail and carve in half lengthways. Brush all over with more brown butter.

Raise the wire rack above the coals. Put the lobster tail back on the rack and place a bowl upside down on top. Put the juniper branches on the coals and gently smoke the lobster tail until medium-rare, allowing the bowl to catch the smoke and heat.

To serve, warm both brown butters. In a small saucepan, warm the red currants in a little of the plain brown butter.

Place the lobster in the middle of a shallow bowl and spoon some of the warm vanilla butter over the top. Sprinkle with a few flakes of sea salt. Spoon some buttery red currants over the top of the lobster and finish with 3 or 4 sprigs of chervil. Serve immediately.

My Girl

by George Ezra

Song: Hold My Girl by George Ezra

I find it very difficult to listen to music I don't like.

As I moved through the ranks of the bigger and better kitchens, the food became more and more serious. And that is a bit like my evolution through music, from listening to pop songs to hitting school discos to getting more into rock bands like Oasis and the Verve. It's like going from the food that we as children would eat or what we consider to be junk food—which I would compare to lots of the music you hear on the radio now these days, the kid pop bands—to the great stuff. You grow out of kid food; you don't want to listen to bad music. It's really similar. There's a world of food being created right now that has a refinement like those legendary bands. What those musicians do now carries on from where their inspirations started. They don't represent a phase; there's a timeless consistency.

It seems like my trajectory mirrors the lifestyle change in many people's current approach to food. The same way people are changing the way they stay at home to cook, they are also no longer going out to eat just to feed the belly. People enjoy dining out as an event more than ever. You go out for a fun dinner and then it takes about four hours! It used to be just a night out at the pub. And things are circling back. Eating at home is now often a more special occasion than being out.

Music has a similar story in many of our lives: At one point, I only listened to music on the radio and TV and my stereo. Then concerts became massive music festivals that last for three or four days and so on. Now it's back to being about finding time to connect with a band or song that really gets to me.

The similarities between music and food run deep. We've got great restaurants in London, for example, where the chefs are as obsessed with music as they are with food. Whatever their music tastes may be, everyone has to listen to it with no choice. It's the atmosphere of the restaurant. I have a friend who has a restaurant where he plays hardcore heavy metal music. Some people can't stand that music, but his food is so good, they deal with it. It really does add to the feeling that he has his vision, he doesn't care what anyone else thinks about his food or his music or anything. Luckily for him his food is really good, so it attracts people. Some restaurants stick to the model of fine dining with light piano playing the same tune in the background all night. It seems to me like no one enjoys it, listens to it, or even picks up on it. But in cutting-edge restaurants today, music is usually crucial in one way or another. The music is really dictated by a lot of the younger chefs now, making it a big part of a restaurant's atmosphere and a big part of the larger restaurant scene.

The music I play in my restaurant is stuff that I personally want to listen to. We play British music—Oasis and others from that era, as well as new English people coming onto the scene, like George Ezra and Tom Walker. Bands that have actual lyrics and actual skill will get onto our playlists. It's rare if two or three people a night don't mention our playlist. A number of the people that come to my restaurant are of a similar age and can relate to the music that they're listening to. They grew up with it, too. I find it very difficult to listen to music I don't like.

My kitchen is open to the dining room, so I hear what the guests hear all night. There's no way I'd be able to listen to piano background music all night, it would just do my head in. The six hours I cook, it has to be what I like.

At the end of the night, when we are finished, I head to my office and the music changes in the kitchen. The kids—I call them "kids" even though they are very much not kids—will put their clean-down music on, and it feels a bit like a rave. I don't know or want to know what the music is called, but it's pretty intense.

ESU LEE AND PHIL EUELL

Esu Lee was born in Ulsan, Korea. He honed his craft in Hong Kong, working in parallel with Jowett Yu of Ho Lee Fook and Le Garçon Saigon, James Henry of Bones, and Jeff Claudio of Yardbird before going to Paris to work with Roman chef Giovanni Passerini. A few months in, he was approached by Phil Euell to be the chef at CAM, a yet-to-be-opened deconstructed Asian food and natural wine restaurant in the Marais neighborhood in Paris.

Phil Euell was born in New York. After quitting the legal profession at twenty-six, he left New York for Mexico City to study at Le Cordon Bleu. Quickly thereafter, he fell in love with a young French woman and spent the next year painting watercolors and traveling through the Mexican countryside before the couple left to settle in Paris.

Objection Overruled Playlist ▶
The theme is universal tribalism and how people form their own tribes through the music they connect with.

Song: This is Not a Love Song by Public Image Ltd.

THIS IS NOT

1.	**Water No Get Enemy**	Fela Kuti
2.	**La La La La**	Orchestre Poly Rythmo de Cotonou
3.	**James Brown Ride On**	Orlando Julius & His Afro Sounders
4.	**Alikali Adajo**	The Sahara All Stars
5.	**Hankuri**	Mad Man Jaga
6.	**Love and Death**	Ebo Taylor
7.	**Lagos Sisi**	Bola Johnson
8.	**Asafo Beesuon**	C.K. Mann & His Carousel 7
9.	**Paint a Vulgar Picture**	The Smiths
10.	**Pretty Girls Make Graves**	The Smiths

SOK CHO BIBIM COLD NOODLES

A LOVE SONG

Recipe Inspiration:
by Public Image Ltd.

When Phil and I were in Seoul together, we would go with all our friends into this basement coin-operated karaoke place that reminded Phil of old-school Times Square peep-show booths. When I was in high school in Korea, I had often gone alone to sing. The culture at my school was kind of limiting my identity, so I had a need to put myself in the karaoke box, sing loudly, and not care about other people's opinions. Just singing like a superstar — and it really felt like I was in concert. Here are our favorite songs for karaoke:

1. **Knockin' On Heaven's Door** Bob Dylan

2. **I'll Be Missing You** **Puff Daddy Ft. Faith Evans & 112**

3. **Brown Skin** **India.Arie**

4. 거꾸로 강을 거슬러 오르는 저 힘찬 연어들처럼 **(Like Those Lively Salmon Rising Against The River Stream)** 강산에 **Kang San-ae**

5. 그것만이 내세상 **(only those are my world)** 들국화 **Deulgukhwa**

Serves 1

■ For the daikon-dashi granita:

30 g *dasima* (Korean dried kelp)

1 daikon, peeled and cut into big chunks

30 g light soy sauce

30 g mirin

10 g fish sauce

50 g *katsuobushi* (dried, fermented, smoked tuna)

■ **100 g clams**

Olive oil, for drizzling

■ For the dressing:

90 g *gochujang*

80 g rice wine vinegar

50 g corn syrup or glucose

50 g sugar

20 g sesame oil

80 g water

■ **1 long cucumber**

30 g salt

About 80 g soba or sōmen noodles

Hard-boiled egg halves or wedges, for garnish (optional)

To make the daikon-dashi granita, in a bowl, soak the *dasima* in 1 liter water overnight in the fridge.

You will be steaming the clams in the dashi water before you finish the granita. Just before cooking them, soak the clams for 30 minutes in fresh water.

Remove the *dasima* from its soaking water, discard the *dasima*, and pour the water into a sauté pan. Add the daikon, soy sauce, mirin, and fish sauce. Bring to a simmer over medium-high heat.

Add the soaked clams to the pan, cover, and cook in the dashi water until they open. Using tongs, transfer the clams in their ▶

shells to an airtight container. Drizzle with olive oil, cover, and keep in the fridge until ready to serve.

Put the *katsuobushi* in the dashi water. Off the heat, let infuse for 30 minutes. Strain the daikon-dashi broth and discard the solids. Transfer the broth to a small metal roasting pan or other freezer-safe dish. Freeze the granita until frozen hard, about 8 hours.

To make the dressing, combine all the ingredients in a saucepan over medium-high heat and bring to a boil, whisking to mix well. As soon as it starts boiling, remove from the heat and let cool.

Peel the cucumber and slice thinly. Sprinkle with the salt and let stand for 20 minutes. Rinse under cold running water for 10 minutes.

Bring a pot of water to a boil. Cook the soba or sōmen until al dente, about 4 minutes. Rinse with cold water and drain well.

In a large bowl, toss the noodles with the dressing. Arrange the dressed cold noodles on each plate. Arrange some salted cucumber slices and 7 or 8 cooked clams on top of each.

Remove the granita from the freezer and scrape with a fork or spoon into more or less uniform shards. Put a scoop of granita on top of the noodles. Garnish with hard-boiled egg, if you like. Serve immediately. Enjoy!

● **Phil Euell** ● Since I can remember, music has been a big part of my life. When I was growing up, my father was always playing music in the car and at the house. Mostly '60s and '70s rock, with some hints at new wave and reggae. The records I heard then sparked a lifelong interest in the power of music to evoke emotions, memories, and experiences. Once, when I was around ten, I was searching through the thousands of CDs my father had collected. Somewhere between the Beatles catalogue, Meatloaf, and the Eagles, I found a live record of the Wailers' *Babylon by Bus*. From the moment I pressed play on the stereo, the music lit something in me: the sound of the drums, the syncopated guitar, the pining lyrical voice. ● Hearing *Babylon by Bus*, almost instantly changed my perception of music from something to keep the mind pleasantly busy in the background on a lazy afternoon at home or on a long car ride from Long Island to Fort Lee, New Jersey, to something more active and alive. The exotic-seeming Jamaican sounds coming out of the speakers that day awoke me to the possibilities of music as a vehicle to understand, in a very deep and personal way, the experiences, pains, struggles, and emotions of others very far away, in an almost quantum, action-at-a-distance sort of way. I was hooked. ● Within a few years, I had forged a path toward my personal self-actualized music identity. An English uncle's boarding-school record collection, which I stumbled across in his basement, exposed me to English punk, post-punk, new wave, and new romantics. When I was twelve, my parents got divorced and we moved. Finding myself alienated in a new school with no friends, I quickly looked for other outsiders to ease my isolation. Fortunately, there was a skater kid named Alex who was really into the Dead Kennedys and New York hardcore. We became fast friends, and within a few months, I went from being a fairly polite and anonymous kid to being an obnoxious, blue-haired skater hardcore punk, gleefully provoking in virtually any way I could in the entire middle school. ● During this time, it was the music that gave me the confidence to be assertive, loud, brash, and authentic. Bad Brains, Minor Threat, Youth of Today, Fishbone, Black Flag, the Minutemen—late eighties punk, ska, skate, surf underground culture was exploding. Looking back, it was a tiny movement compared to the mainstream Top 40 music that most people were listening to. But, curiously, at that moment, there was also a collision happening between the newest movements in punk and hip-hop. In 1989, my friends and I went to a Red Hot Chili Peppers show at Stonybrook University, part of their Mother's Milk tour. To our surprise, they did an entire set of Easy-E songs, with their socks-on-cocks schtick. The crowd went wild for it. It was perhaps the first time I realized the power of contrast and innovation in music. Just a couple of years earlier, this fusion would have been impossible. ● Music surely influences our culinary perspective. At CAM, music is one of the most important interior settings, or maybe the most important. Music shows the direction of a restaurant and its philosophy, and it affects the customers' experience. And personally, music can bring me easily to the fantasy aspect of creating this food and give me a good feeling when I need to be communicating good emotions through the food. And we have thought about the idea of pairing the novelty of sounds with eating to create a new context, with the aim of building a unique sensory association—for example, what if each time you put the chopsticks to your mouth to take a bite of our Vegan Temple Sushi, there's the sound of Tony Allen's drums rolling in the back of your head? ● When thinking about the music for CAM, I had a strong intuition that creating a musical contrast to both the interior design and the food would not just fill a void, but perhaps create something emergent. In design, cuisine, and music alike, there's something rich about contrast and recontextualization. And, in my experience, it's rare to hear Allen's type of African music in a restaurant setting. CAM's playlist is a lot of Ebo Taylor, Fela Kuti, C. K. Mann, Bola Johnson, Pat Thomas. Then compilation records like Afrobeat Academy, Orchestre Poly-Rythmo de Cotonou—it's basically afrobeat, afro-jazz, and highlife from Nigeria, Ghana, and Bénin from roughly 1960 to 1980. There's the peculiar rhythm and composition of afrobeat, especially Fela Kuti. The songs are often twenty minutes or longer, with the lyrics usually beginning five or ten minutes after the beginning of the track. With long compositions like these, we are less disturbed by or aware of the beginnings or ends. The music becomes an almost "intertemporal" experience. This out-of-timeness is well suited to the ambiance of eating spicy, surprising sounds, a blending of kitchen and body moisture, the space itself begins to unify, everything present approaches oneness. ● We play the Smiths exclusively on Sundays. This, again, is a result of thinking about the strength of contrasts. Taking such an aggressively forward stance of the CAM music from Wednesday through Saturday almost necessitates an acoustic break. When I was growing up in New York in the late eighties and early nineties, my friends and I would go to "Club Soda" clubs (no alcohol but a lot of illicit drugs), where the Smiths would be in heavy rotation. At one of these clubs, called the Angle, it was all Smiths on Sunday nights. Then, as now, the jangly guitars and melancholic lyrics stirred bittersweet emotions. I thought this would be perfect for CAM. The Smiths, in all their beautiful sadness, longing, and desperation…what could be better to listen to while eating and drinking late into the evening on a Sunday? ● **Esu Lee** ● Music has always reflected my life and my moods. Music is a great connecter, making it possible to see myself, and also to understand what I want to cook. Seeing the list of music on my phone helps put my feelings of the moment into the food. I have been becoming pickier and more sensitive with everything, such as the sound of music, the taste of food, and even my relationships with the people. I used to feel driven to decide what things are good, like best songs and best food, best restaurants, etc. I have been realizing now that my best picks or choices can be different from what others consider best or even standard, and I realize my choices are equally as valid. Food and music are very personal tastes, so the more the world gets smaller, the more the personal opinion will affect the public market, as people see a lot of things easier and faster. In my opinion, music and food as both art and

boot bnɒ ɔiꙅum
γɿɈꙅubni bnɒ Ɉɿɒ ʜɈod ꙅɒ
ɿɒlimiꙅ γɿǝv ʞool

music and food
as both art and industry
look very similar

food and drinking earthy, natural wine in an often crowded, hot setting. One begins to lose the self—to flirt with the barriers between one and others. When the air is thick with strong food smells, rollicking industry look very similar, as they both get direct and fast reactions and emotions from people, but they also require long, memorable, thoughtful evaluations of taste to enjoy them at a deeper level.

JAMIE MALONE

Jamie Malone has always had a life that revolved around food. She grew up cooking and baking breads with her dad in St. Paul, Minnesota. Before receiving her culinary degree from Le Cordon Bleu, Chef Malone traveled and studied extensively in Hong Kong, Singapore, Vietnam, and Europe, immersing herself in each region's cuisine. In 2017, she opened her first restaurant, Grand Café. She likes cooking French food and drinking sherry.

Songs to Stay Up For Playlist ▶
One way I categorize a great song is this: I'm up late listening to music, I'm tired and ready to call it a night, and a song comes on that is so good, it makes me want to pour another drink and stay up just listening.

1.	Jewel	Moss of Aura
2.	Everybody's Gotta Live	Arthur Lee
3.	I'm on Fire	Chromatics
4.	I Only Have Eyes for You	The Flamingos
5.	We Used to Wait	Arcade Fire
6.	Can't Seem to Make You Mine	The Seeds
7.	Itchycoo Park	Small Faces
8.	I'm Confessin' (That I Love You)	Thelonious Monk
9.	Dracula's Wedding	Outkast ft. Kelis
10.	Sharp Cutting Wings (Songs to a Poet)	Lucinda Williams
11.	Shadowboxin'	GZA
12.	Last Caress	The Misfits
13.	Broken Chairs	Built to Spill
14.	Waiting Room	Fugazi

USA

Grilled Oysters with Cream, Shallots, and Isot Chile

This song is soft and smooth yet powerful, and it builds. These oysters are creamy and subtle, but the deliciousness builds and almost sneaks up on you. Especially if you wash them down with great sherry.

Serves 2

Recipe Inspiration:

Landing Cliffs

by
Explosions
in the Sky

6 East Coast oysters

3 tablespoons very lovely high-fat cream

1 nice fresh shallot, finely minced

Coarsely cracked black pepper, fresh from the pepper mill, and fleur de sel

1 teaspoon isot chile powder

10 Sea Salt & Vinegar Kettle Chips, a little smashed up

■ Very well-chilled Manzanilla sherry in cute cordial glasses, for serving

Build a hot fire in a charcoal grill.

Shuck the oysters, ensuring that the liquor does not drain out.

In a small bowl, stir together the cream and shallot. Top each oyster with a dollop of the cream mixture. Arrange on the grill rack directly over high heat.

Once the oysters are opaque throughout and the meat is pulling away from the abductor muscles, remove from the grill and nestle onto a paper towel–lined plate or a bed of salt to keep the cream from draining out.

Top each oyster with a twist from the pepper mill, a few flakes of fleur de sel, a pinch of chile powder, and scattering of crushed-up potato chips.

Eat quickly while still hot!

Drink sherry.

give you calm

I became aware of music when I was very young. I would sit in my room and listen to the oldies on the radio with my tape recorder, waiting for my favorite songs to come on so that I could record them! The first song I remember NEEDING to record was "The Locomotion" by Little Eva.

●

I really fell hard for punk rock, and it still feels like who I am. I still snowboard and blast Rancid on my headphones. I will always have at least ten pairs each of Vans and Dickies in my closet, and I still crush hard on skateboarders. I listened to punk rock, I went to punk shows, I snowboarded, and now I surf. And that is how I chose my friends. If you were listening to whatever bullshit pop music people were listening to then, there is no way I would have wanted to hang out with you.

●

There is a pretty long list of musicians and bands that I really love, who have influenced me. I use music to navigate life in a lot of different ways. When I have a big day or task that I really need to conquer, that may require listening to GZA or Metallica. Lately, if I need to get into a place of concentration and creativity, I have been listening to Moss of Aura and Explosions in the Sky. If I'm going to put my head down and prep for a while, I listen to Built to Spill, Murder by Death, or Frank Black. The list goes on and on. I have something I like for most parts of the day.

give you power

●

I went through a divorce about five years ago. It's a little cliché, but music was a huge crutch during that time. I listened to a lot of sad country stuff in the beginning, Lucinda Williams and Emmylou Harris. I had a prep table in my living room with whiskeys and a record player, and after work I would just go to that table and drink and play music. Then, once I was ready to get over the devastation, I used music to make me feel powerful and remind me of the person I was before marriage.

make. you happy

I am jealous of music, or the people who can make it, because it can completely take over your emotions in seconds! It can change your whole feeling and perspective! It can give you calm, give you power, make you happy, make you cry. As cooks, we can only dream of being able to do that with our work. I use music in the dining room to control the environment, set the tone and emotion.

Here's a day in music in the Grand Café kitchen:

- Start day, drink coffee, make the stocks.
  Listen to Frank Black and the Catholics.
- Cut fish in the afternoon.
  Listen to the Pixies' *Trompe le Monde*.
- Service at the Grand Café, listen to Dirty Beaches.
- Break down and clean, listen to Robyn.

make you cry

Each of my restaurants has its own playlist and they would NEVER interchange, they are completely different spaces with completely different feeling. They overlap in the way that, as a musician or as a chef, you draw from previous generation's styles and cultures and make it your own. Our goal is the same—to create emotions in people. The music that I love is eclectic; I really love music that is more timeless than experimental, and that is how my cooking is, too.

VIRGILIO MARTÍNEZ AND PÍA LEÓN

Virgilio Martínez was born in Lima, Perú. Though he wanted to become a professional skateboarder, he found his passion in the kitchen. For ten years now, the cooking style of Virgilio at Central, his restaurant in Lima, has spoken volumes about the biodiversity of Perú. He opened MIL (Cusco), overlooking the Archaeological Complex of Moray site, to understand the origins and stories of food in their territory. Central and MIL have become culinary reference points in Perú and Latin America, which a decade ago were barely considered a food destination.

Pía León was also born and raised in Lima. Her interest in cooking began at a young age, when she would help her mother cook for every family meal. She graduated from Le Cordon Bleu Perú in 2007, and in 2009, she joined the culinary staff at Central. In 2018, Pía decided to open her own space, which she called Kjolle. At Kjolle, she showcases Peruvian ingredients by mixing different products from different territories and regions.

Good Days Playlist ▶ With this playlist, we know anyone can start a good day. These songs take us to different moments in our lives with different people, but they all bring us happy memories. And that's what music is for, to help you remember good times with good people.

1.	(I Can't Help) Falling in Love with You	UB40
2.	Beast of Burden	The Rolling Stones
3.	Magic	Coldplay
4.	Pride (In the Name of Love)	U2
5.	All I Want Is You	U2
6.	Me Llamaré Tuyo	Víctor Manuelle
7.	El Cantante	Hector Lavoe
8.	Que Alguien Me Diga	Gilberto Santa Rosa
9.	Yo No Te Pido	Gilberto Santa Rosa
10.	Sweet Fanta Diallo	Alpha Blondy

Sea Bass. Mucilage. Taperiba.

Serves 10

Recipe Inspiration:

AMAZONIAN MUSIC

750 g sea bass fillets

5 gelatin leaves

500 g liquid mucilage

■ For the *taperiba* granita:

1 gelatin leaf

800 g *taperiba* pulp

50 g *cocona* juice

50 g *sachatomate* juice

2 g salt

■ For the *uncucha* crisps:

80 g sliced *uncucha*

200 g salt

200 g *ají negro*

Vegetable oil

■ For the cacao tiger's milk:

5 g fish trimmings

1 garlic clove, smashed

2 g ginger, coarsely chopped

8 g red onion, chopped

4 g celery, chopped

300 g fresh lemon juice

15 g salt

Handful of ice

8 g cilantro (fresh coriander)

5 g cacao powder

■ 1 cacao fruit

Water

Juice of 1 lime

Slice the fish sashimi style. Refrigerate until ready to serve. In a small bowl, hydrate the gelatin leaves in a little bit of cold water.

In a small saucepan over medium heat, heat the mucilage, without boiling. Add the hydrated gelatin. Let the mixture cool down. Refrigerate to let gelatinize.

To make the *taperiba* granita, in a small bowl, hydrate the gelatin leaf in a little cold water.

In a blender, blend all the remaining ingredients until smooth. Pour into a small saucepan and warm over medium-low heat. Once the liquid is warm, add the hydrated gelatin and stir to dissolve. Transfer the mixture to a metal pan and freeze. (You can

use a small amount of dry ice to help freeze the granita faster.)

To make the crisps, thinly slice the *uncucha* and spread on a baking sheet. Cover with the salt and let stand for 30 minutes. Rinse the slices, drain well, and put in a sous-vide bag. Add the *ají negro*. Osmotize the *uncucha* covered in the ají in a vacuum machine. Strain the *uncucha* and confit in vegetable oil at 75°C (165°F). Take the *uncuchas* out with a skimmer and transfer to paper towels to drain the oil. Place them one by one in over a wype all and dehydrate for one night at 65°C.

To make the tiger's milk, in a blender, combine all of the ingredients except the cilantro and cacao powder. Strain the juice ▶|

and discard the solids. Return the juice to the blender, add the coriander, and blend for 3 seconds. Strain again. Discard the solids again and blend the juice one more time with the cacao powder. Taste and adjust the seasoning.

Scoop the cacao fruit flesh into a saucepan and simmer it in 2–3 liters water and lime juice. Remove from the heat, let cool, transfer to a metal pan, and freeze.

To serve, divide slices of fish in the middle of each of 10 chilled bowls. Break the mucilage jelly into big pieces and place them between the fish slices. Pour in a little of the cacao tiger's milk, covering the bottom of the dish without covering the fish. Place a few *uncucha* crisps on top of the fish slices.

At the last minute, break the frozen *taperiba* into big pieces and quickly blend to create a *taperiba* granita. Serve the frozen *taperiba* at the table in the empty cacao fruit.

● **Virgilio Martínez** ● When I go to the Andean world, I listen to Andean music. When I go to the Amazon world, I listen to Amazonian music. This is what happens to me now. I can see this connection with music, landscape, people, culture, story, and tradition. The lyrics are related to all I see and experience around me. When I go to the highlands, I try to listen to music related to it. ● When we started to work in Europe, I could listen to music in the kitchen. There were many songs that would repeat over and over again because of the chefs. I really started to connect with the kitchen from the bottom. The culinary world is huge, and it is associated with different disciplines. Now that I am not so much into music myself, I have had several talks with music producers to help me interpret what I want to transmit, through audio signature, so to speak, in Central—what organic qualities, what actual nature sounds, rhythms, and harmonies exist in music that I can translate into my dining room. ● In the last eight or nine years, I was so focused in the kitchen that when people used to talk to me about music and concerts, I didn't feel it. In the context of my restaurant life, I felt lost about that topic, I didn't have much to say. So, when my son was born, I got connected with music again, since I started listening to it with him. Now I listen to music again with my family, music for children; however, the band I've always listened to and followed is Radiohead. I've listened to all their albums. ● I think it's interesting that when we open a restaurant, we always talk to music producers, who create tracks or playlists related to what I see and eat. We leave that job to the experts, who hopefully see all my attention to and appreciation for the gastronomic and cultural experiences in our dining rooms. If the music is going to be effective, it has to really match what people want to experience, what we want them to experience.

● **Pía León** ● Music has always helped me to connect with people. I remember doing different kinds of trips when I was younger. Even when I didn't know people around me, I would often meet new people through their tastes in music. Knowing different lyrics of different kinds of music really helped me meet and connect with people. ● Music plays a big role in all kinds of cultures. Instruments and music talk about history. If you've heard about the Peruvian *cajon*, our national cultural heritage instrument, you've heard about Peruvian history. The *cajon* was created back in the days of slavery, on the coasts of Perú, and today is known even in flamenco music. However, in Perú, instruments and music can be just like food when talking about regions and territories. You can have the Andean *quena* just as you have different kinds of Amazonian drums. You know where you're standing depending on the type of music you're listening to. ● Music in Latin America often talks about our history, or about the hard past of someone. It's interesting to see how those sometimes painful stories are told with a very cheerful rhythm, and that's what life is about. It's about learning from your past and learning how to see the old days and keep on smiling. For example, if you listen to Ruben Blades or Gilberto Santa Rosa, you will understand what I'm talking about. ● Apart from Latin music, one of the bands I admire the most is the Rolling Stones. In 2016, they did a concert in Lima, and they called me because Mick Jagger wanted to eat at Central. I remember doing all kinds of confidentiality paperwork for him to eat at the restaurant; nobody could believe how excited I was. I met Mick Jagger in person and I remember I was even shaking—it was one of my biggest fan moments! I will never forget it. ● In the kitchen, we play music mostly during pre-service; the team chooses different kinds of music to motivate themselves during the day. We have an open kitchen, so we can't play music during service. But the music in the dining room is a lounge-y kind of music with a little joyful Amazonian twist. At the end of the night, when nobody is in the dining room anymore, we play our music again to clean everything up. ● Personally, I would say music influences my mood very much. That's why I listen mostly to joyful music, and I try creating the same mood in my kitchen so that my team feels comfortable working. In general, I think that *sounds* (not just music) play a big part in the experience I want to transmit in the restaurant, or throughout a meal. Sounds enhance everyone's senses in a lot of different ways, and they will remember a dish, or a restaurant, better if what's happening around them is vivid. It could be music, chatting, even outside noises. Visually, dishes in Kjolle are all about color, and even the dining room is cozy and warm with lots of colors. This is the beauty of Latin music and how it inspires my cooking.

If the music is going to be effective, it has to really match what people want to experience, what we want them to experience.

MATTY MATHESON

Matty Matheson journeyed from early, humble New Brunswick beginnings to becoming a famous chef face on Canadian TV. His shows *Dead Set On Life* and *It's Suppertime* were two of the first original series on the VICELAND television network, propelling Matheson's cooking career to Internet superstardom. In 2018, he released his best-selling book, *Matty Matheson: A Cookbook.*

Recipe Inspiration:

ANOTHER DAY
by Crimpshrine

Music to Do Drugs to Or Not, But You Can Without a Doubt Cook Food While Listening to This Playlist ▶ I want people to enjoy good music while enjoying good food... or whatever they're doing. This playlist will add to any experience.

Song: Another Day by Crimpshrine

1.	**Life Is Cheap**	Flipper
2.	**The Money Will Roll Right In**	Fang
3.	**Hardly Getting Over It**	Hüsker Dü
4.	**Bastards of Young**	The Replacements
5.	**Hooch**	Melvins
6.	**I'm So Tired**	Fugazi
7.	**Swimsuit Issue**	Sonic Youth
8.	**Savory**	Jawbox
9.	**A Salty Salute**	Guided By Voices
10.	**Screaming at a Wall**	Minor Threat
11.	**Big Take Over**	Bad Brains
12.	**Nerves**	Silkworm
13.	**Free Drug Zone**	Seaweed
14.	**Work Hard / Play Hard**	Palace Music

▲ Matty Matheson

CANADA

Clam and Green Olive Pasta

Good food. Good tunes. No pose dogs. Because this song is amazing and it makes me want to cook. If this song doesn't make you want to cook, or at least eat, then I can't help you.

Serves 4

▼ Matty Matheson

3 cups dry white wine

1 shallot, halved

½ celery stalk

3 sprigs thyme

1 bay leaf

3 lb cherrystone or littleneck clams

■ For the bread crumbs:

1 loaf fresh or day-old sourdough, cut into ½-inch cubes

Good olive oil, for drizzling

Salt and freshly ground black pepper

■ Olive oil

3 cloves garlic, sliced as thinly as possible

1 tablespoon good red pepper flakes

2 cups pitted Cerignola olives

½ lb unsalted butter

14 oz good-quality dried bucatini

Salt and freshly ground black pepper

Leaves of 1 bunch flat-leaf parsley, chopped

3 lemons

In a pot over medium-high heat, bring the wine to a boil. Add the shallot, celery, thyme, and bay leaf. Let simmer for 15 to 20 minutes.

Rinse the clams under cold running water for 5 minutes. Meanwhile, set up a large bowl full of ice water.

Drain the clams well, add to pot with the seasoned wine, and put the lid on the pot.

Once the clams are open, using tongs, transfer in their shells to the prepared ice bath.

Once the clams are chilled, pick the clam meats out, put in a bowl, and refrigerate until ready to use. If any clams did not open, throw them out. Scoop out a 6-oz ladleful of the cooking liquid, strain, and keep in the fridge for later use.

Preheat the oven to 450°F (230°C).

To make the bread crumbs, spread the bread cubes on a baking sheet in a single layer and drizzle with the olive oil. Season with salt and pepper. Bake until the bread cubes are a deep golden brown, shaking or stirring once or twice to get even coloring. Make sure to keep an eye on them in the hot oven so they do not burn.

Once done, transfer the toasted bread cubes to a paper towel–lined plate and let cool completely. Put in a food processor and pulse into bread crumbs. Spoon the bread crumbs into a paper towel–lined bowl. Set aside until you are ready to serve.

In a Dutch oven over low heat, add just enough olive oil to coat the bottom. Add the garlic and cook very gently until golden brown. Add the red pepper flakes and stir for 5 seconds. Add the reserved 6 oz clam liquor, the clam meats, and the olives. Raise the heat to medium-high and cook until the liquid is reduced by half. Reduce the heat to low, add 1 tablespoon butter, and stir to emulsify in the sauce.

Meanwhile, bring a pot of salted water to a boil. Add the bucatini to the boiling water and cook until al dente, or longer to your liking. Drain in a colander set in the sink.

Add another tablespoon of butter to the sauce and cook for 1 minute. Add a large handful of chopped parsley and the juice of ½ lemon. Taste and adjust the seasoning.

Stir, stir, stir, and taste again. If you think it needs more salt and/or pepper, do it. Add the pasta to the Dutch oven, drizzle with olive oil, and toss to distribute everything. Divide among plates, add a nice handful of bread crumbs on top, and serve immediately.

● My parents always had music playing. They are massively into music and my dad's an audiophile. He would set up his stereos with subwoofers, preamps, amps, and all this crazy shit. The second my parents woke up, there'd be music on. They love the blues a lot, love classic rock and rock 'n' roll. The first time that music became a big part of my life was when I was in the fourth grade. I was ten years old and my dad started waking me and my brothers up for school every single morning to "T.N.T." by AC/DC. He would just blast that song in the house while cooking bacon and pancakes or whatever was for breakfast. That was the beginning of my love for music. ● My heritage is really all about music and food. My grandparents, especially my dad's dad, always had house parties and always had music there. They're from Newfoundland and PEI, where live music is a longtime tradition, so they always had musicians around. If you ever went to my parents' or my grandparents' house for a party, there'd always be a guy with a fiddle, somebody playing the spoons, or somebody playing a friggin' little accordion. In the Maritimes, when you have a house party, there's definitely live musicians playing there all the time. Music was everything and the food that went along with the music was also really important. ● My culture and my heritage are built around hosting people and having a good time. I always bring it back around to the way that my parents partied. I know some kids in high school weren't even allowed to come over to my house because my parents used to have a good fucking time, and a lot of people are afraid of people who have good times. That mentality of my parents, I'll it take to my grave. ● Growing up, I was a punk and a hardcore kid. The mentality of DIY, doing it yourself, has made my life incredibly easy to navigate because of the ethos that I internalized being in the hardcore community. That attitude really allowed me to find my own way, to always be comfortable in my own skin and do things my way to a certain extent. I looked up to a lot of the New York hardcore bands, like Agnostic Front, Cro-Mags, Leeway, Youth of Today, and Floorpunch. Their attitude and message allowed my brain and my career path to really align. And it was really more than the bands, it was the community that I came to love, because we were there for each other and we stood as one. It was the music that brought us all together. ● I just feel really lucky that I got into hardcore so young and got to make friends with such a diverse group of people. I've always really been into partying and really into meat, but some of my favorite bands growing up were straight-edge vegans, and because of that I've never had a problem with vegans. It's weird to me that some chefs, particularly those who cook meat-heavy menus, always have such problems with vegans. Vegans just eat vegetables; that's not a problem. Hardcore really opened up my eyes to how we can relate to different people who can have completely different thoughts. I was never straight-edge, I was never vegan, but I have best friends who are vegan and straight-edge, and that didn't change our love for each other. ● The very first hardcore show I went to was a Buried Alive show. When I walked in, I saw this packed, sweaty commotion of kids who literally looked like they were beating the shit out of each other. But the same encounter, within all of that really intense chaotic movement, produced a highly peaceful moment for me, and I truly felt like that room was somewhere I belonged. It just clicked… it was true love, and that feeling became forever ingrained in me. The hardcore community is one of the greatest things ever. It is about that unity, it is about people coming together from all over the world. No matter your religion, no matter your gender, no matter the color of your skin, there are all these kids going off, and that is what really made it so attractive to me right from the start. I come from a small town, and I used to wear nail polish, dye my hair, and I stretched my ears—I was a freak. Then all of a sudden, I had a place where I could go have fun and have a release from mainstream society. ● To have a place to go, meeting new people, buying zines, getting stickers—it was this community that you could participate in, it was really collaborative. What I really got out of it was, "You get what you give, and if you want to work really hard at something, I guarantee at the end you're gonna have a really great result." And even if you don't, you're going to be able to keep working toward something, to participate, and I'm a really big believer that if you put good energy out there, you're gonna get some back. That's something I learned from that world. It's something that really made a big impact on my life and how I live my life still to this day. ● Being a weird little hardcore kid in a small town, I was ostracized and called names, but then I was able to find a place where I felt like I actually belonged, that became a big part of my identity. That is something I carry into my restaurants: a belief that everyone is welcome. I like to make food that everyone can eat. It's not highbrow, it's not lowbrow, it's just warm, welcoming food and I feel like that's a big part of hospitality. ● Shit really clicked when I went to cooking school. I had never wanted to be a chef growing up, but again, music was a huge part of the path to my destiny; this time, me cooking professionally. I can't cook at home without music. If there's no music, it makes me feel insane; it really breaks my brain. Music really calms me down, and it seems that was always built into the fabric of my restaurants. We played such loud music in the kitchen during service... it was chaos, just like the restaurant. We would just be jamming to whatever we wanted to play. During prep, all through service, all through cleanup and breakdown, we would just crank music. ● Foundationally, I'll always have that punk "fuck you" mentality of doing it myself and letting my restaurants speak for themselves. Parts and Labour and Odd Fellows were anomalies. Odd Fellows had twenty-six seats with one table made out of marble and it was only open for two years. It wasn't a sustainable restaurant, it was chaos, but it had unity, just like the hardcore shows I would go to. I was twenty-six years old, heavily medicated on drugs and alcohol, and we only listened to loud crazy music, having the best time of our lives. All that comes through punk and alternative music. With Parts and Labour, we wanted to take the experience of that loud, chaotic, small space and make it really big. We wanted to make this big warehouse space, with giant long tables, and treat it like a cafeteria. We wanted to turn the music up even louder! And we wanted to make it crazy, and we did—we created one of the craziest restaurants I've ever seen. ● Music has always been a part of my cooking life. It's all intermingled. That punk mentality was something I took from bands like the Misfits, Bad Brains, and Agnostic Front, which we played all the time. The Sex Pistols and the Dead Kennedys and a lot of fuckin' Ramones. I just like that pace of music, because it matches the pace of our brains. If we were mellow, we'd be listening to Sonic Youth or Screaming Trees or SST. We were just dudes who were the same in spirit as the food in our restaurants. We would always go through phases with the music—we would get into a band and there'd be maybe a month where we literally only listened to, let's say, the Replacements. I remember hearing about Sturgill Simpson and then just listening to him nonstop. ● Sharing the mentality of the independent music scene and the punk scene was extremely pivotal in our restaurants. Everything we did was that style. The way we moved, the way we talked, the way we cooked food, the way we designed restaurants, everything was about that attitude. Everything was about making a chaotic world, but keeping it controlled, tight, welcoming, and that dichotomy always went hand in hand with our creations. ● I'm a punk who became a chef. My food has always been styled after classic French technique but brought to you by Canadian ingredients. When I make pot au feu, I take the joints and the tough meats and put them in water with some vegetables and some thyme and cook it slowly until it's perfect. I'm cooking one of the greatest dishes of all time, but it's just like a three-chord punk song, where you're taking the most basic, most unassuming ingredients and putting your style and your time into it, and that way, you can achieve greatness.

The mentality of DIY, doing it yourself, has made my life incredibly easy to navigate because of the ethos that I internalized

MATTOS

IGNACIO

Born in Uruguay, Ignacio Mattos began his career in the kitchens of Francis Mallmann, Judy Rodgers, and Alice Waters, later moving to NYC in 2006 to be chef at Il Buco and to open Isa in Williamsburg. Mattos is a four-time James Beard Award nominee and author of the cookbook, *Estela.* At all of his restaurants, Mattos cooks food that is comforting and bold, reflecting his varied experiences and the cultures of New York City.

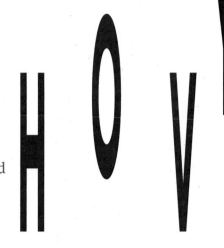

Continental Buffet Playlist ▶ I think the wide range of songs on this list speaks for itself. Perhaps some of the artists are a bit too obscure compared to the ingredients or dishes found on the usual continental breakfast buffet. However, there's a quite versatile and digestible selection of songs included as well that makes the mix fun and interesting. It's a bit like when you go to breakfast in some exotic place and there's always a new and surprising fruit that you've never had. I think this list has a bit of that element of surprise in it.

1.	**Do Your Thing**	Moondog
2.	**A Satisfied Mind**	Bob Dylan
3.	**Evening Breeze**	Emahoy Tsegué-Maryam Guébrou
4.	**Magical Colors**	The Jon Spencer Blues Explosion
5.	**Blues Nile**	Jon Hassell
6.	**Ghetto Defendant**	The Clash
7.	**Only Woman DJ with Degree**	Sister Nancy
8.	**Niandou**	Ballaké Sissoko and Vincent Segal
9.	**Shook Ones, Pt. II**	Mobb Deep
10.	**Sweet and Low**	Fugazi

ANCHOVY Toast

▼ Ignacio Mattos

CAFÉ ALTRO PARADISO, ESTELA, AND FLORA BAR

There are three core ingredients in this toast: bread, tomato, and anchovy. The simplicity echoes that simple, straightforward, and direct punk style. The prep time is also as fast and bold as a punk rock song...it works.

Serves 1

Extra-virgin olive oil

1 thick-cut slice sourdough bread

1 clove garlic, halved

1 tomato, cut in half crosswise

3 or 4 anchovy fillets

Freshly cracked black pepper

Heat a frying pan over medium-high heat.

Add a splash of olive oil to the pan, let it get hot, then add your slice of bread and char on both sides.

Remove the bread and quickly rub one side with the garlic clove and then the tomato half.

Place 3 or 4 anchovy fillets on top of the toasted bread and sprinkle with a grinding of black pepper.

Serve. Repeat for as many people as you've got.

Recipe Inspiration:

53RD & 3RD

NEW YORK, NY

by The Ramones

Music has always been a part of what I do, and I have always connected with the creativity behind it. I can listen to a song for about forty-five seconds and tell you what the song is about, what the artist was trying to communicate. There was one radio station I would listen to when I was growing up that was broadcasted from Buenos Aires, Argentina, called Rock and Pop, and late at night it would play all of this music I had never heard. The station would only come in if the weather conditions were right, so it had to be a little cloudy for me to get a good signal. Just the idea of knowing that I could listen to a radio station to discover music by staying up until late at night, hoping that the weather was cloudy so that I could get a good signal and be able to get some of this nice stuff to come in, was very exciting. Growing up in a small town, it was difficult to find new music at such a young age, like Infectious Groove and Deadboys, a couple of the bands I did eventually find that were so inspiring. I was ten, eleven, twelve years old. ● When I was a young man, no matter what you listened to, you would go and meet up with everyone at the same places. Whether you were a B-boy or into heavy metal or into punk, there was no division. We all hung out at these lofts or underground clubs. One of the bands that was very important to me around this time was Fugazi. They

were such a force, had such a clear vision of what they stood for, and would put that down on their records with such confidence. I respected their socially conscious efforts and their ability to put that in their music, too. What they were asking for was reasonable stuff: equality for everyone, social justice. I connected with their message, and also the way they would do things, their DIY approach. Their philosophy inspired me to take on the same kind of thinking in everything I did and in that way, I made connections with people. Their music today continues to inspire me to do the right thing and try to make positive changes, especially through my restaurants. I try to add to people's mental and physical health and to express my beliefs through my food, giving people a holistic experience, bringing everyone together in one place. ● If I had to pick a band that really influenced me at a crucial moment, it would be listening to the Ramones when I was twelve. The way they played music and looked at the world, they made me see everything in a different way. I remember the first time I listened to them, it was this one beautiful night, where I really connected with their songs. And from then on, they became a vital

part of who I am. Listening to the Ramones and asking myself, "What is going on here? What is this sound?" really opened me up as a person. To this day, that punk aesthetic inspires everything that I do and everything that I approach. ● Seeing the Ramones for the first time when I was thirteen years old changed my life forever. I ran away from home, got a fake ID, and crossed the country, with very little money, to see them play live in Buenos Aires. It's really hard to explain the impact that journey had on me, to live in such a small town and to hear this band play, it was crazy, and I was only thirteen! It was this mind-blowing thing. There was so much freedom in that experience, but it also fed a lot of what I needed to ground me. I am so proud that I did that and thankful that it happened. ● Music and food share such a deep language that is universal, and how we communicate about them is very similar. The soulful connection that I share with both is so personal, it is easy to see how they overlap. Every time someone plays a song or I cook a dish, it is a performance, it's a persona on display. Every day at the restaurant when I open the doors, it is like playing a show, there is a flow and a rhythm to it. A guitar, a knife, they are just instruments one can use to tell a story to create something new. Putting myself out there, it makes me vulnerable, but

Every time someone plays a song or

it also allows other people to connect with what I'm doing. Food and music are a part of life, they are so primal. We need them to nourish ourselves and to connect with society. ● On a personal level, music affects everything I am connected to. For example, if you think about rap or hip-hop and then you think about freestyle, something magical will come out from a personal place, even if you don't know exactly where it's coming from. Then you add those lyrics to a bass line or the scratch of a record and it creates something much larger, something that really taps into so many emotions. A lot of those early rap songs were done by artists with limited resources, but they created such powerful songs. To create something so magical…it reveals to us that you can convey so much with so little. And it is the same thing with food. You can start with something personal and some basic ingredients, but then go on to create a dish that says so much and stands for something. I think about that all of the time. ● Music has shown me that there are a lot of moving parts needed to create a holistic experience. There are so many different elements that go into a restaurant: the materials, the ingredients, the way the ingredients are handled by the chefs, the types of people we hire, the music that we play… it all adds up to what we are trying to say. Then it is

about finding the balance that makes everything work together. ● There was this time when one chef in the kitchen started singing an old Italian opera song about light and darkness. I started looking around at every-one and saw that his singing was making them all so high-spirited. I was in tears, everyone was in tears. I think about that moment and how moved I was about what this person was sharing with everyone. I don't take those things for granted and I try to put that emo-tion back into the food. ● Music is playing all of the time at the restaurant; I am a maniac with the music. You have to be careful; it is about bal-ance. At Estela, we have certain songs for certain times, you cannot be too selfish about what you want to hear versus what you should play. You need to use music to create movement in the dining room, to create a certain feeling, and you have to be very attuned to that. We play a lot of music in the kitchen for prep and then especially for finishing up the night. For service, one example is we play The Clash's "Ghetto Defendant" early in; for mid-service we play Modern Lovers' "Roadrunner"; and late service: Sister Nancy "Bam Bam." ● I can listen to music and understand those

deep emotions, and I also understand that I need to be able to be replicate those feelings through food. I think it is a bit harder task to convey emotion through food, because you do not have lyrics, so I use the food to share my emotions. It is not always about how food tastes, but about how it pleases in a range of ways and how the flavors and texture com-bine, mingle, and follow each other on the palate. When you are in the act of chewing the food I made, I want you to go beyond the flavors and to under-stand what I am trying to say and what it stands for. ● I think about an orches-tra and all of those people being able to play together; it is something that I try to emulate on a daily basis. It is challenging, but it is how I like to run the restaurant. You see all of these human beings performing indi-vidual tasks and you try to make the whole symphony work together as one cohesive piece to create this elevated experience. That sense of openness, when someone is speaking from a place of truth, I connect with that…and it is the same with food. When I eat, whether someone is cooking or I am cooking food, I want people to know immediately that it is com-ing from a place of truth. I have to keep it fresh to keep it interesting. I have felt the same passion about music that I've felt about food since I was young.

I cook a dish, it is a performance

ISAAC McHALE AND DANIEL WILLIS

Daniel Willis grew up in Manchester and has a love of food, music, and photography, all of which have always informed his unusual and creative approach to restaurants. In 2010, he and business partner Johnny Smith created the Clove Club supper club with the help of Isaac McHale and James Lowe of Lyle's London. At the now permanent Clove Club, the trio have created one of London's most contemporary and exciting restaurants, serving thoughtful, precise, elegant food in a relaxed informal setting with a soundtrack curated by Daniel. The Clove Club has been recognized by both the World's 50 Best Restaurants and the Michelin Guide.

Born in Orkney, Scotland, Isaac McHale started his career in Glasgow working in restaurants while still attending high school. McHale went to London in 2003 to work for Tom Aikens and then at The Ledbury for six years. In 2011, McHale, along with friends, formed the internationally acclaimed Young Turks collective. He is one of the vanguards of a high-profile new generation of British chefs.

UNITED KINGDOM

Song: Rip It Up by Orange Juice

▲ Isaac McHale and Daniel Willis

by Orange Juice

All About You Playlist ▶ by Isaac ▶
A quite random selection of songs not meant to be a mix necessarily, just some stuff I love that lots of people won't have heard. It goes from Scottish '80s punk and pop to cockney to Edinburgh to German punk guitar to a glitch remix of German punk-pop by Daniel's big brother to melancholy techno electronic to disco to African disco to a few oldies. And to finish, the otherworldly singularity of my sister, Iona Fortune's debut album *The Tao of I—Volume 1*.

1.	Horrorshow	Scars
2.	Dropout	Urge Overkill
3.	Wet Job	Fingerprintz
4.	Rip It Up	Orange Juice
5.	Eastbourne ladies	Kevin Coyne
6.	All About You	Scars
7.	Up the Junction	Squeeze
8.	Shame	Young Fathers
9.	Eisbär	Grauzone
10.	Auf'm Bahnh of Zoo (Allez-Allez Edit)	Nina Hagen Band
11.	Giant	The The
12.	Dirge	Death in Vegas
13.	A Forest	The Cure
14.	What's A Girl to Do	Fatima Yamaha
15.	Kiss Me Again	Dinosaur
16.	Only You	Steve Monite
17.	Khomo Tsaka Deile Kae?	Marumo
18.	Oh Yeh Soweto	Teaspoon & the Waves
19.	Broadway Jungle	Toots and The Maytals
20.	Perfidia	Phyllis Dillon
21.	Needles and Pins	The Searchers
22.	Qián 乾	Iona Fortune

Warm Blood Orange

with Sheep Milk Yogurt MOUSSE

and

Wild Fennel GRANITA

CLOVE CLUB, LUCA, AND TWO LIGHTS

Recipe Inspiration:

This recipe is inspired by one of Scotland's finest pop moments. A young Edwin Collins in Orange Juice, with their hit "Rip It Up." Every year there comes 'The Hunger Gap,' a period in the UK where very little fresh fruit and vegetables are being grown, usually between January and April. Luckily the European citrus fruit season is in full swing and we do various desserts and raw fish dishes featuring them prominently. My favorite has been with me for a while. I wanted to serve blood oranges warm, but found that if they got too hot, they broke apart and the flavor was lost. It took me forever and the song's lyrics "Rip it up and start again" were ringing through my ears as I tried and failed and adjusted the recipe until I got it right.

Serves 6

Ingredients

6 blood oranges

■ For the sheep milk yogurt mousse:

80 g milk

80 g caster (superfine) sugar

250 ml sheep milk yogurt

40 g yogurt acid powder (we use Sosa brand)

45 g instant food thickened

200 ml heavy (whipping) cream

■ For the wild fennel granita:

900 g water

450 g 1:1 simple syrup

125 g wild fennel

50 g fresh lemon juice

15 ml Pernod

2.5 g ascorbic acid powder

1 g xanthan gum powder

■ For the milk crisps:

500 g milk

50 g liquid glucose

Cut the top and bottom off the oranges, and cut the skin off in strips with a knife, as if you were going to make segments. Instead of making segments, cut the oranges in quarters and cut out the white pith at the core. Put the quarters in a dehydrator at 50°C (120°F) for 3 hours.

To make the mousse, in a saucepan over medium heat, warm the milk with 20 g of the sugar, stirring with a wooden spoon to help dissolve the sugar. Stir in the dehydrated oranges, remove from the heat, and let stand, allowing the fruit to fully hydrate.

Transfer the milk and fruit mixture to a blender and let cool for a minute or two longer if it still seems hot. Add the yogurt and yogurt acid powder and blend on full speed until smooth—but work carefully. There is a point where the thick milk and yogurt mixture is perfectly combined, without lumps; but there is a point past which you can overcombine and overheat the mixture and it becomes too thin and runny. When blended, the mixture should seem like the consistency of a thick stirred Greek yogurt.

In a large bowl, gently whip the cream with the remaining 60 g sugar until soft peaks form. Carefully fold in the yogurt base. Refrigerate the mousse until ready to serve.

To make the granita, blend the water with the TPT sugar syrup. Blend in the wild ▶|

fennel in small batches and strain. Pour into a large bowl and whisk in the lemon juice, Pernod, and ascorbic acid. Use an immersion blender to blend in the xanthan gum. Pour into a metal pan and freeze.

To make the milk crisps, warm the milk and liquid glucose together to 70°C (160°F), about the temperature you want for frothing milk for a cappuccino.

Froth the milk with an immersion blender, then let stand for about 20 seconds to allow the milk to drop out of the froth. Scoop the froth onto a dehydrator tray lined with plastic wrap (cling film). Warm and froth the milk again and transfer the froth in the same way. Repeat until you have filled the tray all over with a layer of foam about 3 cm thick. Pass through a dehydrator for 8 hours, or until dry. Remove the dried froth with a lightly oiled spatula and store in an airtight container until ready to serve.

To serve, scrape the granita to break it up. Place about 60 g (a large tablespoon) of mousse in each chilled serving bowl and make a well in the center. Place the warm blood oranges around the mousse. Spoon the granita into the wells and crack the milk crisps over the top. Serve immediately.

Andrew Weatherall's Gastronomic Plantyfication Playlist ▶ Shared by Daniel ▶ Like so many of my peers, I grew up listening to music Andrew Weatherall had touched and didn't realize until I was a little older; then I came to learn how huge his influence had been. When we first started The Clove Club supper clubs, which brought us all together, we were lucky enough to be friends with some amazing musicians and DJs, who we asked to soundtrack those first few dinners. Andrew was friends of friends but we got through to him and he instantly accepted the challenge and joined us for dinner as payment. He turned up with a CD in this envelope — "Gastronomic Plantyfication" he shoved it into my hands and said — "There you go! — And I didn't do any googles or downloads, not one, they're all in my collection, I bet no one else you asked has done that — it took me fucking ages!" He was, as so many of you described that evening, so humble, funny, and intelligent. I tried to keep in touch and would send him a message every now and then and we tried to get him to come to the opening of the restaurant once we were established but he didn't make it and alas we lost touch. I saw him every now and then in the street but never had the courage to remind him who I was, but I always listened to his show on NTS and kept up with his constant flow of creativity. What a shame to have lost him at such a young age. Cheers to you Andrew, from all of us who met you back then, wherever you are — we raise a glass to you, sir.

1.	Black Olives	The Bad Boys
2.	Sweet Bacon	Julien Covey & The Machine
3.	Bacon Fat	Andre Williams
4.	Garlic Bread	Garry & Larry
5.	Hot Potato	Guitar Red
6.	Gravy (For My Mashed Potatoes)	The Ventures
7.	Peanut Duck	Marsha Gee
8.	Duck Soup	Drumbago's Orchestra
9.	Onions	John Lee Hooker
10.	Fried Onions	Lord Rockingham's XI
11.	Pimento	Heavy Trash
12.	Pumpkin Pie	Kid Congo & The Pink Monkey Birds
13.	Wild Rice	Bill Justis
14.	Peas and Rice	Blind Blake
15.	Sultana	Titanic
16.	(Who's Got The) Tortillas	The Torquetts
17.	Hamburger Hop	Johnny Hicks
18.	Do The Chop	King Khan & The BBQ Show
19.	Meat Man	Jerry Lee Lewis
20.	Chicken Pot Pie	Ken Jones
21.	Puddings & Pies	Gustav Temple & the Blades
22.	My Daily Food	The Maytals
23.	Gastronomic Plantyfication	Bruce Haack

When I was a child, we used to drive to France a lot overnight, and my dad would soundtrack the entire ride. My dad has always loved music—interestingly, he was a DJ at college, where he studied electronics. He even built his own amplifier, which allowed him to connect two turntables and play one record after another—so in a way, my dad invented hip-hop way before Kool Herc. I would say "Don't You Want Me Baby" by Human League was the first song I really loved. Those bands from the '80s like Human League, Talking Heads, Prefab Sprout, Tears for Fears, Eurythmics, New Order, Pet Shop Boys, etc.…they became a sound that was ingrained in my head. That sound became the foundation for what I understood music to be. Unbeknownst to me, later on, the same synthesizers and drum machines would be used to make the dance records I would also fall in love with. That ultimately led me to wanting to make music myself. I even found some of those synth and drum machines and made music with them. ● I was also obsessed with food from a very early age. Music and food in Manchester went hand in hand, and the discovery of good food to be had nearby as well as good music was always something we pursued. I've had the fortune of seeing many amazing bands in really small spaces living in Manchester—like LCD Soundsystem at our student union in a 250-capacity room. Having seen James Murphy play many times, that was probably the best gig I've ever seen him play. Not one word to the crowd, no self-deprecating jokes, just the loudest onslaught of hypnotic rhythm I've ever heard. It had a big effect on me. Becoming friends with James, Nancy, Al, and all of LCD later on is one of those strange circles of life. ● Music is a big part of what we do at the restaurants. My brother and I have created a music consultancy service for the hospitality sector called Double Dutch. We provide the soundtrack to all three restaurants. The sound quality is amazing and the app we have been involved in developing allows us to control the soundtrack over a day. We can set the pace of the music to the busier parts of the restaurant and over a long period of time, we can remove sections of the playlist and bring them back. It means we have a really well-suited, constantly evolving soundtrack that the guests love; at the same time, the staff doesn't get bored. Creating the soundtracks for each of the businesses has been really great fun, too. They all vary. Clove Club is a mixture of classics all across the board. We play a lot of old soul, Balearic classics, afro, disco—but no hip-hop. At Luca, we work on keeping it classic with music from the '50s to the '70s, which has been a nice set of parameters in which to work. Two Lights is more fun: hip-hop, grunge, shoegaze, and now '90s hits! ● Good food is no longer the right of the privileged. In terms of the UK, for a long time in many ways restaurants were places that people who had money went to. This has changed massively; both the Internet and social media have made food a current interest, and a

Good food is no longer the right of the privileged.

younger generation has become much more aware of things like where produce comes from. Generation Z are drinking less and are socializing.

● I've always loved dancing, so from the beginning, the music I was drawn to was always stuff that I could dance to. The first albums I remember having were *The White Room* by the KLF; *3 Years, 5 Months and 2 Days in the Life Of…* by Arrested Development, and *3 Feet High and Rising* by De La Soul, all on tape around 1991 or '92. The first 7-inches I bought were Salt-N-Pepa's "Push It" and the charity single "Do They Know It's Christmas" in the mid 1980s. ● When I was growing up, music was all about tribes. Everything seems so much more fractured now; there isn't the big moment of EVERYONE talking about the new Number 1 on the charts. I went through many phases, from Jeru the Damaja and Wu-Tang and Gang Starr to Orbital and the Future Sound of London to the time that I got my own record player and bought Marvin Gaye's *What's Going On?* and *Trouble Man*. I grew up listening to and loving everything, across most genres: David Bowie, Fleetwood Mac, Talking Heads, Prince, Kate Bush, *Screamadelica* by Primal Scream, Oasis, the Beastie Boys, Queen, A Tribe Called Quest, Aretha, Blondie, and U-Roy, to name a few. ● For some reason, Glasgow always had a strong connection with Detroit and dance music, so in the mid to late '90s I went to a lot of parties in disused underground train tunnels in Glasgow and Underground Resistance gigs in curry houses in Paisley. If my fourteen-year-old self, dancing to Spastik by Plastikman at a Spiral Tribe rave, knew that twenty-five years later Richie Hawtin would be coming to my restaurant and writing emails to me, my mind would have been blown. ● I started cooking at home every day from age seven. I also already loved music by then, but I didn't think of them in the same sphere. These days people think chefs have important opinions on things, in the same way they would ask pop stars twenty years ago. As people have grown more interested in food, and restaurants and dining, it is only natural that chefs who have something interesting to say are being heard. Chefs used to be staff, the people who put in hard work behind the scenes to cook for you, while the maître d' was the important person in a restaurant, or the owner was in the dining room serving you. Chefs cooked what they were told to cook by the owner. As things shifted dramatically and chefs began to own restaurants and to cook creatively, they became the artists, and the general public wants to know more about them and what makes them tick. As we have gone down the path of opening our own restaurants, musicians and DJs have come to eat with us, and in a turning of the tables, those artists are thanking us for an amazing evening. That is something I never expected, but I have come to deeply appreciate it.

DID IT D

MISTRY

PREETI

Preeti Mistry is a two-time
James Beard award nominee
and was executive chef of
the now-closed Navi Kitchen
in Emeryville and Juhu Beach
Club in Oakland, California.
She is the co-author of the
Juhu Beach Club Cookbook.
Born in London and raised
in the United States,
Preeti has held executive
chef roles at the de Young
Museum in San Francisco
and Google headquarters in
Mountain View, California.

Emo Prep Playlist ▶ When I'm
prepping by myself or when
it's chill in the kitchen, I often
like a mix that is easy to sing
along with and that I can get
a bit "into my feelings" with
while working. This list is pretty
indicative of that flow; fun and
bouncy, but a bit deep here
and there.

1.	**Hustler Musik**	Lil Wayne
2.	**Sidewalks**	The Weeknd featuring Kendrick Lamar
3.	**YAH.**	Kendrick Lamar
4.	**Stay**	Rihanna ft. Mikky Ekko
5.	**Hollywood Divorce**	OutKast
6.	**Redbone**	Childish Gambino
7.	**Forgive Them Father**	Ms. Lauryn Hill
8.	**White Ferrari**	Frank Ocean
9.	**Holy Grail**	Jay-Z featuring Justin Timberlake
10.	**Sorry**	Beyoncé
11.	**I Like That**	Janelle Monae
12.	**All the Stars**	Kendrick Lamar and SZA
13.	**All of the Lights**	Kanye West featuring Rihanna
14.	**Headlines**	Drake
15.	**Trip**	Ella Mai

USA

GUJU Eggplant Parmesan SUB

To me, this sandwich captures the DNA of Gujarati cuisine translated into a hot, saucy, Italian-American-inspired sub.

Serves 4

½ cup whole coriander seeds

¼ cup whole cumin seeds

8 to 10 small Indian eggplants (aubergine)

2 teaspoons Kashmiri red chile powder

½ cup rice oil or other neutral oil

Salt

¼ cup fresh curry leaves

2 tablespoons finely minced fresh ginger

1 quart puréed tomato

4 hoagie rolls

Two 8-oz balls fresh mozzarella, sliced

¼ cup freshly grated Parmesan cheese

½ cup roughly chopped cilantro (coriander)

In a spice grinder or coffee grinder dedicated to spices, grind up the coriander and cumin together until finely ground. Mix well in a small bowl and set aside.

Trim the stems off the eggplants and cut in half lengthwise. In a small bowl, mix together half of the spice mixture, 1 teaspoon of the chile powder, half of the rice oil, and salt to taste. Spread the spice paste on a baking sheet lined with aluminum foil or parchment paper.

Preheat the oven to 350°F (180°C). Arrange the eggplants on the bed of spice paste and roast until very soft to the touch, 15 to 20 minutes.

In a saucepan, heat the remaining oil over high heat. Add the curry leaves and stir. The leaves will pop and crackle as they heat up. Add the ginger and the remaining spice mixture. Reduce the heat to medium and fry for about 2 minutes. Use a wooden spoon to stir and scrape the pan bottom; the ginger may stick and brown slightly. Pour in the puréed tomato and season with the remaining chile powder and salt to taste.

To assemble the sandwiches, preheat the broiler. Split the hoagie rolls through the thickness, leaving a hinge like the spine of a book, if you like. Line each cut side with sliced mozzarella. Place on a baking sheet and broil until the cheese melts. Remove from the oven and evenly distribute the roasted eggplant in each roll. Top with the tomato sauce, grated Parmesan, and a sprinkle of cilantro (coriander). Serve immediately.

Recipe Inspiration:

DNA.

by Kendrick Lamar

I think food is culture, just like music. It is a basic necessity; music is not, although the world would be a sad place without music. Like music, the food we cook and eat says a lot about who we are as a people.

My family—and for that matter people of Indian origin in general—loves to sing and dance. It's a big part of our culture; it's in all of our Bollywood movies, it's everywhere. When I think about family gatherings, I think first of food and music. There was always music playing, and singing—or these days, karaoke with songs in both English and Hindi. Oftentimes, when I think of cooking, whether at home or at work, I can't imagine it without some amount of singing and dancing. Both activities are a joyful expression of love.

●

My family is super into music. We took a lot of road trips growing up and I remember always singing along with the radio. My sisters and I would prepare lip-sync dance numbers that we would create to pop songs recorded off the radio and perform for my parents. Music has gotten me through so many hard times. It has always been there for me, whether I'm crying my eyes out or celebrating joys. There is always a soundtrack for what's happening in my life.

●

The music I fell in love with as a young kid was the Beatles. And as time went on, I continued to really relate to their arc of starting off their early years by being catchy and playful and then getting increasingly complicated and innovative. That's how I have approached my journey with cooking. At first cooking was fun and cool and in the spirit of anything goes; but as I've gotten older, I get more focused on technique and pushing myself out of my comfort zone. And I want to make a deeper impact on what Indian-American cuisine is in our world.

●

As a teen, I got into a lot of punk and alternative music—Fugazi, Ministry, the Smiths, etc...—and that definitely shaped my identity as an outsider. I was always hanging with the "weirdos" and wore that with a badge of honor. I fit in with those who didn't fit in. I didn't understand it at the time...I was just drawn to it. But now it all makes sense. I had always felt like an outsider, and that music embodies those sentiments. There's a part of the punk or rap/hip-hop/trap sort of philosophy that is very irreverent, and that still appeals to me and has definitely influenced my approach to cooking: the right

amount of creating something people crave with a healthy dose of IDGAF.

●

Singing along while working in the kitchen is almost mandatory for me, because it helps me do my work and concentrate. I get into a groove of cooking and listening or singing along. And there are different soundtracks for different parts of service. At my restaurants, I would often DJ during service, switching up the Pandora or Spotify stations to fit the mood. I always liked to find a good station to pump the staff up at the beginning of service. During peak service, I wanted something that felt like an "off the chain" party—Lil Wayne, Eve, Missy Elliott, and M.I.A.—to create the right vibe. Kendrick Lamar, Drake, and Lil Wayne speak to me in a way—the right combination of bravado, politics, and emo sort of hip-hop. My fave Pandora station is Frank Ocean, the perfect mix of hip-hop, R&B, and soul.

●

Speaking of IDGAF lessons from my youth, one night during dinner service at Juhu Beach Club, the restaurant was in high, ecstatic gear. It was bumping and diners were having a great time. One of the benefits of being the restaurant's chef and co-owner is that I can play whatever music I want to set the mood and vibe. On this particular night, I chose to play A Tribe Called Quest. There was this guy dining who was going crazy. He said, "This type of music is inappropriate and it's garbage music." He was heated and it was getting racist. I went to the customer's table and introduced myself. I said, "OK, you're being really rude, so we're gonna comp your whole dinner. I don't need your business."

●

I think food is culture, just like music. It is a basic necessity; music is not, although the world would be a sad place without music. Like music, the food we cook and eat says a lot about who we are as a people. Our race, nationality, socio-economic status, upbringing, politics, etc. all influence how and what we eat. I think the more we explore these connections and begin to value the people who make our food, the more our society will have reverence for the folks cooking, just like musicians.

BONNIE MORALES

The first-generation American daughter of Belarusian immigrants, Chef Bonnie Morales grew up in Chicago in a large family that brought with them the distinctive culture of food and drink of the former Soviet Union. She trained at the Culinary Institute of America and in top kitchens in New York and Chicago. Kachka opened in Portland in 2014, inspired by the food of the former Soviet Republics.

with Celery Root, Black Trumpet Mushrooms, and Birch Salt

Kachka Distilled Playlist ▶ This is essentially what drives and inspires Kachka musically. If I had to explain to someone what we cook, using music alone, I would give them this playlist and just walk away.

1.	Belye Rozy (White Roses)	Yuri Shatunov
2.	Шатья Беспризорная	Анатолий Колмыков and Игорь Луньков
3.	Million Roses	Alla Pugacheva
4.	Желтые Тюльпаны (Yellow Tulips)	Natasha Korolyova
5.	Podmoskovnye Vechera (Moscow Nights)	Vladimir Troshin
6.	Zvyozdy Nas Zhdut (The Stars Are Waiting)	Mirage
7.	Vashe Blagorodie	Bulat Okudzhava
8.	Farewell of Slavianka	Red Army Choir
9.	Кони привередливые (Unruly Horses)	Vladimir Vysotsky
10.	Белоруссия (Belarus)	Pesniary
11.	Zvezdnoe Leto	Alla Pugacheva
12.	Gulyanka	Verka Serduchka
13.	Ne Plach, Rodnaya Mat' (Don't Cry, Motherland)	Butyrka
14.	Люди встречаются	Веселые Ребята
15.	Крутится, вертится шар голубой (Krutitsya, Vertitsya Shar Goluboy)	Chervona

▼ Bonnie Morales

Black Cod 'Po Nyomenski'

Recipe: Black Cod 'Po Nyomenski' with Celery Root, Black Trumpet Mushrooms, and Birch Salt

The idea of just "half an hour before the spring" gives me such a very specific feeling. It channels that time in very late winter when it feels like it will never end. It's the bottom of the root cellar. Everyone is tired of the endless white blanketing of snow. But there, in the distance, you see a crocus peeking out. You can't do anything about it yet. The farm vendor lists are still all onions and potatoes, but it's this kernel of hope that pops inside of you. So this dish evokes just that feeling: It is merely the hope of spring.

Serves 4

1 cup cream

1 tablespoon dried birch leaves

Salt for seasoning, plus 1 tablespoon

1 celery root (celeriac)

4 oz butter

2 tablespoons honey

Four 4-oz pieces black cod

1 to 2 oz neutral cooking oil

1 cup black trumpet mushrooms

2 tablespoons celery leaves
(about 20 smaller chartreuse or yellow leaves, not the large green ones)

Birch salt (recipe follows)

In a saucepan, bring the cream to a boil over medium-high heat, then reduce the heat to maintain a low simmer. Stir in the birch leaves. Remove from the heat and let steep for 5 minutes. Strain the leaves and discard. Season the cream lightly with salt. Let cool, then refrigerate until ready to use. (The birch cream can be made up to 3 days in advance.) ▶❙

Recipe Inspiration:

ЗА ПОЛЧАСА ДО ВЕСНЫ

Half an Hour Before the Spring by Pesnyary Песняры

Peel the celery root (celeriac) and slice into 1-inch (2.5-cm) planks. Punch out plugs using a 1-inch-diameter ring cutter. Sous-vide the celery root plugs with the butter, honey, and 1 tablespoon salt for 60 minutes at 185°F (85°C). Have ready a bowl filled with ice and water.

Remove the celery root and immediately place in the prepared ice bath. When cool, refrigerate until ready to use. (The celery root plugs can be cooked up to 3 days in advance.)

Using an immersion circulator, heat a water bath to 122°F (50°C).

Season the black cod pieces with salt and put in a vac bag with the birch cream. Seal, place in the water bath, and poach for 40 minutes.

About 5 minutes before the fish is ready, get 2 sauté pans hot and drizzle a slick of oil in each one. When the oil is hot, sauté the mushrooms in one pan until they have released their juices and are tender with some crispy edges. Season with salt. Transfer to a paper towel to absorb excess oil.

In the second pan, sauté the celery root plugs to brown them. Flip over each plug when the first side is golden brown. When the plugs are warmed through and browned on the 2 flat sides, transfer to a paper towel to absorb excess oil.

When the fish is finished poaching, gently remove each piece from the bag and place in the center of a dinner plate or shallow bowl. Transfer the poaching liquid to a sauté pan and simmer until reduced by half. Gently spoon the reduced liquid over the fish. Place 5 or 6 celery root plugs around the fish, followed by a scattering of the sautéed mushrooms. Garnish with the celery leaves and birch salt and serve immediately.

■ Birch Salt

3 tablespoons dried birch leaves

1 tablespoon kosher salt

In a spice grinder, finely grind the birch leaves. Pass through a fine-mesh strainer to remove any large pieces from the fine powder. Add the salt and stir to mix well. Store the birch salt in an airtight container in a cool, dark place.

▲ Bonnie Morales

you can almost taste the dishes just by listening

● My brother is eight years older than me. He is my only sibling, so of course, I wanted to do everything he did. That meant listening to Iron Maiden and watching *Headbangers Ball* on MTV when I was in grade school and collecting Grateful Dead show tapes in high school. I am pretty sure I was the only kid in my third-grade class that didn't know who New Kids On The Block was, and I sort of wore that as a badge of pride—even then I knew it was a way to stand apart from others rather than connect, to have my own identity. ● I first fell in love with music in fourth grade. My parents got me a CD player for my birthday that year and my brother took me to the store and helped me pick out my first CD. It was *Sgt. Pepper's Lonely Hearts Club Band*. I had never heard of the Beatles before and it just changed everything. But the first song I fell in love with was Madonna's

"La Isla Bonita." I have no idea why, but I do remember dancing on the coffee table when the music video would come up on MTV. The music that has had the profoundest impact though, is the music that my parents would play in the car when I was a kid. An eclectic mix of mid-century Soviet bards, mostly, the most well known of which is Vladimir Vysotsky, often described as the Bob Dylan of Soviet Russia. ● I started playing clarinet in fourth grade and when I was going into high school, I wanted to quit, but my parents told me they would pay for me to go on the marching band trip to Florida that upcoming spring if I didn't. So, I stayed—and ended up forming incredibly close friendships through playing music. I'm not a good musician at all, but I love music, and more than anything, I cherished the camaraderie. I am a bona-fide band nerd, proud of it, and while I was never good at playing an instrument, I loved doing it. I loved being able to understand and manipulate sound to make something. It is empowering and satisfying. When I started cooking, I think it finally satisfied some of those same desires. I see a connection between playing music and making food. Both require a great deal of skill, and when done well, can move people deeply. ● Music plays a significant role at the Russian table. Usually,

as people get a few shots of vodka in, they start singing! Sometimes one of my mom's cousins would bring a guitar or my dad's friend would bring an accordion to accompany the singing. When I hear popular recordings of some of those tunes, I am instantly transported to that dinner table. I love it! In both my cooking and the music I love, I tend to gravitate toward simplicity. I like dishes with two or three components and songs with a simple but strong melody. I like clean flavors and tend to focus on just highlighting their essence by reinforcing them, rather than cooking with a "wall of sound," if you will. I am drawn to certain music and food because of who I am, and not necessarily the music and food I first fell in love with. How they both resonate with me is a reflection of what is happening in my life at the time more so than anything else. ● Music is so moving for me that I can't work when there is any music playing at all. It is too distracting. I allow music to play in our kitchen when we are not in service, so long as it is at a modest volume level, because I don't want to be a stick in the mud. But if it were just up to me, I would want silence. I am constantly reminding cooks that cooking involves all the senses. Out of the corner of my eye, I may see someone using too much force to grate a potato and I know it's not cooked all the way through. I can

hear when a pan is too hot and burning a protein by the sound of the sizzle. And what chef doesn't cringe when they hear the blender being run with something too thick in the pitcher. The frenetic whine of the kitchen printer spewing out new orders can send your adrenaline shooting. When you have music in the mix, the natural soundtrack of a kitchen is muted. ● That being said, I LOVE the Kachka playlist and how invigorating it can be. It's so perfectly curated to match our food that you can almost taste the dishes just by listening. I'm sure that sounds corny, but it's really how I feel. My husband and I are incredibly picky about what kind of music we play. As a result, we hand-pick every song that goes on our playlist, and guests notice. It's all painstakingly compiled from random CDs found in flea markets in Belarus and things like that. ● There are many parallels with music and cooking. Anyone who has an interest in music would naturally find its structure and concepts instructive and inspirational, but I also think that the same guiding principles apply to virtually all artistic pursuits, including cooking. I don't think, for me at least, that influences are restricted to music alone; it's all jumbled up, and that's kind of the point. Art and craft, because while cooking really is a craft in many instances, it has also infinite intersections with art.

▼ Bonnie Morales

Recipe: Black Cod 'Po Nyomenski' with Celery Root, Black Trumpet Mushrooms, and Birch Salt

01:95

YURI NOMURA

Yuri Nomura's venture into the food industry began early in life, with the influence of her mother's traditional Japanese cooking classes. She moved to England in 1998, then, after training at several restaurants, she landed in Berkeley, California, in 2010 to work in the kitchen at Chez Panisse. In 2012, she opened restaurant eatrip in Tokyo. Yuri also writes for magazines, teaches cooking classes, directs catering events, and is a radio MC.

Song: O mio babbino caro by Maria Callas

A "Melancholic" Mood Playlist ▶
I usually save the songs I like regardless of the categories and shuffle them. My playlist this time is a "melancholic" mood that has a tasty theme as well.

1.	Fast Car	Tracy Chapman
2.	Heartbeats	José González
3.	Pink Moon	Nick Drake
4.	Revenge of the Flowers	Malcolm McLaren
5.	New York, I Love You but You're Bringing Me Down	LCD Soundsystem
6.	girls	Masakatsu Takagi
7.	Moon River	Audrey Hepburn
8.	I Dare You	The xx
9.	Thugz Mansion	2Pac featuring Nas, J. Phoenix
10.	Still Crazy After All These Years	Paul Simon
11.	Just in Time	Nina Simone
12.	These Days	Nico
13.	Gymnopédie No. 1	Erik Satie
14.	Condition of the Heart	Susanna and the Magical Orchestra
15.	Blue Moon Revisited (Song for Elvis)	Cowboy Junkies
16.	Walk Away	Ben Harper
17.	Betty Blue	Gabriel Yared
18.	Life Is Just a Bowl of Cherries	Doris Day
19.	This Must Be the Place (Naive Melody)	Talking Heads
20.	Gotta Have You	The Weepies
21.	Drown	Smashing Pumpkins
22.	Coffee and Cigarettes	Augustana
23.	God	John Lennon
24.	Everybody Had A Hard Year	März

Barley and Girl

This is a song of a woman in love, and rich, earthy scenery floats in my head when I listen to it. When I first heard this song, it conjured the image of this dish and I came up with the recipe below.

Serves 2

4 lamb chops

Salt and freshly ground black pepper

2 tablespoons cumin seed

1 red onion, chopped

2 tablespoons neutral oil

90 g barley, rinsed and drained

4 tomatoes

2 bay leaves

1 head garlic, cloves crushed

2 potatoes, peeled and thinly sliced

2 tablespoons raisins, chopped

1 small preserved lemon, halved

2 slices pain de campagne, toasted

3 tablespoons sour cream

Long pepper powder, for finishing

Recipe Inspiration:

O mi^o babbin^o ^o car^o

by Maria Callas

Prick the lamb chops in a few places on both sides with a fork and season with salt and pepper, and cumin seeds. Let them sit at room temperature for 30 minutes.

Stir the onion in a pot with a little oil over medium heat. Add the barley, whole tomatoes, bay leaves and 270 cc water and bring to a simmer over low heat.

In a sauté pan, heat a little more oil over high heat. When the oil is hot, add the lamb chops and garlic cloves and sear well on both sides. Transfer to the pot with the tomatoes and barley.

Add the potatoes to the pot and simmer until the potatoes are almost tender. Add the raisins and lemon and simmer for another 10 minutes. Taste and adjust the seasoning.

Spoon onto 2 plates, dividing everything evenly. Place a slice of pain de campagne alongside and spread with the sour cream. Finish with the long pepper powder and serve immediately.

Song: O mio babbino caro by Maria Callas

▲ Yuri Nomura

Both sound and food are created to be

I became aware of music with my mother singing me lullabies. As I got older, the first few songs I fell in love with were the Carpenters's "I Need to Be in Love," Daryl Hall & John Oates's "Rich Girl," Satie's "Gymonopédie," and "Clair de Lune" by Debussy. I've never seen Jorge Donn dance to Ravel's "Bolero" live, but I have seen Sylvie Guillem and Yasuyuki Shuto's version, and I've watched the video of Donn many times. Their dances stick in my head and create and connect to a lively motion that comes through my ears and into my body. I've learned the strength of the energy that resonates through these connections—the strength to be mixed with many, and the strength of one person. I sometimes rewatch the video of the dances just to stir the power of creativity.

When I started making a living with food and cooking in my late twenties, I soon noticed that music was indispensable in order to enjoy eating, and also for defining the atmosphere and space. At the restaurant, we change the selection of songs depending on the prep time, the opening time, and the day of the week. I will play "Sunday Morning" by the Velvet Underground & Nico on a Sunday morning. I'll also play "Sometimes It Snows in April" by Prince in the month of April. The choice of music is a tool that may better communicate certain thoughts and feelings of a cook. Sometimes it can transmit a stronger and more personal message than the food, even though it cannot be eaten.

One has a chance to get to know another side of a person by their preference for songs and music. My younger self had an equation: good taste in music = good sense. For example, I cannot forget that when my uncle died in the hospital room, he was listening to Frank Sinatra's "Smile" until the end.

Another touching moment I will always remember came when I was traveling in Taiwan. There I heard the Ami, the native people in Taiwan, sing a song in their native language that had been passed down orally. I couldn't stop my tears at that moment. (The same language was sampled by the band Enigma.)

Years ago, I went to Shimanto in Kōchi Prefecture with some chefs and the musician Hanaregumi. There we tried to make a meal with music, serving up songs and dishes, while alternately inspiring and affecting each other. It was a deep lesson for me; in the end, I just found out that the power of music was overwhelmingly too strong, and I could not be still for a while.

I produced a play inspired by food that cannot be eaten called *Shoku-no-kodou-inner eatrip* (which translates to "the heartbeat of the food or meal"). The energy of the food that the audience felt was from the noise and smell: kill → cook → eat. It was a live performance staged to show the circulation of the body, the flow of food and life by combining live music and the sound and smell of the process of butchering, dressing the carcass, and eating.

The relationship between good food and good music is about making time for both to create something special. When I'm by myself in the restaurant in the morning and evening, the music I listen to makes me relax. I will listen to "Marginalia #2" and "Girls" by Masakatsu Takagi. Sometimes, to get my creative energy going, I will loop one song over and over, listening only to that until I get bored. One of those songs is "Thugz Mansion" by 2Pac.

Sometimes a musician whose music we are playing at the restaurant will eat here. When that happens, I listen to their music even more, and add it to my playlist to honor their visit. Once a friend from L.A., an olive oil maker, came to eatrip and had a party. It was May and the weather was good. I found myself I was sitting on the ground with a number of musicians who were also visiting us, and the soundtrack became an improvised live set with all the people at the restaurant. Food and music fit together in a way that I knew would remain in the memories of the people there, creating a place and time associated with them. Both sound and food are created to be experienced and then disappear, but they are things that go inside people. Sounds, foods, and places all come together, and will be a memory of time.

experienced and then disappear

YOSHI OKAI

Yoshi Okai was born and raised in Kyoto, Japan, where he was introduced to the culinary world at a young age through his family's catering company. Because of his parents' hectic work schedules, Okai and his three siblings were often responsible for cooking meals. In 1998, Okai landed in Austin to dedicate time and energy to his band, the Kodiaks. He then began work at Benihana alongside Ramen Tatsu-ya's Tatsu Aikawa and Thai-Kun's Thai Changthong. In 2015, Yoshi was named head chef of Otoko.

Yoshibori Playlist ▶ Play for me!!!!
Rock!! Japanese cuisine!!

1.	**My Dreams**	The Gun Club
2.	**Inca**	Wednesday Campanella
3.	**Contraption / Soul Desert**	Thee Oh Sees
4.	**Hot Blonde Cocktail**	Chrome Cranks
5.	**Third Uncle**	Brian Eno
6.	**Worm Tamer**	Grinderman
7.	**Neat Neat Neat**	The Damned
8.	**Break 'Em Down**	Soledad Brothers
9.	**Confetti**	Cold Cave
10.	**Breathe the Fire**	The Soft Moon
11.	**A Love Supreme**	John Coltrane
12.	**Bela Lugosi's Dead**	Bauhaus
13.	**To Think You've Chosen Me**	Sonny Stitt
14.	**Fire of Love**	Jody Reynolds
15.	**Box Number**	The Boys
16.	**Spoonful**	Howlin' Wolf
17.	**Young Men Dead**	The Black Angels

▲ Yoshi Okai

USA

OTOKO

Just breaking the Japanese cooking rules. Traditionally, you can't sear with charcoal directly on top of any proteins. Even I hold the charcoal when I sear the fish.

Serves as many as you like

Hamachi (yellowtail) sashimi

Olive oil

Soy sauce

Jacobsen or other hand-harvested finishing sea salt

Small sprigs of bronze fennel

Build a hot fire using Japanese charcoal (*binchotan*) in a charcoal grill. Oil the grill rack well.

Sprinkle a few drops of olive oil on the hamachi right before searing.

Arrange the hamachi on the grill rack and sear for 10 seconds on each side.

Transfer the fish to a platter or plates, drizzle with a few drops of soy sauce, and sprinkle with the finishing salt. Garnish with fennel sprigs and serve immediately.

BINCHOTAN SEARED HAMACHI

Recipe Inspiration:

I FOUGHT THE LAW

by The Clash

Service almost feels like

a
live
show

It's hard to say exactly how and when music shaped who I am today, but it has shaped me completely. When I was a kid, animation and TV show theme songs were some of the first songs that hooked me. It was really just me and my family growing up, and music brought us together—that along with my mean piano teacher! I've always listened to and loved so many different types of music—everything from operas, musicals, classical, rock, punk, old school Japanese, and more. I love the band The Gun Club—they were some of the first to mix punk and blues for that country rockabilly!! I think my taste in musical mixes has definitely influenced who I am today.

Before I got into food, I was a musician. I joined my first band at fifteen or sixteen years old, but we never played shows. When I moved to Austin, I gave up landscaping school for music. That was when I became the lead vocalist in the punk rock band the Kodiaks, and we became pretty popular. I also played in a band called Kuroneko (Black Cat). I'm not currently playing in a band, but still love going to shows! Since then, music has always had an impact on everything I do. It's an ongoing big influence, and my musical roots inspire me every day.

For me, music is a big motivator and drives how I work with and think about food. In many ways, food and music are almost the same. You have your own style and preferences, but that can keep changing and evolving. And, both music and good food are for people who know what they want. Still, you have to constantly play with new ideas, or it can get boring! If you compare music from ten years ago to right now, it's totally different. People are the same way in how they crave food, so as a chef, you have to change it up and create new stuff.

Otoko is a seasonal tasting table, so every day it's different and I'm right there with the guests. Service almost feels like a live show—me and the audience. At Otoko, I play the music I need and like; it helps me stay motivated, and that motivation translates to our guests. It depends on the day—sometimes we'll play classic music, some days '80s, garage rock, or psych rock... it just depends on my mood, or my theme. For example, I've done a grilled dish set to "Ring of Fire" by Johnny Cash. I am inspired by the similar tension and relaxation I find in the music I love and the food I cook. Putting them together creates my best work and the best experience for the guests. I love it!

KWAME ONWUACHI

Young Kwame Onwuachi cooked in his mother's catering kitchen in the Bronx, peeling shrimp and stirring roux for gumbo. In 2016, Onwuachi opened modern American fine-dining restaurant the Shaw Bijou in Washington, D.C. In 2017, he moved on to open Kith/Kin in the InterContinental Hotel in D.C., where his food explores the influences of his mother's Creole and Jamaican roots and his grandfather's Nigerian heritage. At the 2019 James Beard Awards, Onwuachi took home the medal for Rising Star Chef of the Year.

Song: Black Cow by Steely Dan

What I Like Playlist ▶ This list is honestly just songs that I can listen to any day. Songs I can listen to in the shower, cooking, or driving. Songs that just make me and the people around me feel good!

1.	**Swagger like Us**	Jay-Z and T.I. featuring Kanye West, and Lil Wayne
2.	**Drip Too Hard**	Lil Baby X Gunna
3.	**Shot Clock**	Ella Mai
4.	**Friends**	The Carters
5.	**Black Cow**	Steely Dan
6.	**Middle Child**	J. Cole
7.	**Neighbors**	J. Cole
8.	**The London**	Young Thug featuring Travis Scott and J. Cole
9.	**Everything Is Everything**	Ms. Lauryn Hill
10.	**Apple Tree**	Erykah Badu
11.	**Twinz (Deep Cover 98)**	Big Pun featuring Fat Joe
12.	**Lean Back**	Terror Squad featuring Fat Joe and Remy Ma
13.	**Get Em High**	Kanye West featuring Common and Talib Kweli
14.	**Jesus Walks**	Kanye West

Black Cow

Black Cow

Recipe Inspiration: **Black Cow**

by **Steely Dan**

This is a nod to Steely Dan and the first song that I ever fell in love with.

Serves 4

3 lb boneless short ribs

Kosher salt

Canola oil, as needed

2 tablespoons tomato paste

2 tablespoons black bean paste

3 tablespoons black sesame seeds

3 carrots, peeled and chopped

1 head celery, cored and chopped

2 yellow onions, quartered

1 garlic head, halved

2 cups dry red wine

2 lb chicken feet

3 quarts chicken stock

2 tablespoons brown sugar

Freshly ground black pepper

Preheat the oven to 300°F (150°C).

Season the short ribs generously with the salt.

In a large ovenproof sauté pan, heat a big swirl of canola oil over high heat. When the oil is hot, add the short ribs and sear, turning as needed, until caramelized on all sides. Transfer the short ribs to a plate. Reduce the heat to medium and add tomato paste, black bean paste, sesame seeds, carrots, celery, onions, and garlic. Cook for about 5 minutes, stirring rapidly.

Add the wine and scrape the bits off the bottom of the pan with a wooden utensil. Cook until the sauce is reduced to a syrupy consistency.

Add the short ribs and any juices accumulated on the plate, the chicken feet, and the stock and stir well. Cover the pan with plastic wrap (cling film) and then aluminum foil and braise in the oven for 3 hours.

After 3 hours, remove the short ribs from the liquid, discard the chicken feet, and strain the liquid. Place the liquid in a pot, add the brown sugar, and reduce until syrupy, about 1 hour. Season the glaze with salt and pepper and pour over the short ribs. Pair with your favorite vegetable or starch.

you
can't
throw
a

Song: Black Cow by Steely Dan

musical
event

without
food

and
you
can't
throw

a
food

I first became aware of music when I was two years old, and music continued to be pretty much everything to me when I was young. The very first song I fell in love with was "Black Cow" by Steely Dan. The entire song spoke to me—the beat, the cadence, the lyrics, everything. At that time, music allowed me to be free in the same way that cooking does today. It accompanied me on the way to school. It was something I listened to when I was happy or sad; whether it was Biggie Smalls, Lauryn Hill, Steely Dan, David Bowie, Hootie & the Blowfish, Nirvana, or Erykah Badu, music was a constant in my life, a way I could express myself and a way to connect with my family. I remember belting out at the top of my lungs "AND IIIIII-I-I-I-I-IIIII!!!!!" from Whitney Houston's version of Dolly Parton's "I Will Always Love You" and my family cracking up at me. That's one of my earliest memories of music letting me be free and express who I really am.

●

As I got older, I really gravitated to Jimi Hendrix, because he inspired me to push the boundaries of creativity. He was just the first of many artists that shaped me and grew the way in which I saw the world. I remember going to see Nas, another artist who taught me about pushing boundaries. It was my first concert and it was so fun. Seeing someone perform songs I had been hearing for as long as I could remember was life-changing, because it took my love of music to another level. It showed me that I could connect with someone's art in real life. I see both music and cooking as a total expression of oneself and one's creativity.

●

My mother was a chef, so food's influence took hold very early on for me. She would teach me recipes, all the while playing classic rock and a lot of Hootie & the Blowfish! In Africa, music is a big part of our culture, especially in celebrations, so music and food go hand in hand. In my village in Nigeria, for big events, we always invite a band and slaughter a goat. These traditions are deeply touching, and basically taught me that you can't throw a musical event without food and you can't throw a food event without music. For me, food and music will always be integral parts of celebrating both creative expression and people coming together.

music

event without

HUGO ORTEGA

Hugo Ortega was raised in Mexico City and Puebla, Mexico, and acquired his love of cooking from both his mother and his grandmother, a revered mole maker. At seventeen, he left Mexico for Houston and began his hospitality career as a dishwasher and busboy at Backstreet Cafe before graduating from culinary school and becoming Backstreet's executive chef and owner, along with his wife, Tracy Vaught. His American dream continued when they opened Hugo's, Caracol, Backstreet Cafe, and Xochi. Hugo is the author of two cookbooks and the recipient of a James Beard Award.

Bike Rides Playlist ▶ This is a portion of the playlist I use when I take bike rides. Some of the songs are upbeat for more energy and others are great for getting my mind off how tired I am. I usually ride with my brother-in-law and our friend who was previously a professional biker. They are stronger riders than I am, so I have to keep my energy up to not fall hopelessly behind. This playlist helps me do that most of the time.

Recipe Inspiration:

Over the Rainbow

1.	**Acceptance**	Set and Setting
2.	**Bohemian Rhapsody**	Queen
3.	**Clocks**	Coldplay
4.	**Desert Rose**	Sting and Cheb Mami
5.	**Kryptonite**	Three Doors D
6.	**Dirty Dancer**	Enrique Iglesias
7.	**Disturbia**	Rihanna
8.	**Grenade**	Bruno Mars
9.	**Havana**	Camila Cabello featuring Young Thug
10.	**Knocked Up**	Kings of Leon
11.	**La Tortura**	Shakira
12.	**Little Talks**	Of Monsters and Men
13.	**Mirrors**	Justin Timberlake

▲ Hugo Ortega

USA

Huachinango
CEVICHE VERDE

This is such a sweet song. Israel was so beloved in his community that after he passed away, the whole town helped to spread his ashes in the sea. This ceviche is a simple one, just like the song—but like the song, it leaves a lasting impression.

Serves 6

by

Israel Kamakawiwo'ole

24 oz red snapper fillets, cut into ½-inch cubes

3 cups fresh lime juice, plus 2 to 3 tablespoons

1 nopal paddle, spikes and knobs removed, cut into small cubes and blanched for 1 minute (to remove the sliminess)

1 cup peeled, seeded, and diced cucumber

1 poblano pepper, peeled, seeded, roasted, and cut into medium dice

½ cup pitted Manzanilla olives, finely chopped

2 tablespoons finely chopped onion

2 tablespoons olive oil

■ For the *salsa verde*:

1 cup cilantro (coriander) leaves, roughly chopped

½ cup flat-leaf parsley leaves, roughly chopped

2 leaves *hoja santa* (Mexican pepperleaf), roughly chopped

1 serrano chile, seeded and roughly chopped

1 garlic clove, roughly chopped

1 small poblano pepper, stemmed, seeded, and roughly chopped

1 cup roughly chopped cucumber

½ cup water

¼ cup fresh lime juice

Sea salt to taste

½ cup vegetable oil

Thinly sliced radishes, seeded and thinly sliced red and green jalapeños, and little spirals of cucumber, for garnish

In a bowl, toss the snapper in the 3 cups lime juice and "cook" in the refrigerator for 30 minutes, stirring every 10 minutes.

Meanwhile, in a deep bowl, stir together the nopal, cucumber, poblano, olives, onion, olive oil, and 2 to 3 tablespoons lime juice, to taste. When the snapper is done, strain in a fine-mesh strainer and add to the bowl with the nopal mixture. Toss gently to mix well. Cover the ceviche and refrigerate until ready to serve.

To make the *salsa verde*, combine all of the ingredients except the oil in a blender and blend for 45 seconds, then slowly add the oil and blend until an emulsified coarse purée forms. Drain the salsa in a fine-mesh strainer.

To serve, spoon the ceviche into 6 shallow bowls, dividing it evenly. Pour a bit of the *salsa verde* around the ceviche in each bowl and garnish with the radishes, jalapeños, and little spirals of cucumber. Serve immediately.

When I first came
to the United States,
I didn't know many
people and didn't
speak the language.

Song: Over the Rainbow by Israel Kamakawiwoʻole

I was

very

lonely.

▲ Hugo Ortega

My great-grandfather played the fiddle, one of my uncles played the trombone, and another played the tuba. There is always music during holidays and celebrations in my house. The traditional music is *música del viento*, which is played during Day of the Dead or when families or communities get together to make the candles to be used on the altars or in the cemetery. There is also an annual patron saint of the town celebration where favorite songs like "Canción Mixteca" by José López Alavez are always played.

When I lived in the countryside with my grandmother, everyone worked so hard every day. My grandmother was a good cook. She was one of a group of special mole makers that traveled to nearby towns to help families make the mole for weddings. There was always music and great food. Sometimes there were so many people that they would cook a whole cow underground. Whenever there was a celebration, there was always music and great food. The people of my region where I grew up loved to celebrate with family and neighbors.

"La Llorona" is a very popular Mexican folk song from about a hundred years ago that people listen to during the Day of the Dead. It is about a woman who lost her children, and her ghost travels along the riverbed crying as she searches for them. Every time I make a traditional *mole negro*, I think of that song.

When I first came to the United States, I didn't know many people and didn't speak the language. I was very lonely. I listened to music and watched television, which helped me learn the language and the culture. I was hungry to understand America when I came to this country. I listened to the radio and learned the song lyrics, and that really helped me to learn English. That's how I came to love Bruce Springsteen. His music is so American. He sings about common working people and he puts so much effort into his music. He helped me understand the ways of Americans better.

I listened to music and watched television, which helped me learn the language and the culture.

CHRISTIE PETERS
AND KYLE MICHAEL

Christie Peters is the owner and executive chef of two restaurants in Saskatoon, Saskatchewan, with her partner, Kyle Michael. Christie and Kyle's restaurants run full circle — they employ a horticulturist on staff and compost all of the waste from the restaurants, which is then returned to the gardens in which they grow their vegetables. They use many ancient and modern preservation techniques to help the produce they grow last the restaurants all winter long.

Song: Benny and The Jets by Biz Markie

Bangers That Keep Banging Playlist
▶ These are the bangers that just won't quit. Music influences everything: the staff's mood, the guests' moods as well as their spending habits, their energy, and how much they eat and drink. This is a playlist I put on when the restaurant is busy and everyone is having a great time. It's pretty incredible how music can change people's entire day.

1.	**Drop It Like It's Hot**	Snoop Dogg featuring Pharrell
2.	**Power**	Kanye West
3.	**King Kunta**	Kendrick Lamar
4.	**Juicy**	Notorious B.I.G.
5.	**Get Free**	Major Lazer featuring Amber Coffman
6.	**Nice for What**	Drake
7.	**N***as in Paris**	Jay-Z and Kanye West
8.	**Goldie**	A$AP Rocky
9.	**Mercy**	Kanye West
10.	**Still D.R.E.**	Dr. Dre featuring Snoop Dogg

TROUT EGGS BENEDICT

W I T H

HOME-CURED ROE

A N D

GREENS

I once saw Biz perform this song, clearly inebriated, and I like picturing him eating this eggs Benny with a hangover and a mimosa.

Serves 4

Recipe Inspiration:

BENNY

A
N THE JETS
D

by
Biz Markie

■ For the citrus-cured trout:

600 g salt

400 g sugar

Zest of 2 grapefruits

Zest of 2 lemons

Zest of 2 limes

Zest of 2 oranges

1 whole trout, about 2 lb, cleaned

■ For the home-cured trout roe:

500 ml water

150 g salt

1 fresh trout roe sack,
you can buy from your local fish supplier

■ For the lemon–olive oil vinaigrette:

600 ml olive oil

200 ml fresh lemon juice

½ clove garlic, finely grated

■ For the hollandaise sauce:

4 egg yolks

1 tablespoon white wine reduction

1 lb butter, clarified

A few drops of lemon juice or water, if needed

■ **2 tablespoons salt**

250 ml white vinegar

10 liters water

8 eggs

4 croissants

Worcestershire sauce, Tabasco, fresh lemon juice, and salt, for serving

4 handfuls spring greens

▶I

To cure the trout, in a bowl, stir together all of the ingredients except the trout. Put the trout on a plate and coat with 3 cups of the citrus-salt mixture coat heavily put a layer underneath the skin. Cover and let sit in the fridge overnight. Remove from the fridge, rinse, and pat dry. Refrigerate until ready to serve. To cure the roe, in a bowl, mix the water and salt together for a 30% salt brine. Rinse the roe sack under cold running water. Place the roe sack in the brine for 1 hour. Remove the sack from the brine and rinse again. Spread to dry, then separate the roe from the membrane and discard the membrane.

To make the vinaigrette, combine the ingredients in a sealable container. Shake to emulsify. Set side at room temperature.

To make the hollandaise sauce, whisk together the egg yolks and white wine reduction in a double boiler until a sabayon forms. Slowly add the clarified butter, whisking to emulsify. Adjust the viscosity with lemon juice or water, if needed. Season with Worcestershire, Tabasco, lemon juice, and salt to your desired taste (we like lots of lemon). Set aside and keep warm.

When ready to serve, poach the eggs: In a large sauté pan, stir the 2 tablespoons salt and 250 ml white vinegar into the 10 liters of water. Bring to a gentle boil. Crack 2 eggs into a small bowl. Holding the bowl close to the top of the pan, slide the eggs into the boiling water. Poach large eggs for 3 minutes and 30 seconds. Using a slotted spoon, transfer to paper towels to drain briefly. Repeat until all 8 eggs are poached.

To assemble, slice the croissants in half through the thickness and arrange on plates, cut side up. Slice the trout into thin pieces. Top each croissant half with trout, then 2 poached eggs. Spoon the hollandaise over all and sprinkle with ¼ teaspoon trout roe. Garnish with Worcestershire, Tabasco, lemon juice, and salt to your desired taste (we like lots of lemon). Toss the greens in the vinaigrette and add a handful to each plate. Serve and enjoy!

● **Christie** ● The first music I fell in love with was Alanis Morissette's album *Jagged Little Pill* and Aretha Franklin's "Respect," which made me feel rebellious and excited. My parents weren't the best cooks and I was taught to just eat what was put in front of me. When I moved out, I started cooking things from scratch, and I listened to Neil Young's "Old Man" on repeat for inspiration. During the early days, I went through a hard time trying to find myself as a chef and restaurateur. I have an '80s and '90s rock playlist that helps me get through the tougher days. They include artists like Alana Miles, Bonnie Raitt, and Chris Isaak, to name a few.

● **Kyle** ● I first became aware of music and the lifestyle that goes along with it at the age of three. My dad was in a blues and rock cover band and my parents would come home from a gig with a crew and make me get out of bed to dance. The first song I fell in love with was "Copperhead Road" by Steve Earle. My mom would blast music while we cleaned the house or got stuff ready for dinner. She says I used to scream "Copperhead Road" every time we got in her Firebird.

● **Christie & Kyle** ● The culinary world is a nonconformist lifestyle, as is the music world. We both listen to music that is underground and alternative, which is reflected in our restaurants. We are known for the music we play and our attitude inspired by that, so it brings the same kind of cooks, staff, and guests to us. Groups and artists like Factor Chandelier, Father John Misty, Aesop Rock, and White Lung really match our aesthetic.
● The music influences the vibe of the night. Nothing gets us going quite like the album *Smash* by the Offspring, start to finish. The last hour before service, when we think we just might not make it, that album gets us running, and when we run, the kitchen runs. It definitely makes us feel like badass, no-fucks-given pirates. We listen to the same music in the front and back, so sometimes we have to shut it off in the kitchen during peak times when things get crazy. As service gets going, we listen to calm tunes and then amp it up as the night goes on, so as it gets later we will play Beirut, the Weeknd, Flume, and Cardi B. ● We have a secret room in our restaurant where we do invite-only shows, for select artists that we really want to hang out with. In doing so, we have actually gotten to connect with some people who made us super starstruck. We got the opportunity to feed them and they were almost as in awe of us as we were of them, which is a great feeling.

It definitely makes us feel like badass, no-fucks-given pirates

QVARNSTRÖM

TITTI

Titti Qvarnström is the first female head chef in Sweden to receive a Michelin star, for her work at Bloom in the Park in 2015. Titti remains in the city of Malmö, where she is developing a new food destination at Folk Mat & Möten, a restaurant, conference center, and event space; and exploring the concept of "Pure Food Camp," with a focus on foraging in the woods and other microclimates in the bountiful outdoors. The natural beauty of Southern Sweden has always been, and remains, a major source of inspiration for Titti. Today her gastronomic vision is to share, through her culinary creations, a small part of the Swedish and Nordic terroir with people all over the world.

Cook It Up Playlist ▶ This is a playlist that my team and I put together in the kitchen a few years back as the ultimate cooking playlist. Since then, it has been added to and extended, but I still prefer this original version for nostalgic reasons, as we had a great time putting it together — and working together in the kitchen.

1.	Lust For Life	Iggy Pop
2.	Don't Look Back Into The Sun	The Libertines
3.	Mr. Brownstone	Guns N' Roses
4.	Johnny B. Goode	Chuck Berry
5.	Mamma Pappa Barn	Ebba Grön
6.	California Über Alles	Dead Kennedys
7.	Solglasögon	Docent Död
8.	Whip it	DEVO
9.	Voodoo Child (Slight Return)	Jimi Hendrix
10.	I Believe I Can Fly	Me First and the Gimme Gimmes
11.	Everything Is AWESOME!!!	Tegan and Sara ft The Lonely Island
12.	I Don't Want to Grow Up	The Ramones

SWEDEN

Zucchini is a nasty little vegetable
that tastes of nothing—until you burn it.
That's when the magic happens.

Serves 4

Grilled Zucchini
with
hummus
and
FETA CHEESE

2 large zucchinis (courgettes)
50 ml rapeseed oil
Leaves from 1 sprig thyme
Salt and freshly ground black pepper
100 g pumpkin seeds
200 g feta cheese, crumbled
400 g hummus
100 g finely sliced red cabbage

Make a hot fire in a charcoal grill.

Cut the zucchinis (courgettes) in quarters lengthwise. On a baking sheet, toss the zucchinis with the oil. Sprinkle on the thyme and salt and pepper to taste and toss to coat.

Arrange the zucchini slices on the grill rack over the hot fire and grill on each side until they are nicely marked with stripes from the rack.

Meanwhile, toast the pumpkin seeds in a dry frying pan over medium heat until they start making a crackling sound. Transfer to a plate and sprinkle with salt while still warm.

Serve the zucchinis on a platter or individual plates with the feta, hummus, and red cabbage alongside, sprinkled with the toasted pumpkin seeds.

Recipe Inspiration:

RING OF FIRE by Johnny Cash

Since music can really get you to be open to sharing a musical experience with others, listening to it can be an intimate experience. As a young person, I was searching for my own identity, yet wanting to connect with others. Music was the perfect tool. Music has played a role in all major happenings in my life, from childhood through my teenage years, in my working life, and in my spare time. From happy events at parties and weddings to the saddest moments of losing a loved one. One of the hardest, yet most important, choices of playlists is when planning a funeral. The chosen tunes will forever have a new meaning and be associated with the loss.

●

Music has always been a part of my life, and not only music played by people on instruments. I have always listened to the music of nature—the notes of wind through the trees, the harsh tones of the sea, or the calling of birds. The first CD that I bought for myself was *Walthamstow* by East 17. One track, "Deep," especially caught my attention, and I played it a lot.

●

As a child and young adult, I had certain preferences about where food and music should coexist. One could say that my taste for both food and music has grown more refined over the last few years. Both music and food play important roles in all large life events for many people and cultures; they interact to create mood and emotions. On important occasions, a program is made where food follows music and vice versa. I love that both food and music might give a first rough impression, but is refined and performed with skill and expertise at a closer look. My restaurants reflect this approach. When cooking *for* musicians, that's when the very essences of food and music get to connect, and when done successfully, a new magic appears. Music and sound in general affect our subconscious, and it is very interesting to study how music can change the impression of a meal. It is a powerful tool!

SoMeTiMeS

it's just nice

to be yelled at

by a singer

At the end of the night, my dining room is quiet, there isn't any music at all. People actually coming together in real life to enjoy each other's company—that's a rarer and rarer sort of interaction these days, and in some ways, we are not prepared for it. So it would not be fair to the music to mix it in with conversation and the food experience. People interacting is a kind of music in itself and needs its own space to blossom.

●

In the kitchen, however, it's a different story. That's where the music is needed as a tool to keep up the pace, to keep a good mood, and to let chefs feel connected. Metallica has followed me through my life and is a band whose music I still very much appreciate today. Metallica is work music for me, and I enjoy listening to some hard beats while working. Sometimes it's just nice to be yelled at by a singer to keep the pace up in the kitchen. Another artist that I keep coming back to is happy Scania reggae artist Peps Persson, because he captures the good and bad in life and our region in a beautiful way. Peps is someone I listen to on my own when I'm either sad or happy, and especially when I was living abroad. I appreciate Peps and his music because it makes me feel a strong connection to this little piece of land that is Scania that I hold very dear.

●

Music is for everyone. Even if you are starving and have no money or instrument, music can be part of your life, if you perform it yourself or just listen to it. Food, however, is a luxury. Very few of us have the advantage of actually choosing what we want to eat, or if and when we want to eat. For most people on Earth, food is still a struggle to get hold of, to have enough and for it be nutritious enough. It is only lately in the history of humans that a few of us have a smörgåsbord of abundance to choose from, making special food a status marker. I feel very lucky to be a part of that.

to keep
the pace up
in the
kitchen

RIZZO

HELENA

Helena Rizzo was born in 1978, in Porto Alegre, in southern Brazil. At twenty-one, she set off for Europe, where she worked as an intern at a few restaurants, most notably at El Celler de Can Roca, in Girona, Spain. She returned to Brazil in 2006, where she opened Maní in São Paulo, showcasing a contemporary cuisine deeply rooted in iconic Brazilian ingredients. Maní has one Michelin star and is listed among the best restaurants in Latin America and the world.

Vaca Atolada (Mired Cow) Playlist ▶ A brief summary of the grooves I listen to and the bands I like!

1.	**Baião de Stoner**	Macaco Bong
2.	**Ratamahatta**	Sepultura
3.	**Ouro de Tolo**	Raul Seixas
4.	**Malandragem**	Cássia Eller
5.	**Sangue latino**	Secos & Molhados
6.	**Juízo Final**	Nelson Cavaquinho
7.	**Waiting**	Meat Puppets
8.	**Almost Fare**	Dinosaur Jr.
9.	**Rape Me**	Nirvana
10.	**Que Estrago**	Letrux
11.	**Son et Lumière**	The Mars Volta
12.	**Roscoe**	Midlake
13.	**T.N.T**	AC/DC
14.	**Moon Wolf**	Type O Negative
15.	**Good**	Morphine

▲ Helena Rizzo

BRAZIL

DA LAMA AO CAOS

Recipe Inspiration:

DA LAMA AO CAOS

by Chico Science & Nação Zumbi

I created this dessert inspired by the aromas and aesthetics of the mangroves. This band was one of the founders of a musical movement called "mangue bit," or mangue-beat. It blends Brazilian rhythms such as *maracatu* with rock, hip-hop, and funk. The dessert is also a blend of different things. It has so many elements: smoked eggplant preserve, goat cheese curd, Palestinian sweet lime zest, orange blossom gelatin, caramelized pistachio, crunchy *kataifi* dough, and black sesame seed ice cream. It combines sweet and savory flavors, different textures and temperatures.

Serves 8

■ For the smoked eggplant preserve:

1 large eggplant, about 400 g (14 oz)

1 green apple, cut into fourths

50 g (1.7 oz) sugar

■ For the Palestinian sweet lime zest:

1 Palestinian sweet lime

100 g (3.5 oz) Base Syrup (recipe follows)

■ For the orange blossom gelatin:

75 g (2.5 oz) orange blossom water

5 g (0.8 oz) Base Syrup (recipe follows)

100 g (3.4 oz) water

1.2 g (0.04 oz) agar-agar

■ For the caramelized pistachios:

100 g (3.5 oz) shelled pistachios halves

80 g (2.8 oz) Base Syrup (recipe follows)

■ For the crunchy *kataifi* web:

100 g (3.5 oz) Base Syrup (recipe follows)

15 g (0.5 oz) black sesame seeds

100 g (3.5 oz) fresh *kataifi* dough

Butter, for greasing

■ For the black sesame seed ice cream:

500 g (17 oz) Ice Cream Base
(recipe follows)

70 g (2.4 oz) black sesame seeds

20 g (0.7 oz) white sesame seeds

■ **200 g (7 oz) goat cheese curd,**
at room temperature, for serving

To make the smoked eggplant preserve, build a hot fire in a charcoal grill. Grill the eggplant directly on the grill rack over high heat until the pulp is soft and the crust is charred. Cut the eggplant in half, scrape out the pulp into a saucepan with a spoon, and dispose of the skin. Process the apple and add the apple juice to the pan with the smoked eggplant pulp. Add the sugar and cook over low heat, stirring constantly until it reaches the texture of a preserve. Remove from the heat and set aside.

To make the sweet zest, using a sharp peeler, peel the Palestinian lime. (Be careful not to peel the white pith; it tastes bitter and should be disposed of.) Julienne the peel very thinly. In a small pot with a little water, blanch the lime zest ribbons twice, adding fresh water to the pot in between. Drain, transfer to a container, cover with the Base Syrup, and store in the refrigerator until ready to use.

To make the orange blossom gelatin, mix the orange blossom water, Base Syrup, water, and agar-agar in a small pot. Heat until it boils, stirring constantly. Pour the mixture into a heatproof container small enough that the liquid is 1 cm (½ inch) deep. Let cool until a jelly forms. Cut the jelly into 1 cm (½ inch) cubes and store in the refrigerator until ready to use.

To make the caramelized pistachios, combine the pistachios and the Base Syrup in a medium saucepan. Heat until the syrup evaporates, stirring firmly. When the pistachios are well coated and caramelized, remove from the heat immediately. Spread on a cold surface to dry.

To make the *kataifi* web, preheat the oven to 170°C (340°F).

In a bowl, using a hand mixer, beat the Base Syrup with the black sesame seeds until the seeds are fully ground. Stretch small portions of the kataifi dough over a flat surface, carefully untangling the threads. Brush the dough with the sesame syrup. Grease the outside part of a silicone hemisphere-shaped mold with butter. Line the area between the 2 hemispheres with dough, to form a long shaped nest. Brush again with the sesame syrup. Bake for about 20 minutes, or until golden brown.

Preheat a frying pan over medium heat. Pour the black and white sesame seeds into the hot, dry pan and toast them briefly, until fragrant. Remove from the pan immediately.

In a large bowl, combine the Ice Cream Base and the toasted sesame seeds. Blend with a hand mixer until the seeds are ground. Strain through a chinois. Freeze in an ice-cream maker according to the manufacturer's instructions. ▶|

To serve, on each of 8 slate boards or other flat serving plates, intersperse 3 teaspoons of the eggplant preserve, 3 teaspoons of the goat cheese curd, 10 caramelized pistachios, and 8 cubes of the orange blossom gelatin. Place 8 ribbons of the sweet lime zest and the *kataifi* web over it. Finish with a quenelle of the ice cream on top, to the right of the web. Serve immediately.

■ Ice Cream Base
Makes 1 kg (2.2 lb)

945 g (33.3 oz) of milk
285 g (10 oz) of heavy cream
230 g (8.1 oz) of dextrose powder
70 g (2.46 oz) of dried skimmed milk
45 g (1.58 oz) of invert sugar
10 g (0.35 oz) of stabilizer
80 g (2.8 oz) of sugar

Pour the milk, heavy cream, dextrose powder, dried skimmed milk and invert sugar into a large cooking pot. Stir with a hand blender and place the pot over a low heat. In a small bowl, mix the stabilizer and the sugar. When the blend of milk reaches 40°C (104°F), pour the stabilizer and sugar mix into the pot. Mix thoroughly with a whisk and let it heat up to 85°C (185°F). Transfer the content of the pot into a bowl and cool it immediately in a cold water bath. Cover the bowl with plastic film and let it sit in the fridge for 24 hours.

■ Base Syrup
Makes 500 g (1.1 lb)

250 g (8.8 oz) of water
250 g (8.8 oz) of sugar

In a large pot, dissolve the sugar in the water and bring to a boil. Remove from heat, transfer to an airtight container and store in the refrigerator.

● My first encounter with music was through ballet. I danced from the age of four to twelve. At the time, I dreamed of becoming a ballerina. I remember going to bed at night thinking about the music and going over the choreographies. Besides dancing, I also took music lessons at school. I was part of the choir; I loved listening to a song and then trying to play it by ear on my recorder. The song that impacted me the most as a child was Gilberto Gil's "Domingo No Parque" ("Sunday in the Park"). At home, my mother was always listening to Maria Bethânia, Milton Nascimento, and Chico Buarque. Back then, I listened to a lot of Brazilian pop rock: Raul Seixas, Lulu Santos, Rita Lee, Cazuza, Jorge Ben, Tim Maia, Kid Abelha. I remember catching Guns N' Roses fever when I was about ten—they were my first rock concert! ● David Bowie had a giant creative influence on me. I watched *Labyrinth* when I was a kid and his music has been part of my life ever since. Over the years, I learned more and more about him through movies, books, and albums. *Low* and *Ziggy Stardust* are my favorites. What I admired most about Bowie was his ability to take in everything that was happening at any given point in time and turn it into art. His ability to change—he was constantly changing! He was a vampire of visual arts, literature, theater, music, and the cultural zeitgeist. ● When I was growing up, there was no Internet. I listened to the radio, watched MTV, went to parties, and shared cassette tapes with friends. Music was always present, and I was happy to hear the songs that I liked. But I didn't pay attention to the names of albums, songs, or artists, especially foreign ones. I don't remember talking to friends about bands and songs at the time. When I was an early teen, music simply came into my life without asking for permission, and it had the power to lift my mood. When I was sixteen, while in high school, I began to work as a fashion model. This led me to move from the state of Rio Grande do Sul, in the south of Brazil, to São Paulo, at the age of seventeen. I shared an apartment with two girlfriends, and we were constantly invited to parties, concerts, and music festivals. We would go to all of them. ● I started cooking to fill up my time, and also because I was shy. I went to school in the morning and didn't have much to do in the afternoons, so I would walk to the supermarket next door and pick something to cook. I would bake a cake, or make cookies or chocolate candy. I would exchange recipes with my neighbors and cut out magazine articles. Whenever there was a party or dinner at home, I would go into the kitchen. I felt useful there, with the

We are realizing that "you are what you eat" goes further;

bonus of not having to chat with anyone. ● My introspection also brought me closer to music. My first job as a cook was at a restaurant that had a small stage for intimate live music. Almost every night there was a different band playing, and I became friends with many musicians. Plus, my best friend worked at MTV, and my boyfriend at the time was like a music encyclopedia. He also played in a rock band. He introduced me to a lot of artists I wasn't familiar with, and I eventually came to like many of them. For these reasons and others I can't exactly explain, I ended up hanging with a crowd of people in São Paulo who were particularly into music. ● There's a band from the state of Rio Grande do Sul that I really like: Os the Darma Lóvers. They are Buddhists. A childhood friend introduced me to them. I lived in Spain for a while and I used to listen to their songs before going to bed. Back then, I was working as an intern at several different restaurants. The groove of their music helped me relax; the songs were like mantras, and helped me cope with the pressure of everyday life. Years later, they played at Maní for an event that I held with some friends, mixing music and food. ● All these influences helped shape my personality and the way that I see the world. Hence, they have also had an impact on how I set up my restaurant, how I work with my team—and most of all, on the food that I create. There is a dessert on our menu at Maní—an iconic dessert at the restaurant—called *Da Lama ao Caos* (From Mud to Chaos). It's a tribute to the great artist Chico Science, from the Brazilian state of Pernambuco. I adore his band, Nação Zumbi (Zombie Nation). Sadly, he passed away in 1997 at the age of thirty. ● I really enjoy listening to music in the car while I drive to work and before I go into the kitchen. But during the mise en place and service hours, I prefer not to play music. I think that the kitchen plays its own natural music. We have some people in charge of creating playlists for the main dining room, but I don't really think this works for Maní. My restaurant is not small (seventy seats), and therefore it is not quiet. We have an informal and laid-back atmosphere and people like to chat. I'm not really into background music. We have started to create an exclusive soundtrack to play all day.

My husband, Bruno Kayapy, had this idea; it will be like a sensory incidental score. ● I have some friends in São Paulo who organize a music festival and bring many bands here from abroad throughout the year. A few years ago, we had a great experience. We invited the bands to eat at the restaurant in exchange for free tickets for those who were interested in going to their concert. I got to cook for musicians whom I really admire, like Mark Lanegan and Thurston Moore. Sometime later, this same group of friends and I organized a music and gastronomy festival at Casa Manioca—our venue for events, right next to Maní. I developed a special menu for each day of the festival, each inspired by the specific guest artist. Brazilian musicians such as Tom Zé, Marina Lima, and Arnaldo Antunes played there. ● Music has always played a unique social and political role in the world, while gastronomy reflects and summarizes everything connected to the act of eating. But now gastronomy is broadening its reach; it is gaining more power and influence in the world from a material perspective. We are realizing that "you are what you eat" goes further; people are also transformation agents for this planet—depending on what we eat, for better or worse and beyond. It depends on one's own mind and philosophy. Our thoughts and ideas are never generic, nor linear. And this is a good thing! ● Music and the culinary world affect us in similar ways. From a sensory perspective, a song can bring about sorrow, joy, an awkward feeling. Food can also cause these sensations, through styles and flavors. Jazz improvisation, a melancholic blues, the authenticity and roughness of punk music, and so on, have their parallels in the eating experience. But most of all they share the "building process," so to speak. It is no surprise that the words "orchestra" and "kitchen" are often interchangeable. ● I am married to a musician and music producer (who loves to cook, by the way). The process of building a song, metaphorically speaking, is very much like the process of building a dish. You think of a melody; that is the base. You mix and master it, and there are also the gestures. The way you "play" an instrument determines the sound it will make. It's the same thing with food!

Recipe: From Mud to Chaos

people are also transformation agents for this planet.

MARCUS SAMUELSSON

Marcus Samuelsson is an award-winning chef, restaurateur, author, and media personality. He is the force behind multiple restaurants worldwide, including Red Rooster in Harlem, and was the youngest person to receive a three-star review from *The New York Times*. He has won multiple James Beard Awards.

My Greatest Hits Playlist ▶ This is sort of a "greatest hits" for me. There are so many artists that have influenced me at various points in my life, and these songs represent some of those who have made the greatest impact.

1.	**Everybody Hurts**	R.E.M.
2.	**Sexual Healing**	Marvin Gaye
3.	**Mountains**	Prince
4.	**Heroes**	David Bowie
5.	**Stir It Up**	Bob Marley & The Wailers
6.	**Lost Ones**	Ms. Lauryn Hill
7.	**Sir Duke**	Stevie Wonder
8.	**Wake Up**	Run-D.M.C.
9.	**Change the Beat**	Fab 5 Freddy

RED ROOSTER

SORREL and SCALLOP

When I'm cooking something elegant, I always hear this song in my head. This dish, with bright, simple flavors and a lovely combination of textures, indeed brings this song to mind with its elegance, and yet it is very straightforward at the same time.

Serves 4

Recipe Inspiration:

Everybody HURTS

by R.E.M.

■ For the hibiscus tea:

½ cup dried hibiscus leaves

4 cups water

■ For the toasted macadamia nuts:

2 oz macadamia nuts

½ tablespoon olive oil

■ **8 sea scallops**, each cut into 6 pieces

Juice of 1 lemon

2 tablespoons olive oil

Salt to taste

¼ cup parsley leaves

To make the tea, combine the hibiscus leaves and water in a saucepan and bring to a simmer. Remove from the heat and allow to steep for 1 hour. Strain and chill.

To toast the nuts, preheat the oven to 350°F (180°C). Toss the nuts in the olive oil and spread on a baking sheet. Set a timer for 5 minutes and place the nuts in the oven. When the timer goes off, shake the nuts and place back in the oven until well browned, about 5 more minutes.

Transfer to a cutting board and chop coarsely. Season the scallop pieces with lemon juice, olive oil, and salt.

Place 1 ounce of the tea in each of 4 bowls. (Save the rest of the tea to drink, or for another dish.) Place the scallops in the bowls, dividing them evenly and making sure some of each scallop is touching the hibiscus.

Garnish with the toasted macadamia nuts and parsley leaves and serve immediately.

Rituals of cooking and dance

MTV had a huge influence on me while growing up in Sweden. Being born to Swedish and Ethiopian parents, I didn't know much about the States until I started tuning in. I remember watching *Yo! MTV Raps*—it taught me how to dress and what was cool in the U.S., not just what the scene in New York City looked like, but other places in America, too. MTV music videos connected me to the U.S. very early on. That's how I began to feel familiar with America.

●

The first time I went to a concert, I was nine years old. It was Stevie Wonder. I went with my two sisters, who didn't want to bring me, but my parents made them. It was such a big deal for us to go as a family. I remember that I couldn't even conceptualize that he was blind—he just made amazing music. The next day in school, I felt like I had seen something that none of the other kids in my school had seen. I knew then that I wanted to explore the world.

●

Growing up in Sweden, my parents always brought me to these amazing musical experiences, and we always had music playing in the house: Marvin Gaye, Stevie Wonder, Miriam Makeba, you name it. Music was so important to my family, we didn't have a fancy car but we had a Bang & Olufsen sound system. We even had speakers out on the terrace, which was unheard of at that time.

●

There are so many artists that have influenced me and my work. I would put Prince and David Bowie at the top, because they both offered "otherness" to me and showed me that I could be unique and different. Being a kid and being black and different myself, I was drawn to that and enamored by the role model they presented. Bob Marley was a big deal, too, because he really talked about Africa in his music and that was big in our family.

When I saw Prince live for the first time, it was a huge moment for me. The performance really affected me; it took me a week to recover from the experience. I loved everything about that concert: I liked the band before Prince, and then him, of course — I wanted to stay afterward and never go home. I honestly walked to school differently the day after the concert — it gave me a whole new kind of confidence. Here was this unique, fully realized being living in his own universe, pushing his own point of view. It was a combination I had never seen before. He was his own thing.

have been around longer

than the borders

of most countries

These artists, along with my heritage, have guided my approach to food to this day. Food and music are deeply intertwined in Ethiopian culture: you cannot have food without music and vice versa. They are both forms of storytelling: about your day, where you're from, where you're going, of celebration and feast. When my wife, Maya, says what tribe she is from, that tells you what style of dance and what style of music they have, what you will eat. Together, they define any event. The best thing to hear after any celebration is, "I danced and ate so much!" Rituals of cooking and dance have been around longer than the borders of most countries.

Food and music were always part of my life, but in my youth, music was king. When I was coming up in the kitchen, we were always allowed to prep with music playing, but during service, it was never allowed. Everyone in Gothenburg, where I grew up, looked to the concert schedule to figure out when they would have jobs. Every kid would work when a show came, whether selling programs, in the kitchen, you name it. These concerts really changed the whole summer for us kids in Gothenburg. I got a job in a restaurant in the city, and on the day of the concert, I would come to work dressed up because I didn't have time to go home to change after work; I needed to stay in town to get to the concert. That's one thing I remember most about my childhood: knowing that I was going to whatever concert was in town, no matter what. If you didn't go to concerts, what were you working for?

AMNINDER SANDHU

Chef Amninder Sandhu has a love for food that is akin to devotion. She is the pioneer of gas-free cooking in India, embracing traditional, ancient methods of slow cooking over wood and charcoal. She embraces traditional Indian cooking practices, locally sourced ingredients, and recipes passed down from generation to generation. She was named Best Lady Chef by the Indian Ministry of Tourism.

Kitchen Confidential Playlist ▶ This playlist has a mix of classics that I listened to with my brothers, a few from when I was studying in culinary school, some that I played at the very first restaurant that I started on my own. There is also a fair share of slightly sad songs in the list that remind me of the tough times in my life, but listening to them now makes me happy that I've moved on from them and am in a much happier space. There are also a few recent discoveries on the playlist, but overall, these songs are those that I can listen to while in the kitchen on a tough day, or even while at home relaxing and sipping on a glass of wine.

Recipe Inspiration:

INTO THE WILD

Soundtrack by Eddie Vedder

1.	All I Want Is Everything	Def Leppard
2.	Thunderstruck	AC / DC
3.	Boom, Like That	Mark Knopfler
4.	Behind Blue Eyes	The Who
5.	Creep	Radiohead
6.	Calling Elvis	Dire Straits
7.	Guaranteed	Eddie Vedder
8.	Heart of Gold	Neil Young
9.	Big Rock Candy Mountain	Harry McClintock
10.	Last Kiss	Pearl Jam
11.	Maye Ni Main Ik Shikra Yaar Banaya	Jagjit Singh
12.	Sailing to Philadelphia	Mark Knopfler
13.	Only Love	Ben Howard
14.	Empty	Ray LaMontagne
15.	Something Just Like This	The Chainsmokers and Coldplay

INDIA

STUFFED MORELS

The *Into the Wild* soundtrack by Eddie Vedder influenced me to create this dish called Morels Stuffed, Kashmiri morels stuffed with minced smoked mushrooms, served on nachni and walnut "sand." I stuff foraged morels or a similar mushroom called *guchchis* with smoked minced button mushrooms, cream cheese, and spices and serve them on a bed of ground walnuts and *nachni*, to warm you up. The spongy, honeycombed texture and earthy flavor of the morel make it one of the most sought-after mushrooms. These elusive varieties cannot be cultivated commercially and grow wild in regions like the Kangara Valley, Jammu, and Kashmir and parts of Himachal Pradesh, including Manali. In this recipe, the stuffed morels are smoked with a touch of clove scent under a glass cloche, to re-create a foggy winter morning when morels are foraged in the wild. To further this feel, I use the *nachni* and ground walnut bed to resemble soil. At the restaurant, the mushrooms are served on a jackfruit tree bark slice sourced from my house in Assam.

Serves 1

14 g dried morel mushrooms	
5 g ghee	
1 g *shahi jeera* (black cumin seeds)	
5 g green chile, chopped	
3 g garlic, peeled and chopped	
5 g fresh ginger, peeled and chopped	
■ 40 g button mushrooms, blanched and chopped	
40 g cream cheese	
4 g salt	
5 g yellow chile powder	
1 g *kasoori methi* (dried fenugreek leaves)	
■ 3 g *jeera* powder (ground cumin)	
50 g full-fat cream	
3 g ground cardamom	
4 g ground white pepper	
1 g black salt	
5 g coriander (cilantro) roots	
15 g *nachni* chips or purple potato chips	
5 g walnuts	
3 g red chile powder	
Micro herbs, for serving	
1 g whole cloves, for smoking	

Soak the morels for 20 minutes in hot water. Remove the stems and chop, leaving the caps whole.

In a sauté pan, heat the ghee over medium heat. Add the *shahi jeera* and heat until the seeds start crackling.

Add half of the chopped green chile and all of the garlic and ginger and sauté for a few minutes. Add the blanched and chopped button mushrooms and the reserved morel stems and sauté until the mushrooms evaporate their moisture and brown.

Add half of the cream cheese and and stir until melted and well blended. Add the salt, yellow chile powder, *kasoori methi*, and *jeera* powder and mix ▶|

well. Remove from the heat and let cool. Transfer the mixture to a piping bag and stuff the reserved morel caps.

To make the marinade, in a bowl, stir together the rest of the cream cheese, the full-fat cream, the rest of the chopped green chile, the cardamom, white pepper, black salt, and coriander roots and stir to mix well. Chill, then marinate the stuffed morels.

To make a bed for serving, grind the nachni chips in a food processor to coarse crumbs. Toast the walnuts in a medium-hot frying pan, then crush coarsely to match the nachni. In a bowl, stir together the crushed nachni, walnuts, and red chile powder. Set aside.

Just before you are ready to serve, skewer the stuffed marinated morels and cook in a tandoor or a hot (200°C/400°F) oven until the marinade starts to brown.

Spread the nachni-walnut "sand" on a serving plate. Place the morels on it and garnish with the micro herbs.

Using the cloves with a smoking gun, smoke the plated morels and cover with a cloche. Serve immediately.

● I'm from the northern state of Punjab, where food, music, and dance are the three vital facets of my culture and heritage. Punjabi culture is vibrant, warm, and welcoming. Sharing our earnings and feeding people is of paramount importance. The Golden Temple at Amritsar feeds 100,000 people a day, and shabads, kirtan, and Paath (hymns) are sung all day. Most of the Punjabi festivals like Baisakhi are big feasts involving bhangra (traditional dance) and Punjabi music.

●

I first became aware of music when I was around six years old. This is when I just started off with school and actually decided to take a keen interest and remember the names of songs. We had an amplifier with tower speakers at home that my dad used on a regular basis. I remember while he was at work, my elder brother used to plug headphones into the amplifier and listen. I soon started imitating him and doing the same, which is when we started fighting over the headphones. My dad realized that I needed my own set of headphones, and he bought me some. The song that I first fell in love with was "Run to You" by Bryan Adams. It's a song that just grew on me after listening to it play at home so many times.

●

I love listening to Bryan Adams; he has been my favorite artist since the time I understood a little about music. By great luck, I got the chance to cook for him in 2004, as he was staying at the hotel where I was working. Before he left, I ran up to him, shouting his name, asking if I could click a photo. There were so many fans around me, but seeing me trying to get his attention, he said, "Can I take a photo with this lovely lady who has cooked for me?" I got the photo printed and sent it to his room to get it signed. When I opened my own restaurant in

> ## I'm from the northern state of Punjab, where food, music, and dance are the three vital facets of my culture and heritage.

Jorhat, Assam, I framed the photo and hung it on one of the walls. (A funny part is that a lot of people who dined there thought it was Chef Gordon Ramsay and me.)

I was a very good student and topped my school in the twelfth standard. My dad wanted me to become a doctor, but after studying six units of life sciences, I decided it wasn't for me. So, one day, while I was extracting DNA in a lab, I discovered my true calling. It was like how it happens in the movies: I just knew that I wanted to become a chef! However, it was extremely tough to go back to my dad to tell him that I wanted to really do this. I went back to my room and really thought it through. I listened to Bryan Adams's "On a Day Like Today" on repeat, and finally gathered the courage to tell my father that I could do this no more and wanted to join culinary school. The lyrics of the song are so meaningful and completely related to what I was feeling at that point in life. The song helped me make one of the most crucial decisions in my life, and I went on to Aurangabad to study culinary arts and kitchen administration at the Taj Culinary School.

However, it wasn't a movie happy ending from there. At some point in my life, I just felt everything going downhill. I had a small restaurant in Jorhat, Assam, and there was an extremely rough month with technical issues in my kitchen, staffing problems, bills to pay. I felt like I was getting nowhere. I was sitting on one of the tables late at night thinking about what I should do next, and if I really wanted to do this anymore. My younger brother was running a dental clinic a few shops away from my restaurant, and he dropped in to check on me once he shut for the day. He saw me sitting there, and I told him what was going on as soon as he walked in. He heard me out, and then he said, "Do you really want things to get better? If you do, then you have to listen to 'Just a Phase,' by Incubus. I just did that and it really made me feel positive and gave me the reassurance that everything hard would be over soon."

Ten years later, both my younger brother and I were living in Mumbai when we heard that Incubus was playing in Pune, a three-hour drive from where we lived. The best part is that it happened to be his birthday on the very same day they were performing. We decided to go on a road trip. I booked tickets for the gig and a hotel for the weekend. While we were on the way, I casually joked with my brother, saying, "What if we bump into them on the trip?" The concert was truly memorable, and I was extremely happy that I saw Incubus live with the person who had introduced me to them. The day after the concert, we woke up and decided to go out for breakfast. When we walked into the coffee shop, we spotted Brandon Boyd, the lead singer, dining there. We couldn't believe it. We said hi to him, sat down at the table, and I got the chance to tell him how I was introduced to his music and how it helped me get through one of the toughest phases of my life.

The music I listen to has influenced the way I think, my beliefs, and even the way I function. Consequently, my thoughts translate into the food I make and the restaurants I open. Music made me realize that I have a great foundation, and that I was doing something right, which I just needed to build on. The concept I am working with has never been seen in the world before with Indian cuisine; and having a custom designed, no-gas kitchen, using ancient Indian methods of cooking over charcoal and wood, and serving ethnic Indian cuisine is something that I really believe in. It has set me on a mission to make others experience, understand, and believe in serious Indian cuisine. The effect I am trying to create is similar to that of most of my favorite songs, as they too possess that level of distinctiveness, authenticity, and self-expression.

NOAH SANDOVAL

Noah Sandoval is the executive chef and partner of Oriole, a restaurant in Chicago's West Loop neighborhood. With the help of his partners and his wife and general manager, Cara Sandoval, Oriole opened in March 2016, and was awarded two Michelin Stars within seven months. Sandoval has been recognized as one of *Food & Wine* magazine's Best New Chefs, nominated for a James Beard Award, and named Chef of the Year by the *Chicago Tribune*.

Recipe Inspiration:

Dischord Playlist ▶
This is a playlist I would have put together when I was just starting out as a dishwasher. I still love all these songs.

IS WHAT THIS YOU WANTED

by Leonard Cohen

1.	And the Same	Fugazi
2.	Weeds	Hoover
3.	Unfold the Leg	Lungfish
4.	For Want Of	Rites of Spring
5.	Spectra Sonic Sound	Nation of Ulysses
6.	Nickelback	Bluetip
7.	Stretched Too Thin	The Crownhate Ruin
8.	Motorist	Jawbox
9.	Here Comes the Judge	The Make-Up
10.	Salad Days	Minor Threat

USA

RYE CAPELLINI WITH YEAST BUTTER AND TRUFFLES

▼ Noah Sandoval

Is this pasta with butter, salt, and truffles what you wanted? Note: *Doppio zero* ("double zero," or 00) is a fine Italian flour available at specialty food shops and online retailers.

Serves 4 to 6

2 cups 00 flour (see recipe introduction), plus more for dusting

¾ cup rye flour

2 tablespoons caraway seeds, ground to a powder in a spice grinder

Kosher salt and freshly ground black pepper

4 large egg yolks

1 large egg

1 tablespoon extra-virgin olive oil

¼ cup heavy (whipping) cream

1 tablespoon active dry yeast

2 sticks unsalted butter, cut into tablespoons

¼ cup black truffle butter

¼ teaspoon finely grated orange zest

¼ cup finely grated Parmigiano-Reggiano cheese, plus more for serving

Shaved black truffle (optional) and snipped chives, for garnish

Sift both flours with the caraway and 1½ tablespoons salt into a large bowl. Make a well in the center and add the egg yolks, whole egg, olive oil, and 1 tablespoon water. Using a fork, gradually whisk the flour mixture into the wet ingredients until a shaggy dough forms. Scrape the dough out onto a work surface and knead until very stiff but smooth, about 15 minutes. Wrap in plastic wrap (cling film) and let rest at room temperature until softened and relaxed, about 2 hours.

Divide the dough into 12 pieces and work with 1 piece at a time; keep the rest covered. Press the dough to flatten. Set up a pasta machine to roll flat pasta. Starting at the widest setting, run the dough through successively narrower settings until it's a scant ⅛ inch thick. Transfer the sheet to a lightly floured work surface and dust with 00 flour. Repeat with the remaining pieces of dough.

Set up the pasta machine with the capellini cutter. Working with 1 sheet of dough at a time, gradually feed the dough through the cutter. Gently toss the strands with 00 flour and transfer the capellini pile to a lightly floured baking sheet. Repeat with the remaining sheets of pasta to form 12 piles/portions.

In a small saucepan, whisk the cream with 2 tablespoons water and the yeast and cook over moderately low heat, stirring occasionally, until the yeast is dissolved and the mixture is very thick, 3 to 5 minutes. Whisk in the unsalted butter 1 tablespoon at a time until emulsified, then season with salt and pepper. Set aside and keep warm. ▶|

Song: Is This What You Wanted by Leonard Cohen

▲ Noah Sandoval

In a large saucepan of salted boiling water, cook the pasta until al dente, about 1 minute. Drain, reserving 1 cup of the cooking water. Wipe out the saucepan.

In the same large saucepan, melt the yeast butter with the truffle butter and orange zest over moderately high heat. Add the cooked pasta, the ¼ cup Parmigiano, and ½ cup of the reserved cooking water and toss until hot and evenly coated with the butter, about 2 minutes. Add a little more of the cooking water, if necessary for a silky sauce. Transfer the capellini to shallow bowls. Top with grated Parmigiano and garnish with shaved black truffle, if desired, and snipped chives. Serve right away.

● Every band I listen to has something different to say. Everybody has a different message, whether it's a very serious or playful message, or just stemming from pure art. And I feel like those different messages influence everything I do—beyond just what I do in the kitchen. As a chef, I have a specific focus and position on things. I take heavy inspiration from music and I see other chefs doing the same thing, both bringing their own passion and pulling inspiration from other art forms. I think it's the same with music, that those artists are pulling inspiration from many places while building their own points of view. ● I was twelve or thirteen when I started noticing the differences between genres of music. My dad bought me a little all-in-one stereo, where the speakers were clamped to the side, and I carried it around like a boombox. I remember listening to the radio on that boombox when I was living in Richmond, Virginia. The first song I fell in love with was "Lithium" on Nirvana's Nevermind album, right around the time it came out. I was young enough to understand what they were doing and how it wasn't necessarily just looking for money. There was an art-centric focus to it—maybe the last real art-focused major label release of that time and since. Growing up, seeing that stuff, I wanted to be an "artist first," too. ● When I was thirteen, my parents were going through a rocky part in their marriage. (They're still together, so it worked out.) It got pretty rough between me and my mom, then me and my dad, and between all of us, we were kind of at each other's throats. My dad was in the military, so that was a lot of pressure; and my mom was really into art, so there were obviously differences in their approach to life—as well as their musical tastes. My mom was very into Nirvana and the Ramones; she was into a lot of really cool music. I remember listening to these bands with her and thinking, most of my friends' parents, if you put on the Ramones or Nirvana or Minor Threat, they would not be into it. They would say, "No, you can't listen to this!" or "This is bad!" or "You know this is the devil's music." But my mom was rocking out with me, teaching me about music and encouraging it. She was the one who shaved my head into a Mohawk for the first time; that was huge. Being raised, especially at that age, by somebody as open-minded and encouraging as my mother, I'll be defined by that for forever. ● Music is definitely a support for me; it's definitely something I can rely on to get me through a creative funk or give me inspiration. My first job was washing dishes in a restaurant, and like all of the servers, all of the cooks, and pretty much everybody who worked there, I was in a band. That's probably a more of a direct association for me, because "Oh, you're a musician, you probably work in a restaurant" or "Oh, you work in a restaurant, you're probably a musician" was so common then. It's not like that anymore, but it was when I was growing up, until I was maybe twenty-five. ● Anybody who listens to the music I listen to and comes from the place I come from is going to name Fugazi as a major inspiration. The music is obviously amazing, very interesting, and unlike anyone else's. It is very dynamic, but all of the songs make sense together, all of the records make sense together. The music speaks for itself. As a parallel to cooking, if you want to become a chef and you are thinking about how to put a menu together, if you can do that like Fugazi did it musically, then you're on the right track. ● There's something else to that band—just the way they go about their personal lives, take care of their business, and run their label, Dischord Records. There's a lot of integrity, and I think that's really more of the influence for me. It's that respect for everyone, the DIY approach, to make sure that people are taking care of each other and to make sure you don't take yourself too seriously. Really to just do right by everybody. That was the most influential thing Fugazi ever taught me. ● Being a chef or restaurateur or cook or server has an extremely high level of professional pressure, just like a musician. If you're onstage and you can't remember the next chord or your voice cracks or you make whatever performance mistake, you can't undo that...and people notice. If you're a cook and you're not perfect all the time, say you screw something up like overcooking a steak, you get yelled at. If a server drops a knife, everybody sees it, and they or the evening are not perfect anymore. It's a black mark on somebody's special experience, which they are paying money for. With that pressure comes a certain amount of respect for the restaurant, which I'm thankful for. Customers used to just go to a restaurant but never think about the people who work there. People now have more of an understanding of what everyone behind their meal actually does, and in that way it's treated very similarly to any sort of performance. ● Music plays a big part in the nightly performance of our restaurants. The cooks get there at 10:00 a.m. and they're there for seven and a half hours before the first diner walks in the door. The servers get in not too long after the cooks, and then there's a huge, constant push to be ready at 5:30 p.m. There's no question about it, there's no doubt about it, and everyone is really good at it. Sometimes we're close to 5:30 but the tables aren't lined up or the kitchen isn't ready and it's a very high-stress situation, so I like to put on something mellow that will make people relax. It's not for the diners, it's for the employees, because I want everybody to understand where we're at. If I put something on with a heavy beat, people are gonna stay stressed out. I really play music for cooks and servers to guide their night, not so much the guests. ● Right at 5:30 p.m. I'll play something like Nick Cave's *The Boatman's Call* or Mulatu

Astatke or *The Black Light* by Calexico, which is something that a guy played for the same reason when I worked at Helen's in the '90s, which was also the first time I noticed music being important during service. When we're getting busy, when we get full, when we're running around and everybody needs to stay calm but also move a little faster, I'll put on something more along the lines of James Brown or first-wave ska. Something that is a little bit more upbeat, like Fela Kuti — romantic and motivating. Toward the end of the night, I like to play music that I would want to listen to when I'm just relaxing or having a beer with friends; I feel like the end of the night should be the best part of the night. Everybody's tired, everybody wants to go, people may be frustrated with each other, and so I want to put on music that is not as calm as the start of the night but not as upbeat as the middle. I usually play Tindersticks or Neko Case. Overall, the music is very, very important to me through the whole arc of service. ● Music has definitely influenced my cooking and the way I work in the kitchen. Growing up in the punk scene made me place a lot of importance on integrity. I won't put a dish on the menu unless I'm really proud of it. I also don't believe in degrading chefs to make them better cooks. I want all of these things to reflect each other: their importance to me, their integrity, that they all send a positive message, and that they are fair. It's essential to me that the music I listen to has all these qualities as well, and that the restaurants I open have all these qualities, along with the people I hire and work with. As much as I can, I try to make these things perfect. If we operated with a concern about money at the center and as the focus, I wouldn't be me, Oriole wouldn't be Oriole, and Kumiko wouldn't be Kumiko. Obviously we have to make money to pay our investors back and we have to make money to pay everyone, but that is not the main driving force. We don't do this for the money. Both the means and the goals are producing genuine art, just like those bands who inspired me by doing the same, with the success coming after that.

Growing up in the punk scene made me place a lot of importance on integrity.

SHANI

EYAL

Eyal Shani's culinary passion was first instilled in him by his grandfather, an agronomist and a dedicated vegan. In 1989, Shani opened his first restaurant, Ocianus, in his hometown of Jerusalem.
Shani is considered one of the leading figures in the Israeli culinary scene, and has appeared on the panel of judges for six seasons of *Master Chef Israel*.

My Inspiration Signals Playlist ▶
When we listen to songs, pop songs or rock songs, I think in the best case, they are a message of something that's happening to you. But when we listen to classical music, it's like what's coming from the universe. It's unending. You can return to a composition all your life without hearing the same thing that you heard the last time. It's a signal to people, a call from the universe, from their creation, their creator, from God. There are many explanations for why classical music moves us, but when it's touching you, you are happening.

This dish was not inspired by a song that I heard; it belongs to a kind of revelation that sometimes arrives for us. This recipe came to me the first time I thought I could combine high-end food with pita.

In Israel, pita pocket bread is very common, mostly used to serve shawarma, hummus, falafel…it's street food. Actually, the main street food in Israel. But I recognize that pita is the most genius bread, because it's not just a pocket but an envelope that is closed on all sides of the bread except for the small opening at the top. That's very meaningful in terms of the possibilities for cooks, because you can put wet sauces inside and they will not make the outside fall apart. One day, for a completely different purpose, I pulled out some shrimp. They were so succulent, without knowing why or what I was going to do, I scalded and peeled them

1.	"Summer" from The Four Seasons	Antonio Vivaldi
2.	Concerto for Four Violins in B Minor	Antonio Vivaldi
3.	Violin Concerto in D Major	Ludwig van Beethoven
4.	The Violin Concertos	J. S. Bach
5.	Impromptu No. 3	Franz Schubert
6.	Arabesques No. 1 and No. 2	Claude Debussy
7.	Piano Concerto No. 5	Ludwig van Beethoven
8.	Keyboard Concerto No. 3 in D Major	J. S. Bach, played by Sviatoslav Richter

Pink

and mixed them with sour cream, some sweet, juicy tomato seeds, and some chile pepper and put it all inside a pita. That was my first pita! I took a bite and the taste was unbelievable. It was so good. Much better, it seemed, than any mixture of those kind of things I could compose on the plate. Then I understood for the first time in my life that with the right recipe, pita can improve any food that we come into orbit with. This moment is also what gave me the idea to open my Miznon places.

My "Pink" is a pita full of shrimp cloaked in sour cream, tomato seeds, and chopped scallions. There are combinations of food called "heavenly combinations"—absolutely pleasing matches of flavor, unquestionably and eternally. Like the combination of vanilla ice cream and chocolate ice cream, or strawberries and cream. This combination of shrimp, sour cream, and scallions is irresistible—but, something seems wrong eating this combination when it is naked. The pita completes it, absorbing the cream, the steamed shrimp juices, and the perfect sweet-tartness of the tomato seeds for perfect balance.

Serves 1

6 to 8 shiny, crystal-fresh shrimp	
1 tablespoonful of cream of yesteryear	
1 scallion (spring onion), finely chopped	
Minced hot green chile, to taste	
Salt	
Sweet tomato(es) such as Maggie, to taste	
1 pita bread	
Aioli	
Peeled green cucumber slices, to taste	
Thinly sliced red onion, to taste	

To clean the shrimp, using sharp scissors, cut a slit in the top of each shrimp shell along the back, starting from the neck and ending with the tail. Remove and discard the dark-colored vein from the slit (this is the exhaust pipe/intestines of the shrimp), being sure to get every bit.

In a saucepan of boiling, well-salted water, very briefly scald the whole cleaned shrimp, with the shells on. Remove the shrimp at the first moment you can see through the shells in the area of the shrimp neck and the color of the flesh turns pink-white, 30 to 60 seconds. Be sure to scald carefully—overcooked shrimp is chewy and plastic in flavor.

Drain the shrimp and let cool until you can handle them. Remove the head and peel off the shells, legs, and tail: Use the scissors to cut starting in the neck area and continue down toward the tail until you can remove all of the shell gently, without damaging the flesh.

Place the blanched and peeled shrimp in a bowl. Add the cream, scallion, chile, and a little salt. Gently squeeze in some seeds and juice from the tomato to the desired consistency. Slice the tomato and set aside. Using your hands, mix the contents of the bowl with the shrimp to coat the shrimp well.

Remove a quarter of the top pita with a knife. Hold the pita with one hand and with the other hand, spread some of the cream mixture from the bowl on one side of the pita and the aioli on the other. Lightly salt the cream. On one side of the pita, arrange layers of cucumber slices, red onion, and tomato. Now arrange the shrimp in such a way ▶|

that they cover the contents of the pita, with a few of the tails sticking out and hinting at what is going on inside. Drizzle more of the cream mixture left in the bowl over the shrimp and sprinkle with more chile, if you like.

To serve, crumple some parchment paper into a small sleeve-style brown paper bag. Place the pita in the paper to help hold it and catch drips. Serve immediately.

● When you begin listening to music, usually you are following influences that other people have passed onto you. That is not the moment that you are discovering your music. Something has to be happening for you to discover music. Music is like a drug: It gets into your blood and changes the frequency of your heartbeat. When the Japanese soak seaweed in water, the water remains water, but a really big change is happening. ● When you're developing your own taste in music, it is a subtle process, because it's not just taste. It's a lot of things dissolved into one big thing in the universe that essentially makes another womb inside your spirit. When you find the right frequency and rhythm for you, something begins to change. ● When I was a young boy, I listened to Deep Purple, Elton John, the Beatles, Pink Floyd, Jimi Hendrix—beautiful creators. Their music touched me, but not in the way that I needed. Then

I began to cook. I was twenty-nine years old and when I went into the kitchen, I was like a priest. I stopped everything. I left my friends. I wasn't with my family. I stopped reading books. I stopped listening to music. I stood at the cutting board for eleven years, trying to analyze what was happening in front of my eyes. ● Around my forty-fourth birthday, I had a customer who was a very old woman, perhaps eighty-five. She had dreamt of being a pianist her whole life, but she never became one. She would dream in the night. One day, she gave me Beethoven's "Piano Concerto No. 4" and the "Triangle Concerto" by Liszt. She said, "Listen to these, it will change your life." ● My first listenings to these works were in my car on my way home after midnight. From the moment I heard them, I could not stop. For eight years, the only man I listened to was Beethoven. I felt like I had found a twin in spirit. Then after those eight years, I discovered Bach. He was complicated…he was like signals from the universe. Most of the time, I didn't even enjoy his music. But there are seconds of Bach's music that are disharmonious and yet combine into such a harmony that you feel the transcendental effect inside your body. I searched out this feeling, so I kept listening to him. ● Then I expanded into Vivaldi, Mozart, and other classical composers. ●

To me, a musical piece that lasts maybe four minutes cannot distract you, you can't experience the magic. When you are listening to a creation of sixty minutes, there is a big story inside it. It is not a story that you can describe in words. It's a story that you can feel without putting your finger on it. Beethoven once said that "Music is not a language. Music is music, and it has to be completely pure." ● People told him, "But you wrote the Sixth Symphony, the 'Pastoral Symphony,' describing the noise of the rivers that are streaming and the noise of the leaves with the wind, describing the landscape of nature." ● He said, "No. It's not the landscape of nature, it's the landscape of my inner feelings. Music doesn't have to serve an idea, it doesn't have to serve anything but itself." ● The most beautiful thing about classical music is that with one creation, you can live with it all your life. Each time, you're touching it again and again from the beginning; it changes inside you and means completely different things. Every day I go swimming in Israel, and every day when I jump in the water, I feel the water differently from the previous day. It touches me in a different way, a different place— it has a different density, a different structure. It's the same with music. You can return over and over to the same suite and hear completely different music. And the depth of the music you hear is telling you about the depth of yourself. ● The first time that music completely entered into my blood, it was very late night at night, after cooking in the north of Israel. I went to my car to drive home to Tel Aviv, but I was completely overwhelmed and couldn't drive. So I stopped the car, and I put on Beethoven's "Concerto No. 5" from the beginning. I closed my eyes and I disappeared. I entered a room that was the music. And I let it touch all the parts of my soul in my body. That was the moment that I shook hands with music. I made it part of my life. ● All my movements in the kitchen, I feel I learn from the movements of music. There is the music. There is the silence, the absent parts. It's like a world that is breathing. When you are making food, it is the same. The energy inside of food is always changing. For example, when you are describing liquid in the plate. "Soup" is a way to describe water that has transformed. Sometimes you cannot make any sound that describes music. Sometimes you can describe music when you make it wait, when there is a silence. Sometimes in food, you describe the strongest idea by doing nothing on the plate except inviting two different ingredients and making a break and that break is expressive. ● Once I worked with a scientist who almost won the Nobel Prize. He was an old man, and the first

time we met, I asked him, "What do you know about science?" He said, "It's all about statistics. Every morning the sun rises, and it will be like that, not because we are promised, but because the statistics say chances are that the sun will rise and we will see it. And there will be no day that the sun will not rise. Mathematics is a light. People stole it from God. It was something they took out of the universe. They felt it and took it for themselves as a chance to understand." ● It's the same with music. It has a shape, it has a form, people are creating it. In the end, when it happens, it's completely transcendental. It belongs to the universe. And there are people who can catch it from the universe and bring it to the world. ● And it's the same with food. There are two different kinds of chefs. There are chefs who believe they are gods. They may take a piece of beef and more or less evaporate it into a cloud, serve it as a cloud above the table. There is another group of chefs who believe that they have to express the food in the most natural way and not change it. I belong to the second party, in the strongest way you can understand food. ● I believe that when I am touching vegetables, fruits, meats, animals, I am serving God in the creator's temple. I have the privilege to see, to touch, to feel, to taste, to understand these creations. Therefore,

I have a big warning not to change the ingredients, just to understand them. Each drop that is coming from the sea is carrying all the characters of the ocean, each vegetable or animal is a complete creation. Darwin said that "a complete creature is one that can bring children to the world that looks like they look." If a cauliflower wasn't a finished process of nature within its seed, then cauliflower seeds could produce elephants, mice, dogs, or people, but possibly not cauliflower. That means when I am working with cauliflower, I am working with a precise structure, a complete creation of nature and all the world is inside it. ● And every time I work while listening to music, it's like a new door is opening. I see different structures and I have to find them each time from the beginning. That is what I learned from music. When I prepare food, I recognize the music, I can hear it in my ears. When I am doing service in our restaurants, which is so complicated, I am not listening to the music…my blood is feeling the music.

And every time I work while listening to music, it's like a new door is opening.

CHRIS SHEPHERD

Midwest-raised, James Beard Award–winning chef Chris Shepherd opened his Houston, Texas, restaurant Underbelly in 2012. He formed Underbelly Hospitality in 2018 to preserve the ethos of his first restaurant—learning about diverse cultures through food—through his three new restaurants UB Preserv, Georgia James, and One/Fifth. Chris's foundation Southern Smoke has donated more than $1.3 million to the National Multiple Sclerosis Society and to those in the food and beverage industry in crisis.

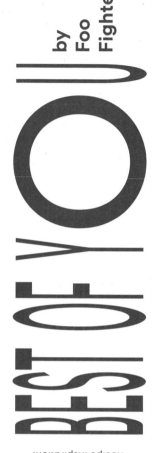

BEST OF YOU

by Foo Fighters

Recipe Inspiration:

1.	**Stranglehold**	Ted Nugent
2.	**Baba O'Riley**	The Who
3.	**Start Me Up**	Rolling Stones
4.	**Detroit Rock City**	KISS
5.	**Hold On Loosely**	38 Special
6.	**Surrender**	Cheap Trick
7.	**Lonely Is the Night**	Billy Squire
8.	**Bulls On Parade**	Rage Against the Machine
9.	**Go Your Own Way**	Fleetwood Mac
10.	**Best of You**	Foo Fighters
11.	**Babe I'm Gonna Leave You**	Led Zeppelin
12.	**Draped Up**	Bun B
13.	**DNA.**	Kendrick Lamar
14.	**Regulate**	Warren G featuring Nate Dogg
15.	**Sicko Mode**	Travis Scott featuring Drake

Georgia James Playlist ▶ I opened Georgia James to provide guests with the equivalent experience of dining at our home on a Sunday night. Cast-iron-seared steaks, vegetables made with local ingredients, delicious wine and whiskey, and, of course, music. I made this playlist for Georgia James while sitting at my dining room table with a glass of whiskey after a Sunday night dinner with friends. The theme? Songs I like. So all of these songs are on the list at the steakhouse.

GEORGIA JAMES AND CRISPY RICE SALAD

I'm a big Foo Fighters fan, and one of their songs, "Best of You," made me go on to open my first restaurant. So here is the recipe for Underbelly's signature dish.

In order to create the desired texture for the rice, we cook it and lay it out to dry overnight. The next day, we coat the grains in rice flour, separate them, and fry them until they're crispy.

This salad consisting of the crispy rice, herbs (they rotate based on what we get from the farmers), tomato, cucumber, Vidalia onion, and radishes tossed in a serrano vinaigrette is a wonderful combination of crisp and crunchy, tender and sweet, bright and spicy.

Serves 4

2 cups short-grain rice, preferably Kokuho Rose

4 cups vegetable oil

1 cup rice flour

1 serrano chile

1 cup fresh lemon juice

1 sweet onion such as Vidalia, julienned thinly

8 cherry tomatoes, cut in half

4 radishes cut into 4 wedges then halved, to make 8 pieces each

2 Persian cucumbers, sliced

4 oz cilantro (coriander) leaves

4 oz dill sprigs

4 oz basil leaves

¼ cup blended oil

Salt and freshly ground black pepper

Cook the short-grain rice according to the package instructions. When cooked, spread it on a baking sheet in a single layer and let cool.

Meanwhile, preheat the vegetable oil in a heavy-bottomed pot to 325°F (165°C).

Once the rice is cool, break up any clumps into individual rice kernels with your hands. Sprinkle the rice flour over the rice and toss to coat all the kernels.

Carefully add the rice to the hot oil, working in batches as needed to make sure the pot doesn't overflow. Stir the rice in the oil and cook until the oil stops bubbling, about 3 minutes. Using a slotted spoon or wire skimmer, lift the rice out of the oil and spread on a baking sheet lined with paper towels to drain.

Meanwhile, slice the chile very thinly. Set aside half for tossing into the salad. In a bowl or glass measuring jar, stir the other half of the chile into the lemon juice. Let stand for about 25 minutes, then strain the serrano out of the lemon juice. Set the infused lemon vinaigrette aside.

In a bowl, combine the onion, tomatoes, radishes, cucumbers, and herbs with some of the vinaigrette and salt and pepper to taste. Toss the rice and remaining chile into the vegetable mixture. Taste and adjust the seasoning and vinaigrette. Divide the salad into individual bowls or a large serving bowl and serve immediately.

Music always has so much power to get us through hard, hard times. It's weird because it seems like when we're sad, we always want to listen to depressing songs... I never understood that. We get our hearts broken, we listen to sad songs. I don't get it, but that's what we want. It's always been one of those things that we do.

●

I'm a big Foo Fighters fan and one of their songs, "Best of You," made me go on to open my first restaurant. When I was working at a restaurant in Houston called Catalan Food & Wine, I would go to the gym in between lunch and dinner shifts and walk for an hour. Every time I got on a treadmill, I put that song on. I'd listen to it over and over again and think, "Someone is getting the best of me! Man I gotta do my own shit." And that's what made me open Underbelly.

●

Foo Fighters played the night before Super Bowl LIII, and we got to see them. Billy Durney of Hometown BBQ knows the guys, so we got to go backstage. Just sitting there talking to Dave Grohl, the lead singer, was surreal. Going from working in a restaurant to opening restaurants to hanging out with these dudes to having a conversation was one of the most amazing things. That song specifically got me back then; and twelve years later I was sitting with him. I couldn't tell him, though, I would have freaked out if I did that.

I started my career later in life, when I was twenty-two or twenty-three, working at Brennan's. I was going to culinary school and listening to Rage Against the Machine every day. I couldn't afford to live inside Houston and go to work, so I lived about forty-five minutes outside of it. Every day driving in, I would listen to Rage, Metallica, Slayer, because I knew I was going to get my ass beat. It was just gonna be busy with four hundred covers every night. My best friend lived outside of the city as well. We'd ride together, and it was like that was the music you listen to—to make you move faster and be more efficient. Metallica across the board. They've influenced generations of restaurant staff at this point.

●

Food touches people's emotions just as music does. That's what has come to the forefront over the past decade. As much as you want to go see a show by a band that you really want to hear, you want to go eat at a restaurant with a chef whose food you want to eat. I don't know whether to blame or praise the Internet and how it has made things so accessible to people now. Before this era, you couldn't find chefs in just any city. Now you can find restaurants that you want to go to pretty much no matter where you are traveling, similar to shows that are popping up in cities you aren't familiar with, or vice versa. Lots of us have lists of restaurants we want to go to and shows that we plan way ahead to go see. There are special occasions and there are things that you want to do all the time. There's an emotion that gets attached to everyday life: Everybody eats, everybody listens to music. Food, or restaurant dining, just came more to the forefront than electrician or dentist stuff; they haven't gotten up there yet.

At the Georgia James, every day I walk in, it's like a concert. That kitchen line is the most animated and music-driven set of cooks I've ever seen in my life. How they move and how they get ready for service...there's a regimented set of songs that they really love to listen to and it's absolutely amazing to see the combined effect. Whoever gets there first gets to put the playlist on for that day, but everyone has their go-to playlist, so we hear a lot of the same things over and over. The selection bounces between country, rap, metal—it bounces through everything. One day I asked, "What are you listening to?!" They said, "Chef, it's performance jazz!" That was a new one for me.

Music always has so much power to get us through hard, hard times.

I may not like it, but they all have their ways of doing things; each kitchen is that way. During service, music can definitely set a tone and a mood. One of the oddest dining experiences we had recently was *no* music playing. It was cool, it was very thoughtful. Most of the time, however, I put the playlist together for all the restaurants, and depending on the spot, depending on the time, I want it to be fun and fun-loving.

•

To make a good playlist, you've got to have a sense of the place. I try to go on beats per minute, depending on how we want the restaurant to move, whether or not the guests actually know it or under-stand it. There's a beat in their head and it sets the tone of thinking, is it gonna be a fast-paced and in-your-face kind of dining experience or a very low-key and relaxed experience. Sometimes I see the guests walking in and I tell the staff, you have to change the song, you're killing the mood here, it's like you're physically making people's souls scream. They will put something different out, and you can see the effects. People are moving faster, or they flutter, they're eating and they're having a good time. They're smiling and their souls are peaceful because they're listen-ing to French versions of '70s love songs.

BEN SHEWRY

Ben Shewry grew up in a musical household, with a strong sense of environment and personal identity. After moving to Melbourne, Australia, in 2002, Ben began working at Attica restaurant in 2005.

He took full ownership of the restaurant in 2015. Ben has dedicated his time at Attica to discovering what it means to be a cook in Australia from a cultural, community, creative, and committed perspective. His journey has been fueled by a deep love of music.

Attica Pre-Service Playlist

▶ I created this playlist for pre-service in the kitchen. A pre-service playlist should be like getting into bed with an electric blanket turned on high on a cold winter's night. At first you think, "Oh, this is so comfortable," but then about thirty minutes later, you are too hot. But you can't just pull out the big guns at the start of a playlist — you need to ease into it and build a heavy crescendo that just hypes the hell out of everyone and gets them super motivated to absolutely crush service. I know what you are thinking: "What's that Tom Petty song doing in there so late in the set?" Well, who the hell doesn't like Tom Petty? That song makes you feel alive. Heaviness comes in different forms and has different tones, folks. Just get cooking and crank this list.

1.	**Are You with Me Now?**	Cate le Bon
2.	**Bad Girl (Part 1)**	Lee Moses
3.	**You Said Something**	PJ Harvey
4.	**Magic in Here**	The Go-Betweens
5.	**Sweaty Fingers**	Cave
6.	**And the Glitter Has Gone**	Yo La Tengo
7.	**Born in the Wrong Time**	The Great Unwashed
8.	**Kyeo**	Fugazi
9.	**Dead Moon Night**	Dead Moon
10.	**Sex Beat**	The Gun Club
11.	**Beautiful Delilah**	The Kinks
12.	**Don't Do Me like That**	Tom Petty and the Heartbreakers
13.	**Head like a Hole**	Nine Inch Nails
14.	**Dark Arts**	The Nudge
15.	**Your Hollows**	Heron Oblivion

Song: Green Arrow by Yo La Tengo

▲ Ben Shewry

AUSTRALIA

Bolognese of Kindness

Recipe Inspiration: Green Arrow by Yo La Tengo

When I think of kindness in food, I think of Bolognese sauce. It takes time and care to make a really good one. Bolognese is something so common that when people are served an exceptional one, they are often really moved. You've got to put your heart into it and be patient, it can't be rushed. Like a friendship. This recipe was inspired by the Yo La Tengo song "Green Arrow." It's nourishing and healing. All the ingredients should ideally be organic and free-range. Cook it while listening to "Green Arrow" and pay the love forward. Serve on top of your favorite pasta, and you should be able to make a lasagna with the leftover sauce!

Makes enough to feed a band as large as Broken Social Scene (8 + people)

80 g olive oil

750 g beef, coarsely minced

750 g pork, coarsely minced

100 g peeled and finely chopped garlic

150 g peeled and finely chopped shallot

150 g peeled and finely chopped carrot

40 g finely chopped celery

500 ml whole milk

750 ml dry red wine

3 fresh bay leaves

30 g whole thyme sprigs (stems and all)

200 g finely diced prosciutto

700 g tomato purée

700 ml thin tomato water, made by rinsing out the tomato purée can with fresh water and reserving

Salt and freshly ground black pepper

Sugar, if needed

Heat the olive oil in a heavy-bottomed cast-iron saucepan over medium heat. Sauté the beef and pork until lightly browned. Use a wooden spoon to break the meat up and make sure that there are no lumps. (Lumpy mince in Bolognese is a cardinal sin in my book, and people who "choose" to do so are of very poor character.)

Add the garlic, shallot, carrot, and celery and sweat for 4 minutes.

Add the milk and simmer until the liquid is completely evaporated.

Add the wine and simmer until reduced by three-fourths.

Add the bay leaves, thyme, prosciutto, tomato purée, and tomato water. Bring to a low simmer and add salt to taste. Cover with a tight-fitting lid and cook for 30 minutes. Taste and adjust the seasoning with salt, pepper, and a little sugar, if necessary.

Simmer gently until rich and tender, 4 to 4 ½ hours longer. Check the seasoning again.

Serve with your favorite pasta.

● I grew up in a musical household. My dad was into "hi-fi" and built his own speakers. My uncles Kerry and Tracy are musicians, and Uncle Kerry ran New Zealand's longest-running folk festival, the Tahora Folk Festival, for about thirty years. It was always held just after Christmas, starting on Boxing Day, and went through to New Year's Day. It took place on a farm in backcountry, New Zealand; hundreds of musicians played there over the years. Everyone would camp in tents, and there would be communal dinners and lots and lots of music. These festivals had a big influence on me because there was this sort of beautiful freedom going on. ● The year I was ten at the Folk Festival, it was decided that there was going to be a big *hāngī*, a traditional New Zealand Māori banquet that called for a certain method of cookery. You dig a pit in the earth and lay branches across the top of the pit with rocks on top, and light a big bonfire. Eventually everything falls into the pit. When all the timbers have burnt out and it's just embers and rocks, it's insanely hot in the pit—over 1,000°C (1,800°F). You remove the rocks with a shovel, trying not to get burned, and clean the ash out of the pit. Then you put the rocks back, lay a pile of flax (a haylike plant) across the rocks, add the food on top, then more flax, and then you cover the whole thing with earth. You leave all that smoldering for about ten hours. It's really an amazing way to cook for a large amount of people—but you need a lot of food to put in the pit. ● My uncle told us we had to harvest a couple of wild geese. A lot of the people that attended the folk festival weren't from the country; however, I was born and raised there. There's a way that you handle yourself in the country. If you're raised the right way, with respect to animals, then understanding that animals need to be respected comes naturally. My father would never let us hunt for sport; the only reason why you would hunt for food was if you needed it. We had a big farm with a lot of bush on it and Dad would actually put himself between the animals and the hunters. People from the city don't understand this relationship between humans and other animals—man's umbilical cord to nature. We are animals as well. It's about respecting everything in the natural environment that you are a part of and connected to. ● A group of men and boys gathered, and I went with them. There was an air of excitement as they gathered weapons like baseball bats and sticks. Somebody had an axe, another man a hammer. After about forty-five minutes of hiking, we came across the wild geese. The men chased the geese up the side of a hill into a gully. The men kind of went crazy; I would liken their behavior to bloodlust. They lost their minds momentarily and they basically slaughtered all of the geese. My uncle had asked for two and they killed of thirty or forty of them…they bashed them to death. It was extremely brutal and crazy. I stood and watched, feeling sick inside, and I began to cry. When the men calmed down as they came off their adrenalized high, they realized that they'd done the wrong thing. They only took two of the geese back with them and they left the rest to rot in the paddock—another thing that my father never would have tolerated, a pointless and mean loss of life and food. ● We walked back to camp shamefully and it seemed nobody was going to say anything. I went to my uncle and I told him the story. And man, he lost it. I thought he was going to kill somebody. He spoke to those men the way I have seen farmers speak to their working dogs when they're really angry with them, when they're trying to muster the sheep and they can't get the sheep in the pen. He made them walk back, pick up all of the dead animals, and pluck all of them. They all went into the hāngī. Under the earth went forty geese. That smell of goose fat coming out of that steamy pit in the ground is something I'll never forget my whole life. ● And so it goes: music and food have always had this very close relationship for me because of those early experiences at the Tahora Folk

Festival. ● I created a dish early on at Attica around that memory. Cooking is very much about hiding the brutality of what we've done. If you were presented with a raw cut of beef cheek or something like that as a dish on a table, you'd be disgusted by it. Cooks hide the brutality by transforming the raw meat into something that's delicious and beautiful looking. Most people are disconnected from the fact that an animal died to provide that food. By cooking those geese in the hāngī at the Folk Festival, we hid the brutality. ● From the goose slaughter during the Folk Festival, I created a simple dish of potatoes cooked in the earth they were grown in. There's a symbiotic relationship between potatoes and soil, which might sound a bit flowery, but the same soil that flavors those potatoes when they are growing is then reflected in the flavor that emerges when they are cooked. Earth is a great conductor of heat; it holds a very even heat, so you can cook the potatoes in an earth oven. The consistency is unbelievable because they come out from tip to tip cooked exactly the same. That's impossible to do pretty much any other way when you are cooking a potato. This method inspired by the hāngī presents a unique texture and flavor inspired by traditional Māori cooking. And it became a dish that helped make the restaurant. ● Music is a big part of culture and life in New Zealand. There's always been a reggae kind of Rastafarian influence. We grew up with reggae, which turned into dub, which is a really big feature of the landscape. In addition, there is Māori music—Te Pūoro Māori and influence of the Pacific Islands. Culturally, the biggest influence on me has been the record label Flying Nun, which was founded in New Zealand in 1981. It's still in existence and is now owned by Neil Finn and the label's original founder Roger Shepherd. It had one of my favorite bands of all time on its roster—the Clean, who are a revolutionary New Zealand band that influenced a lot of other bands worldwide. The Flying Nun label just punched so far above its weight. It was a different time, Internet free. At that time, New Zealand was so disconnected from other parts of the world, geographically and therefore in terms of news, social media, and the like. ● There is a deep well of creativity in New Zealand that we call kiwi ingenuity. People here have to innovate because we don't have a lot of the same commercial opportunities that people have in the States, England, or even Australia. Our nation had to innovate twice as much just to be even slightly noticed. The Flying Nun musicians were not creating music with any intention of becoming commercially successful. The music was pretty pure. It was a sort of innocence. That label is an influence on me because as a cook, I've always been influenced by things from my part of the world. I've always held creative Kiwis and Aussies in the highest regard. Europe was not an inspiration to me because I'd never been there. It didn't relate to my landscape or my upbringing. I looked to local chefs and to Australian chefs because they were my part of the food world—and sort of my music world, too. ● Punk music also really helped shape me. The idea of self-publishing, making everything yourself, on a small budget, of course—just making a small amount of money go a really long way. And the no-excuses approach is part of Attica's DNA. That plus a healthy amount of us-against-the-world mentality laid down the foundations and attitude of how we would approach everything—from honest relationships with suppliers questioning everything to DIY art projects inside the restaurant made by family to collaborating with up and coming artists and makers to the actual music that is playing in the dining room. At the restaurant at that time, we had no money. So rather than whine or complain, we made things. My father and I found an old fridge on the side of the road and turned it into the first cold smoker. We didn't have nice plates, so when important people came to the restaurant, I would ask friends who work for more corporate venues to loan me plates. My budget to set up the kitchen when I took over here was $1,000 dollars. Rather than complaining, I took that and made the most of it. I found plates that no one else wanted but which were different looking, and which I could use until we could gain enough momentum to afford to buy things—the whole time just remembering all those core values of punk. ● I think when you've grown up in a strong culture, it influences how you view the world. For me, one thing that music said to me was, "Let's go—let's get in it, question everything, and make the most of life. Let's not make ANY excuses about why we can't, let's get on doing, let's make something beautiful out of nothing. And let's never forget where we came from." Attica started with two staff in the kitchen and two staff in the dining room. Now we have forty-two full-time employees. We have grown our restaurant, but we have always stayed true to who we are. Thank you, Ian MacKaye. ● From punk music and my parents, I learned to not give up. Another lesson I learned from music was kindness. ● Attica brought an additional sphere of influence to my life that includes musicians, art projects, skateboarding, and research, a combining of all these passions. I've found a way to bring together all of the things I am passionate about by making short films, and these always combine food and music. They are arty, and take on darker topics, like mental health or sustainability and overfishing. They were professionally made with a filmmaker friend; I'd write the story and I'd choose the music. That was always really important—but I didn't know about music rights. ● I was about thirty years old and I had been at Attica for a few years. It was a super desperate time financially, personally...just all around intense. I was scared that we were gonna go broke all the time. Amidst all that, I made this film about the intergenerational passing of knowledge, inspired by where I grew up in New Zealand. We harvested shellfish from the coast, but my father taught me how to do that the right way, with respect, as his father had taught him. I wanted to pass that on to my young son, who was about four or five at the time. We made this film about the overfishing of abalone on the south coast in Victoria. There was one song that I wanted to use by one of my favorite bands, Yo La Tengo, called "Green Arrow." We made the film and the song fit perfectly. ● We didn't sell it or anything, but we posted it on YouTube. As we started to make more films, I learned that if you use someone's music, you need to get permission and you need to pay for it. No one from Yo La Tengo ever said anything, but I felt bad, as I was a major fan, so I just took it down. A year later, I became friends with Jesper Eklow, the guitarist of a band called Endless Boogie, and Yo La Tengo came up in conversation. He was cool with them, so he

Well, what would Yo La Tengo do?

put me in touch. I sent them an email saying this is what we do, and this is what we're about. I asked Ira, one of the members, if there was any chance that we could get permission to use "Green Arrow" in our film and I didn't hear back. I neglected to say that we had already used it. ● Then, basically one year to the day, I heard from Ira, saying he was having a hard time reconciling the violation that he felt when he found out that I'd already used the song. It felt like a knife stabbing into my heart. I didn't know how to respond, so I just left it for a few days. I was gardening in our vegetable garden across the road from Attica about a week later when another email came; it was Ira again. "We're in Melbourne now. We're playing a show in two days. Would you like to come? Let me know. I'll arrange tickets." ● I responded straight away, saying I felt so embarrassed about my behavior, and humiliated. I said I didn't feel like I deserved to come to their show, but that I would love to come. They were playing at Hamer Hall. It's a beautiful venue normally used for classical music. When I got the tickets on the back was written, "Ben—come see us afterwards, we'll be at the merchandise desk signing." I came into the auditorium and it was obvious that he'd chosen my seat himself because it was one of the best seats in the house, right in the middle. A perfect bird's-eye view. ● When the show began, I started getting really paranoid; the whole time, through the whole concert, I'm thinking, *It's going to be like that Phil Collins show where he stops the show to call out that guy who saw the other guy drowning and didn't do anything about it.* I thought Yo La Tengo was going to stop playing and be like: "That guy stole our music! You should beat him up!" But that didn't happen. ● It was an amazing performance. Afterward I did go to the merchandise desk, and eventually I was the last person there. We met face to face, and we talked for about twenty minutes, the entire time I'm thinking, "Wow, why are you being so nice to me?" At the end I had to ask why they were treating me with such kindness after what I did. Ira said simply, "Yeah, but I can tell you're not a bad person." ● And after that we slowly became friends. Subsequently, we catch up around the world; whenever we're in the same town when they're touring and I'm doing public speaking or cooking somewhere, we'll catch up for dinner, and it's just a lovely friendship. ● I'd never experienced kindness like that before, because most people when wronged turn around and try to wrong the person who wronged them...and maybe up to that point in my life, I'd been more vindictive myself. This was really the first time that a stranger that I'd done the wrong thing to turned around and, instead of anger, there was this wonderful gift. I learned about kindness from Yo La Tengo. There's this kind of saying we have at Attica: If there's a decision to be made that's a tough decision and we don't know what to do, I'll say, "Well, what would Yo La Tengo do?" I try to remember that act of kindness always, because it had a really profound effect on me. It actually changed me, and from there I went on to do a lot of other things based around kindness and inclusiveness. It's just flat-out rare to experience that kind of treatment. Generally, most people who've been wronged want to hurt someone in turn—they want to retaliate. Yo La Tengo just operate on a different plane to the rest of us. Exceptional humans.

NUMRA SIDDIQUI

Numra Siddiqui is the founder of Empress Market, a British-Pakistani food pop-up and events caterer. Numra launched Empress Market to share a fresh perspective on modern Pakistani identity through her grandmother's recipes. Numra currently operates a street food residency at the Pitch, an outdoor terrace in Stratford, and hosts curated dining experiences and private events across London.

EM Choons Playlist ▶
This music will take you to the places I've been, to where I currently reside, and along with me on the journeys I have yet to make.

1.	**Mogoya**	Oumou Sangaré
2.	**Cranes in the Sky**	Solange
3.	**Sweet Honey**	Peyton
4.	**Time Can Wait**	Leo Kalyan
5.	**I'll Call U Back**	Erykah Badu
6.	**Spanish Joint**	D'Angelo
7.	**Bibi Sanam Janem**	Zeb and Haniya
8.	**Jibal Alnuba**	Débruit and Alsarah
9.	**You're the One**	Kaytranada
10.	**Boom Boom**	Nazia Hassan
11.	**The Perfect Blues**	Jesse Boykins III and Melo X
12.	**Jogi**	Fariha Pervez and Muazzam Ali Khan
13.	**Love Will Tear Us Apart**	Joy Division
14.	**Ruby**	Ali Farka Touré and Toumani Diabaté
15.	**Je Pense à Toi**	Amadou et Mariam

Song: Ruby by Ali Farka Touré and Toumani Diabaté

▲ Numra Siddiqui

UNITED KINGDOM

Baingan Ka Bhurta

Clean, simple. Both the song and the dish will take you far away, perhaps to a place where you are sitting around a smoky, open fire under the desert stars without a care in the world.

Serves 6

Smoked

Aubergines in Onion and Tomato Masala

3 large eggplants (aubergines), about 1.5 kg total

1 large Spanish onion, about 600 g

5 vine-ripened tomatoes, about 600 g total

100 g vegetable oil

20 g salt

10 g red pepper flakes

5 g ground turmeric

Cilantro (coriander) leaves, for garnish

Naan bread, for serving

Recipe Inspiration:

Ruby

by Ali Farka Touré and Toumani Diabaté

Pierce the eggplants (aubergines) in a few places with a fork and place over an open flame, preferably a hot fire in a charcoal grill, but a gas burner is just as effective.

Let the flame burn the skin off the eggplants, turning them every minute or so using tongs, until charred on every side.

When all the sides have been burnt, gently take the eggplants off the flame and place them in a bowl of cool water. Peel away the burnt skin, rinsing off under water if needed, leaving behind the soft, cooked flesh. Discard the stems.

Meanwhile, finely dice the onion and tomatoes. In a frying pan over medium heat, fry the onions in the oil until they are soft and translucent. Add the salt, red pepper flakes, and turmeric and cook, stirring until the oil separates. Add the tomatoes and cook until the water evaporates and again, the oil separates.

Roughly chop the cooked eggplant flesh. Add to the onion and tomato masala and cook until the eggplant flesh is tender and cooked through. The color will change as you cook the dish through and the oil separates. This stage of cooking is called *bhunna*.

Sprinkle the dish with coriander leaves and serve with fluffy naan bread.

My eclectic taste in music

Song: Ruby by Ali Farka Touré and Toumani Diabaté

Music was always playing around me growing up. My mum listened to South Asian classics, my dad liked the Eagles, and my elder brother was a massive Madonna fan, so there was a real mix of genres playing around me! The Eagles's "New Kid in Town" is my all-time favorite song. I remember drifting in and out of sleep to Glenn Frey's crooning as a child on family road trips during the summer. At times, the song was the soundtrack to my dreams!

●

Other songs have really shaped chapters in my journey. I was obsessed with Hanson for a brief period during my early teens. I bought all their albums, dancing to "MMMbop" on repeat, plastering my walls floor to ceiling with their posters. Alt-J's cover of "Lovely Day" carried me through rainy market days when I first started my business. Amadou et Mariam's "Je Pense à Toi" sets the mood for the late hours of the dinner service at the Empress Market restaurant residency. And I've lost count of the amount of times my team and I stopped cooking to dance to "You're the One" by Kaytranada! These songs are the soundtrack to my life.

●

My obsession and dedication to certain artists and songs has really shaped the way I manage the things I care about. The passion for my craft as a chef, my focus as a businesswoman definitely comes from my teen musical obsessions. My eclectic taste in music, from Hanson to Nas, has allowed me to connect with all sorts of people. It ties in with my multicultural identity, being from more than one place and being able to identify with different things. You can always get along with people and engage with their story if you enjoy their music.

has allowed me to

●

The summer I launched my business (then it was a food stall called *Bun Kabab*), one day, it started pouring down rain. It was one of those heavy summer showers and I wasn't prepared for it at all. Everything was drenched… and yet somehow my sturdy Bluetooth speaker carried on playing music. (And still works to this day!) I was near tears as I struggled to protect my new equipment, to keep my stock of bread dry, when suddenly Alt-J's "Lovely Day" came up on my playlist. I couldn't help but laugh at that moment, and realized I had to let the elements have their way with me. Whenever I feel a little bit helpless, I listen to that song and I'm reminded to let go and let things ride their course.

Food is more than a means for filling your belly; it's also a way of creating an experience. The music I play during my food service really creates the mood for each course. I spend a lot of time curating my Empress Market playlist, pairing each song with the food like a good wine or cocktail. And it's not just about playing songs from the ethnic origins of the food. My cooking is an expression of who I am. People are always amused when the songs shuffle from Nas to Asha Bhosle. Food and music are integral to any Pakistani gathering and entertaining. You need to have good food and a solid playlist because that's the only thing people will remember. I've always loved entertaining friends, and part of that is having the perfect menu and curating the perfect playlist! The two go hand in hand for me.

Personally, I need good music when I'm in the kitchen. I can't work in silence, so the tunes I'm listening to really set my rhythm. It can't be too hectic during prep; I'd find that stressful. But then, a bit of drum and bass during the busy service is everything! You'll find me bopping my feet, dancing around the kitchen when I'm in my element! So, music is really important for getting the right mood in the kitchen.

As for the service floor, I like music to be quite relaxing to start off with, generally; then maybe some upbeat numbers during the peak hours and some classics as service begins to ease off. I do love it when guests recognize an obscure classic song or even ask what songs I'm playing. It means they are part of the larger experience and all the elements are coming together toward the hospitality I provide.

One night during service, a table started singing "Boom Boom" by Nazia Hassan. It was a group of young Pakistani people, so they instantly engaged with the nostalgia of the song. By the end of the five minutes, the whole restaurant was singing "Boom Boom," whether they knew the song or not. It did feel quite special!

Music and food are both about creating a mood and evoking certain emotions. Good hospitality is more than just serving a plate of food. I like my guests to feel almost like they have entered my home and are experiencing a part of who I am; and this can only be achieved through the atmosphere I create around what they eat. Music is so integral to this process, where the songs become part of the lasting memory of the overall experience.

connect with all sorts of people

CURTIS STONE

Curtis Stone began his career in his homeland of Australia and later honed his skills at Michelin-starred restaurants in London under renowned chef Marco Pierre White. He opened his first solo restaurant, Maude, in 2014, followed by Gwen Butcher Shop and Restaurant, with his brother Luke. Curtis has appeared on top-rated programs in the U.S. and Australia and is a *New York Times* best-selling author with six cookbooks.

T.N.T. by AC/DC

Song: T.N.T by AC/DC

Firestarter Playlist ▶ We often find our identity through music, but tastes change and develop over time, quite like our palate. When I was young, I liked everything loud, but more recently my wife and my kids dictate my choices. We dance a lot as a family—in the kitchen, or buckled up in the car. This is a bit of a smorgasbord, but these cuts have range, while taking me back to what we listen to now.

1.	Anarchy in the U.K.	Sex Pistols
2.	Firestarter	The Prodigy
3.	White Light / White Heat	Lou Reed
4.	Summer	Calvin Harris
5.	What's Love Got to Do with It	Tina Turner
6.	1999	Prince
7.	The One Thing	INXS
8.	Ddu-Du Ddu-Du	Blackpink
9.	Stitches	Shawn Mendes
10.	Cole's Memories	Pyramid

▲ Curtis Stone

USA

BBQ MARRON with Wakame, Kombu and a Saltbush Dukkah

GWEN BUTCHER SHOP & RESTAURANT

From Maude's Western Australia menu. I think most people forget that AC/DC are Aussies. This song just takes me back.

Serves 10

■ **For the wakame powder:**

250 g dried wakame seaweed

■ **For the court bouillon:**

2 lemons

100 g celery, medium dice

100 g carrots, peeled, medium dice

150 g onion, medium dice

50 g shallots, medium dice

2 fresh bay leaves

30 g parsley leaves

50 g dry white wine

4 liters water

■ **For the BBQ sauce:**

500 g Worcestershire sauce

500 g rice wine vinegar

250 g fresh lime juice

50 g grated garlic

10 g Tabasco sauce

■ **For the kombu oil:**

4 full sheets kombu (dried kelp)

500 g grapeseed oil

■ **For the *dukkah*:**

60 g hazelnuts, toasted and chopped

10 g coriander seeds

3 g cumin seeds

5 g dried parsley

To make the wakame powder, in a heatproof bowl, pour boiling water over the dried wakame and cover with plastic wrap (cling film) immediately. Let steep for 30 minutes until vibrant green. Wring out all the water through cheesecloth until dried. dried. Separate the rehydrated wakame on non-reactive trays (or lined trays with parchment) in a single layer.

Dehydrate the wakame at 160°F (71°C) for 8 hours, or until vibrant green and dry. Blitz in a food processor to a powder. Reserve in an air-tight container with silica packets.

To make the court bouillon, combine the juice of the lemons along with the spent rinds, the celery, carrots, onion, shallots, bay leaves, parsley, white wine, and water in a pot and place over medium heat. Bring the mixture to a boil and then reduce to a simmer. Simmer the mixture lightly for 30 minutes. Strain through a fine chinois and chill. Reserve.

To make the BBQ sauce, in a heavy-bottomed pot, combine the Worcestershire, rice wine vinegar, lime juice, grated garlic, and Tabasco. Simmer over medium heat until reduced by three-fourths. Remove from the heat and reserve.

To make the kombu oil, preheat the oven to 350°F (180°C).

Toast the kombu on a baking sheet in the oven until nice and crispy and fully dried, with a nutty aroma, about 30 minutes.

Once toasted, cut the kombu with scissors into manageable pieces. Transfer to a blender, add the grapeseed oil, and blitz on high for 5 minutes, or until smoking. Strain through 3 layers of cheesecloth and reserve.

To make the *dukkah*, on a baking sheet, toast the hazelnuts in a 350°F (180°C) oven until fragrant and all the oils are released.

Chill and chop to the desired consistency. In a small, dry frying pan, toast the coriander and cumin seeds separately until the oils are released. Let cool ▶|

LOS ANGELES, CA

and put through a spice grinder until well blended.

In a bowl, mix the chopped hazelnuts, coriander, cumin, and dried parsley together. Place a silica packet in the mixture and reserve.

To blanch the marron, bring the strained court bouillon up to a simmer. Prepare an ice bath and set aside.

Prepare a grill on medium high heat while processing the marron.

Place the dormant marron in the court bouillon and blanch for 90 seconds. Immediately transfer them to the prepared ice bath for 45 seconds until cold throughout. Cut the marron In half through the head and tail keeping them intact. Remove the tail meat from the shell and place a small piece of butter in the tail shell. Remove the head meat from the shell and discard, place a small piece of butter in the head as well. Place the tail meat back in the shell on top of the butter.

Separate the claws from the body of the marron and carefully remove the claw and knuckle meat and place inside the head of the marron on top of the butter. Baste the flesh of the marron in the BBQ sauce with a pastry brush until well coated.

Now grill the half bodies of marron flesh side up until the butter begins to froth and the marron turns a slight pink, about 2 minutes. Baste the meat after one minute of cooking and right when it comes off the grill.

Drizzle with the wakame oil, coat with the dukkah and dust with the wakame powder. Serve.

● Music's been such a big part of my life, it's so emotionally connected for me; it always has been. When I actually dig right down to the very first songs that I remember, I grew up in the '80s and my mom was a single mom. It was right when a lot of those slow, sad songs were big, like "True" by Spandau Ballet. It was all about heartbreak, and I can remember her playing music that was kind of sad and depressing, but it was also comforting. In our home and in our culture, food and music shared a togetherness that came as one. My mom would set the table, turn off the television, play some music, and light a candle, really creating this moment around eating. She always made food and eating together a special occasion. Music certainly helped set the scene, so I've always had music in my life. There's always music playing in my house and in my restaurants, it's just part of who I am. ● When I was a teenager, I listened to and connected with stuff that was super rebellious punk music, like the Sex Pistols, and bands that allowed me to throw some of my personal stuff off. I was feeling very rebellious as a young man, as an adolescent, and I was never exactly sure why. Maybe it had something to do with my upbringing or my personal situation. I didn't like going to school very much, so I wanted to rebel, and music gave me that avenue, that vehicle to do so. Whether it was listening to the Dead Kennedys or the Clash or the Who, they gave me time to stop to think about the world. It gave me a reason to pound my fist into my chest and believe in something different than what was being taught at home or at school. That music also allowed me to be a little bit more independent. Music gave me a sense of belonging. Going out to watch a band, I felt like part of the same club as other people who felt the same way I did or who were maybe going through the same stuff. It is an interesting tribal thing, especially when you're listening to that genre of punk, as it is quite alternative and quite different. When you're among other people who are into the same music as you and as much as you, it allows you to be a part of your own community. ● When I was growing up, I always loved to eat; food is something I've been obsessed with since I was a kid. I started cooking when I was really young because I wanted to understand how to make something delicious. My experience in the kitchen has continued to evolve, because the importance of cooking to me never went away. I started when I was eighteen, and my love of music has always been side by side with it. Music has always been in sync with food for me, both the preparation of food and being lucky enough that I've worked in restaurants that allow music. A lot of the kind of restaurants I grew up in

▲ Curtis Stone

MUSIC GAVE ME A SENSE OF BELONGING

MUSIC GAVE ME A SENSE OF BELONGING

didn't allow it, but tellingly enough, I was drawn to places where people enjoyed having music on in the kitchen. ● Cooking is also a very nurturing thing. Being a parent, that's the one thing that you create for your family, for your children, that is all about survival. That means safety and continuity, all wrapped around food. There's nothing more primal than that; but I do feel music is similar. I grew up in Australia, where our native people, the Aboriginal people, have performed *corroboree*, a mixture of music and dance to tell and celebrate their stories, for fifty thousand years. Their stories get passed down through music, as do stories around food about what you can and can't eat. ● It's like that across all cultures. If you ask someone, "What's your favorite thing you've ever eaten?," 90 percent of people answer with something like, "My mom used to make this chicken dish," or "My grandma made this veggie dish," or "My aunt used to make this beef dish." It's that personal connection that people have to food that's so special. ● When you're a chef, you're telling a story through your food, but it's more than that; you're actually telling a story or creating an environment through the experience that you offer. It's multifaceted—it's how low the light is, what sounds are coming out of the stereo, what smells are wafting from the kitchen, what's on your plate and then tasted. All of those elements have a big influence on us. ● When I briefed the designers for Gwen, one of the first things I spoke about was how I wanted this restaurant to feel a certain way. Before I even had an idea of what I wanted the design to be, I knew the vibe I wanted, so I created a playlist of the kind of music that I wanted to play. I wanted it to feel a little random, I didn't want to have a particular style. I wanted to play the blues, I wanted to play rock and roll. I curated thirty songs that were in the brief to the designers. It was a range of artists, everything from Al Green to Local Natives to Yeah Yeah Yeahs to Cat Power to the Strokes. I can remember sitting with the design team when they read that first paragraph, which spoke about the music, and they totally understood what I was looking for. They knew exactly what I wanted to create, and that playlist helped express the vision. ● Music is super connected for me in terms of my mood, so however I'm feeling, you'll know it by my music selection. When it comes to my work, we play rock and roll in the morning—quite loud, really aggressive music. I like bands like Queens of the Stone Age and Rage Against the Machine to get us moving and jiving around the kitchen, because we're getting ready for service. On the other end of the spectrum, on a Sunday morning, if I'm at home cooking for my family, that's when I'll play classical music. I also like Jack Johnson, because his music puts me in my happy place more than anyone else. It's very chill, very calm, and it makes me slow down a little when I am in a kitchen, when we're not like pumping around getting ready for service. ● Pre-service is very much "we're here, we're at work, let's go," so that's when we put on high-energy music. I work with some chefs who don't like the music to be too abrasive first thing in the morning, but I'm like, "Crank it, let's go, let's get down to business!" I like music to be super energetic—I can listen to dance music or I can listen to punk or I can listen to rock and roll, but it's got to have a lot of energy. During service, it depends on the restaurant, because each one has very different characteristics. Maude is very romantic, very intimate, and the music mirrors that. We play things like Etta James; there's a real sophistication to that dining room and therefore to the music choices. It's about creating a really beautiful environment every single night. People are coming there for their birthdays and anniversaries, so we try to set the atmosphere to suit those occasions. ● I approach cooking food the same way a musician layers a song. The different sounds are like the ingredients, and I layer them over each other, manipulating them in different ways to fine-tune their flavors or change their textures. I arrange them on top of or alongside each other to create a dish that is meant to tell a story or make you feel something. It can be something that is straight-up delicious, or something that is really hot, crunchy, spicy, and salty, so a little more complex. I find lots of similarities in the two processes—maybe that's why we have so many musicians who come to our restaurants, because they see the creative process we share.

JEREMIAH STONE

AND FABIÁN VON HAUSKE VALTIERRA

Jeremiah Stone and Fabián von Hauske Valtierra, chef-owners of Contra and Wildair, pride themselves on cooking ambitious yet accessible food. Inspired by their personal histories and the culinary traditions found in New York's Lower East Side, in 2014, they opened Contra, a tasting menu–only restaurant, which has held one Michelin star since 2016. Wildair, a casual wine bar, followed in 2015 and quickly gained recognition from the *New York Times*, which awarded it two stars, and *Bon Appétit*, which named it a Best New Restaurant 2016.

strawberries

Evolutions Playlist ▶ This is a playlist of bands we really like, and sort of tries to show the evolution of their work: The first songs are the earlier stuff and then it dives into how the band has been evolving. We love all these bands; they all have very different sounds, but they have a lot in common in the way they build their songs.

1.	Deadbolt	Thrice
2.	In Exile	Thrice
3.	Blood Clots and Black Holes	Thrice
4.	Golden Haze	Wild Nothing
5.	Blue Wings	Wild Nothing
6.	Breakers	Local Natives
7.	Blue Blood	Foals
8.	Spanish Sahara	Foals
9.	White Onions	Foals
10.	Ebolarama	Every Time I Die
11.	Map Change	Every Time I Die

Fabián ▶

This dessert is inspired by driving through Irapuato on the way to see my mom's family in Guanajuato, Irapuato, the strawberry town of Mexico. We would always listen to "Down Under" by Men at Work when my dad was driving, so memories of that drive and this song always take me back to thinking of strawberries.

Serves 4

■ For the granita:

4 liters strawberry juice

Salt

Sugar, for seasoning

Fresh lemon juice, for seasoning

■ For the corn mousse:

200 g dried blue corn

1.2 kg cream

315 g milk

70 g sugar

100 g trimoline

50 g milk powder

5 gelatin sheets

260 g egg yolks

■ For the popcorn powder:

3 cups popcorn kernels

100 g sugar, cooked into caramel

■ **16 small strawberries,** for serving

Irapuato
strawberries

Recipe
Inspiration:

Down
Under

by Men at Work

To make the granita, season the strawberry juice with salt, sugar, and lemon juice to taste. Freeze in a square container overnight. When frozen, scrape with a fork into more or less uniform shards. Reserve the granita in the freezer.

To make the corn mousse, cold-infuse the blue corn with the cream overnight. Strain and reserve. Make a custard with the rest of the ingredients and let cool. When cool, add the cream and reserve the base in the refrigerator.

To make the popcorn powder, pop the popcorn and toss with the caramel. Let cool, then process to a powder in a mixer or food processor.

To assemble, put the mousse base into a whipped cream canister and charge twice with No. 2 charges. Pipe a mound of it in each of 4 frozen bowls. Arrange fresh strawberries on top. Place 2 tablespoons of the granita on top of each mousse and sprinkle the popcorn powder on top. Serve immediately.

● **Jeremiah Stone** ● Hip-hop was my true love, starting at age ten. Then I started DJing when I was thirteen, in middle school, and that really shaped and formed who I was and who I hung out with. I was going out to shows at fourteen, fifteen years old and I used to travel with people who were in their twenties and thirties, so they took me under their wings and took me out to the clubs. It was a normal part of the scene, the concept of sharing hip-hop culture. DJs wanted to make sure that their world had younger people coming around to support them. I wanted to pay my respects, show them I knew their stories, and that was a large part of all of my life growing up. I didn't really feel like I fit in with kids at school, so I plugged into a lot of the older folks' scene, and they took me around and showed me the ropes. ● I would go to different shows, different clubs, and I was exposed to a diverse crowd at a young age. Without music, I would have been a little bit more ignorant or close-minded to certain things. I'm first-generation Chinese—my parents immigrated here, and what I was exposed to at home was very homogenous. But as I grew up, most of my friends were all connected through music, even though everyone had a different background and upbringing. ● One of the reasons I started cooking was that I wanted to be a DJ. When I was seventeen, one of my close friends, who was twenty-seven, was already established as a DJ. He was much better than I was, so he basically warned me about becoming a DJ and told me how hard it was, that there was a lot of competition. He encouraged me to get a day job to make money on the side, and that was really what led me to getting my first restaurant job, right out of high school. ● I had worked other jobs, but that first restaurant job made me realize that being a professional musician was not really my path. When I got into cooking, that same friend helped me do everything from writing my essay to get into cooking school to encouraging me to stick with it. As I started my career, it was so great to have somebody supporting me who I had met through music, through DJing, and who had lived a full

life. He had traveled the world spinning and producing music. And he was there for me, to coach me and encourage me to continue my love for music, but to stick with cooking. So that's how I got into the restaurant world. ● Music influences our culture, our scene, and our cooking because everyone we're around is always listening to music. Even though everyone has different tastes, you can get an idea of the food they cook by what they listen to. For example, if someone really loves classical music, their food might be a little bit more fine-dining or there may be a certain kind of beauty to their plating. If they like hip-hop music or certain kinds of rock music, maybe their food's a little more loosened up, with funky combinations and something a little bit more casual. ● The food that we make has a certain seriousness to it, but it is also fun and simple, and that's what our restaurants represent. And I think that combination of sentiments can be found in a lot of music I listen to. I don't like overproduced music; I like very kind of simple things, like jazz or country. There are a lot of similarities between the type of music that I like to listen to and the food of our restaurants.

● **Fabián von Hauske Valtierra** ● The reason I fell in love with music is that while my father is a serious man, on weekends he would always have his buddies at home and they would have great hangs with music. I remember him always playing Men at Work, songs like "Dr. Heckle and Mr. Jive." It's one of the songs I remember the most; I would always go to his studio just to take out that vinyl and play it again and again. ● My father always listened to a lot of Bob Marley, too, while we were driving to see my mom's family in Mexico. On the way there, there was this really famous market in Irapuato, which had these amazing strawberries and cream. It's a flavor that I use in many of my desserts because they remind me of my mom—and then immediately, I think of Bob Marley, because of my dad. It's funny how sounds, smells, and flavors will bring you a memory. I'll try something or I'll hear something or I'll smell something, and it brings me back to that dessert from that moment in my life. Like right now, I'm picturing myself in the back of a car, listening to fucking Bob Marley and hearing my parents talk about strawberries and cream. ● When I was a kid, my parents forced me to play in the orchestra in school. Like Jeremiah, I'm very obsessive, so I became obsessed with playing drums and I started a hardcore band. I always just wanted to find something, and I realize that I was always looking for an artistic point of view in my life, rather than wanting to be an accountant or something like that. That's how I got into cooking. ● Thrice (who Jeremiah also loves) and Wild Nothing are two bands that I discovered and listened to at stages of my life when I was really young and sort of weird. It's an intense thing when you find a band that progresses the same way you do…I like those two bands because every album they've put out is different than the one before. I felt like their changes were very similar to my stages of life—like the first record they put out was super hardcore and really heavy, and then they got even heavier. I was at that point of my life where I really liked that heavy music. Then around the time I started to get into design and photography and all those things, those guys became super abstract and started releasing records that were very out there, which was like my art. We've become friends with them, and their music still aligns and resonates with me. Now their music is much more straightforward and much more refined, which is like how I feel about my cooking these days. ● Creation in our kitchen and the creativity in music give me the same sort of feeling, especially if I look at them through the perspective of art's visual interaction with society. There's an equation in my mind, where the things that I listen to have visual connotations to me. I'll listen to a song and visualize it in a very geometric way, where I can really find the small subtleties.

"Now I take what's mine, from the ground that I cultivate."
— O Brother

I think about that artistic approach in the same way when it comes to our food. When I come up with a dish, it's very simplistic, but in a very chaotic way, and that's the kind of music I listen to: songs like "White Onions" by Foals, "Black Honey" by Thrice, "Breakers" by Local Natives. That's the same reason I'm drawn to the kind of design work I do; and I look at our food like any type of art with an attached visual medium. ● There's a band called O Brother and in my email signature, I have used a quote from them: "Now I take what's mine, from the ground that I cultivate." We were doing this interview for *Vogue* and I mentioned how I liked this band to the interviewer. Then two days after the article came out, one of their managers contacted me. He lives in New York and he said, "Man we just saw this and we are stoked. The guys are in New York and they're playing a show if you want to come, we'll get you some tickets." And I was like, "You guys should come in for dinner." They came in and we met them, including Fred Feldman, who owns Triple Crown records and is such an amazing guy. That all started from me putting a quote from a song that I love in an email, and then I got to meet one of my favorite bands. ● When I get into a band, I listen to their first record and then I listen to their most recent one. Even if they're extremely different, at the same time, they're very much the same because they were created by the same people, which is so interesting to me. With our food, you could look at it in the same way. Here are these chefs who started cooking one way, but they have kept at it for years and they have a lot of experience, so their food changes, but the fundamentals are the same. The changes may seem like they represent very different approaches, but it's all coming from the same basic ideas and point of view. There are a lot of layers that have to be built to create something that sounds very specific, and that's the way we approach our cooking. You need to understand simple ingredients to build bases, but you might not see them in the final dish. A plate might look simple, in the same way a song might sound simple, but so much work goes into it.

MARSIA TAHA

Bolivian chef Marsia Taha graduated from the Hotel and Tourism School (Bolivia) and the Center for Hotel Studies of the Canary Islands (Spain). She had professional internships in restaurants such as Studio, the Standard, and Geist. In 2013, she joined the Gustu team, and in 2017 became head chef. At Gustu she works toward making Bolivian gastronomy an engine of socio-economic progress for her country, and promotes the use of forgotten native ingredients.

Picante Mixto Playlist ▶ The creative process in gastronomy depends on several aspects, such as the personality and mood of the chef. This process is as diverse as the musical taste or preferences in certain moments.

1.	**Karma Police**	Radiohead
2.	**Say It Ain't So**	Weezer
3.	**Ni Tú Ni Nadie**	Moenia
4.	**Déjate Caer**	Café Tacuba
5.	**Zoom**	Soda Stereo
6.	**Todos Los Dias De Sol**	Mimi Maura
7.	**Nunca**	Zoé
8.	**Ritual Union**	Little Dragon
9.	**Wildfire**	SBTRKT featuring Little Dragon
10.	**Pure Morning**	Placebo
11.	**The Bitter End**	Placebo
12.	**Clandestino**	Manu Chao
13.	**Starlight**	Muse
14.	**Ojala**	Silvio Rodriguez
15.	**Munasqechay**	Los Kjarkas
16.	**Embriágame Suavecito**	Grupo Nectar
17.	**Perfect**	Alanis Morissette

▲ Marsia Taha

BOLIVIA

NIXTAMALIZED FRIED CORN SPHERES ON HOMEMADE SRIRACHA

with Avocado–Ají Gusanito Emulsion, Goat Yogurt, K'Oa, and Fresh Cilantro

This dish reflects the cultural richness and biological diversity enclosed in the warm Bolivian valleys, with their great productive potential and amazing native ingredients, as well as the roots of our national identity.

Note, the homemade Sriracha needs 2 weeks to ferment.

Serves 10

Recipe Inspiration:

WARMIKUNA YUPAYCHASQAPUNI KASUNCHIK

by
Alcoholika La Christo
& Luzmila Carpio

■ For the homemade Sriracha:

1.5 kg fermented yellow chile paste

4 kg carrots, peeled and cut into big chunks

600 g sunflower oil

200 ml fresh lemon juice

10 g salt

50 g sugar

■ For the yellow corn spheres:

3 g sugar

5 g salt

15 g apple cider vinegar

500 ml warm water

400 g yellow corn flour

■ For the black corn spheres:

3 g sugar

5 g salt

15 g apple cider vinegar

500 ml warm water

400 g nixtamalized black corn flour

■ For the black corn crunch:

3 g sugar

5 g salt

15 g apple cider vinegar

500 ml warm water

400 g nixtamalized black corn flour

■ For the avocado emulsion:

250 g avocado pulp

1 g ají gusanito chiles

5 g salt

20 g lemon juice

■ For the goat yogurt:

1 litre goat yogurt

Salt

■ 10 g dried koa leaves, for serving

50 g cilantro (coriander) stems in brunoise, for serving

▶I

To make the Sriracha, ferment the chile paste at room temperature for 2 weeks.

Cook the carrots in boiling water until very tender.

Process all the ingredients, including the chile paste and carrots, in a food processor until a smooth and homogeneous paste forms. Transfer to a bowl or jar(s), cover tightly, and reserve in the refrigerator.

To make the yellow corn spheres, in a large mixing bowl, dissolve the sugar, salt, and vinegar in the warm water. Add the flour and stir until a consistent dough forms.

Shape the dough into spheres of different sizes: 3 g, 8 g, and 10 g. Freeze until firm, then fry in a deep pot of oil heated to 180°C (356°F).

Make the black corn spheres in the same way as the yellow.

To make the black corn crunch, in a large mixing bowl, dissolve the sugar, salt, and vinegar in the warm water. Add the flour and stir until a consistent dough forms. In a deep pot of oil heated to 180°C (356°F), fry dollops of the dough until they rise to the surface. Once fried, drain the excess oil by pouring the preparation onto absorbent paper.

To make the avocado emulsion, in a bowl, blend all the ingredients together until smooth.

Strain the yogurt until it has reduced its weight by about 60 percent. Mix with salt to taste.

To assemble, spread a circular base of 40 g of the Sriracha on each plate. Using cooking squeeze bottles, dot 40 g each of the goat yogurt and avocado emulsion. Sprinkle the yogurt and avocado dots with 1 g of the koa leaves and 15 g of the black corn crunch. Spoon 5 g of the cilantro (coriander) stalks in brunoise on top. Place 5 or 6 corn spheres of different sizes on the plate. Serve immediately.

Music says a lot about a person. It seems like all the music I have come to love is because of the people I've been surrounded by who have influenced me both in my life and in music. I grew up listening to '80s music when my parents were students and we were living in a student apartment in Sofia, Bulgaria. This meant that there were a lot of meetings, study sessions, and friendly gatherings going on in that apartment— with a constant accompaniment of music, of course. According to my parents, I loved "Another Day in Paradise" by Phil Collins. Music was a common factor that made me understand who the right people were to connect with. The style or styles of music you like usually says something about who you are as a person. ● Music is also related directly to our heritage in Bolivia. Music reflects the different states the country is in or has been in at any given moment. There is music related to the seasons, certain days and nights, and many other rituals we celebrate. If there is a celebration of any kind— birthdays, holidays, change of season, harvest, funerals—there will always be food and music. Music enhances the feelings we show while we dance and we feast. ● For me, music also helps balance work and my personal life. A large number of bands and artists influenced me early on in my career; Radiohead, Café Tacuba,

Bob Marley, Soda Stereo, and Manu Chao are definitely the ones who have meant the most to me. Not a lot of international bands come to Bolivia to play, but one time, Radiohead was going to play in Chile, and I wanted to go. My boss at that time wouldn't give me permission to travel—so I quit. I'm so happy I did. The concert was amazing. It was truly worth it! ● Music plays a huge role in terms of our daily work at the restaurant, as we use it to set a rhythm while we cook. However, the front of house staff often feel out of the vibe of the restaurant during service. During prep, you need to create a good energy within the team. This is often driven by playing music that fits the different personalities in the kitchen—often by finding music that a majority can relate to and sing along to. Just before the service begins, we usually need an energy boost, and that often comes from deep rhythms or high tempo, something like hip-hop; Kendrick Lamar's "HUMBLE." is a favorite. ● During service, the front of house is extremely aware of the vibe inside the restaurant. They may begin with music choices that have soft but steady rhythms. Later on, when further into service, the ambiance often lifts a bit and the music gets a bit faster; then it slows down a bit toward the end of service. At our restaurant, we believe that afrobeat often

gives the best vibe to go along with the type of experience we offer. A good example is Fela Kuti (and the tons of followers he has inspired). After service, it's free game. When the last of the guests have left and the last finishing up has to be done, the music is often turned up. The team pretty much chooses what is played for the rest of the night. ● I think food has reached such a celebrated status because of the people who cook. As we cherish or appreciate music composed by someone, we now appreciate food cooked by someone—same as music, it could come from a celebrity, a rock star, a Michelin-star-awarded chef, or the celebrities in our own families, like our grandmothers, mothers, or partners. I believe in gastronomy as a living cultural expression that represents a region, a country, and its people. Therefore, my creative process is influenced by as many cultural manifestations as possible. Music is probably part of the most important ones.

> my creative process is influenced by as many cultural manifestations as possible. Music is probably part of the most important ones

TALDE

DALE

Dale Talde's passion for cooking began at a young age in Chicago, where he learned to cook alongside his mother in the kitchen. A builder and inventor at heart, Dale Talde drives the creative process for his hospitality group, Food Crush Hospitality. The proud son of Filipino immigrants, he grew up immersed in his family's cultural heritage while also enjoying the life of a typical American kid. Dale applies that distinctive Asian-American experience to his menus and design aesthetics.

Eggplant Emoji Playlist ▶ I think this list paints a pretty accurate picture of me...or who I thought I was in high school when I had one pant leg rolled up and wore a bubble vest and Timbs (Timberland boots) in my suburban town. It's the perfect playlist to make sweet, sweet, sweet love to or smoke a blunt. Enjoy.

1.	Good Morning	Kanye West
2.	Let's Go Crazy	Prince
3.	Til I'm Laid to Rest	Buju Banton
4.	Passin' Me By	The Pharcyde
5.	93 'Til Infinity	Souls of Mischief
6.	Electric Relaxation	A Tribe Called Quest
7.	Award Tour	A Tribe Called Quest
8.	Check the Rhime	A Tribe Called Quest
9.	Big Pimpin'	Jay Z featuring UGK
10.	Who Shot Ya?	The Notorious B.I.G.
11.	Ante Up	M.O.P.
12.	If It Isn't Love	New Edition
13.	Just Friends	Musiq Soulchild
14.	Lady	D'Angelo
15.	Flamboyant	Big L

▲ Dale Talde

USA

bacon, GOOSEFEATHER
egg,
and cheese
fried rice

A bodega-style bacon, egg, and cheese sandwich is the remedy for any hangover in New York City, full stop. Grab one with a cup of coffee, blast "Check the Rhime," and tell your hangover to fuck off.

Makes 1 solo shame serving

8 oz bacon (streaky), cut into 1-inch pieces	
1 medium onion, diced	
3 cloves garlic	
1 tablespoon finely minced or grated fresh ginger	
4 eggs, beaten	
4 slices American cheese	
3 cups cooked white rice (preferably from leftover Chinese take-out)	
1 bunch scallions (spring onions), sliced	
Your favorite hot sauce	

Recipe Inspiration:

Check
THE
Rhime

by
A Tribe
Called Quest

The night before, make sure you go out drinking and party hard AF. Go to a show and make some questionable decisions with some sketchy "friends." Barely make it home, and please don't remember how you got there.

When you wake up, ignore all of your text messages, especially "Yo man, where did you go?" and in a large cast-iron pan over medium-high heat, cook the bacon to the desired crispness. Transfer the bacon to paper towels to drain.

In the bacon fat, sauté the onion, garlic, and ginger until aromatic, 2 to 3 minutes.

Add the eggs and scramble, making sure you don't brown them, then add the cheese and rice and raise the heat to high. Stir-fry for 3 to 4 minutes, then add back the bacon and fold in the scallions (spring onions).

Serve with as much hot sauce as you can handle.

Lastly, ghost any and all plans and friends for the day and go back to sleep.

One day when I was thirteen or fourteen, I was watching *BET Rap City* and A Tribe Called Quest's "Check the Rhime" video came on. Seeing that video was the first time I felt like, "I like this shit. I'm *into* this. Phife looks like me. Phife is five feet tall, so am I. He's dressing in a way that I want to look like. He looks mad cool. I don't know where Linden Boulevard is, but I want to go there." It felt like there was some form of angst, and I was such an angst-y teen, it was like finally someone understood what I was talking about. ● I used to go to shows at the Metro in Chicago, and one of the best was Common. I felt like, "Holy shit, this is it!" It was such a wild night. I was an intern at the Four Seasons at that point, and I got so hammered that I called in sick *from the* show. Common was in the background with me leaving a voice message from my phone: "Hey, it's Dale and I'm not going to make it in because I'm sick." I was twenty years old, and it was such an epic, positive moment in my life...it defined me. There was no way I was going to leave that show to get ready for early a.m. breakfast service at the Four Seasons. It was a once-in-a-lifetime show that I was never going to be at ever again. It was one of those moments that I knew I couldn't leave because the music was changing me. ● Hip-hop is the music culture I relate to the most. When it started, it was pretty marginalized. I feel like to some degree, we Filipinos have been the most marginalized Asians in America. To help fit in, I wanted to be a part of this music culture, and that is what hip-hop did for me. ● What drew me to the music was my personal angst, from a lack of identity. "Hey, you're Filipino and your parents are Filipino, but most of the Asian people or most of the white people and black people and anyone who's not Asian, think you are 'Oriental,' or think you're Chinese. They

don't really know what you are, right?" And then in our community, you speak the language, and your mom, your dad, your aunts and uncles, their friends, are from the Philippines. And they themselves will say, "Oh, 'they' are not Filipino, they are Filipino-Americans." Growing up in this culture of "Where do I belong?" made me, I think, want to eat American food just as part of trying to belong—and rebelling against eating rice and chicken adobo all the time was crucial. I wanted to eat what my white or black friends were having. At that time, they were eating fried chicken on the South Side and so that is what I wanted to eat. ● The music of A Tribe Called Quest allowed me to fit in somewhere. I was American because these guys were out there—they felt the same way I did. When I was in English class, we had to write stories about our lives—what dinner was like the night before, for example, or the conversation that we had at dinner. My Filipino friends, when talking about a regular dinner at one of their houses, were like, "Oh, my mom made a pot of chicken adobo and steamed vegetables, with a pot of rice." Then when I heard what my white friend ate, it was like: "Oh, my mom gave me twenty bucks and told me to go to this place called the Works, and I could order whatever I wanted, so I ordered a gyros plate with everything on it and a side of cheese fries and a Coke. And there was no conversation...I ate by myself, because my mom and my dad had already eaten." It was weird, because I just thought, "That sounds so awesome! That's so cool, you got to order whatever you want." There's this freedom of choice, this American value of, "No one is telling me what to eat or what to listen to." There's a freedom in just growing up. No one is censoring me, so I'm going to listen to what I want to listen to. ● All my friends, every single one of us, grew up in these immigrant families, where Filipino food was eaten at the house every single night because it's what your mom cooked, it's what your dad wanted to eat, so we ate that every single night. And so—I'm talking about a crew of twenty Filipino kids—the minute we left the house, and the minute we started making our own money, it was like, "No, I'm not eating Filipino food—I'm not even eating Asian food!" We ate fucking pizza. We ate Italian beefs at Al's. We went to Wiener's Circle...anything but Filipino food. I think we felt like, "Hey, we've been missing out on this shit," all the dope-ass street Chicago food, so we were crushing it. I'm pretty sure every single one of my friends had this affinity. ● But we loved Filipino food. We happily eat it when we go to each other's family things—when our moms are cooking for each other, or for your kid's first birthday or whatever. But when we get together, it's like, "Yo, we are going to Pequod's and doing four or five pizzas. We are going to Al's Italian Beef and getting down on the cheese fries and a combo Italian with double dips." And it was very...it was always understood. That was the craziest thing. We played ball, we'd go to concerts, and we never even had to have those discussions like, "Where are we going to eat?" We just headed to Al's, or to Buffalo Joe's to crush a couple hundred wings. ● The moment I realized that food has the same pop culture status as music was when I was listening to Goodie Mob's "Soul Food." If you know that track, the chorus is "Come and get yo' soul food, well well, Good old-fashioned soul food, all right" and then Cee-Lo comes in spitting this verse: "A heaping helping of fried chicken, macaroni and cheese, and collard greens" and it's just like, *boom*! That's exactly the song that I've always wanted, that's the song, that's the

anthem. They tied food and entertainment and hip-hop all together—all my favorite things into one verse, and it's like...it's not even talking about it in a weird abstract way, he is talking about eating chitlins and eating grits and collard greens and fried chicken hot sauce and it's like, "Yeah, man!" That's it, and that to me is when I knew that food in entertainment is real and positive. I know that people are thinking about it the same way as me. ● The whole message of staying positive in hip-hop that stuck with me is the same positivity I have found in house music. I'm a big Derrick Carter fan. He's the godfather of hip-hop and of house music in Chicago, and those are kind of my two favorite genres. I think of how smooth Derrick Carter is when he plays a session...the transitions are so smooth. He takes you through this ride, this up-and-down ride. That's how I create menus; I try to create menus that are just that smooth as silk. It's like house music but it has that jazz quality to it, and that inspires the flow of service. ● That's my dream, to be as smooth as Derrick Carter's cuts. I hope people leave our restaurant smiling, the way I feel like a lot of the hip-hop I listened to back in the day left me smiling. Going through a Derrick Carter set, listening to him jam out for three hours at a music festival, leaves me smiling, leaves me in this upbeat mood. That's what food and eating and creating menus and creating dishes that take you through the highs and lows is about; good food should be an experience that takes you through all those highs and lows, the ups and the downs that music can bring you through. I hope you eat my food and by the time you're done with it, there's a little bit of sadness that there isn't any more left, but you're walking out with a smile.

good food should be an experience that takes you through all those highs and lows, the ups and the downs that music can bring you through.

LEE TIERNAN

Lee Tiernan spent almost eleven years working his way up through the ranks of Fergus Henderson's St. John restaurant group, taking the position of head chef at St. John Bread and Wine in 2011. Lee founded Black Axe Mangal in the Bakken Nightclub in Copenhagen with his wife and business partner, Kate Tiernan, in 2014. In 2015, BAM, as it has become affectionately known, opened its doors for business in North London. Black Axe Mangal cuisine reflects London's vibrant multi-cultural communities.

Fuck 'em All Playlist ▶ I use music to focus and escape at the same time. This playlist helps me revert back to being a cook after being a dad all day, and vice versa. I'm usually in the weeds from the get-go, but I find this style of music gets me into a certain groove and helps me dig myself out of the shit. Parts of this playlist are pretty "hard," but playing grime in the dining room at the volume we do is not for the diner's benefit—it is for mine. The fact that the kitchen and the dining room are extensions of each other is neither here nor there. We used to play exclusively metal at BAM, but when that became mundane, we started to play a wider variety of music, and then our menu offerings broadened. That's when we really started to put whatever we liked on our menu: Music shapes things at BAM.

THAT'S NOT ME

by Skepta Ft. JME

Recipe Inspiration:

1.	**Round Ere**	Black Josh
2.	**Polaroid**	Slowthai
3.	**Lock and Load**	Milkavelli featuring Bakar
4.	**Sell Drugs**	Lee Scott
5.	**Where and When**	P Money featuring Giggs
6.	**Thiago Silva**	Dave x AJ Tracey
7.	**Seein' Double**	CASisDEAD
8.	**Revvin'**	Ocean Wisdom featuring Dizzy Rascal
9.	**BABY**	Giggs
10.	**Pulse 8**	JME
11.	**It Ain't Safe**	Skepta
12.	**Know My Ting**	Ghetts featuring Shakka
13.	**Ladbroke Grove**	AJ Tracey
14.	**Born On Your Own**	Maxsta x JME
15.	**Part Deux**	Cult of the Damned
16.	**Je t'adore**	Milkavelli featuring Lee Scott and Trellion
17.	**Vossi Bop**	Stormzy

▲ Lee Tiernan

UNITED KINGDOM

COCONUT LAKSA & PICKLED POMEGRANATE

▼ Lee Tiernan

When we opened Black Axe Mangal, I wanted to only play rock and heavy metal. I wore a bandana and painted the wood oven that dominates our tiny restaurant with the faces of the band Kiss. My vision for BAM was a kebab shop — a vision that changed the moment we opened our doors. Since opening, we've wanted to shed limitations and become a genre-fluid restaurant. This took time, but as our confidence grew, we dropped more and more of our mainstay menu options in exchange for new dishes. A long-term thorn in my side was to master decent vegetarian and vegan options. We opened with falafel being the only veggie main course. Granted, the falafel was hugely popular; but it always felt like a creative low point, a confidence-casualty dish. Eventually, we were confident enough to scrap the falafel and replace it with dishes like Laksa and Mushroom Mapo Tofu, which was a turning point in the evolution of BAM.

As the food evolved, our attitude toward the music we were playing was changing, too. We don't play a particular genre any longer. Grime has become a big part of BAM's identity and is a better representation of what we are trying to achieve. If Skepta, a self-produced Grime artist, can win the Mercury Prize and capture the imagination of the nation, we can definitely put laksa curry on our menu.

Everything in this dish except for the rice can be made days in advance of serving, so give yourself the time to enjoy bringing the dish together —

no need to stress out pulling it all together last minute. This curry is great to serve in the colder winter months, to warm everyone through when you've got a house full of mates over for a few drinks.

We serve this laksa with roasted bone marrow, smoked mutton, pulledham hock, or even pastrami on occasion — all of which work extremely well, as does any fatty, salty, smoky meat. Most recently we have been serving this as a vegan option with smoked and grilled aubergine alongside roasted sweet potatoes. We have some hardcore regular customers, most of whom come for the smoked meats and offal, so it's been nice to surprise them with a vegan option that has as high an impact of flavor as the meat-heavy options.

The pickles make this dish sing, so be generous with them. If you can't be bothered to make pickles, use a selection of your favorite shop-bought ones and fresh pomegranate or even pineapple. All the other garnishes add layers of texture and flavor as well as color. I personally love adding fish sauce to this recipe, so please don't feel obligated to keep it vegan if you're not that way inclined. Also the sweet potatoes are just a suggestion — green beans, new potatoes, corn, okra, roasted cauliflower, or pretty much any veg works well with the base sauce. Don't let my suggestions hinder your imagination.

This dish keeps well for over a week in the fridge.

Serves around 8 hungry people ▶|

■ For the *laksa* base:

4 star anise

3 tablespoons coriander seeds

8 green cardamom pods

5 banana shallots (echalions), peeled and roughly chopped

10 cloves garlic, peeled

40 g ginger, peeled and chopped into small dice

10 long red chiles, stemmed and roughly chopped

100 g coconut oil

1,200 ml coconut milk (three 400-ml tins)

100 g grated palm sugar or Demerara sugar

Bulbs of 3 stalks lemongrass, bashed up a bit

4 kaffir lime leaves

About 50 ml fish sauce, for seasoning (optional)

Fresh lime juice, for seasoning

■ **2 large sweet potatoes,** peeled and cut into 1-inch chunks

Olive oil, for coating

Salt, for seasoning

1 large or 2 smaller eggplants (aubergines), diced into 1-inch chunks

Steamed rice, for serving (plain, or I add a teaspoon of turmeric and a couple of star anise and green cardamom to jazz it up a bit when I'm feeling racy)

■ **For the garnish:**

Leaves or small sprigs from 1 bunch cilantro (coriander)

½ cup store-bought crispy shallots

½ cup toasted coconut flakes

1 teaspoon red pepper flakes (optional)

Pickled pomegranate, or a selection of your favorite pickles and fresh pomegranate

To make the *laksa* base, toast the star anise, coriander seeds, and cardamom pods in a small, dry frying pan over medium-high heat until fragrant. Transfer to paper towels to cool, then blitz them in a spice grinder and pass them through a fine-mesh sieve to remove any skins or pod fragments. Set aside.

In a blender, pulse the shallots, garlic, ginger, and chiles to a smooth purée.

Fry the ground toasted spices in the coconut oil over low to medium heat until melted, warmed through, and very fragrant, 3 to 5 minutes. Reduce the heat to low, add the shallot purée, and cook to reduce, stirring occasionally to prevent sticking, 10 to 15 minutes.

Add the coconut milk and stir to mix well. Add the grated palm sugar, the bruised lemongrass, and the kaffir lime leaves. Cook the laksa over low to medium heat, tickling and stirring occasionally, until reduced to a nice sauce consistency and the flavors have developed, 30 to 45 minutes.

While the curry is simmering, preheat the oven to 180°C (350°F).

Toss the sweet potato in a dash of oil, season with a pinch of salt, and transfer to a baking sheet. Roast until soft, with a pleasing bronze color on the edges.

At the same time, fry the eggplant (aubergine) in a similar way: Toss the chunks with a dash of oil and a pinch of salt and fry in a large frying pan (in batches of you don't have a big frying pan) until blackened and soft.

Finish the curry with the fish sauce (if using) and lime juice to taste.

Serve the laksa and vegetables warm in a deep dish with a big serving spoon, with the rice alongside or underneath. Garnish with the cilantro, crispy shallots, toasted coconut flakes, and red pepper flakes, if you like it spicy. Serve immediately.

● My earliest music memory was listening to Culture Club in my front room, with my mom dancing about. She had me when she was eighteen, actually, so we kind of grew up together. I just remember going mental in the front room listening to Boy George. "Karma Chameleon" definitely resonates with me and brings back a lot of good memories. ● Others of my warmest memories are fishing with my dad. We were never any good at catching fish, but we never ran out of things to say to each other or laugh about. We had two cassette tapes: Billy Joel's *An Innocent Man* for the journey there, Carole King's *Tapestry* for the way back. Those albums are special to me and

I reckon I can sing each song word for word. ● I always loved music, but when I first discovered Skid Row, Mötley Crüe, and Guns N' Roses, I totally immersed myself in all of that. That music always stayed with me. I was sixteen years old when Nirvana released *Nevermind* and Pearl Jam released *Ten*. The arrival of those two albums has had a lasting effect on me. I've always been quite heavily influenced by American culture, even though I'm very British. This all went hand in hand with skateboarding and that aggressive "dick out" rock philosophy, which was my attitude toward life at the time. ● My taste in music was different from the other kids on the estate I grew up on. At my school, there was a spot called the Crypt where local cover bands played songs by bands like Pearl Jam, Nirvana, and Red Hot Chili Peppers for fun. When I started going there, I didn't know who was going to be there or what I'd find, but it was mostly older kids from my school. There were loads of people that I didn't know but I had seen around school or skateboarding. We all shared these common interests in music, getting drunk, and moshing for hours. That was definitely a nice life moment when I realized that I wasn't just into this shit alone and there were others like me. ● I come from a large Irish Catholic family and I have been around traditional music my entire life. When I go back to Ireland, traditional is the type of music that I like to seek out if I can find a session close by. I'll go have a session in the pub and listen to that music; my wife loves it as well. It's the nicest community, and the musicians from the village come together in the pub to play together. Sessions like that make for a good sense of occasion and everyone gets into it. People start singing along and it's a great way to spend the night. It's not something you see too often in England. There aren't really pubs where you can go and see a bunch of people just playing instruments in a corner, having a laugh. ● There isn't much food at the pubs for those sessions; the fare on offer is usually a bag of chips afterward or something like that. There used to be a place in Ireland, where my dad's family comes from, called Fat Squans. They would do "spud balls," which were deep-fried "champ" (mashed potatoes and spring onions). They just ball the batter up and chuck them in the deep-fryer. The hardest bit was waiting for the balls to cool down before you could eat them. Perfect after Guinness and whiskey! ● I came into food by accident. I was attracted to the camaraderie more than what was going on on the plate. Then I found that I was actually quite good at cooking. I started to get more interested in food and started taking it very seriously from the age of about twenty-two or twenty-three. I have always liked food, but I didn't have any interest in cooking until then. ● When we first opened Black Axe Mangal, we were playing lots of Pantera, early Metallica, Black Sabbath—anything heavy and dark. And those sounds did have an influence on me. What I was seeking to do was match the sort of energy that music has with what I was transporting into people's mouths, as well as the vibe that music gives off. It definitely influenced me as far as a benchmark for flavor to match the punchiness in the songs that inspired me and to punctuate the flavors the way music stirs feelings within people. ● More than any of those artists, though, Tom Waits has had the biggest influence on my attitude. He leads by example; he's not conventional in any way, which I admire. He's not mediocre in any way. He's not afraid to change tack and style. You can't

really categorize him in a particular genre, and I think his voice is always going to stand the test of time. He's like a Chanel suit: He never gets old. ● If you ever come to my restaurant, Black Axe Mangal, you'll hear we play really loud music. We get a lot of complaints about the noise levels in our restaurant. We get people who sit down, then get straight back up and walk out pretty much every night, because we won't turn the music down. One of the reasons why I started playing really loud music during service was because of my insecurity about not really knowing what I was doing, so I created all these shields to hide behind. When we first started, turning the music up really loud gave me comfort and helped me keep it together. After that, we became known for it—our food and loud music became synonymous. Famously, the two elements can be enjoyed at the same time; and when you play certain music in a restaurant, it affects the vibe. Loud or not, music is a critical component of Black Axe Mangal. ● These days, our menu is more balanced, which has come not just from me hiding behind thrash metal to get me through the prep list or creative process. We don't just play metal anymore; the music at BAM is broader now, and this has definitely affected my mood—which in turn is reflected on the menu. Our tastes are more diverse, and I think our menu and playlists have become more diverse as a result. I don't take guilty pleasure in music; I'm too old to worry about what people think of my tastes. I hate a lot of music, but I love more music than I hate. I have a soft spot for Spice Girls, but I'm not embarrassed about that. There have been occasions where we have played Spice Girls in the restaurant and the whole place has gotten up and danced. It's fun. I want our restaurant to be fun. Like the first time I went to that gig at my school, I realized I'm not the only Spice Girls fan. We try and remain genre fluid with our food, and I want to always apply that to the music we play. ● Our restaurant is tiny, so the front of house and back of house are kind of one united space. We play music before service, throughout service, and then after service. If it's been a big night, we might put on something a bit more chill or a completely different genre from what we've been listening to during prep and service. Some of the songs we play during service are "Pat Earrings" by CASisDEAD, "Too Fast For Love" by Mötley Crüe, "Vossi Bop" by Stormzy, "Jump" by Van Halen, "Custard Pie" by Led Zeppelin, "Tempo" by Lizzo, "Work It" by Missy Elliot, "Toxic" by Britney Spears. If we have a quiet night, we might curate the music a bit more to fit the vibe or pick an album that we really want to listen to. Basically, we listen to what we want, and if I'm there, I usually override the system if I'm not into what's being played—but that's just because I'm a bit of a diva sometimes. ● After service, when I'm in the car, I like listening to Joni Mitchell's *Blue* on the way home, especially when it has been a tough service. The cooking part of my job is easy; I love it. It's all the other stuff of running a business that stresses me out, so I need something to bring me back down and relax. I've found that singing along to Joni definitely helps. I struggle to reach some of the higher notes, but I try. ● Food and music are so intertwined, I wouldn't feel comfortable if we didn't have music in our restaurant. It is a major, major factor in our vibe. If the sound system goes down, it really fucks with the vibe and stresses me out. We've never done service without the music at BAM; they're completely fused. The restaurant, the food, and the music, it is all one.

our food and loud music became synonymous

BRIANA VALDEZ

Briana Valdez is the owner of HomeState, a Texas Kitchen in Los Angeles. By her own account, she "carved her way into the restaurant business," driven to share her story of Texas and to bring high-quality food and hospitality to Los Angeles neighborhoods.

Andy Valdez moved from Austin to L.A. to pursue a career in the music industry. After years of success in talent management and music marketing, she brought her expertise to create a unique brand identity for HomeState.

Home Playlist ▶ A small taste of some of our favorites and what you might hear at HomeState.

1.	**La Grange**	ZZ Top
2.	**Needed Me**	Rihanna
3.	**Run (Live)**	George Strait
4.	**Marina del Rey**	George Strait
5.	**Truth**	Kamasi Washington
6.	**Maps**	Yeah Yeah Yeahs
7.	**Still Not a Player**	Big Pun featuring Joe
8.	**Moonlight Lady**	Julio Iglesias
9.	**Ay Te Dejo En San Antonio**	Flaco Jiménez
10.	**Promises**	Eric Clapton
11.	**Borrachera**	Little Joe Y La Familia

Andy and Briana Valdez

CHICKEN

PEANUT BUTTER

Our mom often cooked this dish for us on Sundays, always while playing Julio Iglesias.

Serves 4

¼ cup neutral oil

8 pieces bone-in chicken

Salt and freshly ground black pepper

¼ cup flour

3 cloves garlic

½ cup creamy peanut butter

1 tablespoon chile powder

1 teaspoon ground cumin

1 teaspoon ground onion powder

1 teaspoon paprika

12 to 16 oz chicken or vegetable stock

Heat the oil in a large Dutch oven or heavy pot over medium heat. Sprinkle the chicken with salt and pepper.

Arrange the chicken in the pan and cook for about 15 minutes, turning once, until brown on both sides. Transfer the chicken to a platter.

Recipe Inspiration:

Whisk the flour into the oil in the pot and cook until the flour is caramel in color. Add the garlic, peanut butter, chile powder, cumin, onion powder, and paprika and whisk until the peanut butter is melted and the mixture is smooth. Stir in enough broth to achieve the consistency of a thick gravy.

Return the chicken to the pot and turn to coat. Simmer over medium heat for 20 minutes. Taste for flavor. If needed, adjust the salt and chile powder. Spoon onto plates or into shallow bowls and serve immediately.

Paloma Blanca

by
Julio Iglesias

Recipe: Peanut Butter Chicken

Music has always played a large role in our lives and has a deep connection to food for us. As kids, we'd visit our grandparents on the weekends. Our dad and his brothers would sit in the dining room—dad on guitar, grandpa on accordion, an uncle singing—while our grandma made tortillas a few feet away. Every Sunday after church, our mom played Julio Iglesias while she made enchiladas or a roast. Our parents had a record player, and we'd often lay around it, taking turns picking LPs. One of our first favorite songs was "Sneaky Snake" by Tom T. Hall, an incredible songwriter. We have that song in rotation at HomeState as a reminder of that time in our lives. Even today, every time our family gets together, in either San Antonio or Austin, we can count on listening to George Strait and all of us singing along. We can also count on playing our favorite Tejano jams and taking turns dancing with our mom and dad.

●

We grew up in a small town on the Gulf Coast of Texas. There wasn't a heck of a lot to do there, but we found a large world to explore through music. Our friends were in bands, and we hosted shows for bands touring from other cities and states. There was a lot of focus on building community through music. Briana was a band nerd. In Texas, in order to play music, you also had to be a member of the marching band, which meant practicing outdoors in the summer heat, memorizing the Russian classics and thousands of field coordinates. All this while wearing a top hat and a cummerbund in 100-plus degree heat and humidity. It taught her discipline, resilience, and pride, since we had to work as a collective to achieve a great performance.

Music is an opportunity,

●

For Andy, music was always her compass. In high school, she spent her free time ordering records, listening to records, going to shows with friends, and convincing our parents to drive her to shows in nearby towns. When she got to college, she and her friends would often take road trips to other states to see concerts—in Chicago, New York City, etc. Music was a portal to experience other people, places, and cultures. After college, she moved to Los Angeles to pursue a career in the music business, while still going on the road to see shows like Modest Mouse in Albuquerque, Braid and Karate in Chicago, Ida in New York—having the pleasure of seeing hundreds of shows in venues ranging from storage rooms to stadiums.

●

When Briana decided to really make a go of turning HomeState into a reality, she knew she needed to start with the flour tortilla. It would become the foundation of the restaurant. She didn't know how to make tortillas, so she pulled out a picture of our Grandma Lala, blasted Tejano music, and channeled her spirit.

●

Food owners and operators over the last decade have been approaching restaurants in different ways than in decades past—breaking the mold, finding new voices and ways to tell their story that are nontraditional. That has created a culture within restaurants in a big way where there wasn't culture in restaurants before. Restaurants now tell stories and represent specific points of view. People can connect to that in a way that has not been accessible before. It was status quo that didn't resonate with individuality. Music is something that has always given that connection to people. People have personal connections to a band or genre that has crossed over to relationships with restaurants.

For us, it's about creating an environment that transports our guests to a place and a feeling. It's so personal, but growing up in Texas, there are so many great memories. A lot of them involve gathering with friends and family around a table with music playing. That has absolutely influenced the menu at HomeState—the design of the space and the music programming. We look at every service the same way we would if we were hosting a party or a get-together at our house. What would we play to make people feel happy and welcome? We always refer to music at restaurants as the ultimate finishing salt. After all of the work that goes into making a space great—great food, the music playing as a guest enters, orders, sits down, and takes that first bite of queso or drinks a margarita—it matters. If it's good, we've done our job. If it takes away from a guest's experience, the song has got to go.

just like the food,

Music is an opportunity, just like the food, to have a voice.
At HomeState, we handpick every song that is played in the restaurant. Whether it's a country song that we love from the '80s or a new hip-hop track, it's all part of our perspective and individual personality. For a song to be added to one of our playlists, it has to *feel* like HomeState. When selecting songs, we will often close our eyes, imagining ourselves sitting on one of our patios or being back home in Texas with our family, and ask ourselves if it evokes a feeling of happiness, nostalgia, or fun. Our playlists are structured for different times of the day, but also including the different vibes. A Saturday afternoon where people are lounging and drinking margaritas might call for Waylon Jennings, whereas a Monday morning where people are coming in for a quick breakfast taco before work might call for Gil Scott-Heron. If the patio is full on a Sunday morning, you can expect to hear some Texas-style conjunto, Tejano, or country music. If the patio is jumping on a Friday night, you might expect to hear some '90s hip-hop. The kitchen is open, so everyone is having a collective experience.

to have a voice.

Back in 2015, we launched HomeState's Band Taco program. The idea was to create limited-edition tacos whose profits go to charity, with bands whose music we loved and who also happened to be regular guests. It turned out to be a dream come true. Our first Band Taco was a collaboration with the Austin, Texas, band Spoon. It was a *migas* taco, a favorite of lead singer Britt's, and we called it "The Ranchero." Britt created a playlist of his favorite *ranchera*-style songs, which we played in the restaurant. We also collaborated with Local Natives, as they are longtime guests of the restaurant and approached us in advance of their latest album being released. We sat at a picnic table on the patio and tried about a dozen different ingredient options before deciding on the perfect combination. The guys were so excited about the collaboration and wanted to do everything they could to raise awareness to drive sales of the taco, with all profits going to support an LA-based organization that helps get homeless into homes. We hosted the band for an intimate, acoustic performance on the patio of our Highland Park location where fans were only able to access by donating directly to charity. It was a beautiful evening, and really the culmination of our lifelong love for food, music, and community.

CHASE AND CHAD VALENCIA

LASA was founded by Filipino-American brothers Chad and Chase Valencia. The word *lasa*, meaning "taste" or "flavor" in Tagalog, had a lot of meaning in the Valencia brothers' upbringing. Food was always a centerpiece of any gathering. Their journey began in the summer of 2013 as a series of intimate backyard dinners. In 2016, they caught the attention of Chef Alvin Cailan, who offered the Valencia brothers a weekend residency at his Chinatown culinary incubator, Unit 120, at the Far East Plaza. In 2017, LASA took over the culinary incubator space to make it its permanent home.

Iseo Naps Playlist ▶ Chad ▶ I made this playlist for my son, Iseo, when he was born. Like me, I realized he loved ambient noise, and he would often fall asleep to certain songs in this vein. Three years later, I still use this playlist to help aid nap time, and we even play this at the restaurant every now and then during prep.

1.	**Replica**	Oneohtrix Point Never
2.	**Water Wheel One**	Julian Lynch
3.	**Was**	Vincent Gallo
4.	**Felt Tip**	Teebs
5.	**Makes**	Lukid
6.	**Tezeta (Nostalgia)**	Mulatu Astatke
7.	**You and Me In Time**	Broadcast
8.	**Gala**	Ahnnu
9.	**Auntie's Lock / Infinitum**	Flying Lotus
10.	**Im halbhohen Gras**	Misel Quitno
11.	**AM**	Mndsgn
12.	**Couch**	Shlohmo
13.	**Untitled (Piano)**	Gang Gang Dance
14.	**Title Track**	Dakim

F

Chad ▶
Simply put, this song reminds me of the ocean, and the flavors of this dish do the same, with a hint of tropical vibes. It's a take on the Philippine classic sour soup/stew called *sinigang*. Here we use rhubarb as the souring agent; in California, it's in season during the springtime.

Serves 4 to 6

RHUBARB SINIGANG WITH SLOW ROASTED OCTOPUS AND BRAISED DAIKON

Recipe Inspiration:

■ For the slow-roasted octopus:

1 Spanish octopus, 6 to 8 lb, thawed if frozen

1 large yellow onion, quartered

1 head garlic, halved horizontally

½ Fresno chile, seeded

■ For the rhubarb *sinigang* broth:

4 quarts cold water

2 lb rhubarb, cut crosswise into slices ¼ inch thick

½ cup thinly sliced yellow onion

1 full sheet kombu (dried kelp)

5 garlic cloves, smashed

½ Fresno chile, seeded

4 tablespoons fish sauce, or to taste

Salt

■ **2 lb daikon**, peeled and sliced into ¼- to ½-inch-thick rounds (if the daikon is on the larger size, you can halve the rounds into crescents)

Salt

■ **Neutral oil**, for searing

Torn red shiso, chile oil, and puffed rice, for garnish

E L T T I P

by Teebs

Preheat the oven to 250°F (120°C).

To make the octopus, fill a heavy-bottomed stockpot three-fourths full of water and bring to a boil over high heat. Using your hands, carry the octopus by the head and dip the bottom half of the tentacles into the boiling water in and out until the tentacles curl. Once blanched, remove the head by slicing under the eyes. Cut off the bottom half of the head and invert. Remove the beak.

Place the onion, garlic, and chile on the bottom of a braising pan. Add the blanched and cleaned octopus, suction side up, on top of the aromatics, as well as the inverted head.

Cover the braising pan with plastic wrap (cling film) and then aluminum foil and bake for 2 hours. Check for doneness/tenderness with a cake tester. If the flesh is still bouncy and the cake tester does not slide in and out easily through the thickest part of a tentacle, re-cover and keep cooking, testing again at 10-minute increments. (If the octopus is closer to 8 pounds, do your first check after 2½ hours.)

When the octopus is tender, remove from the heat and let cool at room temperature in its braising liquid. Once it reaches room temperature, drain well. Portion the octopus into individual tentacles and coat with any neutral oil to prevent the tentacles from sticking to one another. Cover and store in the refrigerator until ready to sear.

To make the rhubarb *sinigang* broth, combine all ingredients except the fish sauce and salt in a heavy-bottomed pot, starting with the cold water. Bring to a very gentle simmer. (Think in between steeping and simmering.) DO NOT let simmer aggressively or come to a boil! Let "steep" for 30 to 45 minutes, or until the rhubarb is completely cooked through but not falling apart or disintegrating. Strain the broth through a fine-mesh sieve, gently pressing the rhubarb and aromatics to get all the flavor and liquid out. Season with fish sauce and salt to taste. The broth should taste savory, tart, and of the ocean.

To make the daikon, in a heavy-bottomed pot, bring 1½ quarts of the *sinigang* broth and the daikon to a simmer. Let braise until the daikon is cooked through but still keeps its integrity. This can take anywhere from 30 to 40 minutes. Season with salt to taste. Using a spider or slotted spoon, remove the braised daikon and set aside to cool. You can use the braising liquid to fortify the rest of the rhubarb broth, once it's cool.

To assemble the dish, heat a cast-iron pan over medium heat and add just enough neutral oil to coat the bottom of the pan. Cut each tentacle into 4 or 5 pieces; this will help ensure an even sear throughout the length of the tentacles and make them easier to eat. Slowly sear the octopus until it is crispy on the outside and warmed through.

(Grilling is also a great way to warm and crisp up the octopus. We prefer the slower gradual sear over medium heat to let the skin render a crispier result. A high-heat sear can also yield a great result, but for this dish, intentional char as opposed to a slower caramelization can take away from the nuances of the broth and even the dish overall.)

In a saucepan, warm the rhubarb *sinigang* broth and braised daikon over medium-low heat. This will warm through before the octopus is perfectly seared if you time it correctly. Keep the broth and daikon warm.

Once everything is ready, have your serving bowls ready near the hot broth. Use a slotted spoon to transfer the daikon to fill the bottom of the bowls. Since the daikon is cut on the thicker side, you can place some up the pieces upright to give some dimension and height.

Place the seared octopus on top of the daikon pieces. Spoon or ladle hot broth into the bowls, or if you fancy, save this step for last and pour the broth tableside. Garnish with the red shiso, chile oil, and puffed rice and serve.

● Music was a pretty big part of us growing up, it really shaped who our friends were and how we lived our lives, and that is still true today. We grew up in the '90s and the influence of hip-hop is ever-present in who we are today, it's our base and foundation, it's our reference point. We can easily say, '90s hip-hop and R&B are a big part of the Filipino-American experience and community. Without a doubt, our community out here in SoCal was heavily influenced by it. We grew up with dance crews, party crews, car crews, etc., and Tupac, Snoop, Biggie, and Wu-Tang were our soundtrack. Music helped us connect heavily with others simply because we were going to shows, collecting records and cassette tapes, and finding a common voice. To this day, we each have a closer-knit social circle connected to music than we do to food. That may change one day, but that's still what it is. ● When we were in high school, like every adolescent, we believed that the music we associated with defined who we were. We were so adamant about "being" hip-hop and of course back then, that meant you were a B-boy, DJed, MCed, or tagged. All we wanted was to be able to do a little bit of all of them. The older we got, however, the less we felt connected to these specific ideas. Chad especially wanted to discover more experimental, weirder shit. Not for the sake of being weird or experimental, but because he craved the new and different, expanding on the golden era of boom bap. The boom bap era let him explore where artists found samples for their beats and then it helped him open up to find more music. Hearing the source of the sample was always so interesting, being able to get into the mind of the producer and seeing what they did to that particular snippet to make another song was something cool. We both started to dig deeper and, in the end, it opened us up to soul, Latin, and other world genres. ● As we got older, we really got into '60s and '70s Latin music artists such as Caetano Veloso and Arthur Verocai, as well *cumbia*, salsa, and bands like E.S.G. and other groups with a similar sound. Some artists we always put on repeat are the Ethiopian jazz great Mulatu Astatke or afrobeat god Fela Kuti. There is something about their approach and how they made their own sound, representing a culture and doing something inspired from their own culture, that inspired us. Mulatu and Fela really influenced our work, because at LASA, it's a vibe and energy we strive for in the dining room. The way these artists created their music, with soul, purpose, texture, and their unique time signatures and beats based on

Create a vibe, a time and place, an energy, but do it your own way.

their cultural references being Ethiopian and Nigerian, respectively, is something we try to take in. Create a vibe, a time and place, an energy, but do it your own way. ● Don't get us wrong, we will always love Tribe, De La Soul, Wu-Tang forever, but we really found ourselves in music when we realized there were slightly more experimental or alternative versions of the genres we already loved. This also inspires Chad when he is making his own music. When his second album, *ANAK*, came out on vinyl, it was one of the greatest music moments of our lives. Chad makes music more from the production side of things, experimental, ambient, sample-based stuff with tripped-out beats. He is an artist above all, with food and music as his outlets. It was crazy seeing him evolve and grow from making beats in his bedroom to putting out an album...to have completed such a huge side project while pursuing food and LASA, that's something incredible. ● As clichéd as it sounds, every dish at LASA is a song, in the sense that there are distinct parts. For us, a close to perfect dish always has fat, salt, acid, and texture. There can always be additions of say heat or a flavor profile in herbs, but we always use those four as the driving force. Like a song: Every great one has its own distinct parts, drums, or a rhythm/groove, bassline, melody, and vocals. Chad models a lot of his creative approach after J Dilla, who is his favorite producer, because nobody has ever influenced hip-hop beats and production like that man has. Boom bap rap was an already perfect sound and formula, but Dilla brought attention to finding the swing in a perfect loop from a sample; he took everything to another level. ● Like music, with food, there can always be innovations and additions, so we are always trying to find our own way to take Filipino classics to a new place. Almost all the music we love is a progressive version or take on something that is timeless or classic, and we hope to do the same with food. We will always love the classics, but we will also always have the drive to create something new with an homage or nod to those classics and traditions.

ED VERNER

WAGYU

Ed Verner is chef-owner of Pasture restaurant, a six-seat unique fine-dining restaurant in Auckland, New Zealand. Having spent a year in Japan in his twenties, he was soon inspired to follow a life in food. Opened in 2016, Pasture is known for its creativity, attention to detail, and whole animal butchery. In 2018, Pasture was named Restaurant of the Year by *Metro* magazine.

The Best of Pasture Playlist ▶ Some lesser and more well-known tracks from Pasture's playlist, these are the songs that define our dining room.

1.	**It's Bad You Know**	R.L. Burnside
2.	**Dance**	ESG
3.	**Oh Yeah**	Yello
4.	**Another Life**	Kano
5.	**Mr. Roboto**	Styx
6.	**Sleeper In Metropolis**	Anne Clark
7.	**Just Like Honey**	The Jesus and Mary Chain
8.	**Try**	Delta 5
9.	**Ça plane pour moi**	Plastic Bertrand
10.	**Lost in the Supermarket**	The Clash

▲ Ed Verner

NEW ZEALAND

▼ Ed Verner

BEEF

with Roasted Koji-Vinegar Sauce

This preparation is based on our first cow to arrive at Pasture. Completely unaware of how heavy a cow is and the work involved in butchering it, we decided to name him Nigel.

Makes 1 perfectly aged Wagyu cow

1 whole best-quality Wagyu cow, with low marbling and good fat cover

About 100 g aged beef fat

1 kg aged cow trim, leftover from previous cows you've worked with

100 g salt

80 g koji yeast

10 kg aged cow bones, leftover from previous cows you've worked with

Aromatic vinegar such as elderflower, to taste

Quality salt, to taste

Manuka wood, or the best burning and aromatic wood from your country

Recipe: Wagyu Beef with Roasted Koji-Vinegar Sauce

Break down the cow into 6 or 8 large parts and hang in a humidity- and airflow-controlled chilled room.

Cover the carcass in aged beef fat after 1 week. Leave to age, ideally for 3 months, checking frequently for any bad mold growth.

In a large pot, combine the trim, 100 g salt, koji, and 300 g water and age at 60°C (140°F) for 3 months to create a garum for the sauce.

After the beef and the garum have aged 3 months, roast the bones, then simmer in a large pot in a large pot over low heat for 8 hours. Chill overnight, then remove the fat. Reduce the sauce again, slowly, until thick.

Mix the sauce with the garum and aromatic vinegar of your choice.

When ready to cook, cut your favorite steaks from the aged carcass and bring to room temperature.

In a large grill, wood-burning oven, or fire pit, build a large fire and burn it down to ember stage. Using a lot of glowing embers, fan violently until the highest temperature possible is reached.

Cover the steaks in ridiculous amounts of the best salt you have. Over high heat, sear both sides until charred hard and medium-rare.

Serve with just the sauce, because it doesn't need anything else.

MAKING PLANS FOR NIGEL by XTC

Recipe Inspiration:

If you listen to music and you love music, I feel you're someone who's in touch with your feelings. Making food is a very creative and emotional thing, and I see the two as very similar. I know that feeling I get when I'm listening to music is definitely the same one I get when I'm cooking food. It's tapping into the same thing. When you're cooking something amazing or you're listening to music that's special, it's a kind of buzz, an excitement. It's that feeling inside that something great is happening and it just makes you feel really good.

●

When I left home, I was still making dance music, but I had to find a real job. Making music was my creative outlet, and electronic music was something that I connected to and could create with. Electronica was the start of me being able to put something out into the world. Then when I was in my twenties, I started to focus more on food — the kitchens I worked in were pretty serious, no music zones! I'd say music became my own space outside of work, especially on my pedal bike, heading to and from the kitchen. Music is still a really emotional thing for me; these days I listen to music in the kitchen for many reasons... sometimes to give me the push I need, during the highs and the lows.

Becoming a chef wasn't something that was a clear-cut decision for me. I just started getting more serious about cooking and more focused on a life with food at the center. I didn't have time to be looking for new music and I literally disappeared 100 percent into kitchens. Even lately, for the most part, nothing else happens in my life beyond the food, but more recently, music has crept back into my life more and more. At Pasture, I can play whatever I want, when I want, and that has taught me to be a little less intense, to find more balance. I used to work long hours under someone else and I couldn't just listen to whatever I wanted to, but now I have the freedom to listen to a lot more music. I also encourage our staff to get involved, and that's often how we discover new music and tracks that might eventually hit the restaurant playlist. I also feel it helps build strong connections between us.

●

When I was younger, music was often the opposite for me, something I could reach out to and make my own space. I think music became very personal for me as I was growing up. But these days, I definitely use music to connect with customers, as well as staff, at Pasture. We're a fine-dining restaurant, but anything goes with the music, from AC/DC to Grandmaster Flash. It's a way to get people comfortable and to understand that we like to have fun.

Music is a huge part of Pasture. There isn't one minute when we're not listening to music there. We'll take turns putting on what we want to listen to, and we definitely have our favorite tracks. There are a few bands that I associate with Pasture and that flows through to our playlist. Over the years, the playlist has developed into something quite unique. I'm always adding to it; I'm also dropping off tracks that I don't think work anymore. It is a constant honing, just like we refine the menu and the cooking.

●

I take the music so seriously at Pasture because it relaxes people. Even if a person has never been to the restaurant, when we're playing great tunes, people automatically relate to what we are doing and they understand what we stand for. It allows people to enjoy the experience more and it cuts away any pretension by breaking down a bit of a barrier between the customers and me. I cook right in front of them every night, and will have conversations with people about music, or people ask which band is playing, and that all creates the symbiotic environment that I want Pasture to be. I want it to be fun, because that connected feeling is very important to me.

It's also important to me that during the day, we all get to play what we want and what we love to listen to, and at the same time, I'm always hoping to find that next track to play in service. Then as the prep day continues, the pace of the music gets faster. As we get past 4 p.m., the music usually builds into something to push us through to service—usually techno. I still listen to electronica, so that's really pumping during late afternoon, right up until the first guests arrive, when someone usually remembers to switch it over to the Pasture playlist! Since we have a seasonal menu, we add and remove tracks to and from the service playlist for certain times of year, as well.

●

Music has a deep creative influence on the food and drinks we serve. We include three band names at the top of the menu, which are the names of the cocktails that we have in rotation. We see it as a fun way to get into the menu and to relax the guests. We have served up the Presidents of the United States of America, a drink inspired by the band's song "Peach": our house peach vermouth that we make from scratch, plus peach juice that we ferment for a year. We have a piña colada–inspired drink called Rupert Holmes, inspired by his song "Escape."

We also print the name of the cow we are serving that night on the menu. We work with whole animals and we always name them, using the titles of favorite songs. We've had cows named Jolene, Roxanne, and Layla, and of course Nigel in the recipe above. He was the only boy cow we've ever had. We named him after "Making Plans for Nigel" by XTC. We also like to pair songs with specific food, and have fun matching tracks to the dishes.

●

We do two seatings a night at Pasture, with two groups of six. We have six people who come in at 5:45 p.m. and then the second seating is at 8:15 p.m. By the second seating, it's usually dark outside. We kill all the lights and the music gets louder. It's pitch black in the restaurant when I drop the beef on the fire. When I'm putting on a piece with a lot of fat, like a sirloin, we put on AC/DC's "Hell's Bells." There is a flash fire when the beef goes on and the guests feel this surge of heat. Then AC/DC kicks in and it's just so much fun. Another great track to play is Yello's "Oh Yeah," which we've played as customers are eating the beef, because that's the reaction they have when they eat it: It's probably the best piece of beef they've ever had. It's all very rock and roll. It's a little bit of theater and we love it.

We also put song credits on the back of the menu. The music that we play and how we tie it into the food and drink makes for a really interesting and integrated experience. Food at a certain level is just the same as music. People get the same feeling from food as listening to great music. Both experiences allow one to be taken on a journey where one doesn't necessarily know what's going to happen next, and that's very exciting. I've always loved music and it's a big part of what I do today. It's always been a part of my life and built into my creative makeup.

We include three band names at the top of the menu, which are the names of the cocktails that we have in rotation.

We also print the name of the cow we are serving that night on the menu.

MARC VETRI

Marc Vetri is a chef, restaurateur, author, and philanthropist. His critically acclaimed restaurant, Vetri Cucina, has set the standards for modern Italian cuisine since opening its doors in 1998 in Philadelphia. In 2018, Marc debuted Vetri Cucina's much anticipated second location at the Palms Casino Resort in Las Vegas.

A Bluesy List Playlist ▶ There are just some songs I can listen to over and over again. This list is basically my go-to for anything that I need to get super motivated for. These songs just get me going. Some live, some studio versions, but they all get in there and move my soul. The Marcus King Band is the newest music that I can listen to for days on end!

1.	The Lemon Song	Led Zeppelin
2.	Whipping Post	The Allman Brothers
3.	Mary Had a Little Lamb (Live Version)	Stevie Ray Vaughan
4.	You Can't Always Get What You Want	The Rolling Stones
5.	Do You Feel Like We Do	Peter Frampton
6.	Everyday I Have the Blues	John Mayer
7.	Dyin'	The Marcus King Band
8.	Midnight in Harlem	Tedeschi Trucks Band
9.	Soulshine	Gov't Mule
10.	Have You Ever Loved a Woman	Derek & the Dominos
11.	Ask Me No Questions	Albert King and Stevie Ray Vaughan
12.	Come and Go Blues (Live)	Warren Haynes

▲ Marc Vetri

LAS VEGAS, NV, USA

Simple Strip Steak

My wife loves when we make steak for dinner. It's simple, easy, and always a hit. And this song has always reminded me of her.

Serves 2

2 aged NY strip steaks, bone-in, each about 2 inches (5 cm)

Salt and freshly cracked black pepper

2 tablespoons olive oil

1 tablespoon butter

1 rosemary sprig

Generously season the meat with salt and pepper. Heat the oil in a large cast-iron skillet over medium heat.

Once the oil is hot, place the steaks in the skillet. Add the butter and the rosemary. Let the steaks come to a nice dark brown color on the bottom while constantly basting the top of the meat. After 6 or 7 minutes, flip the steak and repeat the basting process. Then, cook the fat side of the steak, fat side down, for 1 or 2 minutes so the fat can render out.

Remove the skillet from the heat and place the steaks on a baking sheet with a drip rack. From here, the steaks can simply rest or can go right into the oven at 350°F (180°C). Roast for about 10 minutes, or until the internal temperature is 123° to 135°F (50° to 57°C). Take the steaks out of the oven and let them rest for about 30 minutes in a warm place. While the steaks rest, the internal temperature will go up to 130° to 133°F (54° to 56°C), which is perfect.

Slice the steaks on a bias on the width to create shorter slices. Season each slice with salt and black pepper to taste.

Tips:

■ I prefer to use grass-fed beef, but this technique for steaks also works great with a grain-finish cow. It's important to get a thick cut. I typically go with a minimum of 2 inches (5 cm) and sometimes 2 ½ to 3 inches (6 to 7.5 cm).

■ Leave the steaks out at room temperature for about 90 minutes before cooking so they come to room temperature. This will help the steaks cook evenly, ensuring the center of the steak is not cold.

Recipe Inspiration:

She's a Rainbow
by The Rolling Stones

People can put too much on a plate

My grandfather was an oboe player in the Philadelphia Orchestra in the 1930s and '40s. My dad tried to follow in his footsteps later in his life, but he never really got there. But there were generations of an appreciation for music in my family; still, no one tried to push the oboe on me. Funnily enough, my dad still tells me he thought the guitar was going to be a vicious waste of money and that I would be done in a month.

●

Since I was eight or nine, there has always been an entanglement of music and food in me. My interest in both came at the same moment: My father's mom and dad were from Sicily, and when I was a kid we would head down to South Philly to this old row house for those huge Sunday meals—meatballs, lasagna, the roast, everything. Those are some of my earliest memories—classical music on the stereo and eating this big meal. Around age eleven or twelve, I started sleeping over to help cook, and got my first lessons in stuffed artichokes, macaroni, lemon chicken, etc. In my first cookbook, there is a recipe for Jenny's Ricotta Pie, which is named after my grandmother, a dish I learned to cook with her.

Up until eleventh grade, I was a loner. High school was just survival for me. When I got home from school, I was like the Spinal Tap guy—turn the amp up to eleven and just blast Deep Purple's "Smoke on the Water." You could hear it for blocks. My guitar was my friend. I played with some people, but I was too shy to be in a band and play out in public. In eleventh grade, however, I started to be more open about it. We had to bring in something to share in social studies class. I had just returned to my old school, which I had left two years earlier, and everyone was like, "Oh, great, it's Vetri the weirdo." So instead of talking about where I'd been, I played Lynyrd Skynyrd's "Sweet Home Alabama," and then they started to like me a little bit more.

●

After college, I still loved guitar and decided that I wanted to go to the Musicians Institute in Los Angeles. This was in 1990. You had to mail in your audition tape: my Side A was Steve Howe "The Clap Song" and Side B was a heavy medley mix mash to show I could shred. I got accepted, moved out to Los Angeles, and went to school there for a year. Obviously, while I was there, to make money I worked nights in a restaurant.

●

Halfway through music school, while I was the line cook at North Beach Bar & Grill, I heard Wolfgang Puck was opening up Granita in Malibu and something clicked for me: I just wanted to work for Wolfgang. I applied for a job, got it, and that became my cooking school. I used to go in early to study and learn—how to fillet fish, butcher an animal, make all these different stocks and sauces. That was a big shift for me. I was mesmerized. I was still doing the music thing; I had started a band called Mild Mustard and was playing shows now and then. But cooking was becoming a larger and larger part of my life.

After my first year at Granita, I started to work as the morning chef to make time for Mild Mustard. You need a flexible job to be in a band, just to figure out how to try and make it work. We could get the least expensive studio time from midnight to 5 a.m. My schedule was something like: recording studio, live show, rehearsal, and then work the morning shift at Granita. I played all night and then I just went to work. There's no thought of balance when you're in your early twenties; I just did it and didn't think. It was always *food and music*. On one side of it, I was this starving musician, and on the other, I was getting deeper into the high-end food world, with Wolfgang Puck as my mentor.

●

Pretty soon the band saw where I was going with food. Some of them had a chance for a record contract with another band, and they took it. There were no hard feelings; everyone just saw where my life was heading. After that, Wolfgang set up a stage for me at Taverna del Colleoni & dell'Angelo in Bergamo, Northern Italy. I took a backpack of clothing and my Martin guitar and that was it. It was a long eighteen months; I was lonely over there. I was twenty-five years old and I didn't know anybody. But the Martin helped me relax whenever I needed it. It came everywhere with me; it was nice to play for everyone, and in many ways, the guitar was my security blanket. Everyone from that chapter of my life still remembers me as the guy with the overalls and the guitar. What I remember is how I leaned on my love of guitar during this period to help me get through the difficult aspects of my career.

●

This lifelong love of music carries through everything I do in my culinary life. I definitely feel more creative when I'm listening to music. If I'm making stuff in my house and everyone is running around, I'm going to stick some Allman Brothers on or some Led Zeppelin. When I'm cooking at Vetri, with the table covered by a whole bunch of books from Italy, and I'm working on menus, I listen to melodic jazz. Songs that have interesting solos and are a little bit more complex, those inspire more restaurant-style dishes. Those kinds of tunes make me think a little more out of the box because the solos often get out of the box, versus rock and roll, where the heart of everything is more in the pocket.

like they can put too many notes in a solo.

When there's an interesting solo in a song, the musicians are playing outside the game. They're using all sorts of other scales and they're challenging melodic normalcy. A lot of the time, rock and rollers pretty much use one, four, five chords and stay inside the scale. You're just driving ahead then, and it's nice because it's a flow, you know what's coming. But old jazz artists, or modern interpreters like the Punch Brothers, push the limits and take you out. When you're in a solo and it makes you a little bit uncomfortable, and then it kind of brings you back into the melody, and then it's, "Oh, wow, that was kind of a rush. Like, where is that going?" And then, "Oh, there it is."

●

When I get home after a long service and my family is asleep, I go for my guitar to help me unwind and think. Some people go for other things, but this is mine. I'll work on a solo or practice some lick while I think about recipes and push myself to think outside the box. From a young age, I realized that food and music were the same creative outlet for me. Making a melody is the same thing as making a sauce or decorating a dish. People can put too much on a plate like they can put too many notes in a solo, and it makes it messy. Lessons from both worlds continue to help me be a better chef. I get the same satisfaction from being able to listen to a song and learn the solo as from cooking and creating a new recipe. There's a complementary feedback loop between each other, but they also allow me to push different creative buttons.

●

It's so easy to just make something simple that you've made before, to rest on your laurels. You've got your handbook of winter dishes and spring dishes and summer dishes and all dishes. A lot of chefs think, "I can always make this. It's straightforward. It's safe." But perhaps if you're listening to jazz, or another piece of inspirational music, something that takes you out of your comfort zone, you may think, "Let me start to change it up a little. Let me take this dish in a different direction, use a whole-tone scale or a little flat tip or something diminished in there. Just kind of snake it to make it a little bit uncomfortable, but then bring it back home."

●

Listening to music, it pushes me. So many chefs are so smart and so thoughtful, but they can get stuck on the same steady thing. Where is the inspiration? What's their method?

●

I remember one night when I asked one of my pastry chefs, a veteran of the pastry field, to make something special for the evening. He made this really nice fancy, Frenchy, layered kind of a thing. Some chocolate, booze, and layers of stuff, real shiny. But ultimately, it was something that you would find in every French bakery. While it was wonderful, I looked at it, and I looked at him, and I asked, "Why do you think I'm not happy with that? It's nice, but why is this lame?" And he's looking at me. "I don't know you're talking about, Chef. It's nice."

Our chef didn't understand. We gave him the freedom to create something new for our restaurant, told him to take this solo for a walk. But he didn't. He had a creative opportunity to make something different, but he just made one of the same things that he's made a thousand times before. That's the issue with this type of thinking. I could name a thousand chefs who can make that same shiny, layered dessert. The diner eats it but likely ends up feeling like it was well done, but somehow...the same. Wouldn't you want to eat something that's just, "Oh, this is really awesome! This could have been that same thing that everyone makes, but he took it here! How did he do it? I never thought about it this way. This is the same, but different."

●

I think that listening to out-of-the-box music takes you and just makes you think of that next level. Maybe our pastry chef should have been listening to Miles Davis or something while he was creating that.

●

We had an event with Sam Calagione, the founder of Dogfish Head Brewery. Sam told me that when he was just out of college and he was writing the Dogfish business plan, he got the record *Bitches Brew* by Miles Davis. His dream was to have Dogfish in some small way stand for the same thing in the beer world that *Bitches Brew* stands for in the jazz world. The record is considered a landmark that showcases a turning point in the fusion of jazz and experimental music. Almost seventeen years later, in honor of the fortieth anniversary of the original release of *Bitches Brew* and as a tribute to the record, Sam stood on top of a craft beer empire and made a beer by the same name.

●

Sam knew I was a jazz guy, so he went to his chiller and got a whole bunch of old vintage stock for me to cook with. You don't always think of beer as vintage, but it's incredible—it comes out rich and chocolatey, and it's amazing. We took that vintage stock and made smoked short ribs with celery root (celeriac) purée. The sauce was reduced beer with some chocolate in it, which came out as a really rich, thick, thick sauce. We served it while playing that Miles Davis album on repeat all night. It was mind-blowing for the guests who experienced food and music on multiple levels. *Here's the song, here's the album, the actual beer was named after it, the food was inspired by the beer, and this is the record Sam was listening to when he was starting his company.* So many levels and depth. It was full circle right there.

AND SHIN HARAKAWA

JEROME WAAG

Jerome Waag worked for Chez Panisse in Berkeley, California, for twenty-five years. While in Berkeley, he co-founded a collective called OPENrestaurant, where they make "happenings" about food and culture. Now he lives in Tokyo, where he has his own restaurant, the Blind Donkey.

Shin Harakawa is the co-owner of the Blind Donkey in Tokyo and the former chef-owner of Beard, also in Tokyo, which won the 2015 Monocle Restaurant Award.

Mind Traveling Playlist ▶ Shin
▶ This playlist is for complete relaxing mind travel. It also goes well with a simple, casual dinner in a relaxed setting to really enjoy the time and open your senses. Just be yourself instinctively; these songs will help you to really connect with whomever you dine with.

1.	Peace Piece	Bill Evans
2.	Like Someone in Love	Bruno Major
3.	Elephant Gun	Beirut
4.	Bachelor	Kevin Krauter
5.	Holding Out	Adrian Underhill
6.	You Already Know	Bombay Bicycle Club
7.	Vampire	Okay Kaya
8.	Me in You	Kings of Convenience
9.	Bolerish	Ryuichi Sakamoto
10.	Zebra	Beach House
11.	Set in Stone	Milk & Bone
12.	Beret Girl	Bibio
13.	Yellowknife	Conner Youngblood
14.	Imagine	Eddie Vedder
15.	Intuition	Feist
16.	The Long Day is Over	Norah Jones

Lullaby Playlist ▶ Jerome
▶ For middle-of-the-night, "can't sleep, won't sleep" kind of hours.

1.	Zodiac	Baby Fox
2.	Life in a Glasshouse	Radiohead
3.	Overcome	Tricky
4.	Teardrop	Massive Attack
5.	Roads	Portishead
6.	Papi Pacify	FKA Twigs
7.	Ivo	Cocteau Twins
8.	Ali Mullah	Natacha Atlas and Transglobal Underground
9.	Tembang Sunda	Imas Permas and Asep Kosasih

JAPAN

PORK ROAST SONG

Jerome ▶

This recipe is a song, not inspired by a song. Listen to the fat and juices sputter as the pork is getting golden and delicious. I like to cook by listening: the sound of a roast in the oven or vegetables getting dry in a pan, a pot boiling too hard…listening to the whole kitchen and hearing focus or distraction.

Serves 6 to 8

One 1kg pork loin,
preferably from closer to the shoulder

Salt

---

1 sprig rosemary

---

1 lemon

Season the pork loin with salt the night before. Place in the refrigerator overnight.

The next day, remove the loin from the fridge and let come up to room temperature.

Preheat the oven to 400°F (200°C).

Chop the rosemary and grate the lemon zest. Rub the rosemary and lemon zest generously over the pork loin.

Roast until the meat bounces to the touch, about 130°F (54°C) at the center. Let rest for 20 minutes. Slice and serve.

ROASTED RED BEETS with CURED JAPANESE UME PLUM and YOGURT SAUCE

Shin ▶

Both this song and this recipe reflect an exotic and nostalgic mood, something that represents a mixing of cultures.

Serves 4

2 medium red beets

---

30 ml red wine vinegar

---

1 big Japanese pickled *ume* plum, chopped

---

100 ml plain yogurt

---

30 ml light olive oil

---

1 bunch dill

Steam-roast the beets. Peel the skins and cut in half.

In a bowl, pour the red wine vinegar over the beets and let cool.

In another bowl, mix the plum, yogurt, and olive oil.

Serve the beets and yogurt sauce together, with chopped or small sprigs of dill.

Recipe Inspiration:

ELEPHANT GUN
by Beirut

● Shin Harakawa ●

I have been surrounded by music my whole life, and I'm always listening to music now. All that music has bonds with a lot of my childhood memories and has had a strong impact on my life, so much so that I could almost say that I cannot live without music. Music plays a huge role to set my tone and mood. When I was a child, we used to go driving often as a family. My parents listened to a lot of music, like Stevie Wonder, Diana Ross, Lionel Richie, the Beatles, the Carpenters, etc.

●

I still like to travel a lot, and right now, Beirut's music helps me travel in my mind while I'm cooking. It helps me to connect to certain memories or moods when cooking. Music supports and complements traditional rituals, and can support, inspire, cheer up people as they go through different stages of their lives. Also, when we celebrate something, there is always music. Music helps me be a person who cares a lot about atmosphere and ambience. When I host parties or dinners or when I'm driving, alone or with companions, I always play music to set some tone of the space.

●

Music definitely motivates me in my cooking and my work, and it definitely plays a big role in our—and any—restaurant's scene. I play music to put myself in a certain mood while cooking, and I also select music for our restaurant depending on the vibe from day to day. It relaxes me and my staff (although sometimes not? lol) during our prep. I play many varieties of music in the restaurant, depending on the tone of the customers or of the day, and it definitely helps to create the desired atmosphere in the restaurant. Our restaurant is an open kitchen in one open space, so the dining room hears what we hear. We play mainly alternative music, but different tempos and moods, depending on the situation each day. Once we cooked a diner for Ryuichi Sakamoto at the Blind Donkey; he was my dream artist to cook for. I made a super-simple vegetable soup and salad, served with natural wines—and of course, music we thought he would appreciate.

MUSIC SUPPORTS AND COMPLEMENTS TRADITIONAL RITUALS

Jerome Waag

Music was always there when I was growing up. My friends' and my tastes were very eclectic, so we listened to different kinds of music together. We would smoke weed and listen to the Gladiators or Dr. Alimantado or Fela Kuti. Airto Moreira and Miles Davis gave us a sense of sophistication. We liked Genesis and Kate Bush. Later it was Grace Jones and Kid Creole and the Coconuts; then came Tricky and Portishead. Bob Marley was everywhere; he was a big influence. Some artists were more personal— I listened to John Coltrane or David Bowie's *Low* by myself. There has been so much music in my life, it's really tough to narrow down my favorites... there are way too many to pick one, it really depends on my mood or the time of day. I do love "Duet for Two" by Arthur Blythe; but "Out to Lunch!" by Eric Dolphy is probably closer to what's happening inside my head. One of my favorite memories is listening Salvatore Adamo on a small radio in my dorm room in the south of France; another is of playing a Donovan album on my mother's record player. In my mind, these are not songs, it all hit me more like a voice.

Many of my childhood memories are tied to music. When I was around fifteen years old, I had a friend whose mother would leave for long periods of time, a week or two. They lived in a beautiful house, an old mill with a small stream running underneath, so we would all stay there when her mom was gone. We had no money, but we ate pasta with butter and had big parties, where we blasted Stevie Wonder's *Songs in the Key of Life*. A few years later, we packed a friend's car and drove three hours to the suburb of Marseille to see an Iggy Pop concert. I don't think I knew who he was, but I did after that. Also, seeing Pharaoh Sanders playing at the Keystone Korner in San Francisco barely three feet away from where I was sitting was magical. And Don Cherry. And Sun Ra.

But through all that, food was my other passion. I always liked to eat and to cook. My mother is a really good cook; I owe her gratitude for opening me to much of what I love about cooking. But only later did I understand that we are what we cook. It became political. Food has always been more popular than music: We eat three times a day. But with new audio technologies, music started to catch up. Now, arguably, food and music are even—and tattoos are required for both.

I also think performative food events are great for combining with music gatherings. Like burying a pig wrapped in wild fennel in a hot pit for 24 hours, then gathering everyone to take it out and taste what happened while the music plays. But music or no music, the Blind Donkey is dedicated to nature, the living soil, and the farmers who take care of it.

As I said above, I like to cook by listening. Service requires listening, too—the dining room getting crowded, too loud, or too quiet. This is music to me. It's a great emotion to listen to the hum of a restaurant kitchen when everyone is focused, and everything is in its place. The music of food becoming delicious.

ONLY LATER DID I UNDERSTAND THAT WE ARE WHAT WE COOK

DYLAN WATSON-BRAWN

Dylan Watson-Brawn is the head chef and co-owner of ernst, an intimate produce-driven restaurant that he set up with fellow Vancouver-native Spencer Christenson in the north Berlin neighborhood of Wedding in late 2017.

At ernst, we don't have many complete dish recipes. Instead, we work with a series of base recipes, from which we build our dishes. Our menu changes daily, and much of the work goes into sourcing the products we work with. This dish is centered around a very special person who gives us the opportunity to work with some of the most pristine shellfish in the world. When we went up to visit him for the first time, "Beautiful Day" was the song he played after picking us up from the ferry.

Mise Playlist ▶ A playlist like this is our go-to before service. It puts us in the right frame of mind: It's energizing and keeps us positive and gelled as a team. In the buildup to service, that's key.

1.	**Emotions**	Mariah Carey
2.	**Tradin' War Stories**	2Pac featuring Outlawz, C-Bo, CP-O, and Storm
3.	**Shape of My Heart**	Sting
4.	**Looking Forward to You**	Jack J
5.	**Elevators (Me & You)**	OutKast
6.	**Lazy Bones**	WITCH
7.	**Motivation**	Kelly Rowland featuring Lil Wayne
8.	**Yes Indeed**	Lil Baby & Drake
9.	**Wicked Games**	Chris Isaak
10.	**Business Is Business**	Lil Baby & Gunna
11.	**One in a Million**	Aaliyah
12.	**In Limbo**	Radiohead
13.	**March Madness**	Future
14.	**This Charming Man**	The Smiths
15.	**Marvins Room**	Drake

arctic razor clams in lovage vinegar ponzu with pickled lovage stems

ERNST

This very simple recipe relies on using the best possible ingredients from farmers in the area, artisans in Japan, and our diver in Norway. Note, time is of the essence here. The heady vinegar needs to be cellared for a year, while the fresh clams should be plated and in front of your guests within 5 minutes of shucking them.

Serves 6

■ For the lovage *ponzu*:

20 g Lovage Vinegar (recipe follows)

100 g Niban Dashi (recipe follows)

5 g juice from grilled Sicilian lemons

Light shoyu, to taste

Dark shoyu, to taste

■ **6 large Artic razor clams**

Finely diced stems of young lovage, for garnish

First, find yourself someone who is incredibly passionate and obsessed with their craft — someone who is crazy enough to dive above the Arctic circle. Bother them by phone and email for a year until they're ready to work with you.

To make the *ponzu*, first prepare the Lovage Vinegar (give it a year!) and Niban Dashi. In a bowl, whisk together the Lovage Vinegar, dashi, lemon juice, and light and dark shoyu to taste.

Just when ready to serve, shuck the live razor clams. Separate the primary muscle from the skirt. (Save the skirts for use in a sauce, or dry them to preserve.) Slice the clams crosswise into thin rounds. Divide among the serving bowls and dress with the diced lovage stems and spoonfuls of *ponzu*. Serve immediately.

■ Lovage Vinegar

200 g barley *koji* vinegar

100 g young lovage shoots

Combine the vinegar and lovage shoots in an airtight container. Infuse for 1 year in a cool, dark, well-ventilated place.

■ Niban Dashi

12 g kombu (dried kelp), preferably ma-kombu

1 liter filtered water

20 g freshly shaved *katsuobushi* (dried, fermented, smoked tuna)

In a saucepan, combine the kombu and water. Simmer at 60°C (140°F) for 2 hours. Remove from the heat, let cool, then chill and strain.

In a clean saucepan, bring the kombu broth to a boil and add the *katsuobushi*. Reduce the heat to maintain a gentle simmer, cover, and cook for 40 to 60 minutes, until the dashi is very flavorful.

Recipe Inspiration:

BEAUTIFUL DAY
by U2

Music is definitely our source of fuel to keep things going.

▲ Dylan Watson-Brawn

Growing up in Canada, my relationship with local music was tumultuous, because the radio stations have to play a certain percentage of Canadian music. Many big Canadian artists are prolific—so you'd get a lot of a select group. Consequently, I listened to a lot of Neil Young and Rush. I actually rebelled against the music that I grew up with, gravitating more toward hip-hop groups like Wu-Tang Clan and Outkast.

●

All of this created in me an obsessive need to understand the totality of a genre, as well as its roots. I listened to the people who first influenced the formation of hip-hop, and really appreciated the depth to which I could explore. My dogmatism toward music, being such a hard-liner, eventually led me to appreciate diversity and variety in everything. Learning to appreciate and not completely write off any one genre (like pop music) also helped me grow up personally.

●

For example, to be honest, I didn't start appreciating Drake until I'd been living away from Canada for a while. Now his music totally suits our hard-working environment at ernst.

●

When I started working in my first kitchen, I had to work pastry because I was too small to work on the line. Because of that, I was in the back of the restaurant—the upside was, that was the only part of the place where we got to listen to music all the time. I got to listen to lots of different kinds of music, and that was the first time I got to experience an environment like that. On the other side of the spectrum, when I worked in Tokyo, there was no music—just silence. There is so much to learn from both styles.

●

At ernst, we as individuals listen to an incredibly eclectic selection of music. We're a young team, from all different backgrounds, and our tastes range from hip-hop to musical theater. It gives us the energy and the vibes that allow us to continue to develop and push relentlessly. The music we play follows the intensity level of that moment of the day. During service, we work with a mellow energy that suits us, but while we're prepping, there's more high energy; we're using music to create a comforting and upbeat vibe. After service, we crank up the music again for cleaning the restaurant. Music is definitely our source of fuel to keep things going.

WEY
TUNDE

Tunde Wey is a Nigerian immigrant artist, chef, and writer working at the intersection of food and social politics. He engages systems of exploitative power while working to ameliorate the disparities they create. Tunde's food work has been written about in the *New York Times*, *Washington Post*, NPR, *Vogue*, and *GQ*. His own writing has been featured in the *Boston Globe*, *Oxford American*, *CityLab*, and the *San Francisco Chronicle*. He is a 2019 *TIME* magazine Next Generation Leader.

Chukwu Olisa

by Umu Obiligbo

Testosterone JM Playlist ▶
This was my second attempt at a playlist for a friend who had complained that the first playlist I shared with her was testosterone heavy. I tried to share some of my more chill faves. That said, I guess this list is still overwhelmingly male. The next one will be better.

1.	**Things Are Getting Better**	Cannonball Adderley, Milt Jackson
2.	**I Wish I Knew How It Would Feel to Be Free**	Nina Simone
3.	**Atomic Bomb**	William Onyeabor
4.	**Akula Owu Onyeara**	The Funkees
5.	**Life's Gone Down Low**	Lijadu Sisters
6.	**Digital Kids**	Vicktor Taiwo featuring Solomon
7.	**All**	Umi Copper
8.	**Cold Little Heart**	Michael Kiwanuka
9.	**Betray My Heart**	D'Angelo and the Vanguard
10.	**On the Ocean**	K'Jon

USA

Ukpo Ogede with Figs and Pistachios

Recipe Inspiration:

Ukpo ogede is a southwestern Nigerian delicacy. Similar to *moi moi*, which is steamed bean cakes, *ukpo ogede* uses overly ripe plantains as the main ingredient. The plantains give the dish its characteristic sweet flavor, balanced by the savory umami from the other ingredients. Traditionally large, fanlike green leaves called *uma* are used to wrap the batter for steaming, but corn husks work as well.

Serves 5; 2 *ukpo ogede* each

1 package dried corn husks

3 fingers overly ripe plantains (black skins, soft, but not rotten), peeled and roughly chopped

½ onion, roughly chopped

1 red bell pepper, stemmed and roughly chopped

½ habanero chile, stemmed and roughly chopped (remove seeds as you like for less heat)

1 tablespoon ground *iru* (fermented locust beans)

¼ cup palm oil

Salt

8 oz fresh figs, quartered or chopped, if desired

¼ cup crushed pistachios

Place the corn husks in a heatproof container and add hot water to cover. Let sit for 45 minutes to soften.

Place the plantains, onion, bell pepper, and chile in a blender and add ½ cup water. Blend until smooth and thick.

Transfer the batter to a bowl. Add the *iru*, palm oil, and salt to taste. Stir the batter until thoroughly mixed.

Lay the rehydrated corn husks on a clean work surface. Scoop 2-ounce portions of batter onto each husk. Fold the husk over the batter widthwise and then lengthwise. Turn over so the seams are on the bottom.

Fill a steamer pot with a few inches of water and bring to a rolling boil over medium-high heat. Carefully place the filled corn husks in the steamer basket and cover. Steam for about 45 minutes. Make sure to keep the pot filled with enough water.

To check for doneness, slide a knife into an *ukpo ogede*. If the knife blade comes out clean, they are ready.

Serve the *ukpo ogede* garnished with the figs and pistachios.

In 2018, my professional life was not very fulfilling. I felt like I needed to transcend the work that I was doing, which was just hosting dinners and talking about race. I wanted to do something more, I knew that there was a second or third gear I could go into, but I didn't have the means, the capacity, the financial resources, or the connections to take my idea to the next level. I was very broke. I was also under a lot of stress because of my immigration situation. ● It was just a whole lot of shit. ● I decided to take a risk and open up a restaurant stall, based on the theme of racial wealth disparity. The idea was crazy and didn't make any sense, but I felt compelled to do it. There was little validation along the way, and also at this time, terrible things were happening on the personal front, big and small. I jammed my finger in a door, my bike tire got stolen, and then I almost didn't get the license to open up the business for a month because I'm an immigrant. ● But through it all, I just kept listening to Nipsey Hussle's song "Victory Lap," which is the opening track to his record. It's this soaring, amazing song, and I would just keep repeating the opening to myself. This one line says:

I'm prolific, so gifted
I'm the type that's gon' go get it, no kidding

Saying all that. I just needed to hype myself up, and that whole album got me through the month. I just listened to it over and over again. Nipsey Hussle's music provided me with a lot of support at a particular moment in my life when I needed motivation and inspiration. *Victory Lap* was so instrumental for me personally. Since he died, just revisiting his music, listening to the songs again, revisiting the themes and messages but then finding new ones, has been both sad and pleasurable. ● Music was always just a part of my life. I clearly remember my disinterest in using music as a currency for influence; I wasn't trying to be cool. When music was fun, I would dance, and when it wasn't, I wouldn't. That was my specific relationship with music, and I would say that who I am influenced that relationship as opposed to a song

influencing me. ● But in my teenage years, my interest in music really set in. The way I saw it before, music was consumed as a status symbol, so that people could tell other people what they knew about music and which music was good. What I have come to understand now, twenty years or more removed, is that those songs that we were consuming subconsciously went into the fabric of our being, and then became nostalgic. I may have not been self-conscious then, but now they're part of my history. I tell folks that Puff Daddy raised me. The whole Bad Boy/Puff Daddy era was huge when I was growing up in Lagos, in Nigeria. All of those songs, I was eager for every little tidbit. Just so eager to hear it. ● When I started cooking Nigerian food professionally, I didn't really know how to cook, so I was learning on the job. This is how I operate: my work is oppositional. I wasn't mainstream; at best it was looked at like a curiosity. My work and my food were "exoticized"…but I was trying to normalize the food. I listened to a lot of Nigerian rap music because I was cooking the food and I just felt so disconnected from my cultural heritage. Reconnecting with the music was amazing. ● I started following all of this music that I had historically discredited. I had felt much of it was a cheap imitation of rap music or poor mimicry. But it wasn't. It was complex, it was rich, and it was powerful. It was also spiritual for me to connect to the music and to the people who were making the music. Most of them were young men who were also creating the traditional protest music that Nigeria is known for, especially with Fela Kuti. ● They weren't fearing for their music, but the need and the worry in my mind was how to protest the infiltration of our country and continent by Western European wars. I felt like I was doing the same thing with my food: providing a counter narrative to the dominance of Eurocentric European white food. I connected viscerally with the work that these Nigerian musicians were doing on a conceptual and emotional level, but also on an energetic level. The music invigorated me and propelled my cooking. ● Most of my dinners, I cook

The music that I love is honest, brash, vulnerable, and singular

alone, and I'll cook through the night, probably acclimated to the weird times that I had to cook at the donated restaurant spaces. I'll find myself alone at 2 a.m., cooking for fifty people and nowhere near done. Sometimes I'm tired, sometimes I want to start crying. But I just turn on the music and I get a second wind. I'll cook till 5 a.m., sleep on the bench somewhere, wake up, and finish up. I go take a nap, then come back and serve for the pop-up. That's what music did for me—provided so many levels of validation. ● When I'm cooking, I have my headphones in my ears—music is everything. When people come into my dining rooms, I want the music to be blasting. I know it can be uncomfortable and people are trying to have conversations, but I'm sending messages to the folks: This is raunchy, these are all the things that rap is about, so now you know what you are walking into. At the end of service, it's mostly the same high-energy music. Soft music is rare in the joint. When I am having a conversation at a table, we turn the music down, but when people go back to their pockets of tableside conversations, the volume goes back up. People are able to take refuge in that sonic canopy. They don't have to be emotionally engaged, they can just vibe out to the music; or they can talk to somebody who may not necessarily hear them, but that's okay—it facilitates a certain kind of freedom. ● I do not think food is as powerful as music. Food is consumable—literally, once you consume it, it's gone. It doesn't have the potential viral effects of music; it can't be broadcast. It's not media in that way. It's limited. I think what makes food similar to, but nowhere near the power of music, are the ideas it represents. For a lot of people who cook, the ideas are very small. We talk about the food or what's on the plate, and in most contexts, those ideas don't change the world. But music changes the world. It speaks with notes and melody, it moves people, it speaks with lyrical content. Name a chef who has been as influential as Bob Marley, Lauryn Hill, Erykah Badu, Fela Kuti, Nipsey Hussle, or Jay-Z, and I'll concede the point. ● Still, one of

the defining moments for why I started to cook was when my partner and I opened up this restaurant. It was a place to push the boundaries of certain ideas. I wasn't even sure *what* I was trying to push…it was just, something. The food I was serving was prix fixe, multicourse American food. The people we served it to were middle-class white suburban folks who appreciated the dining experience in this historic storefront in a neighborhood that was fading. It was different from what they had seen. The walls were bare and we were playing rap music. ● In those days, we started the evening playing John Coltrane. Then I would get bored, so I would switch to Biggie Smalls. One night, an older white woman called me over and asked if I would mind changing it back to jazz, because she felt that music was more appropriate for what they were eating. ● I was stunned by her lack of cultural awareness—not realizing that what jazz was in its day was what hip-hop is now. Jazz is black music. It made people uncomfortable. It was jarring. She wanted this whitewashed idea of black music. In that moment, I knew this was not the environment I wanted to be in. It struck me as something I wanted to challenge. That's when I started cooking my own vision, my own dinners, in my own dining spaces. ● For a chef, using music can be an extension of your message in the dining space or in communicating what your message is and what you are selling. Sometimes the message is unfortunate, or sometimes the message is uplifting. There are so many ways that music can be used to signal certain ideas, when mingling with food. The music that I love is honest, brash, vulnerable, and singular about what it is. I'm talking about rap, afrobeat, Nigerian pop music…which is kind of like rap, reggae, and dub. It fuels the work I do. It makes my food what it is. It makes me bold and aggressive in conveying my message—not aggressive as in being disrespectful, but being forthright. Cutting through fear, cutting through the lack of confidence, or cutting through the doubts to show confidence in the food and the message.

It fuels the work I do

KARL WHELAN

AND WILL DEMPSEY

GRAVEL PIT

by Wu-Tang Clan

Chef Karl Whelan worked in Michelin-starred restaurants from France to Australia before returning home to Dublin and spending time at popular restaurants like Chapter One and Luna. Meanwhile, Will Dempsey, his friend since childhood, had honed his craft as a DJ and promoter, throwing some of Dublin's best parties for many of those years. The duo founded Hang Dai Chinese in 2016.

1.	**Jimmy, Renda-Se**	Tom Zé
2.	**Travelin' Light**	J.J. Cale
3.	**Foggy Notion**	The Velvet Underground
4.	**High Tension Line**	The Fall
5.	**Blindness**	The Fall
6.	**Baby's On Fire**	The Creepers
7.	**Bela Lugosi's Dead**	Bauhaus
8.	**The Mexican**	Babe Ruth
9.	**Acenda o Farol**	Tim Maia
10.	**Black Pepper**	Yoruba Singers
11.	**I Shot Her**	Ngozi Family
12.	**Flight 2**	Angelo & Eighteen
13.	**Medina's Magic**	DJ Cole Medina
14.	**They Call Me Country**	Sanford Clark
15.	**I Won't Hurt You**	The West Coast Pop Art Experimental Band

Magic Cloud Playlist ▶ There are a lot of different genres and tempos in this playlist, but I think it gels in its current order and also works on shuffle. All of these songs get a lot of play around us. Some are suited to Hang Dai and some are better at a house party. It's hard when you have a lot of music you love and you try to squeeze it into one list. That's what we tried to do with Hang Dai, too: merge our love for food, music, socializing into one project. Our project name until we came up with the name Hang Dai was Magic Cloud.

WU-TANG CLAMS

(REAL SURF CLAMS FROM THE SHAOLIN, HOT SAUCE)

(REALLY SPICY CLAMS FROM THE SHAOLIN ISLAND WITH WEST OF)

HANG DAI
CHINESE

We call the toilets in Hang Dai "the hip-hop Jaxx." They have their own sound system and we blast out old school, fast hip-hop tunes. People tend to have their own little parties in there; and this tune seems to always kick things off. The Wu-Tang Clams were born out of a love we have for the band, and, well, a tip of the cap to our toilets.

Serves 2

In a wok over a medium heat, melt the butter in the sesame oil. Add the crushed rock sugar and cook until melted and caramelized. Add the ginger; onion; garlic; and green, red, and bird's-eye chiles and cook for 1 minute, stirring constantly.

Stir in the broad bean chile paste, hot chile powder, and Sichuan chile powder and cook for 1 minute longer.

Add the clams and toss everything together. Add the wine and toss once more. Turn up the heat and cover. Steam the clams for 3 minutes, or until they have all opened.

Add the sherry vinegar, toss, and serve. Spoon the clams into shallow bowls or serve directly at the table from the wok. Sprinkle with some chopped cilantro and spring onions for freshness, if you like. Add a little habanero if you want your head blown off!

---

20 g butter

2 tablespoons sesame oil

5 g yellow rock sugar, crushed

20 g fresh ginger, peeled and thickly sliced

40 g sliced onion

2 cloves garlic, sliced

10 g sliced green chile

10 g sliced red chile

7 g dried bird's-eye chiles

10 g fermented broad bean chile paste

1 teaspoon hot chile powder

1 teaspoon green Sichuan chile powder

1 kg surf clams, scrubbed

50 g Xiaoshing wine or dry sherry

8 g sherry vinegar

Chopped cilantro (coriander), spring onions, and habanero, for garnish (optional)

Song: Gravel Pit by Wu-Tang Clan

▲ Karl Whelan and Will Dempsey

Music plays a huge part in Irish culture. It has always been how we tell stories and comment on what is happening to us in our lives. The songs we sing hold the history of our culture. And—singing makes you hungry. Will and I were each inspired by music very early on in our lives. Will's dad was a big music fan—there was always music on, especially on weekend drives out to Dalkey, on Dublin's south coast, listening to people like Stevie Wonder, Neil Young, and Billie Idol. The first song Will ever loved was the Talking Heads "Once in a Lifetime," but it was CAN's "Mother Sky" (the 12-minute version) that opened his ears, eyes, and life in a big-time way. For Karl, the Velvet Underground's *White Light/White Heat* changed everything for him—listening to it on repeat, being really taken by how poetic and stunningly dark it was, those dark lyrics and sweet repetitive melodies. It was mind-blowing and cracked him right open, the realization that music and poetry

was an art form and an incredible form of expression. It played a huge part in his creative development—and encouraged him to dig deeper.

●

After our introduction to '60s music and deeper sounds, we started to think about where these artists came from and what influenced them. This opened us up to so many different genres. And then along came electronic music. It was 1994 in Dublin; we were seventeen years old, and we dove headfirst into the newly emerged underground dance music scene. We dropped all the rock and immersed ourselves in techno. Tonie Walsh (DJ) was running charity gigs for the Dublin Aids Alliance in the Ormond Multimedia Centre with a collective called the Horny Organ Tribe with Aoife Nic Canna and Eddie Kay (we play them all at Hang Dai now). We were only teenagers, but we got put on the guest list by a family friend, and we were thrown straight into the deep end.

This scene and time really shaped us; it was a super exciting time in Dublin, and we were a part of it. It was also so special because it was another world, one where you could feel completely free. We were part of the community. We made lifelong friends in those days, and learned so many valuable life lessons.

●

At the same time, food's importance started creeping in. We were living together, we started eating out, and we would throw a lot of dinner parties. Music was still a big part of this: Karl would cook, Will would pick the music... and that was the birth of Hang Dai, in a sense. The type of music would usually be quite seasonal. If it was Christmastime, a lot of doo-wop would get played; soul music in the summer; that sort of thing. One cold, damp Sunday in Autumn, Karl picked up some game and mushrooms, so Will made a mix of purely '80s wave music, the slower, darker stuff. I remember the track of

music   service

food   décor

the day being "Living in Vain" by Snakefinger.

●

A few years back, there was a night in a restaurant when Karl was working when James Murphy of LCD Soundsystem and 2ManyDJS came in for dinner. They ended up hanging out until late, talking about food and music. They were touring with "Despacio," which is their super high-end audiophile club that they bring around the world, and they were playing a festival the next day. They invited us to come along, so we ended up cooking a barbecue and drinking amazing wine and hanging out with them all day. Eating a barbecued lobster sandwich in the DJ box with those guys was nuts. Plus, we got top tips on building the sound-system end of things, which really helped with the sonic aspects of Hang Dai.

●

Music plays a huge part in the experience of our diners at Hang Dai. We build the atmosphere up throughout every night,

and on weekend nights, a DJ comes on and people start dancing until the early hours. This priority really steered the design of Hang Dai. The sound system and the acoustics of the room are of music-studio quality. The music can be heard but is not intrusive on your conversation. It's like a futuristic nightclub and restaurant that catches you off guard. The food, as a result of its planning, is playful and unique to the environment you are in.

●

In Hang Dai, we have an open kitchen, so the sound system can be heard everywhere. We experience the vibe along with the customers and the front of house staff. During pre-service, we could be listening to anything from jazz to punk. It will invariably get faster throughout the day. We have had so many nights where all the kitchen staff are full-on dancing once the DJ gets going toward the end of service. Serious buzz! At Hang Dai, we offer more than just food. Our craft has evolved so

much over the years. It is the immersive and escapist nature of modern restaurants that has really touched people and elevated food, chefs, and restaurants alike. People now want an experience when going out: food, music, décor, and service are all an important part of this event. That is, taste, sound, smell, touch, and visual experiences all bring us back to certain times in our lives and have a huge influence on what we do today. I read that Aretha Franklin once said, "music is transporting"; and culinary experiences are as well. All the music and food that we have absorbed over the years has an influence on what we do today.

sound   touch

taste   smell

ED WILSON

Ed Wilson is the chef and owner of Brawn restaurant. Established in 2010, Brawn is a neighborhood restaurant serving a daily written menu of seasonal, ingredient-led, cultural European cooking. There is also a wine list focusing on producers from around the world who work with sustainable practices and a gentle hand in both the vineyard and cellar. The restaurant has a vintage sound system and plays vinyl on a single turntable. The selection spans a broad church of music, and albums are played in their entirety.

Mornings at Brawn Playlist ▶ These are current staff favorites being played in the restaurant. Mostly old stuff with a bit of new. With a constant changing selection of vinyl, this is a snapshot of how we like to kick off the summer season.

1.	I love you S	La Perversita
2.	Was Dog a Doughnut?	Jellybean
3.	Coro Miyare	Fania All Stars
4.	War is Coming, War is Coming	War
5.	Brothers on the Slide	Cymande
6.	Parev' Ajere	Nu Guinea
7.	Estrelar	Marcos Valle
8.	Be Free	Dr. Togo
9.	I Want Your Love	James Mason
10.	Adventures in Success (dub)	Will Powers
11.	Prophecy	Fabian
12.	Civilised Reggae	Burning Spear
13.	We Need Love	Johnny Osbourne
14.	Jazz (We've Got)	A Tribe Called Quest
15.	Natural Sci-Fi	Steve Spacek

Song: Everybody Loves the Sunshine by Roy Ayers Ubiquity

▲ Ed Wilson

UNITED KINGDOM

LEMON POSSET

Classic summertime vibes are reflected in both the song and the bright, zingy set lemon cream.

Serves 6

Recipe Inspiration:

Everybody Loves the Sunshine

by Roy Ayers Ubiquity

600 ml double cream

200 g sugar

Zest of 3 lemons

100 ml fresh lemon juice

Fresh summer berries, for serving

In a heavy-bottomed pan, add the cream, sugar, zest, and lemon juice.

Bring slowly to a gentle boil and simmer for 3–4 minutes, making sure the cream doesn't catch.

Pass the cream through a fine sieve (to remove the zest) into a jug.

Pour the cream into individual bowls or glasses.

Place in the fridge and allow to cool (at least 3 hours).

As it cools, the cream will naturally set.

Remove from the fridge and serve with fresh summer berries.

Stick on Roy and chill.

Song: Everybody Loves the Sunshine by Roy Ayers Ubiquity

It's now
more than ever
that I see
how important
that time was,

and it did
bring so
many people
together

across
so many
types
of music.

▲ Ed Wilson

I was in awe of my Dad's collection of jazz, which was on vinyl and tape recordings. I wasn't particularly into the music itself, but loved the different pictures and artwork on the sleeves. I think the first song I really fell in love with was Gerry Rafferty's "Get it Right Next Time." I remember it being played really loud and singing along with my sister.

●

My first real music love was hip-hop and I remember at the age of thirteen getting De La Soul's 3 Feet High and Rising. It was the first time I really connected with music and it was so new and fresh. I guess looking back, hip-hop exposed me to the music I listen to now. As I grew older and started to hear the original tracks that were sampled, I realized how deep these producers would go to sample and loop music from everywhere in the world and give it new life, meaning, and exposure.

Then came the music of Gil Scott-Heron when I was around nineteen. His music changed the way in which I listened to and bought music. It covered a wide spectrum from jazz, soul, and blues, to poetry and spoken word. His intelligent songwriting made me question and discover new worlds of music.

●

In 1996, I was living in Newcastle in the northeast of England. Gil Scott-Heron was due to play and at the last minute the gig was cancelled. He apparently got turned away at the border. The gig was sold out and we were told to keep the tickets and they would reschedule. Some three months later they announced his return and it was a cold Tuesday night down by the riverside. I think there must have only been about 60 people in a 300-person capacity room. His performance was intimate, engaging and moving. To have witnessed something that special made me realize it doesn't matter how many people are there, you have to give your all at all times.

I grew up in the north of England, and during my teenage years in the early nineties it was an incredible time for new and emerging music. There was the second wave of the acid house scene. American house music DJs from New York, Chicago, and Detroit were regularly coming over and playing in clubs and bringing a whole new sound. There was an emerging drum and bass scene and hip-hop was in its golden era. British acts like Massive Attack and Portishead brought a different but relevant tempo that still remain timeless to this day. It was also the time of Nirvana and Primal Scream. I personally don't think there has been a richer time in music since. It's now more than ever that I see how important that time was, and it did bring so many people together across so many types of music.

●

I believe people are inspired by their senses and creativity. Food and music are two crafts that still require a large element of human input and people will always connect more with that. There are more artists and musicians that are inspired by food and wine. They are informed, knowledgeable, and well travelled. Combine that with chefs who have the same passion for music, and we are beginning to see collaborations between the two.

And you have to have soul. It's the most important element that connects food, space, music and people who work in each medium. It's not a tangible measure. It comes from within.

JANICE WONG

Janice Wong was born in Singapore in 1983. After studying economics at the National University of Singapore and graduating from Le Cordon Bleu in Paris, she eventually studied under Pierre Hermé and Oriol Balaguer, and opened "2am:dessertbar" in Singapore in 2007. 2am:dessertbar is now in its twelfth year, redefining the dessert experience and pushing the boundaries between sweet and savory with carefully researched progressive dishes.

My Classics Playlist ▶ This is a small collection of tracks from my go-to genres. It's a playlist that sums up my music preferences at a glance, highlighting the types of music that influenced me the most when I was younger. Most people shuffle their playlists, but because my musical tastes are so varied, I would recommend a listener to enjoy mine as-is. It should bring one on a journey starting from the classic Coldplay, transitioning smoothly into trance with Armin van Buuren's "Overture", and then winding back down with some jazz and country tunes.

1.	**Yellow**	Coldplay
2.	**Overture (The Best of Armin Only)**	Armin van Buuren
3.	**This is What it Feels Like**	Armin van Buuren featuring Trevor Guthrie
4.	**Wild Wild Son**	Armin van Buuren featuring Sam Martin
5.	**My One and Only Love**	John Coltrane and Johnny Hartman
6.	**'Round Midnight**	Thelonious Monk
7.	**The Girl from Ipanema**	Frank Sinatra
8.	**On an Evening in Roma**	Michael Bublé
9.	**Cheek to Cheek**	Tony Bennett and Lady Gaga
10.	**Take Me Home, Country Roads**	John Denver
11.	**Speechless**	Dan + Shay
12.	**Queen of California**	John Mayer

SINGAPORE

CHOCOLATE H2O

The Chocolate H20 is a comprehensive chocolate dessert made from many individual components, much like the jazz standard "Cantaloupe Island," which has such distinct melodic lines for each instrument, but all working together in harmony to create a single masterpiece.

Serves 6

Recipe Inspiration:

CANTALOUPE ISLAND

by Herbie Hancock

■ For the burnt caramel parfait:

745 g caster sugar

100 ml water

1550 ml cream

33 g gelatine

240 g egg yolks

550 ml milk

■ For the salted caramel sauce:

960 g caster sugar

160 ml water

800 ml cream

34 g Sel De Guerande

160 g unsalted butter, cubed

■ For the yuzu sorbet:

1000 g ice

200 g yuzu juice

350 ml yuzu paste

1000 ml water

240 g inverted sugar

80 g glucose syrup

200 g sugar

20 g pectin

■ For the yuzu-kalamansi gel:

480 g Boiron kalamansi puree

440 ml yuzu liquid

800 g glucose syrup

200 g trimoline

20 g agar agar

■ For the chocolate soil:

280 g unsalted butter

170 g caster sugar

10 g flaky sea salt

120 g egg whites

400 g Valrhona cocoa powder

■ For the chocolate water:

500 g Inaya Chocolate 65%

500 ml water

10 g egg white powder

100 g egg whites

■ For the grey spray:

200 g cacao butter

70 g white chocolate

5 g black coloring powder

3 g Mycro cacao butter

▶l

■ Make the burnt caramel domes:
Combine 400 g of the caster sugar with the water to make a caramel. Cook to 200°C or until dark brown. Warm 500 ml of the cream and stream into caramel stirring continuously. Bloom gelatin and whisk into caramel. Whisk the egg yolks with the remaining 345 g sugar until it forms ribbons, then fold into the caramel mixture. Beat the remaining 1000 ml cream until soft peaks form, then fold into the caramel. Pipe the mixture into silicon half-dome molds and freeze.

■ Make the salted caramel sauce:
In a large pot, combine the sugar and water to make a caramel. Warm cream and stream into the caramel, stirring continuously. Stir in the salt, then allow mixture to cool to 40°C. Stir in the butter then blend by hand and strain. Transfer to a squeeze bottle and reserve in chiller.

■ Make the yuzu sorbet:
Combine the yuzu juice and paste with the ice and set aside. Make the sorbet base by bringing the water, inverted sugar and glucose to a boil. Mix the sugar and pectin together then blend into the sugar mixture. Place into a paco tin and reserve in freezer.

■ Make the yuzu-kalamansi gel:
Combine all ingredients together in a pot and bring to a boil. Blend, strain, and rapid cool. Reserve in chiller.

■ Make the chocolate soil:
Place butter, salt and sugar in an electric mixer fitted with a paddle and mix well. Add the egg whites and mix to incorporate, then add the cocoa powder. Mix well, then chill the dough for 1 hour. Spread the dough on a baking sheet to a thickness of 1cm, and bake at 180°C for 15 minutes. Cool to room temperature and transfer to a processer and blitz into crumbs. Reserve in an air-tight container.

■ Make the chocolate water:
Mix water and egg white powder together to hydrate. Place over high heat and bring to a boil. Mix melted chocolate into the egg white mixture and blend well by hand. Add mixture to a siphon and charge twice. Shake well and reserve.

Line GN container with plastic wrap, then pipe mixture into container and freeze.

Place 16 caramel domes and salted caramel onto the semi-frozen chocolate water mixture. Freeze mixture and cut frozen chocolate water and assemble. Freeze chocolate water blocks. Ready for spray.

■ Make the grey spray:
Melt the cacao butter and bring to a temperature of 55°C. Pour the melted cacao butter over the white chocolate. Add the black coloring powder and blend the mixture by hand. Add the Mycro to temper the spray and check that temperature is between 30 and 35°C. Once mixture is ready, spray all sides of the chocolate water blocks.

To assemble, place 1 tablespoon of chocolate soil onto a plate. Place 1 portion of Chocolate H20 mousse onto the plate and allow to defrost for 8 minutes. Pipe yuzu kalamansi sauce onto the plate and pipe salted caramel onto the chocolate H20. Quenelle one tablespoon of yuzu sorbet onto the chocolate H20.

Music and food create a unique dining experience; I think it is all about making magic together.

Music was essential in helping me to connect with myself and others emotionally. When I was young, I would share my favorite music with my best friends and vice versa. It was the art of sharing and connecting with one another through music that created everlasting bonds in my friendships. Music helped me to be exposed to and learn about other languages and cultures. ● I first became aware of music when I was three years old. We had moved to Japan, and I vividly remember going to Disneyland and hearing all of the tunes that were played; they were happy memories. The first song I fell in love with was "It's a Small World After All" by Disney. I was also in Sunday school in Japan, and in Sunday school the first music I heard was "Jesus Loves Me," which was love at first listen. ● Over the years, so much music influenced me and caught my attention. I liked *Phantom of the Opera* when I was twelve or thirteen years old, which was the first musical that I had ever seen. I was fascinated with the music because it was so powerful, one-of-a-kind, and I found it incredibly beautiful. ● When I played sports competitively, I would listen to jazz and country music, with the occasional Coldplay songs. I remember the song "Yellow," which I used to play over and over to keep me focused. ● Some of the songs I have connected with have helped me through competitive sports wins and losses. As a Christian, gospel music has been close to my heart since I was young. It has helped me through the death of my grandmother when I was thirteen years old. Trance music has also helped me a lot with my greatest fear — the dentist. When I'm in the dental chair, my go-to music is always trance. ● Trance music influences my emotions and I feel more energetic when I'm working. The energy that I get from it gets transferred to the creations of the dishes. When I'm in the kitchen and experiencing a high-pressure environment, I will listen to trance music, particularly Armin Van Buuren's radio show "A State of Trance." I feel that the power of music connects your senses and emotions. It has such a powerful influence over one's dining experience. I listen to music every day and I am sensitive to sounds as it is also essential in creating the right ambience in our restaurants and art installations. In 2am:dessertbar, we play lounge chill out, bossa nova, big band, and jazz. ● We have certain themed events where music plays a big role in the dining experience. One of them was the "5 senses dinner," which we put together for the National Museum of Singapore, Gallery 10. All food courses were curated with the theme of the six elements: water, earth, fire, wood, metal, and air. Together with projected visuals, music, lighting, and other elements, the dinner experience stimulated all five senses. ● The "5 senses dinner" also showcased how music influenced the creations of the dishes for the event as a whole. The course for the dessert was a crowd favorite and partly due to the music curated by Lucas Vidal. It was light, feminine, fun, and cheeky, and enhanced the dessert taste and flavor and the experience for the guests. ● Music and food create a unique dining experience; I think it is all about making magic together. Having one without the other would be incomplete.

Having one without the other would be incomplete.

SHOHEI YASUDA

Shohei Yasuda is from Okayama. His dad was a French chef and Yasuda came into contact with cooking from a young age, which naturally led him to become a chef. After working at Kadeau in Copenhagen, he opened Kabi in Meguro, Tokyo.

Shabu-

Song: X0004000X by 999999999

Kabi Playlist ▶ This playlist is part of one that I use at Kabi. It starts with Japanese music that we really love, and the beat energizes our work, without interfering with the meals we are preparing. It's a nostalgic playlist that was made with suggestions from the whole team of the kinds of music they like.

X 0 0 0 4 0

1.	Rapt in Fantasy	Takkyu Ishino
2.	1000 Knives	Yellow Magic Orchestra
3.	Neo Geo	Ryuichi Sakamoto
4.	If You Please	Chinese Man
5.	If You Only Knew	Jurassic 5
6.	Firecracker (U.S. version)	Yellow Magic Orchestra
7.	Japan Air	Skee Mask
8.	Foreign Bodies	Herbert
9.	Snowcaps	Larry Heard
10.	A Day The Life Of A Day	Jeff Mills
11.	Café De Flore	Doctor Rockit

Black

Pork

I listened to this song when I was trying to come up with how to use this delicious black hog (kurobuta, Berkshire pig) pork from Nagano.

Serves 2

Shabu

O O X

Recipe Inspiration:

by 99999999

60 g Nagano black hog pork

5 g wild seri herb

3 g Blue Mussels Miso (see below)

50 g Ichiban-Dashi (see below)

1 g Mikan Peel Oil (see below)

100 g Fermented Mushroom Ponzu (see below)

1 g Roasted Malted Rice Oil (see below)

10 g raw daikon radish, grated

2 g arugula flowers

■ Blue Mussels Miso

1 kg blue mussels

1 liter cooking sake

1 kg Terada Honke koji (rice malt)

Seaweed Salt 5%

Heat the mussels in cooking sake, then leave to cool.

Mix the mussels with Terada Honke koji (rice malt) as well as seaweed salt (about 5% of the total ingredients). Leave at room temperature for between six months and a year. (Ideally, prepare in mid-winter and leave until the following autumn or winter.)

■ Ichiban-Dashi

Kombu (dried kelp) 10 cm x 10 cm

50 g katsuobushi (dried bonito flakes)

Soak kombu (dried kelp) overnight in water.

Bring to a boil and add katsuobushi (dried bonito flakes).

Turn off heat, then leave for two minutes before slowly straining.

■ Mikan Peel Oil

100 g mikan citrus fruit peel

150 g canola oil

Place equal amounts of mikan citrus fruit peel and canola oil in a food mixer. Blend for five minutes, then strain. ▶|

■ Fermented Mushroom Ponzu

Seaweed Salt 2%

1 liter mushrooms

50 g mirin

Kombu 10 cm x 10 cm

50 g katsuobushi

Sudachi

Add seaweed salt equivalent to 2% of the quantity of mushrooms and seal in a vacuum bag, leaving to ferment at room temperature for 3 to 7 days.

Add mirin, kombu (kelp), and katsuobushi (dried bonito flakes) to the fermented mushroom juices, then bring to a quick boil.

Add sudachi citrus of an equal amount as the fermented mushroom juices.

■ Roasted Malted Rice Oil

200 g terada honke koji

300 g canola oil

Roast Terada Honke koji (rice malt) in an oven at 180°C for 30 to 40 minutes.

Add canola oil and seal in a vacuum bag.

Place in a steam oven at 80°C for an hour until the fragrance has permeated.

Plating
Thinly slice the Nagano black hog pork. Wrap with wild seri herb and homemade blue mussels miso.

Parboil for one minute in ichiban-dashi (soup stock/broth made from dried kelp and bonito flakes) and place on a plate.

Sprinkle mikan fruit leaf oil and fermented mushroom ponzu sauce, and roasted malted rice oil. Finish with grated raw daikon radish and arugula flowers.

Black Pork Shabu-Shabu

Without music, I wouldn't be who I am today, and I probably wouldn't have started Kabi. ● As a child I'd watch DVDs of arena concerts by the likes of Queen or Oasis, and really aspired to be like those artists, which has led to who I am today. My dad was a French trained chef who loved Queen. Their music was always playing in the car or when he was working. Without a doubt, the first song I loved was "Under Pressure" by Queen. The music I listen to these days is so different from back then. My playlist now is full with Mama Snake, Sugar, Niki Istrefi, Anetha, Takkyu Ishino, Ryuichi Sakamoto, and Haruomi Hosono. Their music is essential to me when I'm thinking about cooking or preparing food. ● Music artists and chefs think about the same things. At the end of the day, we enjoy expressing ourselves and the customers get a good time out of it. We have a good time seeing them enjoying themselves. ● When I was working at Kadeau in Copenhagen, I used almost entirely unknown ingredients for the sake of creativity. When work was over, I would go out to a club and encounter music I'd never heard in Japan. So, the two are linked in that I want to know the unknown. ● Now, when I think about cooking, I do it right by the speakers at a club or while relaxing at a hot spring. Creative music gives me creativity. I think my cooking includes elements of music. Like trance or techno, you can taste all kinds of different flavors in your mouth. It's like sour or acidic tastes are the treble, while umami is the bass. ● All the team at Kabi went to see Peter van Hoesen when he was playing at UNIT in Tokyo. We had the best night dancing to the music right in front of the speakers during his set. The next day, he showed up for dinner at Kabi and I was so surprised I almost leapt into the air. He ended up having a great time at Kabi and even made us a playlist. ● I think a restaurant without music is not a restaurant. Alongside the decor, the drinks, and the food, you have music. Without music, I cannot work—it's just no fun. I play music while Kabi is open, while preparing food and even while thinking about what food to make. What's interesting about this is that there is a "nightclub" element to thinking about food with the style and approach I take to cooking changing depending on the day's music. ● Never forget—a chef is also an artist.

Never forget— a chef is also an artist.

■ Author Acknowledgments

This book was written at a time of global uncertainty. We dedicate this book to the chefs, restaurateurs, bartenders, baristas, small business owners, farmers, grocers, journalists, writers, podcasters, publicists, purveyors, publishers and the millions of members of the food industry who continue to be a daily inspiration. Thank you to Mom and Dad, who gave us our original love of food and music, and who have supported us in all of our wild endeavors. Thank you to our wives and kids, who make every day a little more delicious: Anna and Josephine; Molly and Louise-Amelia; Shannon and Felix. Thank you to every chef, musician, restaurateur, bartender and artist who's ever sat down to share their story with us. Finally, thank you to everyone who helped lift this boat over the mountain: Sarah Abell, Fernando Aciar, Carter Adams, Ali Altinsoy, Kimberly Chou Tsun An, Adi Anand, Joey Arak, Carolina Arantes, Caitlin Arnell Argles, Tyler Arrivillaga, Jennifer Baum, Rachel Becker, Emily Benson, Siobhan Bent, Peter Berard, Aimee Bianca, Kate Bittman, Karmelle Biyot, Annie Black, Sai Blount, Linda Bouchard, Maxwell Britten, Adi Brock, Tommy Brockert, Royce Burke, Brooke Burt, John Bush, Alex Calderwood, Andrea Campos, Mike Caputo, Carlos Carneiro, Luis Cerón, Carmen Chan, Sue Chan, John Chao, Janie Chartier, Justin Chearno, Jessica Cheng, Dhruv Chopra, Agnes C. Chung, Frank Cisneros, Taylor Cohen, Loren Daye, Juliana de Oliveira, Parker Dean, Amanda Dell , Ken Della Penta, Kerry Diamond, Ben Dietz, Christian Dortch, Amani Duncan, Kristy Edmunds, Farley Elliott, Aaron Espinoza, Erin Fairbanks, Anthony Falco, Janaina Fidalgo, Vanya Filipovic, Alexis Florio, Food Book Fair, Jonah Freedman, Andrew Friedman, Jake Friedman, Laryl Garcia, Aaron Garvey, Peter Gaston, Philip Gilmour, Marcus Glover, Anne Goldberg, Matt Goldman, Jeff Gordinier, David Graver, Erin Gray, Kate Green, Josh Greenberg, Ellie Groden, Deepali Gupta, Brendan Hannah, Julia Hasting, Cesar Hawas, Travis Hayden, Rami Haykal, Vickie Hayward, Heritage Radio Network, Orlando Higginbottom, Luther Himes, Vitor Hirtsch, Christina Hollenback, Amy Hordes, Erik Horn, Josh Horowitz, Susan Hosmer, Diana Hossfeld, Brandon Hoy, Leiti Hsu, Jack Inslee, Hannah Jacobs, Kat Johnson, Lisa Kanamoto, Kevin Kearney, Christine Sun Kim, Julie Kim, Sam Kirby, Laura June Kirsch, Evan Kleiman, Lisa Klipsic, Amanda Kludt, Lexie Komisar, Keith Kreeger, Jon Kurland, Ilexa Landau, Matthew Langille, Angela Law, Paizley Lee, Ellie Levine, Nick Liao, Joy Limanon, Amy Ma, Kate Marriage, Lila Martin, Richard Martin, Patrick Martins, Sam Mason, David Massoni, Alix McAlpine, Monica McClure, Sean McGuinness, Travis McMichael, Ben Miller, Natalie Minerva, James Moody, Lesley Moon, Joao Mota, James Murphy, Maggie Mustard, Carrie Bradley Neves, Phoebe Ng, Laura Nolte, Patrick North, Now Serving, Chris O'Connell, Shereen O'Donnell, Elena Occhipinti, Evan Orensten, Jessica Orozco, Ben Palmer, Cameron Parkins, Matt Patterson, Jeet Paul, Seth Peterson, Andy Petr, Liz Pierson, Chelsea Place, Anna Polonsky, Kat Popiel, Sumaya Prado, Rickey Reed, Elise Reinemann, Matt Reynolds, Luke Riffle, Roberta's, Niki Robertson, Matt Rodbard, Jesse Rogg, Tracey Rosen, Jordana Rothman, Josh Rubin, Suzy Ryoo, Farideh Sadeghin, Becs Sanders, Cameron Schaefer, Kyle Schmitz, Ryan Schreiber, Nikki Scoggins, Ben Shapiro, Jeremy Shockley, Rebecca Siegel , Amrit Singh, Ben Sisto, Liz Smith, Sarah Sporn, Eric Strauss, Jay Strell, Emily Takoudes, Andrew Tarlow, David Tatasciore, Terence Teh, Xavier Tera, Emilia Terrangi, Mike Thelin, Guilherme Umeda, Amaechi Uzoigwe, Caity Moseman Wadler, Lex Weibel, Nat Weiner, Dawn White, Ngahuia Williams, Tom Windish, Samantha Wong, Shelley Wright, Sophia Yablon, Nahoko Yamashita, LinYee Yuan, Kimberly Zerkel, and Bridgette Zou.

■ Recipe Notes

The recipes in this book use both metric and imperial measures, depending on the preference of the chef, and have been printed as they were submitted. Cooking times are for guidance only, as individual ovens vary. If using a fan (convection) oven, follow the manufacturer's instructions concerning oven temperatures. Exercise a high level of caution when following recipes involving any potentially hazardous activity, including the use of high temperatures, open flames, slaked lime, and when deep-frying. In particular, when deep-frying, add food carefully to avoid splashing, wear long sleeves, and never leave the pan unattended. Some recipes include raw or very lightly cooked eggs, meat, or fish, and fermented products. These should be avoided by the elderly, infants, pregnant women, convalescents, and anyone with an impaired immune system. Exercise caution when making fermented products, ensuring all equipment is spotlessly clean, and seek expert advice if in any doubt.